HOW TO BE A BITCH* WITH STYLE

▲ BEING IN TOTAL CONTROL OF HERSELF

DR. VIKKI ASHLEY

ATALARIA PUBLISHERS

None of the material contained in this book is medically prescriptive. Individuals are asked to make choices about their lives, including their health. Such choices should *always* include a partnership with the right health professional, regardless of training or title, for the individual situation. All health professionals are encouraged to continue to learn about alternative and complementary healing practices, and herbal, magnetic and electrical technologies in order to have a wider range of information and knowledge to bring to the client/patient relationship. All individuals are encouraged to *take control of their lives and make health their highest value.*

FIRST EDITION 10,000 Copies

Printed in Canada, 1999

Library of Congress
Cataloging-in-Publications Data Available

ISBN 0-9669493-0-7

Published by Atalaria Publishers,
P. O. Box 15349
New Orleans, LA 70175
www.atalariapublishers.com

DEDICATION

To Bob with whom I have gone around countless lives,
who loves me just as I am and whom I love with true consciousness
and energy. You're my Anchor. I'm your Kite!

To Donald and Donna, my natural children,
whose presence, love and respect in my life insured
my growth and spiritual development.

To Alan, my son, whose life, and death at 30 from AIDS,
put the finishing touches on my growth and
showed me the light in the darkest moment of my life.

To Steve and Dee, Allen and Bridgett, Judy and Michael and Lynn,
my spiritual children, whose love and acceptance of me has been
heartening as Bob and I brought two families together without strife.

To Shawn, Kara Shea, Rebecca, Emily, Zachary, Barret,
Carlin and Mariah, and Mahea Lani, my grandchildren, who have
presented endless opportunities for love, teaching and learning.

To Herb and Sybil York, whose presence in my life, then and now,
provides a crystal clear window of love, support and transition
for me that made all the difference in my growth.

To my mother and father, Vivian and James T. Henry, Sr., who did the
best they could with what they knew. I now know how to love you.

To my younger eleven brothers and sisters who each
have to trod the path they chose, I love you.

To Father Alphonse Schumacher, Ms. Martha Clark
and Uncle Carl Henry, thank you for being the inspiration
my soul needed in the early days.

To my Aunt Gerri Jester to whom I owe the
deepest and most profound love and gratitude.
You had, by far, the deepest and greatest impact on my life.
"I did it, Gerri. I completed the book. Just like I said I would!"
She never doubted me. Ever.

*To Eunice Lockhart-Moss who has walked
with me through Hell in a gasoline shirt and
I with her—we made it through together, girl!*

*I thank all of you for joining me on this
round of my circle of life, bringing me the opportunity
to love, learn, teach, share myself and grow.*

*I am grateful that y'all heeded my call and came into my life.
My vision is that I will continue to give you something of value,
as you have given me.*

The journey continues.

CONTENTS

PREFACE

I n many ways, this book "wrote" me. I began preparing notes in the Houston airport on February 27, 1988 at 6:00 P.M. between flights from San Diego to New Orleans. The very first thing I wrote was, "I've just been given the Bitch of the Year Award. And, I've decided to take it. Why? I'm a Bitch *with Style!*"

This thought was in my mind because I had just done battle with the doctors, hospital care staff and some of the administrators of University Hospital in San Diego to keep my youngest son from dying of pneumocystis pneumonia! Once my deathly ill son told me he wanted to live, I promised him I would move heaven and earth to help him do so. I share this experience in the Introduction. It became obvious to me each day I arrived at the hospital and told the nurses and doctors about something *else* that wasn't being done "right" for my son that I could "hear" them say, "Here comes *that* bitch, again." I was inspired by this reality, obviously, whether it was *my* projection or *their* perception.

I've been called "bitch" many times: sometimes by my first husband because I wasn't behaving as he thought I should; often in the workplace because I wasn't behaving as others thought I should. It occurred to me many years ago that this "name" was applied almost exclusively in situations in which another person's desires and mine clashed or were totally incompatible. In the workplace, especially, I found that *my* approach and style, if interpreted by others as being even a slight bit on the self-assured (read, arrogant) side of the ledger, would be labeled "bitchy" in a heartbeat. So, "OK," I thought, "What's so bad about being *called a bitch?*" For years I have wanted to write about women who control their own lives, but had no idea I'd be writing *this* book until that very evening.

After boarding the plane to New Orleans that evening, I continued to ask myself the same question: "What's so *bad* about being *called a bitch?*" I wrote down everything I could think of that would describe **B-I-T-C-H.** Let me share a few of those ideas with you now to demonstrate what I found *good* about being called a ***bitch***!

Phrases

1. Better to be Bold and Independent Than Considered Helpless.
2. Blessed Is The Caring Heart.
3. My Boundless **Intellect** Thinks Constantly of Heaven. (Also say Him.)
4. Bad Information and Thoughts Can Hurt.
5. Beautiful Informed Thoughts Can Heal.
6. Be Impressive, Thoughtful, Collaborative, Healing.
7. I have Beauty, Integrity, Talent, Competence, and Health. (And Humor)
8. I am Bold, Idiosyncratic, Thoughtful, Centered and Haughty. (And Healthy)
9. I am also Believable, Informed, Trustworthy, Compassionate and Helpful. (And Healthy)
10. I am Blessed, Infinite, Thoughtful, Cherished and Holy.
11. I am Blameless, Innocent, Trusting, Creative and Heaven-bound.
12. I have Brains, Influence, Taste (Style), Choice and Health.
13. This is the Best Informed Training Curriculum Here (on Earth!)
14. I am a Beacon, Initiator, Teacher, Conductor, Harmonizer.

I thought of all the positive ways to describe **bitch** and my pen flew over the page.

Words

Bright	Blessed	Boundless
Independent	Inner Directed	Intense
Thinking	Transformed	Tuned In
Caring	Certain	Communicator
Humble	Happy	Home

Bountiful	Bold	Being
Integrated	Imaginative	In
Truthful	Thankful	Total
Contented	Complete	Control of
Holistic	Heedful	Herself

And then, it hit me: **I am a Bitch *With Style!* And it is *beautiful!***

I have already covered all the various ways I thought **bitch** could be positively represented. Next I went to the word **With**.

WITH = Will It To Happen!

Next I wrote out **WILL**

WILL—Wonder Illumination Light Love

Then I wrote out **STYLE**

STYLE = Self-Esteem Thinking Youthful Love Energy!

And *then* I wrote:

1. Self-Esteem that Yearns to Lead/Love With Energy!
2. Self-Esteem = Thoughts from you that radiate love and energy, enthusiasm and enlightenment!

Results

I could readily see that the Universe was sharing insights with me that indicated a **bitch *with style*** has the moxy to *will it* (anything she wants) *to happen*; is a person filled with *self-esteem—"a self-esteem that yearns to lead and love with energy!"* She is *thinking, youthful, and full of love and energy.* Furthermore, her will is based on wonder (curiosity), illumination (seeking information, knowledge and experience), light (she has worked with her shadow and integrated *it* into the light, and is full of the knowledge that *love* truly begins with love of Self.

My thoughts on self-esteem kept coming. I consider self-esteem to be an outgrowth of answering the question, *Who am I?* But there are many more facets of this question to explore and I do so in the book. I kept on writing that fateful evening: "*Self-esteem* supports thoughts from me that radiate love and energy with enthusiasm and enlightenment."

I vowed then to write this book and to share what I knew. Well, I made all those notes in the back covers of the soft-cover edition of **A Course in Miracles**. As it says in **Miracles**, "I want another way of looking at this." (T, 583) Because I wanted another way to look at the word **bitch** and my own life, you are reading this book today.

Alan sent me a birthday card on October 13, 1989. The cover was a picture of brass instruments reaching into a brilliantly lighted sky. It was a year of robust health for him following his close call in 1988, and he continued playing his CDs, recording and listening to music, which we both love. In his own hand, he wrote:

> *Dear Mom,*
> *The instruments represent a symbol of music and the sound of love, the love that fills my heart like a symphony!*
> *Have a glorious birthday.*
>
> > Your son,
> > Alan Rickman

If only one person in the world *decides* to change her or his life because some word or phrase or story *hits home* or *inspires* her or him, then I am more than one step further along the loose gravel path of life and am heading in the right direction. Toward enlightenment!

This book is *my* symphony of music and love.

> —*Vikki Ashley, PhD*
> *New Orleans, LA*
> *December 29, 1998*

Meet the Bitch *With Style!*
Vikki Ashley, PhD

To all of those whose information I have been reading, learning and applying for lo! these many years and lives, I thank you for putting pen to paper or papyrus, as the case may be. It is by your sharing that a great deal of my learning and growing has been inspired. There is so much more to learn, write about and integrate that I still feel "unfinished." I promise to write more. Still, I trust that I have made fair use of available resource materials and that you will forgive me should there be any transgressions in its use.

To the Universe, "Ain't it grand?"

ACKNOWLEGMENTS

I must first acknowledge the *Vital Essence* of the Universe that **IS** represented in my person on this earth. I continue to be in awe of the wonder of it all. I also want to acknowledge that this *Vital Essence* **IS** knowable.

Bob Daniels, you are a wonder to me as well. You came into my life at a time when it was necessary for us to grow and you have stuck with it all in good spirit, fun, sorrow and, yes, wonder. You are my anchor and have been my port in stormy seas. Thank heaven we have found a calm cove in which to rejoice in our walk together on the loose gravel path of life.

Eunice Jean Lockhart-Moss. Girl, you are the spark plug I needed at the end when the going was *really* rough and when Michael was telling me the publication date was, well, a bit much to ask for at that time. You jumped on a plane in the nick of time and together we focused our emotions to achieve this result. That's called *love*, my friend.

Michael Ledet, I cannot thank you enough for your professional expertise and warm friendship in the production of this book. You *know* what you are doing, my friend. As a result, the design and layout of this book are more than even I *ever* anticipated. Thanks for being on my team.

Mimi Pelton, my friend, I now *know* why *you* are in *my* life. It has nothing and yet everything to do with this book. May you discover why I am in *yours*.

INTRODUCTION

Tough Love, Tender Love

*"...Your children are not your children.
They are the sons and daughters of
Life's longing for itself.
They come through you but not from you,
And though they are with you, yet they
belong not to you ...* [1]

Khalil Gibran, The Prophet. "On Children."

Alan Rickman
After the first crisis

Christmas, 1988

"**M**om? This is DQ. I just took Alan to the Emergency Room at University of California, San Diego (UCSD) Medical Center. He has pneumocystis pneumonia. You know what that is? AIDS!" The date: February 4, 1988. The caller: my oldest son, Donald.

My heart almost stopped beating! God, no! I shouted inside me. Yes! Yes! Yes! Why be surprised? I had known in my heart it was coming. The blood test Alan had taken during the Christmas holidays that showed him HIV negative had buoyed us up for a few weeks. Somehow, though, I was not convinced. I was uneasy as Bob and I left San Diego for New Orleans on January 2, 1988.

Before, during and after Christmas, Alan had been coughing and running fevers. He had been treated by a San Diego physician for nearly two months. If only the doctor had known how to diagnose pneumocystis he would have been able to detect the first signs of this pneumonia that was soon to terrorize the family and almost take Alan's life. It is the "almost"—that "parenthesis in eternity" that makes this story worth telling.

> *You may give them your love but not your thoughts,*
> *For they have their own thoughts.*
> *You may house their bodies but not their souls,*
> *For their souls dwell in the house of tomorrow,*
> *Which you cannot visit, not even in your dreams.*
> *You may strive to be like them, but seek*
> *not to make them like you.*
> *For life goes not backward nor tarries with yesterday.*[2]

The Challenge

Sharing the following events is a heavy challenge for me. It is like a "reality check" I conduct with my clients. It covers love, process, language, individual and group effort and impact, timing, crisis intervention (process and strategy), organizational development, cultural (gender) behavior, how a health-oriented and human systems' community (read, medical center/hospital) responds to human need, or not; how an individual can impact individuals and systems when driven by needs, values and love; how personal truth confronts medical truth (both "true" in their individual perceptions); and how one empowers self as a change agent in a seemingly insensitive and hopeless situation.

All of these elements are here to be viewed through my life experience as expressed in what follows during my "twenty-five days in February, 1988."

As I write this, my whole body is charged with emotion. The energy field around me is literally moving. I am, to be sure, reliving this in my mind. It is not easy to share. But important to do. Why? Ultimately, it was my battle, and Alan's, with the *institution* of medicine that held the balance of his life.

My oldest son, though frightened for his brother and for him Self, "took over" as he had done so many times when I was not there, and handled the initial admission and treatment process for Alan. He advised me by phone that he did not trust the "asshole" resident who had a smart mouth and negative attitude towards "this AIDS patient," *my* son! Of course, Donald doesn't suffer fools or arrogant individuals gladly, being very much the latter him Self. Mirrors are

Alan, Vikki, Donald
May, 1988

hard for him to handle! I took his negative view of the resident, who was the only one handling Alan's case at the time, as partly true and partly a reaction formation on Donald's part. I was to soon find out, Donald was 100% right!!! For once!

My husband was dean of the LSU School of Medicine. I discussed with him whom I should consult with in New Orleans. As a psychologist and management consultant, my first act is always to "get the data first." Bob directed me to Dr. Robert Marier, who is an infectious disease specialist and headed the AIDS unit at Charity Hospital in New Orleans. Rob was sympathetic, compassionate and very helpful. He assured me that UCSD, as a training hospital and a national center, had everything it took to keep Alan alive. Rob gave me names of individuals to talk to when I landed in San Diego, so I would have a network link that would provide easier access to the doctors.

I had been following the AIDS literature and various television specials because I knew Alan might get this disease because of his lifestyle. He had tested HIV positive almost two years before and did, I know from personal conversations between us, "worry" about the possibility. That is why the HIV negative diagnosis by a very reputable lab during Christmas holiday had us all confused. I have since learned that the virus can "hide" and remain undetected—no one knows how long—and eventually show up—well, no one knows *its* timing. How tragic, I thought. How many people "think" they're clean, but are not? Such was the case with Alan on January 2, 1988. I have no evidence, even to this day, that he did anything to prevent getting AIDS; he watched many of his friends die from it, however. Just one month and two days later, Alan's own odyssey would begin!

I decided ten years ago that there was nothing I could do to *prevent* my children from following their own paths. "I've done my best with what I had," I told my Self. All I can do now is provide continuing love, feedback, information, encouragement, and—over the past five years—a type of tough love absent in our earlier lives together. This tough love found its way into my consciousness when I determined, finally, that I, out of my own issues of guilt and wanting to be loved, tended to support my children's negative behavior around money. How was that? As a divorced single parent of three (two boys and one girl-in-the-middle), I had vowed they would want for nothing materially and that I would do my very best to provide values and developmental guidance that would make them responsible, thinking, individuals—capable of making choices and consciously accepting the consequences of their actions. Just like I had learned to do . . . finally!

Well, they found out how to play my personal need for them "not to go without" like a violin and, over the years, borrowed money, made contracts with me for cars, promised to repay or, in the case of cars, make their payments on time, or pay their tickets (parking, mostly, with an occasional moving violation). Did they keep those promises? No way! Did I stop helping them? No way! Did I rationalize and tell them I was going to give them another, then another, then another chance? You bet I did. Knowing, I repeat, *knowing*, it was I and not they who was doing what I wanted to do and was allowing them to be irresponsible in relation to me.

I was thinking about all of the bailouts and the occasional personal rejection I had received from my children, including Alan, when I allowed my mind to accept the possibility that my youngest son could die, and soon; he would never know the joy of having a career that counted; he would never marry; he had not yet, at age 27, and would not, now, have a permanent love in his life because of the AIDS; and he was going to suffer greatly and all I could now do was see that he got the best care and the most comfortable circumstances in which to suffer, as opposed to living life long and well as I had hoped he would do.

But I must tell you. I was besieged by thoughts of how I would live what I knew to be my truth at this stage of my own knowingness, regardless of the past:

1. There is a God within each of us and that god-part of us, the soul, never dies. That energy ensures us continued life. The body is just a vehicle for living out the "heaven on earth" part of our mission: to know and manifest who I am on this earth.

2. We each have our own set of life experiences through which we gain, if we are conscious, wisdom, that "pearl of great price," which allows us to know and love our individual selves and thus those we mirror in our every contact each day.

3. Alan is not *mine* (reference Gibran, above). No one belongs to another human being, in spite of the various games we play for control of one another. I had made that determination years ago when I recognized, understood and accepted that my son was gay. I love and accept him now as I did then, no matter the path he chose for him Self. He must, however, answer for whatever he chose. As must we all. As I had done, and would do for the remainder of my stay on *terra firma*.

4. I love my children enough to respect their individuality. After all, was that not a strong value I instilled in them? Didn't I make them make decisions, choices, and pay the prices exacted for those choices, whether or not they brought joy or sadness? Isn't that really what life is all about?

5. Could I, now, walk my talk . . . and just BE what I know to be my truth?

"Lord God of my Being, if ever I needed strength to truly *be* what I *know*, be with me *now*," I prayed as I went to bed two nights (February 9) before my trip back to San Diego. With tears in my soul I prayed I would have the strength to do what I *must* do for Alan, for me, and for my two other children who were in fear and terror at the thought of their brother's death. Both Donald and Donna had not truly processed their father's death of a stroke two years before. They had not yet confronted the issues playing their Selfs out before their very eyes related to codependency, abandonment (their father's during their lifetime and in death; mine, emotionally and often physically because of my work and responsibility to support them) and the whole syndrome of adult children of alcoholics (their dad). But even more than this, both their father and I were children of dysfunctional families and I could now accept and share with them the devastating combination of background they were facing. I had just come out of ten years of growth, including therapy and a two-year spiritual sabbatical where I engaged my own odyssey and "dark night of the soul." And, now this. Could I handle it?

To add to the question, "Can I handle it?" was the realization that my husband had just finally accepted a diagnosis of Parkinson's disease as a reality. Though a doctor, and knowledgeable about the disease and its potential crippling effect, he hates medication, and could not accept the idea that his strength, stature, and independence could be robbed by so potentially devastating a disease. I wasn't upset about this because he has always had a tremor since I've known him. The issue, of course, was: Would I love him? Would I still always be there? Yes, yes, yes. But the question for him really was "Can I accept my Self and love my Self with this disease?" That is not for me to answer.

The Intervention: February 7, 1988 about 6:00 P.M.

This message greeted me on my answerphone: "Mom! Do something! They're moving me to a ward with a lot of sick people. Mom! Help me! I don't want to be with other sick people. Please do something!" Tears. Choking.

It was Alan. I couldn't stand the sound of his voice. It was so weak and puny. I could feel the tears. What to do?

I called Donald at work. He said the doctor had ordered the shift to the four-bed ward because Alan didn't have any insurance and they needed semiprivate rooms for "paying" customers, not AIDS patients. I could feel my anger rising. I was not going to have my son treated this way. I know how I would feel being shuttled around with no one to look out for me in such an environment. I had to do something. During this week, my company had sponsored a Neurolinguistic Programming Seminar, with out-of-town people attending. I had no backup and couldn't leave and, up to this minute, had felt things were essentially under control with Donald at the helm. I was wrong.

When I telephoned Ward 6, on 6E at the UCSD Medical Center, Alan had been in the new room an hour and a half crying. He said he was told the semiprivate room 'was needed for a patient who had to be isolated. I could hear coughing in the background and busy noises. He was asking me to rescue him from the sounds of death and despair. "Rescue me, Mom. You've always been there for me. *Do something, please?*"

I promised him I would. But what? I'll talk to the nurses, I thought. They should be able to help. Wrong again.

After reaching the nurse's station on the Sixth Floor, I found my Self talking with a nurse who could *barely* speak English. I asked to speak to someone who could tell me why my son had been moved. She gave me another nurse. And another. And another. Finally, I strongly and angrily insisted they locate someone on that floor who could tell me what was going on. I would wait until they did.

Finally, an English-speaking nurse told me Alan had been moved because he "is not covered by insurance and cannot remain in a private room." (So much for needing the room to "isolate" a patient. Also, until then, I had thought it was not semiprivate. Turns out the nurse was wrong. It *was* semiprivate.) "Who gave the order?" "I don't know." What's his or her name?" "I don't know." "Doesn't it have to be a doctor?" "Well . . . yes, usually . . ." "Usually? Don't you know?" "Well . . ." "Look at the order. Who signed it?" "I don't know."

By now I could not believe what I was hearing. I asked: "Who's on call on the floor?" A Doctor Golden. "Beep him," I fairly screamed into the phone. Answer: Not available. "Who's the chief resident?" Dr. Fierer. "Page him, *now*! Dammit!" Answer: "not available." "Get me somebody, *now*!" I shouted. "*Now*, goddamit!"

It was quite clear to me at this point that I was not walking my talk nor being civil, nor being the calm person I thought I could now be. *No one, absolutely no one* in that hospital was available. After what seemed to me an eternity, a voice indicated she would now be able to page a Dr. Zev Nash who was a pulmonary fellow working on AIDS cases and was the doctor (read, "asshole" resident) who had admitted Alan and appeared to be the person who knew the most about his case.

The Encounters

Dr. Nash, obviously briefed on my hostility, which, by now was bordering on hysteria based on the incredulous conversation I had just experienced, approached me on the phone like he was talking to an idiot. He told me Alan had been started, finally, on Septra for "presumed" PCP (Neumocystis Carinii Pneumonia) but that he wanted to do a bronchoscopy to make sure. However, they had done a silver stain in the meantime and it came back positive PCP. "Please slow down, Dr. Nash. Speak English to me and explain."

"I thought you were a *doctor?*"

"I am a psychologist, a PhD, not an MD. Even if I were an MD, you can't presume I know that much about AIDS. From what I can tell, no one does," I hissed.

"OK. Let me continue."

"This type of pneumonia is seen with people who have AIDS," he said. "I've got *that*," I said.

"Tell me about the lab test Alan took in December that was negative," I asked.

He countered with Alan's statement from his history taking indicating a positive HIV two years ago. "This means he's been exposed, and he also told me he was gay," said Nash. "Once he's had PCP, *he has AIDS.* (His voice was really saying 'I know what I'm doing and you don't. You're not even here!') Right now he is stable but fatigued. He is being premedicated with Ativan, a tranquilizer that makes him sleepy and makes him vomit."

"What's the outcome of this medication? Side effects?" I ask.

"Depends on the patient, how he handles all this. This is an *incurable* disease, you know. The patient eventually dies. No one can be completely cured. Medically, an AIDS patient is a difficult patient to take care of. So much can go wrong."

"Well, what are *you* doing for him *now?*"

"I will keep him from getting antibodies; support oxygenation; keep up his nutritional status, and, hopefully, keep up his spirits. The hospital staff can help (How? I thought. Most of them don't even speak English, for God's sake!) . But Alan's mental attitude is important and a supportive family is important. He obviously has *that*. Donald is here all of the time and, when not here, he's on the phone. Your coming out will provide critical support. His friends come by every day. He's getting calls and flowers. So all of this is important and helps keep his spirits up. Well, I hope I've helped some. I've got to go. I'm being paged. When did you say you were coming? Sorry . . . " Hangs up.

This was my introduction to the wonderful world of the UCSD Medical Center care. The nurse had indicated that they had not completed Alan's tests (not scheduled yet!) but the wheels were in motion for him to get California Medical Insurance and other social services that are automatically provided once the AIDS diagnosis was confirmed "so that these things could be 'taken care of.'" (Read: paid for.) Three days already and this is where they are? "Oh my God," I thought, "he may be dead before I arrive—the way things are going."

I called Rob Marier back and I told him what I knew. He advised me to go directly to the head of the center at UCSD when I arrived and get Alan into the experimental program where AZT was being administered. Of course, he advised, they would have to clear up the pneumocystis first, but he assured me that *if* Alan survived the pneumocystis and *if* he were accepted into the Center's experimental program, he had a chance, but no guarantees. Not all, but a good many, patients being treated with AZT and aerosol pentamidine were remaining free of contamination for longer and longer periods. He provided comfort by stating that with all of the research under way, there is hope that within the next few years more drugs would be given in tandem—effective suppressants—that would allow people to live in remission for long periods of time. "All this means, Vikki, to be honest, is that we're trying to buy some time. We're not without hope. Better times and days are coming." "Thanks, Rob, I thought. Now, what do *I* do in the meantime?

My answer, for now, was to remain in daily telephone contact with Alan, Donald and Dr. Nash.

On February 10, I spoke with Dr. Nash for the last time before flying to California. I had talked with Alan and he felt, drugged as he was, that he was not being treated well. The tests had not all been run. He was being essentially ignored and his experience in the ward was depressing him. With this in mind, I asked Dr. Nash "if Alan had not told him he was gay, would Alan have received better treatment?" No response. Nash indicated that, in any case, clearance from me was required for extensive changes in treatment and that the sooner I could get there the better. "*We're* doing all we can to clear up this pneumocystis and to cope with keeping him breathing and his strength up. He's not eating. In short, I think your presence will help."

I told him my expected arrival on February 11 and said I would look him up immediately. I also asked why I had not been contacted by him or a representative of the medical staff *if* my approval for treatment was so important. No answer.

I asked who ran the center (Dr. Chris Matthews) and would he be available? Nash said that he knew more about the case than Matthews and that I should speak with *him* first, not Matthews.

I got the picture immediately and vowed to find Matthews the minute I arrived at the UCSD hospital.

Dr. Chris Matthews was not easy to find. After repeated pages, we connected. He agreed to meet me in the cafeteria within fifteen minutes.

He was pleasant, as was I, but I peppered him with questions about Alan's treatment, Dr. Nash's role, and resident supervision in the hospital. He assured me Nash was supervised and doing as good a job as possible. The UCSD hospital was the only place AIDS patients could get care in San Diego County. Private physicians were not touching these cases at all. Too costly and reimbursement for care was too low for private physician care. Alan was very fortunate to have a caring, loving family. Most AIDS patients brought there didn't have *that*, or most any, type of support. That, he assured me, was in Alan's favor, for starters. (Little did he know!)

Matthews spoke about a case just the previous week where a father brought his son into emergency with pneumocystis and, in the presence of Matthews, told his son: "I hope you die in here," and left. The son has not seen nor heard from him since. He assured me such negative behavior by parents was more typical than not. "So, you see, your concern and presence, especially coming from such a distance, is both reassuring and helpful to Alan and to us." (Is it any wonder so many AIDS patients never leave alive? Who cares, really?)

I told Matthews about Dr. Marier, whom he didn't know, and indicated my desire to have Alan in the Center and on the experimental program after the pneumocystis was licked. (Positive thinking!) I also gave him a quick review of my background and noted that my husband was a physician and dean of a medical school. I did this deliberately. It provided Matthews with an "excuse" to extend "professional courtesy," though I did not directly ask for such a response. But I know that, psychologically, Matthews got the message and understood what I was saying. He did. He assured me that, *if* Alan made it, he could be in the Center program. I said, "Not *if*, but *when* . . . ."

". . . You are the bows from which your children
as living arrows are sent forth.
The archer sees the mark upon the path of the
infinite, and He bends you with His
might that His arrows may go swift and far.
Let your bending in the archer's hand be for gladness;
For even as He loves the arrow that flies, so
He loves also the bow that is stable.[3]

The Bow That Is Stable

It helps to have been a management consultant at a university hospital. I knew the structure and knew where to go directly for help. My next stop was the Patient Relations Office where I met with the director, told her what had happened to my son, indicated who I was and who his stepfather was and then said I wanted a semiprivate room for him *now.* "*How* can you help me accomplish this?" I asked firmly, maintaining eye contact. The director asked me to wait. When she returned, she had already ordered Alan moved to a semiprivate room where she said I could then see him. Fast action, to be sure, but I did make it clear I would not take *no* for an answer.

When I saw Alan in his new room, he smiled and reached for me. We hugged and cried and said nothing. We just held one another knowingly. When I composed my Self, I told Alan about my trip; indicated, by sweeping my hand around the room, that I had "stopped off to take care of some business" (he smiled) and then, holding his hand, said: "Alan, darling, I must know. Do you want to live or die? I'll support you in whatever *you* want. But this is *your* life, *your* pain and *your* decision. If you want to die, I'll see that you die with dignity and without pain to the extent that can be accomplished. If you want to live, darling, I'll do all in my power to provide the support for life. But you'll have to fight for it and keep in your mind that it is life that you want and life that you choose. Do you understand?" He answered tearfully, "Yes, Mom." "Alan, what is your decision?"

"Mom, I want to live. Help me to live." Tears streamed down both our cheeks. "I will, Alan. I promise I will do *my* part. You must do yours. Understand?" He whispered a feeble, "Yes." With that "Yes," Alan and I made a bargain for life. He told me he did not want any life-support system introduced. If he got to that point, he just wanted to be made comfortable and allowed to transition peacefully. He insisted that he also wanted to be cremated—"but make sure I sit long enough for my soul to leave my body before cremating it," he cautioned. I agreed, kissed him, and then started the process that would earn me a reputation as an outrageous bitch.

The Work

First I introduced my Self to the nurse supervising 6E. I emphasized the "Dr." knowing she would never ask "Dr. of what?" I gave her my card on which I had put my San Diego number and then asked to go over Alan's chart to make sure all the information was correct regarding family, telephone numbers, etc. Next, I asked who was supervising night duty and when she came on board. I indicated I would return that night to meet her and to be sure she understood that I wanted Alan watched and taken care of. Next, I talked by phone with the head of the nutrition and diet division. Alan had not been eating and was losing weight very fast. Dr. Nash said that was not unusual, but he had not consulted with the nutritionist to see what could be done. I found I could bring Alan food that he liked that was not available through the hospital. For the next 14 days I provided him with fruit smoothies and salads from his favorite health food store. (It helped him gain weight.)

Next, I conferred with Nash and had him explain to me what had been done for Alan to that minute, what was planned, what were side effects of medications, and what other tests were going to be run and why. Nash was testy but responsive. It was obvious I wasn't going away. I finally told him that my husband was a physician and that no invasive procedures beyond intravenous feeding and medication were to be done without talking with Bob first. A protection against unnecessary processes just because they are learning about AIDS, I thought.

With these steps, I began my comings and goings at University Hospital—at odd times, to see how Alan was doing and how he was being cared for and treated. I noticed how slowly nurses responded to the beeper on Alan's various "machines" attached to his body. I finally asked to be shown how to take care of the equipment, in case I needed to do so, since their response time was so slow. This didn't endear me to the floor nurses, but, over time, as they began to know me and understood that I was not going away, they were more helpful, responsive and, above all, more pleasant. I insisted on pleasantness by *my* pleasant interaction and greetings. I noted the "institutional attitude" toward some of the other AIDS patients. Not good, I thought. Their attitude was: They're (AIDS patients) using more than their share of care time, MediCal payment for their treatment ensures loss of money to the hospital for the rooms and treatment, and the personnel are "running scared" of the disease. Not an ideal place to heal, I thought, but a great place to die! And "the sooner, the better," the environment seemed to whisper!!

Alan's friends, his brother and sister, and I kept him happy with our presence. My friends all over the country sent flowers and assured him they were praying for his recovery. Members of the family we hadn't heard from in years telephoned him to assure him they knew he would get well, and soon. Colleagues of mine called Alan and told him they were holding good thoughts for him. He was buoyed up by us all and it helped him to *know* he is loved. Basking in that knowledge, he began to gain weight, feel better, and sound like his old self.

Donald, Donna and *their* friends saw Alan every day. The three of us talked about the problems I was encountering with treatment, doctors and the system. I asked how they were handling Alan's illness and how they were *feeling*. Donna admitted being afraid. Donald was angry, but could not really express his feelings in words. There was tension in our survivor group.

Donald had never accepted Alan's gay lifestyle. He had "warned" him that he was going to "get in trouble." Of course, his own feelings about death and abandonment had never been worked through because of his denial about his true emotions toward his father and me; he was still angry deep inside with me about all the responsibility I had "laid on him" as the oldest *in loco parentis*. He was an eruption waiting to happen. Just like I had been eight years before. Mirror, mirror!

Donna appeared to be more accepting and personally understanding. She has a dominant personality and was more outspoken, picked at both Donald and Alan all the time, and did not like Alan's friends. But it was she who had called me that fateful January 26 to tell me Alan had lost 25 pounds. "Mom, I think he's dying. I found him crying today. His pants are baggy, his face is drawn, he acts irrational, and he is so stressed out from coughing he can't work. Dr. Zirpolo is treating him for bronchitis, but this doesn't happen with bronchitis, does it?" "No," I responded, "Keep an eye on him and if he doesn't get better in 24-48 hours, he should go into the hospital. Keep me posted."

She had caused me much pain in her teen years—to get my attention—and had not processed how much she felt left out of my affections in favor of the boys (her perception, thus her truth). Still, she has a deep concern for each of us in her own way, though at times her brothers think she has a strange way of showing it. And yet, I would not have had *any* warning except for her call.

I, too, was tense and wasn't taking care of my own emotions. Too much to do. But it was time to stop and face our Selfs, together. I enlisted the help of a psychologist friend, Ann Jennings, and the four of us convened for a Saturday afternoon group therapy session. It was honest, brutal, emotional and draining. But it helped us cut through a lot of crap that had built up over the years and permitted us to begin openly communicating with one another on new levels and with new expressions of love. The healing had begun and continues to this day. *Tough and tender love.* Hard work—all around. Alan's crisis had been a much-needed catalyst for the rest of us.

> *"You have been told also that life is darkness,*
> *and in your weariness you echo what was said*
> *by the weary.*
> *And I say that life is indeed darkness save when*
> *there is urge,*
> *And all urge is blind save when there is knowledge,*
> *And All work is empty save when there is love;*
> *And when you work with love you bind your Self to*
> *your Self, and to one another, and to God . . .*
> *Work is love made visible . . .* 4

The Crisis

Without warning, Alan began to run very high temperatures that would not come down. I arrived at the hospital Sunday, February 14, to find Alan with a bright red rash all over his body. He was having difficulty breathing. I urgently called Drs. Nash and Matthews. Nash was the first to arrive and said the rash was a reaction to the septra. They had to change his medications right away or Alan could go downhill fast. Nash indicated he would put Alan on pentamidine. He noted there were risks, even with pentamidine, but that Alan's reaction to septra would lead to death for sure. I asked if that rash had been there during morning rounds and Nash said there had been some sign, but nothing like what I found. The nurse who had helped him with his change of clothing and bedding *must* have seen it, but did not report it. I was truly upset. Nash wrote new orders and the change in medication was put in process. With the change in medication, Alan's temperature returned to normal within 24 hours. And so it went for the next two days.

By February 17, the doctors had agreed that Alan was doing well enough to go home and become an outpatient. I felt they were pushing their luck so soon after the "rash" incident, but I was assured all would be well. Dr. Nash wrote the orders releasing him, he was given instructions on taking medication, a schedule for his first visit and I was called to pick him up. Even as I was checking Alan out of the hospital, I felt he was not strong enough to leave but the doctors assured me that was not the case. So, on Wednesday, February 17 at 4:00 P.M., I took Alan home. He had lost 30 pounds and weighed about 120, but he looked much better, though still "emaciated" in my view, and was glad to leave the hospital.

I was very uncomfortable with Alan's breathing and had that nagging inner sense that all was not well. The first night home, he had a very high temperature reading—102. Thursday morning his temperature returned to normal. I called Dr. Matthews and asked him what to do. High temperatures meant trouble. He indicated that if it persisted, Alan would have to come back to the hospital. Friday night his temperature climbed to 104 and stayed there. At approximately 3:00 A.M., I readmitted Alan to the Emergency Room at UCSD hospital. To say I was upset is an understatement. The resident on duty who drew Alan's blood in the Emergency Room was tired and kept poking the needle around trying to find a vein. Alan cried out in pain, but this didn't faze the resident. I told him to go easy and asked what was wrong with him? He asked me to step outside. I didn't do it. I held Alan's hand but couldn't stop the doctor's bungling. After this procedure, I went to the desk and asked about a private room. The nurse said there weren't any available. I left the desk and went immediately to the Patient Relations Office where, without any flack for once, I arranged for a private room on the eleventh floor. It was done. Satisfied, I returned to the Emergency Room, advised the nurse of the room arrangement, then went into the cubicle where Alan was waiting. I told him the private room was arranged. He smiled and said, "*Do* it, Mom. I *knew* you could do it." I smiled and squeezed his hand. We sat in silence until the team was ready to move Alan upstairs. Then the phone rang. I could here the nurse's conversation. "The room's already been assigned. Yes. We're getting ready to take him up there now. Oh? There is a reassignment? To what room? I think we've got a problem here. I'll get right back to you."

The nurse called me over and told me Alan had been reassigned to the 6th floor again. "*Over my dead body,*" I said. "Don't move him until I return." I flew out of the Emergency Room and went to Patient Relations (by now it was 7:00 A.M., Saturday, February 20). I asked for the director. She was waiting for me. I told her that one of my skills was training people like her to handle people like me but that at this moment I was prepared to do everything in my power to get the private room for my son, up to and including talking with the hospital administrator and then the dean of the medical school, if necessary. I explained Alan's unfortunate dismissal, his relapse, the problems with the nurses, the bungling resident who had drawn his blood that morning—everything that he had encountered. "How do people survive in this, or *any*, hospital without someone who both understands the place and is willing to advocate and orchestrate activities and treatment in their behalf?" I asked. "Listen, Dr. Ashley. I understand. You are a mother. This is your son. No explanation is necessary. The truth is those without caring and knowledgeable family or friends have a rough time of it. If I were in your place, I would do exactly what you are doing. Just sit there a few moments and let me make a few calls." In ten minutes, the director returned and indicated that she had intercepted the orderlies and Dr. Nash on their way to 6E and had redirected them to 11E, Room 20. She assured me Alan would be there *until discharged*. (You're damn right, I thought. Until he goes out feet first or walking out. No one is going to push him around again in this hospital.) I thanked her with tears in my eyes, told her I was not sorry for my behavior, indicated I hoped she didn't take it personally, and assured her I would do it *again* under the same circumstances. She smiled knowingly and said she understood and did *not* take what I said personally. She repeated, "I'd have done the s*ame* thing under the *same* circumstances."

When I arrived in Alan's room on the private patient Gold Coast, Dr. Nash was already giving him the most thorough examination he had received since first being admitted. Nash looked sheepish and subdued when I asked what had happened. "Quite frankly, Dr. Ashley, I don't know. He had a severe reaction to pentamidine and we're putting him back on septra. We may have to add steroids, though that is also a high-risk medication since it depresses the immune system further. We just don't know what to do about this, but we'll do everything we can. I am personally sorry about Alan's relapse since I was the one who certified that he was well enough to leave. Be assured we'll keep him here this time until he's fully recovered from the pneumocystis. I've already talked to Dr. Matthews and we're going to do a bronchoscopy to determine what's going on. He's scheduled for 3:00 P.M. We're going to test him again for everything. We're hopeful we'll learn something more."

In front of Alan I told Nash that I was holding him personally responsible for seeing that no orders were given to move Alan out of the room or off that floor. "When he leaves this room he'll either be dead or walking out on his own steam, do you understand?" Nash nodded agreement and said that he'd see to it.

When he left the room, I walked out to the corridor with him and said: "If you fuck over my son, in *any* way, not only will you answer to me, I'll see to it that you *pay* for it dearly. Do you understand me, Dr. Nash?"

"Well, I wouldn't have used *that* word, but I understand you loud and clear. Don't worry, Dr. Ashley. I will see that he gets the best of care and Dr. Matthews is taking over his case *personally*. He knows a lot more than I do (No kidding! I thought) and we'll all work together, including the team that is now in Pulmonary. Go home, Dr. Ashley. Get some rest. I'll see you here for the bronchoscopy. I'll call you if anything changes."

"Well," I thought, "seems like the worm has turned!"

I returned to the room and held Alan's hand. "Honey, you're in bad shape and they don't know what to do. You're going to have to reach down inside and think "health" and "living." Visualize your Self as whole and well. Can you do that?" He nodded yes. Then he made him Self talk. "Mom, I don't want a life-support system. Promise me you won't let them put me on a life-support system. Please? If it comes to that, I just want to be made as comfortable as possible before I die." We were both crying. I promised and then asked him if he would accept life support if it were only temporary and there was hope of recovery. He said he would, but only up to 72 hours. If I don't recover in 72 hours, pull the plug, he said. "OK, honey. I will do as you say." The nurse came in and proceeded to hook up the oxygen. Alan could barely breathe; I left to take a nap. It was going to be a long day and night.

As I left the hospital, a policeman was in the corridor outside the Emergency Room asking about the car parked in the Emergency Room slot. I told him it was mine and explained the circumstances. "Move it, *now*," he said. When I reached the car there was a ticket on the windshield. Later I wrote a letter of explanation about why it was there. It was refused. Months later, I chose to pay the fine . . . $57! So much for humanitarian treatment and understanding. No patient slots outside Emergency. Do all seriously ill patients arrive in ambulances?

The bronchoscopy was painful to watch, though Alan did not seem to mind. I was there in the operating room behind a lead apron. Because it was Saturday, (February 20) the nurses usually available to help the doctors weren't on duty. The doctors had trouble finding their equipment. Alan told the lead physician not to start until he had *everything* he needed. That made us all laugh. It was the first laugh I had had since arriving in San Diego eight days before. What irony!

The tests, again, indicated PCP, a small problem with his blood and a severe problem with his breathing. When I had approached Matthews after the operation, he indicated nothing new was indicated, but that Alan was going downhill, and fast. He was unable to eat solids and was on intravenous feeding. They had begun septra again because he was clearly not doing well on pentamidine. His mouth was full of sores and he was having trouble sucking the troches to stave off Candida Esophagea (sores in his mouth). He was having trouble with his bowels and getting up to use the bath was painful. A bedpan was indicated but I had to request it!

Alan was very, very weak and could hardly speak. For the next four days I watched my son begin his private death march, though I would not label it so. He had been so pickled with needles in both arms, he was in danger of vein collapse. I had spent a night with him to monitor his night care. It proved to be unsatisfactory and when one of his machines went off, I just sat there to see how long it would take for someone to answer and check. After ten minutes and no response, I checked the hall and saw no one in the corridor. When I arrived at the desk, the nurse was there. I asked her why she had not answered the beep. She looked surprised to see me standing there and without a word hurried down the hall to Alan's room. All I could think about was how lucky a person is to get out of a hospital alive! No wonder those who can afford it hire private duty nurses for their loved ones while they are in the hospital!

I complained to Nash and to Matthews. They indicated they were short of staff at night and were doing all they could do under the circumstances. I noticed that Matthews glared at me, as he was beginning to do regularly. I said I could appreciate that, but I didn't want my son harmed because of *neglect*!

The Culminating Experience

So this is how things went until February 24. Early that morning my aunt, Geraldine Jester, called and told me she had heard a report the night before about an experimental drug released for use on AIDS patients by the National Institute of Allergy and Infectious Diseases (NIAID). She spelled the name: trimetrexate. She had an

800 number for me to call, (800-342-7514), so I hung up and at 6:00 A.M. PST called for information about the new drug; the operator was very helpful and provided a citation for the only article published about it at that time. The treatment sounded like it was just the thing that might work on Alan's pneumocystis. It was designed to knock out the PCP virus and to protect the rest of the body with leucovoran (folic acid). The information operator also provided the name of Debbie Katz at NIAID and her telephone number: 301-496-8210. She indicated Debbie could make decisions related to the release of the IND (investigative new drug).

I immediately called Ms. Katz. Eureka! She answered the phone. After telling her Alan's condition and what he was up against, she indicated that he sounded like a perfect case for the IND. What I had to do was get Dr. Matthews, as head of the Center, to call Ms. Katz to verify the diagnosis and agree to the treatment protocol for the new drug.

After determining her availability in her office all morning, I contacted my daughter and asked her to go to the library and get a copy of the literature citation. She promised to drop it by the apartment that evening.

Next I called Matthews at his home. After saying "hello," and determining it was I, he told me he didn't want to be called at home. "What do you want?" "To see you as early as possible at the hospital. I have some good news." "Page me when you arrive" he fairly shouted. I was stunned. "How did you get my number?" "I asked for it," I said as I hung up the phone.

In spite of Matthews' attitude, it is hard to express how I felt, but I *can* say that I was excited, apprehensive, happy and floating. I hardly remember driving to the hospital. Alan and I had agreed that he would "try anything" that seemed like it would work. What did he have to lose but his life?

I met Dr. Matthews in the corridor outside Alan's room around 10 A.M. February 24. He and Dr. Kipper, the chief resident, pulled me aside and told me they had concluded Alan had no more than 48 hours to live. They wanted to start life-support *immediately*. Matthews said that if they didn't, he had no more than 48 hours *at the outside*. I looked him in the eye and said, "Well, then, *you're* going to tell him.

Not me. I am dedicated to his *life, not* his death. *I won't tell him."*
Matthews: "I'll tell him. Let's go."

He stood at the foot of Alan's bed with the resident. "Alan, can you hear me?" Alan nodded "Yes." "We were just telling your mother you have no more than 48 hours to live. We know how you feel about the life-support system, but we have to let you know that without it, you have no chance at all. Are you willing to give it a try? Perhaps we can do something once you are on the system that will make a difference. If we do nothing now, there is *no chance at all."*

Alan's eyes welled up in tears. He looked at me. I could see death staring back at me. "Alan, there's some news I haven't even told the doctor—until now. I spoke with a Ms. Katz in Washington just this morning. There is a new investigative drug she thinks will help you. Darling, are you willing to try it? If Dr. Matthews will call and confirm the diagnosis, she assured me they can fly it here within 48 hours. Can you hear me, Alan? What do you want to do? After all, it's *your* life!" Alan nodded "Yes."

I turned to Dr. Matthews who was fidgeting and upset, clearly. Matthews: "Alan, this is a new drug. I know your mother is excited about it, but *we* know nothing about it. There's no evidence it will work. We have you on steroids, now, and with the extra life-support, we think we can pull you through." Was I hearing right? This is the man who had just told me and Alan he had 48 hours *at the outside* to live? *I was furious!* "*No!* I want *you* to call Ms. Katz right away and discuss this with her." My voice was firm, steady and powerfully even. "Here is the telephone number. She is *waiting* for your call, now. Will you call her, *now?"*

"Yes, I'll call her. But I *will* not promise you I will use the drug, even if we can get it."

"Just call her now, please. And let me know what she says. That's the least you can do."

Matthews walked stiffly out of the room, followed by Dr. Kipper. I sat by Alan and held his hand. We did not speak. The thoughts running through my mind were mixed with anger, hurt, and, yes, fear for the callous way this eminent physician was responding to an *opportunity* to save my son's life. All I wanted was a chance. If we were going to race the clock for Alan's soul, it was clear *my* way was better than Matthews'. He had all but said the *Dies Irae* over him not twenty minutes ago!

After sitting with Alan for two hours, I called my husband and told him the situation. He explained to me how Matthews must have been feeling. I had been directly interfering all along with the treatment plan and *now* I had *really* done the unforgivable. I had interfered at the national level in the office where the Center probably got approval for their research designs and funds and certainly received go ahead for use of investigative new drugs. I had probably done something even Matthews could not do. After all, Bob explained, the Centers had to wait for their allocations of investigative drugs and it was a roll of the dice who got them when they arrived. Furthermore, the availability had just been announced within the last 24-48 hours. How had I made the contact with the decision-maker so soon? Through my aunt who was checking every possible source for help, I explained.

I told Bob I understood how the system is *supposed* to work but that right now I was grateful that I had the guts to move ahead and intervene. This is a crisis! *I want Alan to live!* To hell with how Matthews or anyone else feels, my soul screamed! To hell with the whole damn system. If I have to fly to Washington and return on the next flight, I'll do it. *Whatever* it takes. Alan will *not* die because of some stupid medical protocol or ego requirements! I cried so hard I thought I would go blind.

Bob said he understood, supported me 100% and that I was doing the right thing, no matter what Matthews thought. His rational self just wanted to be sure I recognized how far I was going out on a limb. I knew. But did I care? No way.

"Vikki, doctors see so much death, they become inured to the emotional impact on families. In our system there are so many demands, it is better to *try* to treat everyone alike. Individuality does not count unless someone is *making* it count. The situation with AIDS is probably wearing all of the doctors, including Matthews, pretty thin. Any disease without a cure tries their belief in healing. Regardless of his hostility, I am sure he doesn't want to see Alan die. I also believe he doesn't want you getting in his way. After all, what do you know? You're not a *medical* doctor, right? Nevertheless, my dear, remember that you are a formidable person on your *best* behavior. In these circumstances, I would not like to be in Matthews' shoes. Do what you have to do. I love you." That night, Bob and I went through this scenario again. He was, and is, supportive, thank God.

To keep my Self busy that afternoon, I used Alan's phone and made some quick calls, talked with my best friend, cried with her, and sat by the bed of my dying son. He'd occasionally open his eyes and just look at me, then drop off to sleep again. He was heavily drugged.

At 1:11 P.M. I had not heard from Matthews. I decided to call Debbie Katz directly again to see if he had called. He had. "But, Vikki, I don't know what you said to him but he was very hostile and angry with you and said so to me. Nevertheless, Alan fits the profile and the trimetrexate is already *in the air*. It will be there early tomorrow morning." I thanked Debbie and told her I would let her know how things went. (A month later I did.)

> *Individuality does not count unless someone is **making** it count.*
> —Vikki Ashley

Before she let me go, however, she explained that it was a 21-day treatment and that Alan should stay on it 21 days for expected results. I told her I would see to it that no shortcuts were made. She laughed and said she was sure I would. She also said that, in my circumstances, she would have done the same thing.

I jumped for joy. Then I put my head down and cried like a baby.

My heart was thumping so hard I could hardly speak as I woke Alan to tell him the medicine was on its way. He reached up, smiled and said, "Thanks, Mom. You did it *again!*" Then back to sleep he went. This time, though, I detected a much stronger smile.

To prepare for the use of the drug (no way was Matthews *not* going to use it), I left the hospital, went to my oldest son's apartment, and drafted a legal release form. I called Donald and Donna and told them the good news, reinforced the importance of Donna picking up the article so we could all read about this drug and its side effects. In the early evening I had Allisyn, Donald's friend, who is an attorney, review my draft. It was legal.

The night of February 24, I took the release form to the hospital, woke Alan, explained what I had done, read it to him and then went out in the hall and looked for someone to witness our signatures and sign as a witness. I had dated the release form for February 25, the date the treatment was to begin. There was *no* doubt in my mind that trimetrexate would make the difference. I would be ready.

Dr. Matthews called me at the apartment around 9:00 A.M. February 25. He told me that the medicine had arrived and that he had decided to administer it. First, however, I would need to come in and sign all the necessary release forms before he could proceed.

"I anticipated this," I stated as calmly as I could, "and you will find a signed copy in the drawer beside Alan's bed. You can proceed as soon as possible."

"We're getting ready now, but I want you to understand there is *no guarantee this is going to work.* Even if he improves, we won't know whether it is the trimetrexate and leucovorin or the steroids," he stated in a clearly commanding, hostile voice.

"No matter," I said. "After all, just yesterday you advised me he had no more than 48 hours to live. Let's get on with it. I'll be there in an hour."

When I arrived, Alan was being tested and prepared for the pre-medication. I was to wonder later how long "preparation" really took. He began the trimetrexate treatment at 10:15 *P.M.* on a one-hour drip followed by leucovorin—every six hours. I was so glad the treatment was under way, I allowed my Self not to worry about the long time in between receipt and implementation!

The next morning I called Matthews and thanked him for going ahead with the treatment. I also said: "I feel you are angry and upset with me. Is that true?"

"No. I'm not upset with you. I just do not want you to expect more than we can do. We'll see how this new treatment works, but if there is *any* problem, we will pull him off it and return to the septra. That's the way it is."

I bit my tongue and mumbled something about being glad to know he was not upset with me and my behavior (I knew he was lying) and that I wanted him to give this new drug every opportunity to work. I let him know I understood Alan was the first patient in San Diego County to get the drug. *That* way he *knew* I had talked with Debbie Katz and *knew* that *I* knew he had not given me the courtesy of closing the loop after he had talked with her the day before. But I left a "way out" for him and never confronted him directly regarding lying. He *had* taken Alan on personally as his patient—at least for the investigative phase, and even I knew that was unusual with both his medical and administrative responsibilities. Besides, I had achieved my goals. I wanted to be able to talk with him later and count on him to respect the fact that he was not dealing with an idiot. More than even *that*, I wanted Alan to get the very best of treatment the Owen Clinic had to offer. Matthews would see to it. I felt confident of that now.

Death And Rebirth—A New Beginning

As they say, the rest is history! Alan began to improve almost immediately. Two days later he was sitting up and beginning to ask for food. He even asked if I would rent him a TV! I did. Gladly.

Well, I thought, maybe I can hop that plane today. Alan is on the mend. He's lucid, smiling, breathing more easily and asking for a chicken salad sandwich. The plan according to Dr. Zev Nash, who by now was talking and acting like a concerned human being, was to keep Alan on the trimetrexate/leucovorin protocol for 21 days. He didn't see any reason why I needed to be there. The crisis had passed. He promised to stay in touch by telephone. He told me that he had learned a lot from Alan's case and had even come to like and respect me. After all, I taught him a nonmedical thing or two. He also hoped someday we could be more friendly and even, perhaps, that he might call me Vikki. I smiled, said I too had learned a great deal. I assured him I would do the same thing over again. He laughed and said he *knew* I would. "And, *no*, you may not call me Vikki . . . yet."

"Let me make a suggestion, though. When Alan is released, I think he should go to Mercy Hospital's clinic and enroll for the aerosol pentamidine program. He's eligible and we don't have the program here. From what I am reading, it is doing a really fine job of keeping PCP patients' lungs clear. That, together with the AZT treatment here, should give him a real chance at a good life, in spite of the AIDS." I thanked him for that "special information" and asked him to reinforce it with Alan. He promised me he would. And he did.

I flew home that night in peace.

It was hard to leave Alan. But, at 27, he had to take charge of his own life now. I had done what I could. It was no small feat.

On February 29, I received the following telephone report from Dr. Nash:

"When I checked at 7:00 A.M., Alan's lungs were all clear. The pneumocystis is gone. He's looking good and was even able to discuss his case with me. I gave him a rundown on what was happening. Haven't seen Matthews in three days."

On March 2, I received a call from Nash saying Alan was being discharged and that I shouldn't worry. He was being set up to continue his daily treatments of trimetrexate/leucovorin through a home nursing program. A social worker would be looking in on him daily for a while and in two weeks he would be coming regularly to the UCSD Owen Clinic for blood tests and checkups. I mildly protested but recognized that the deed was done. Matthews had signed the order for his release.

Nash indicated Alan is "lucky." "We have a lot of AIDS patients with PCP who are lingering and may not make it. 'But ole Al did!'"

"It's possible Alan will have intermittent problems. But it's important that he maintains a positive mental outlook and have good nutritional habits. This, together with the AZT and aerosol pentamidine treatments will allow him to live. He must do the most with what he has, if he is to live well. Clean living will help."

"To be honest, life expectancy right now is two-to-three years from the onset of diagnosis. The average is five years. Some beat the numbers; some don't. I hope Al does. With you on his side, he's got one hell of a head start, *Vikki*. He beat the Reaper this time and this is when many AIDS patients 'buy the farm.'"

"Regarding limits? Well, really there are none. He shouldn't permit him Self to tire. He will always need rest and should take it *when* he needs it. Exercise, especially walking. Eat well, and keep mentally and as physically fit as possible. Oh, I suppose he shouldn't scuba dive or sky dive; beyond that, he can do whatever he wants. Swimming is OK, in fact, it's good for his lungs as long as he starts out slowly and builds up his stamina. Also, no smoking or hanging around smokers. And that includes you (chuckle)."

"Well, that's just about it. Oh . . . Alan got teary eyed when I told him good-bye. We've become pretty good friends. The people at the Owen Clinic *will* take good care of him and you'll be glad to know Dr. Matthews is taking a special interest in Alan and will be his physician (surprise for me!). I know how you must feel about Dr. Matthews, but this guy is very strong but reticent. He deals with death and dying all the time. If he got emotionally involved with every case, he'd be an emotional wreck. As a psychologist, you can understand that, I'm sure.

"Oh, yeah. I want to tell you personally that the relapse Alan had was unfortunate. It's the first time that's happened to one of *my* patients. And I've only lost one patient to date. I believed Al would turn around all along. But the day before the trimetrexate arrived, he had inflammation of the pancreas. (No one had told me.) He *was* in bad shape. Still, I believed in his recovery to the bitter end."

"A social worker will see him before he leaves the hospital today and the home health care nurse from the Visiting Nurses Association will check on him each day and administer his medicine. He has his troches for his mouth, thermometer—he must take his temperature twice a day—and Chris (Matthews) will talk to him again and set his limits.

"It's been nice knowing you and Dr. Bob. I'm leaving the floor. My rotation is over. But I'll be in town so I'll check on Alan once in a while. Good luck. Thanks."

"Good luck to you, *Zev*. And thanks."

Chris Matthews called after Zev.

"Alan is doing nicely. We'll continue trimetrexate for seven days at home. In one week he will come to the Owen Clinic. We'll see him twice a week for about a month. There he'll get psychological support, physical care/exercise and nutritional direction. Luisa Stone will handle home care. Don't worry. He's in good hands at the Owen Clinic."

"Thanks for your help. Barbara Peabody thinks highly of you and so do I, in spite of our differences. (Matthews had me call her for support. She'd had a similar experience, but her son died.) I did what I had to do. So did you."

"Well, if it matters," said Matthews, "Even though I cannot say for *sure* that trimetrexate made the difference, I think *you* did the right thing. I'll stay in touch."

I smiled as I put the receiver down.

Evaluation And Debriefing

Love is the *only* thing, I thought. Love of self that brings self-esteem and the courage to do what *you* think is right in spite of everyone and everything. Love of your child whose path is not yours but whose desire to live permitted you to join in the struggle without guilt. A sturdy bow from which to shoot the arrow, I thought, with pride.

Love of the Lord God of my Being that provided the energy to "see" the right thing to do at every turn. And, strangely enough, a tough kind of love that *allows* others to be where *they are*, whether I agree or not, so that there is no hate, only *allowing*.

It is, in the end, my own acceptance of my Self that made it possible for me to be an "outrageous bitch" and to redefine what it means to be a "bitch" within the context of love and not hate—of anyone or of the system. That redefinition? A female who *B*rings *I*t *T*o *C*onclusion *H*appily. I had to resist saying *Herself*, though that might be appropriate under different circumstances. I had lots of help, in the end.

After all, as an organizational psychologist and management consultant, systems are "my thing." I suspect I have left my mark at UCSD, no matter *what* they called me behind my back. I felt like that person who said, "You can call me anything. Just be sure you know how to spell my name!" Perhaps because of my efforts, the doctors, for one small moment in time—that "parenthesis in eternity" we were given (my family and me)—perhaps they, too, in spite of their Selfs, secretly admired the effort I launched with

> **There is only the now. One moment, one day at a time.**
> —Vikki Ashley

my son to cheat death, against the odds. And, yes, against the medical establishment's processes in *that* hospital. The paradox is that help finally came from two "outside" sources: my Aunt Gerri and

Debbie Katz of NIAID. And yet, I know I made a difference because of my knowledge of systems and process.

Our knowingness, Alan's and mine:

>*There is only the now.*
>*One moment, one day at a time.*
>*One foot in front of the other.*
>*Live life to its fullest in the now!*
>*Through living and just being, each of us*
>*can stretch that "parenthesis in eternity"*
>*into forever!*
>*You control your own reality.*
>*Make it what you truly want.*
>*It's our choice!*

A Son Dies! A Bitch **With Style** Is Born.

Being a **Bitch** *With Style* started in the beginning of my life, literally. It began by my living it without putting a name to it or claiming it. I began to put my thoughts to the idea twenty-five years ago and began actively doing research and writing about this concept ten years ago when the idea of this book was born. In my case growth occurred as a result of crises, chaos, and significant emotional events (SEEs) in my life. This book was begun out of pain.

The Rest of the Story

My son Alan's crisis with pneumocystis pneumonia in 1988 passed. Service in the hospital went from shit to first class. Alan recovered and walked out on his own two feet. We enjoyed three years of relative freedom from worry until 1990. That's when he decided he just had to have a kitten. He wanted something to cuddle, touch and hold. It was his greatest sorrow that he would never have a child to put his or her arms around **his** neck. The kitten would have to do, along with me. Within three months of the kitten's arrival, Alan began coughing and having trouble with his lungs. He had to let his kitten go. The fumes from changing the litter had become a source of danger to his fragile life line.

It was the beginning of the end of this earthly existence for him. Once more I had to engage in my **bitch, *with style*** methods at University Hospital because there was a whole new crew who had to be "trained." One chief resident, in January 1991, told Alan he'd have to go home because he was "taking up" expensive bed space. "You can be transported by ambulance each time you need a treatment," he said. After Alan informed me of *that* decision, I went into action. I told the chief resident it was none of his damn business how long Alan held that bed and that he was totally out of bounds talking to a dying patient in that tone and with those words. Besides, the cost of ambulance transportation, the discomfort for Alan would kill him faster than anything I could think of. "I won't have it," I told him and promptly found the attending physician. After I had recounted all the *faux pas* that had been occurring *this* time, I asked the attending physician to call a meeting of all of Alan's caregivers and to permit me to talk to them all. He did and I did. I shared all of the problems and issues with each one of them, pointing out the final act of the chief resident that set me off. I told all of them that I hoped some day they would have a child or relative in crisis and have to rely on the health care profession to "do the right thing." By the time I was through, most of us were crying. The chief resident came up to me, apologized and told me that all I had to do was call him any time of day or night and he would come to Alan at home. Chris Matthews, that wonderful doctor so dedicated to the care of his patients that he had to keep some detachment or not be able to function, offered to come to Alan at home at any time, and did.

Alan requested that he die at home in his own bed. I had the morphine to ease his pain. He didn't need too much of it nor did he ask for more than he needed. I would have been willing to give him that and more if he had asked me. The night of January 21, his brother, sister and several friends gathered around his bed, making jokes and talking to him when he suddenly pointed up to the ceiling and told us there were three women looking down on him. Three spirits come to help him over into his new dimension, I thought. That night I slept with Alan. I hugged him and kissed him one last time. The next morning I got up early to do some laundry. Just as I returned to his bedside, he transitioned January 22, 1991 at 6:15 AM.

He had waited for me, just as he promised he would. I held my dead son and sobbed and sobbed and sobbed. I knew he was all right, but I was feeling the pain of loss so deeply that only crying could bring me momentary release.

The nursing aide arrived shortly thereafter and helped me clean Alan up. I called the children and his friends and told them we would all say good-bye to Alan together before I called the undertaker. They all arrived within an hour of my call. We drank coffee, recounted our own experiences with Alan, all of us around his corpse, laughing, crying, talking, celebrating this "love" of a man who gave so much love to each of us. This impromptu posttransition session took some of the sting out of Alan's immediate death. It also gave his spirit time to linger in love with those he left behind.

I deliberately put Alan's body in storage for seven days to permit his spirit time to "make it over" before the cremation. When I saw him wrapped in a shroud before the cremation, I thought how serene and beautiful he looked. He looked like a Buddha! And then they shoved him into the furnace. Ashes to ashes, dust to dust.

The memorial for Alan was held on January 29th at 11:00 A.M., with the music he had selected and recorded and the service he had designed. I know he attended. It was a beautiful, sunny day. That evening all his friends gathered to each in turn take handfuls of Alan's ashes and scatter them into the wind and the ocean off the rocks of Herb and Sybil York's home in La Jolla, Ca. As I took Alan's ashes into my right hand to hurl into the wind and water, I looked into the western sky and saw a shooting star. "Bye, darlin," I said to my Self. "God speed."

The collage on page 34, I designed with the assistance of Dr. Jackson Townsend at LSU School of Medicine, New Orleans. It was part of a creative project I developed and chaired in 1994 at the end of my grieving/healing process. The show, was called *The Future of Healing**, and displayed photo art of various elements of basic science research being done by academic investigators at the LSU medical school in New Orleans. It was a juried show and selections were made by professionals who run the Louisiana State Museum in New Orleans.**

---

*Was sponsored by the LSU Medical Center Foundation
**It's still on display in the auditorium of the medical school.

Alan Vincent Rickman
September 21, 1960—January 22, 1991

From lower left to right: (1) The family: Donna, Donald II and Alan Rickman and Vikki Ashley (Taken during the almost three years of Alan's health after the first crisis in 1988). (2) Alan's last stay in University Hospital. (3) Christmas, 1990—Alan's favorite time of year, at his home! (4) The HIV (Human Immunodeficiency Virus)—a beautiful piece of art and deadly virus. (5) Alan and Vikki at Christmas. (6) Alan Getting Worse. (7) The night before transitioning (family and friends were with him). (8) Burial at sea— throwing Alan's ashes into the win and te sea, a mother's last responsibility. All of us, his family and friends, are gathered to each throw a handful of his earthly body into the wind and into eternity on the rocky shore of the home of Herbert and Sybil York in La Jolla, Ca.

It was a wonderful way to demonstrate the beauty of nature and how art imitates nature. The bottom line for this **bitch** *with style* was my spiritual and soulful release of my agony with the hanging of Alan's AIDS collage in the auditorium of the LSU School of Medicine. The whole project, this work, was one of love (focused emotion) and the completion of Alan's collage was an act of love released into the ethers for anyone and everyone to see and learn from. It was my own way of saying, again, but this time in public: I *love* you, Alan. Always have and always will. *Thank you* for being my teacher. *Thank you* for coming to me when I called. I *love* you. We *love* you. We miss you.

After Alan's first encounter with the medical community around AIDS (1988), I flew home to New Orleans to be with my husband. I was spent, down, depleted. It was in the airport in Houston between planes that I began the idea for this concept and started my notes identifying all the positive words one can develop using the letters **b.i.t.c.h.**

I turned to the back inside cover of my **Course in Miracles** paperback and began to write. In the **Bitch's Book Bag** at the back of the book is a copy of the original notes I wrote. I thought that being a **bitch** wasn't so bad after all if it meant something good was taking place. I began to feel very good about what I was considering and the more I talked to my Self about being a **bitch**, the more I liked what I felt.

I added *with style* because I recognized immediately that I was dealing with my own style of behavior, how I handle my emotions, values and perceptions. Every act I triggered to support Alan's living was an act of love. I took all of my masculine **and** feminine energy and focused each in turn like a laser beam on the challenges and issues that confronted us both. My *masculine* I used for action. I initiated, identified, relayed information and perceived that, in reality, I was working against my doctor's ego and for my son's recovery. I turned that scenario around and began to change the environment (a hostile one) to match **my** intentions around my son's survival and his recovery from that bout of pneumocystis pneumonia. I focused the attention and response of the nursing and orderly personnel toward doing

L to R: Donna, Donald, Alan Rickman. Vikki Ashley, May 1988.

their jobs on my son's behalf. I had already indicated to the Patient Relations manager my intention to have my son housed on the "best" floor of the hospital, or I was going to take my information above her head. She moved like lightening to take care of everything.

My feminine energy was used to love, nurture, cuddle, touch, talk with and support my ailing son, his friends, his brother and sister and my friends. It seemed endless, that love. The more I spread around, the more I had. I even mentally sent love to all the hospital staff (including *all* the doctors!)that were giving my son trouble. Whenever I saw one of his nurses, I mentally said "The Christ in me salutes the Christ in you." I did this repeatedly. To everyone. Still do. Only difference today is that when I greet *anyone*, I know that it is The **I** (spirit) I am greeting *in* everyone.

It's important to report that throughout all of the foregoing odyssey, I did not blow up nor did I curse anyone out. Aren't you surprised? I got angry as hell, but when I get *really* angry, look out!. I get very, very intense. I slow my speech down and my eyes get like laser beams as I look directly at whomever I am talking with. I thought about verbally kicking ass but concluded, rightly, this was neither the place nor the situation, nor would it help me to accomplish our (Alan's and mine) goals for his health. To tell you the truth, I felt like acting an ass might allow someone to take it out on Alan and I did not want to entertain that possibility. I know medical personnel think of their Selfs as healers, but that's a title that is earned and not automatically conferred by dint of MD or a starchy white uniform.

During this odyssey, I was direct, intense, powerful and concise. I was directive and asked questions that required direct answers, usually "yes" or "no." I was my most powerful Self in the service of love. I was, indeed, a **bitch**. I have no regrets. That's how this book began, finally, to be written.

Where Do We Go from Here?

Chapters Two through Four share information about the **bitch *with style's*** possessions, values, ways of handling and using information and relationships and establishing psychological as well as physical roots. Chapters Five through Seven will discuss the importance of the power and energy in self-expression, risk taking, love given, sexual energy and its importance in creating "children of the mind" as well as real ones, enthusiasm, taking care of business (TCB), working with details, perfection, work, health, balance, beauty, relationships, and singing *your* song. Chapters 8 through 10 cover sex, rebirth, death, transformation, higher learning, traveling in the mind and foreign lands, the **bitch** *with style's* career, her public position, organizing her life. Steps 11 and 12 relate to friends, self-mastery, love received, detachment, imagination, relaxing, cleaning out our closets (figuratively and in reality), enlightenment, the importance of the subconscious and the formula for success. Step Twelve is also about holding the hand of God.

A Bitch *With Style* Is A Woman Who:

---

1. Loves her Self and is able to love others.
2. Is self-accountable and accepts responsibility for all aspects of her life—ALL.
3. Is conscious and awake! to Life—healthy in spirit, mind, emotions and body. Or, is walking into health!
4. Walks her talk!
5. Initiates, pioneers and is willing to walk where others have not trod.
6. Leads and influences people with her vision, thoughts, ideas, suggestions *and* applications of her thoughts.
7. Manages her own day-to-day life and takes care of business. She thinks for her Self.
8. Looks at her **S**trengths, **W**eaknesses, **O**pportunities and **T**hreats (**SWOTs**) fearlessly and often.
9. Is courageous in small things and large. She acts "as if" she already has what she envisions. She "walks" into her fears "as if" they were already gone and they disappear.
10. Is independent and assertive. She walks on her own two feet.
11. Is warm and vital, cooperative and caring.
12. Is youthful—in energy, regardless of age—and lives in the *here and now*.

ASHLEY MAXIM

You create your own reality. Make it what you TRULY want!

February 25, 1988

TO: Dr. Chris Matthews

FROM: Alan Vincent Rickman

SUBJECT: Treatment and Life Support

I have asked my mother, Dr. Vikki Ashley, to prepare this letter in my behalf.

Because many patients being treated for pneumocystis pneumonia have required more than one regimen because of either FAILURE OF OR INTOLERANCE TO primary therapy, as soon as it is determined that the current therapy is ineffective, and based on the results of tests and the bronchoscopy that indicates I have a severe case of pneumocystis, I desire that I immediately receive Trimetrexate that is specifically designed as an experimental treatment for severe pneumocystis.

I understand from my mother that enough medication for a 21-day treatment course is being provided. I want every opportunity to lick this PCP and I am clear that this is not a CURE for aids but specifically an experimental new drug for pneumocystis.

I have decided that should it become ABSOLUTELY necessary to put me on an inhalator (life-support) system, such effort, IF REQUIRED AT ALL, will last no more than approximately 72 hours UNLESS it is determined my condition can be turned around. IF MY CONDITION CANNOT BE TURNED AROUND WITHIN APPROXIMATELY 72 hours, IT IS MY DECISION TO TAKE ME OFF THE LIFE SUPPORT SYSTEM AND MAKE ME COMFORTABLE FROM PAIN IN A PRIVATE ROOM, UNTIL I TRANSITION.

My mother is to be IMMEDIATELY informed of any action, day or night, leading to the use of life support equipment and she is my agent
in this whole matter, knows my wishes, and can speak for me if I cannot speak for myself re treatment, et al.

cc: Dr. Vikki Ashley
     Dr. Robert S. Daniels
     Donald C. Rickman II
     Donna Rickman
     Allisyn Thomas

Alex Rickman

Vikki Ashley

Jane C. Godden
Witness

2308 Albatross, #5
San Diego, CA 92101

237-1714

Alan's consent to begin the trimetrexate treatment.

TWELVE
STEPS
TO
BITCHHOOD

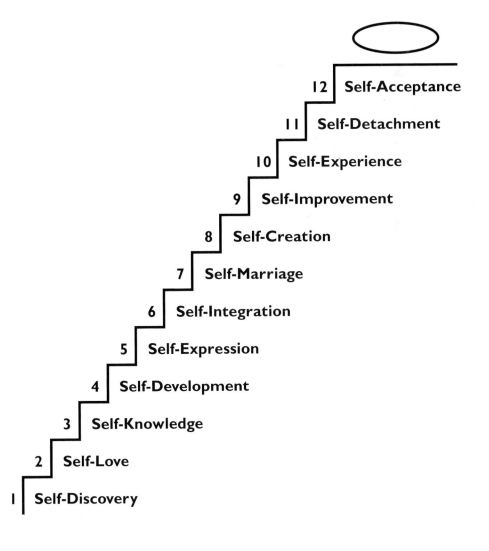

12	**Self-Acceptance**
11	**Self-Detachment**
10	**Self-Experience**
9	**Self-Improvement**
8	**Self-Creation**
7	**Self-Marriage**
6	**Self-Integration**
5	**Self-Expression**
4	**Self-Development**
3	**Self-Knowledge**
2	**Self-Love**
1	**Self-Discovery**

*The Bitch **With Style** Hat Racks*

*Vikki and Bob On the Way to
Australia—1997*

*Young Love—Vikki and Bob
and Cherry Blossoms—1992*

PART ONE

Laying the Foundation:

Who Am I?

STEP ONE

I Am A **Bitch**!

You create your own reality.
Make it what you truly want.

Hold that Tiger! Vikki in Red, again!—1997

THE FIRST STEP TO BITCHHood:
Self-Discovery.

This book is about *health, love, knowledge, power, error, igno-rance, pain, growth, Be-ing, death and rebirth, transformation and resurrection.* Yours and mine.

Like ingredients on the label of food and pharmaceutical products, the most important ingredient is *always* listed first, the next, sec-ond, and so on. I promise you "truth in packaging" so you can count on these ingre-dients to be absolutely essential to living. Guaranteed! So *health,* as the leader, is the foundation for all other ingredients in this package called "life." *Health* is the integra-tion of the spiritual, mental, emotional and physical energies that constitute spirit, mind, and body. *There are no exceptions to this defi-nition of health,* as I have come to understand it. Health cannot be bought, sold or invested. You *can* buy organs, treatment and care, but not health. You can't even buy a cure because ultimately a cure is in your thoughts and your body, which cures *itself,* if treated right. You and I are in charge of our health and it behooves us to make sure we have the tools and information in our book bags as we travel this path to **BITCHHood**. A **bitch,** *with style* is healthy.

> **Health** *is the integration of the spiritual, mental, emotional and physical energies that constitute spirit, mind, and body.*
> —Vikki Ashley

Without health, you have *nothing!* And the premise of this book is that *with* health, the **bitch** *with style* has *everything* she *truly* wants! Want that?

You will meet the "New You" that has a very special and unique purpose in life. Be-ing a **bitch,** *with style* is a state of being requiring acts of conscious love, will and desire for your Self. A **B**eing **I**n **T**otal **C**ontrol of **H**erself with style! But first, there's an old saying: "Love starts at home and then spreads abroad." You're going to rethink your thoughts of love at home (home is *you!*) as we go along and nothing you ever do will matter more than using love as one of

> *Love starts at home and then spreads abroad.*
> —Anonymous

the most potent emotions and tools in becoming a **bitch,** *with style.* What a difference it will make in your life. You'll see.

I want to warn you though, not everyone out there *wants* to walk the path to **BITCHHood** in this life. It's not in their blueprint, but, they can gain information that will help them the next time around. The soul will carry the energy that is put into their growth, no matter how far down the path they choose to use it. Until they *decide* to put their feet on the loose gravel path of life firmly pointed toward the North Star, they're going to be walking through hell in a *gasoline* shirt! While "hell" is a place the devil throws you into—we were taught—on this earthly plane, it only occurs in the experience of each of us according to the way we "see" our Selfs. Why not, then, "see" life differently? A **bitch,** *with style* does! It doesn't matter your station in life, age, race, culture, religion, job, or career. To be "in health" and to be a **bitch,** *with style* requires that we get out of the "hell" of our own making and begin to use that *gasoline* to fuel our imaginations to raise our sights! Health Elicits Light and Love.

> **It's a soul thing**
> —Vikki Ashley

Crossing the Burning Sands

The journey of self-acceptance (**BITCHHood**) *is* "crossing the burning sands." *When* that trip is taken has nothing to do with age. It's a soul thing, an experience that turns you in a new direction. The "New You Review" is part of the **Bitch,** *With Style* **Tool Kit** for which an order form is in your **Bitch's Book Bag.** It will help you on your way, should you choose to travel the path of self-acceptance.

The Gasoline Shirt

While my son Alan was going through the third year of health after his pneumocystis pneumonia crisis, several simultaneous events occurred in my life: Avis Johnson, my best friend and another mother to me, made her transition in November, 1990. On December 22, 1990, my dad died of lung cancer; On January 22, 1991, Alan made his transition at 6:15 A.M. On April

11, 1991, my mother died of bone cancer. On October 14, 1991, a dear friend and colleague, Bill McGrane II, made his transition. Then, to top it all, somewhere between January 1, 1990 and January 1991 I lost my desire for sex. Lost it, do you hear? Is that something to grieve or what? Poor Bob, I thought. This is serious. What on earth am I going to do about *all* this?

To me, this was chaos, big time. I had been working on my Self for years, spiritually. Had even taken what I called a spiritual sabbatical. Actually had the gall to think I *knew* my Self! After all, I had a PhD in psychology, was well known as a civic activist, politician, management consultant, and was also a divorced mother of three doing my best to keep it all together under the circumstances. Now I was recently married. My marriage was shaky for a number of reasons and it did seem to me that the gasoline shirt was about to consume me, not enlighten me. But while I had an academic PhD, I didn't yet have my PhD in the *Permanent Health Department* of the Universe. The gods were about to kick my ass, but good.

"Whoa, there, Vikki," I thought. "What's happening? What does this *mean?*" I was exhausted mentally, emotionally and physically. I just wanted to crawl up in some warm hole and hibernate for a while. It was a natural inclination that would never be satisfied physically, but I decided I had to satisfy it psychologically. Got to go into therapy, I told my Self. Got to have some help to orchestrate all this stuff that's going on. What does it all *mean?*

I was going through hell in a gasoline shirt and it was burning my butt instead of lighting my way. I had a decision to make: to get out of one hell (**H**abit **E**licits **L**aziness and **L**oneliness) and into another (**H**ealth **E**licits **L**ight and **L**ove). Getting into Hell #2 proved to be a learning ground; a place to make my way across the burning sands of life without *getting* burned. Therapy would eventually provide the asbestos shoes I needed to make my way for the next year through my life, my relationship with Bob, my spouse, and my grieving for my son, parents, and friends. Into therapy I went, practically breaking down the door to get in after checking around for a very good and strong therapist. It's a bit like people who go to those training sessions intent on walking across burning coals. Everyone who has the balls to do it, makes it across with or without help. Some make it across *without* burning their feet. Some get burned. What's the difference? Mind set. My mind was set on getting across without burning up. It was close!

> *Once a **bitch** sets her mind to "go," she grows.*
> —Vikki Ashley

Once a **bitch** sets her mind to "go", she grows. So I decided to move on toward Heaven, on the fast track, if there was one. (**H**ealth **E**licits **A**wareness, **V**itality, **E**nthusiasm and **N**uminosity.) (Note: Numinosity means being a deity; God. Having a deeply indwelling force or spirit.) I was convinced with all the death in my life, I had just been hit with a *Cosmic Mack Truck*! I was totally laid out and had to have spiritual treatment right away. I knew the sickness was in my soul but I could tell it was taking over my body as well. I was *tired,* y'all! *Just plain tired!* **And . . . .** revelation of revelations: *there ain't no fast track!* None! Got to do it moment-by-moment, day-by-day!

Now I *knew* in my soul this was a critical turning point in my life. I just didn't know how long it would last. The lessons of the Universe are not ours to time. It was *my* time to apply, once more, the knowledge of "how I wanted to 'see' things." It was time to put one foot in front of the other one moment-in-time, after another. And that's what I did, dragging ass to be sure. I was a **bitch, *with style***, and I was about to learn the greatest lesson of my life: how to own something by taking the comma *out* of my perception of who I AM. I was about to learn the difference between being a **bitch, *with style*** and a **bitch *with style*!**

How often have you heard the phrase "Heaven on Earth?" versus the phrase "hell on earth." When you're on vacation in Maui and walking the beach, you say to your Self "this is heaven on earth" and mean it at the moment. I've done that. Such a wonderful *feeling* inside when you say that phrase. It has good energy. Now, you've probably also said "this is hell!" when nothing goes right and every-thing that can go wrong, does. You verbally or mentally have said it a thousand times, and meant it. I have. Who hasn't? It just seems like Hell #1 (**H**abit **E**licits **L**aziness and **L**oneliness) sometimes, does-n't it? This phase doesn't *feel* so good. It's a downer!

So, y'all, "Welcome to the University of Life, Schoolhouse Earth." The curriculum, **BITCHHood 101** is set but the decisions about the courses we take are in our hands. As a result of this cur-riculum, we can set our minds to think, do, see, and become *anything we want.* We will go from kindergarten through the PhD (*Permanent Health Department of the Universe*) whether we want to or not. The only question now is "How much time do you want to take to get your PhD in **BITCHHood?**" Your coin of life may say "hell" on both sides but each side may have totally different meanings depending on *your* view. Or, your coin may say "chaos" on one side and "opportu-nity" on the other. Keep in mind that *Chaos* was a Greek god of the shapeless void that preceded the creation of Earth. Chaos, in "life" time creates a shapeless void for each of us (organizations as well as individuals) that affords us a time to reorganize our thinking, behavior, values and perceptions in order to form a new creation of our Self. And, you can do it more than once! I call chaos the "silly putty" of life because once our lives "break down," if we have the love, will and desire, we can shape our new lives

> **Chaos:** *the "silly putty" of life.*
> —Vikki Ashley

any way we want. Earth is where the lessons are learned that will bring all of us **bitches** to an understanding of our power and ability to *know* Self. I warn you in advance: you can run but you can't hide! A pre-requisite is an open mind.

The Foundation for the Curriculum

The cement a **bitch** uses to pour her foundation for the "New You" is based on the answer to the question, "Who am I?" To find that out, a **bitch**, *with style* knows her behavior, emotions, values, and perceptions of *her* reality. She seeks and finds how best to know and use information about her **S**trengths, **W**eaknesses, **O**pportunities and

Threats (**SWOTs**). She is conscious of her efforts to use her strengths, compensate for her weaknesses, seize her opportunities and eliminate her threats. She thinks of fear as **F**alse **E**xpectations **A**ppearing **R**eal. Remember that what you fear, appears! Always. Why? Your thoughts of fear magnetize the very thing you fear to you. Thoughts are things and have energy. What you think *is* what you are, and a **bitch,** *with style* knows this and monitors her thoughts because of her knowledge of her Self and what she represents to her Self.

As we grow, we learn that *everything* in life is about the use of consciousness and energy which create the nature of our reality.

Turning A Corner

When I was the assistant to the chancellor of the newly designated UCSD campus in La Jolla, I was in a unique position. To be the number two employee in such a highly anticipated great enterprise, was an honor. Can anything good come out of Xenia? Well, yes. That experience was part of the tool kit in my book bag that got me there. I was organized, knowledgeable, conscientious, and aggressive.   Sometimes, too aggressive. Back then (1961) in a developing organization, I knew it was important to take initiative and get things done. The staff initially was small and there was a lot of work, all of which I enjoyed. I saw my Self then as an executive doing her job. Lots of people saw me as the chancellor's secretary— important, but not hardly as important as I saw my Self! I *knew* in my soul that this work was a position made to order for me and I enjoyed it and learned from Herb York and all the other outstanding professionals I met.

> *Consciousness and energy create the nature of reality.*
> —Ramtha

I was hired in part because of the attitude I projected and the confidence with which I put my skills before the recruiter and finally the chancellor. I'll never forget her— June Saleeby. She saw in me what I saw in my Self but had never defined; she saw in this young mother the energy, intelligence and capability that belied her years and would grow with time. She *saw* this and later told me that the way I presented my Self was so far and away above the other applicants in the final selection pool, that she insisted I be seen by the chancellor. The requirements for the job were, by the way: over 35, children out of the way, able to work long hours if needed, knowledgeable about higher education, shorthand past 120 wpm, typing over 75 wpm, articulate, and (not written down) very presentable to and effective with the public. I was 27, married, with three children, six, five and six months, but otherwise, qualified. Now that I look back on it, my youth and the baby should have knocked me out of the first round, but my background and skills kept me there until the interview. This position was truly a turning point in my life at all levels. However, it was also another Schoolhouse Earth course for me—at the graduate level! And I shall never forget when some of the newly hired professors and several of the "older" administrators decided I was too big for my britches and complained to the chancellor. He essentially told me about it and suggested that I tone down the "bull in a china closet" perception some (not all) people had of me. "Other than that," he said, "carry on." I later learned from Sybil, his wife, that he went home after interviewing me and told her I was "head and shoulders" above the other candidates. "And pretty, too," he told his brother-in-law! I was 27 years old!

But I wasn't *fully* awake would you believe! I didn't know my Self the way I do today because I didn't have anyone to tell me about the *curriculum* for **BITCHHood**. But I plowed through what I had and what I could find and put that information together with experience. I was a young **bitch a-borning!**

The Orientation

Today is the first day of the rest of your **bitch** life. It's a new day and new world. Each day is what you make it, so "starting over" really means you have a chance to correct whatever needs correcting and make each day new within your understanding of "new." When you finish this curriculum, you will know that living in the *here and now* is how you make your world what you want it to be.

The **bitch, *with style*** looks in the mirror and decides, at some point in time, to cross the Red Sea of her life (chaos, crisis and SEEs) by parting the waters of confusion and calmly walking through the morass of ignorance, social conformity, poor information and lack of self-esteem onto the shores of knowledge, power, individuality and enlightenment. No more wandering in the wilderness on the banks of the Red Sea (mental pandemonium, muddle-headedness, relational snafus and screwed-up ideas). No more miracles, either. A **bitch, *with style*** *knows* that a miracle by any other name is knowledge of *who she is* applied to the natural processes (spiritual, mental, emotional and physical) she has learned to use. When Moses led the Israelites across the Red Sea, he led them out of mental captivity and onto the shores of a new land filled with new ideas and a new way of thinking. That's what this biblical metaphor *means!* And so it is with the curriculum for **BITCHHood.** Out of mental captivity and into the light!

Ashley Maxims For How To Be A Bitch *With Style*

---

1. **Your thoughts control your life.**
2. **Your decisions determine your destiny.**
3. **Your perception of reality *is* your reality until new information changes *your* perception.**
4. **You create your own reality. Make it what you *truly* want.**
5. **You are *never* late for your appointment with destiny.**

Twelve steps to BITCHHood

---

1. **Self-Discovery**   I *Am* that I Am.
2. **Self-Love**   I *have*, therefore I Am.
3. **Self-Knowledge**   I *think*, therefore I Am
4. **Self-Development**   I *feel*, therefore I Am.
5. **Self-Expression**   I *create*, therefore I Am.
6. **Self-Integration**   I *choose*, therefore I Am.
7. **Self-Marriage**   We *are*, therefore I Am.
8. **Self-Creation**   I *desire*, therefore I Am.

9.	**Self-Improvement**	I *seek*, therefore I Am.
10.	**Self-Experience**	I *build*, therefore I Am.
11.	**Self-Detachment**	I *see*, therefore I Am.
12.	**Self-Acceptance**	I *know*, therefore *I Am.*

The Curriculum

1. *Health* is the most critical and important process in the world. Without it, a **bitch** will not be functional. She **must** be healthy to become a **bitch, *with style!*** Until she earns *that* name, she'll just have to be content to be "walking into health!" That's all right, too, because it puts you on the right path to seeking your own higher good. So what is health? Simply your ability to be in control of every aspect of your spiritual, mental, emotional and physical energies. That's right, *energies!* Doable? You bet it is, because if it isn't, that litany of wonderful phrases heading up this book are for naught.

2. *Love* is essential because it makes everything we do worthwhile. But it must begin with you. I define **love** as **focused emotion** and every woman I know has been looking for it in all the wrong places without knowing what it truly is. A **bitch, *with style*** knows what it is and where and how to find it! Guaranteed!

3. *Knowledge* is information for use in the service of your own *visions, goals* and *objectives* in life. Repeat, *your own visions, goals* and *objectives.* Regardless of what they are. You've known for a long time that some of the information medical doctors and researchers have been feeding us is garbage where women's health is concerned. There's still not enough of it to make a dime's worth of difference in whether or not we use hormone replacement therapy pills, a vaginal estrogen ring, vaginal estrogen creams or estrogen skin patches. And then there's that wild yam tea, wild yam extract and on and on it goes. This is just a contemporary example of a health issue that is physical but has a mental and emotional load to it that is devastating because of the

implications of side effects of the medications and, worse, the continual fear that cancer lurks somewhere in the shadows of our titties, vaginas, and stomachs. Whose responsibility is it to sort out what happens to our bodies and how we use our energies? The doctors? No way! *That* responsibility belongs to us—you and me. And there's help out there if you **bitches** will take responsibility for your Selfs.

4. *Power!* A **bitch**'s best friend except most don't know it or use it positively. Power is the energy to choose or not choose, to decide or not decide, what we want to do with our "Selfs." It is the creation of a perception in other people's minds that we *know* what we're doing. Power is energy that oozes from our pores. We just know when we're in the presence of a powerful woman. But, if we were to sit around a cafe with a cup of coffee or tea in our hands, we'd skirt the subject of power and dance around its essential ingredients because to be a powerful woman is to truly be called a **"bitch"** (with all the negative meanings) behind your back and we don't want *that*, do we? Even women dislike women who seem to be sure of their Selfs, who make decisions easily, leave groups of women to take care of *their own* business, and who seem to intimidate others with their style and energy. Be honest. Don't we "talk" about these women behind their backs (. . . haven't got the guts to tell 'em to their faces?) But that's coming if you aspire to be a **bitch, with style**. We may admire these women, but basically we don't like them, do we? Well, that will change once you take the course and learn to love your Self.

> **Power is the energy to choose or not choose, to decide or not decide, what we want to do with our "Selfs."**
> —Vikki Ashley

5, 6, 7. *Error, ignorance and pain* belong together because they are the "three horsewomen of change." Central in our lives, they create the chaos that becomes the seed bed for change and growth. Really? When was the last time you thought of change on a bright sunny day when things were going your way and you were having a good time? Think about it seriously and tell the truth: Never! Only when there is crisis, chaos or significant emotional events (SEEs) do we even give change a chance and yet our bodies are changing their Selves over completely at various levels *con-stantly.* In seven years we'll have an entirely new internal cell structure. Like it or not, healthy or not. The important point for a **bitch** to remember is this: Nothing in your life will change until *you* make it happen! That's right, until you *do it* for your Self. Until you *think* for your Self and *act* for your Self. Until then, you are subject to error,

> *Error, ignorance*
> *and pain*
> *are the three*
> *horsewomen*
> *of change.*
> —Vikki Ashley

ignorance and pain, struggling across the burning sands in that gasoline shirt!. And it's *your* responsibility, *whatever* happens to you.

    Error is a mistake, a blunder, a slip, a transgression and an indiscretion. **Bitches** are prone to such behavior as they trod the loose gravel path of life. What makes the study of error important to this curriculum is the willingness of a **bitch, *with style*** to look at her Self *truthfully* and name, claim and ultimately, reframe what she "sees." This willing-ness is a key element of taking responsibility for Self. It's the "readiness" state, often induced by crisis, chaos or significant emotional events (SEEs), that opens her mind to new infor-mation. Readiness is a precursor to change and change is what error, ignorance and pain force all **bitches** to confront. (See the "Be Readies" on page 284.) If you've never made a mistake, been indiscrete, made an unfortunate slip of the tongue, misread a person's intent and blundered in your interaction, or transgressed the laws and covenant of your belief system or religion, please raise your hand! I want to study *you* because you're definitely "out of this world!"

    Pain is a more or less localized sensation, tension, dis-comfort or distress, sometimes agony, resulting from the stimulation of specialized nerve endings. All pain is a protective mechanism that permits each of us who has it to find a way to eliminate or withdraw from the source of that pain. Pain, therefore, is a good thing when it permits each of us to find out what is going on in our body, mind, and spirit! Yes, a good thing. If it were not for pain, there would be no opportunity to bring our bodies back into balance and health. However, once the **bitch,** *with style* is *aware* of how her body functions and how each system affects the other, she then knows that eliminating pain from her body must be a conscious process and not one that is masked by drugs and medications that eliminate that localized sensation and thus allow the negative effects of the pain to continue ravaging the body. "The treatment was a success but the patient died."

It is the *process* of the elimination of pain that is critical to the development of a **bitch,** *with style.* That process involves thoughts, words, deeds, choices and decisions

8. *Growth* is the process of taking steps to self-knowledge on four levels: spiritually, mentally, emotionally and physically. As in nature, each season of our lives (which means each day, or if you go by moon changes, every seven days, for humans) we can choose to plant new seeds in our minds and create young new thoughts that will change our lives. Just as in nature, these seeds must be cared for, nurtured, watered, pruned as necessary and finally enjoyed in the full bloom of their development (when we apply and use the information that generated the new thinking,) at all four levels. We care for the seeds of thought by reading, discussing with friends, attending seminars, buying cassettes and videos, and participating in experiential opportunities, like yoga, Tai Chi, running, etc. Growth goes on constantly in the body and our physical Self benefits from our knowledge about healthy thoughts, foods, exercise, meditation, relaxation, visualization and all those alternative, complementary and psychological processes that keep our physiques, internal organs and bodily mechanisms moving together as the greatest symphony on earth. The orches-

tration of the body is mind boggling and any **bitch** who aspires to graduate into *"style"* will make it her business to find out "what's going on" in there.

Growth can be stunted by negative thoughts, retarded by inadequate nourishment of the mind, as well as the body, reversed by total negativity, and, finally destroyed momentarily by loss of faith in Self. The flame of life can be reignited, however, when one receives the wind of inspiration from others who love and care about her more than she cares for her Self—a holding action, though, until she can walk on her own two feet!

9. *Be-ing* refers to the state of *knowing* that you exist fully in the *here and now*. Be-ing refers to the name that only you can call your Self. *I Am* . . . and then you put whatever name you have either accepted as given to you by your parents or the name that you have given your Self. Your name carries *your* energy. As you grow in knowledge of the energy in the Universe, you will become aware that the letters of your name and the numbers they represent provide information about your life. That is called numerology and is used by people the world over to assist individuals in their struggle to answer the question "Who am I?" A **bitch** *with style* determines her own **be-ing** and decides who she is and what she wants to be called. She may accept her given name, change it, add to it as in hyphenated last names in marriage, or substitute another name socially, as in most traditional marriages. She may marry and keep her own name, as many of us have done. It's her choice.

Be-ing is a state of consciousness centered on the undeniable knowledge of who one is. Thus, a **bitch,** *with style* knows she is a spiritual being having an earthly experience. The curriculum has, as one of its goals, the proof of the *underlying idea* related to the soul that *it always was and always will be.* So what does that *mean?* What is the soul, anyway? I explain this at the end of this step.

Regarding her name, She "be's" who she wants to "be" so long as she **knows** she's God!

10. *Death and rebirth* is a controversial segment of the curriculum but it is also one of the most important. Levels of knowledge go with readiness to consume information new to your perception. Should you not be ready, the information will not "take." You will reject it because of your values, religion, socialization, whatever. Nonetheless, it is a critical learning ground for a **bitch** and most essential for a **bitch,** *with style.*

Death is one of the last taboos in our society and ranks right up there with other crucial issues that must continue to be discussed in a new frame, such as women's health and control of women's birth process and abortion. **Death** is a transition into a new dimension where you continue to live and grow in knowledge. **Death** on this earth, then, is *not* the end. We do not write *finis* and call it a day. Even reason rejects that thought when you consider that plants can renew their Selfs totally from year to year. Why not people, the crown jewel of all God's creations? The planets continue in their paths without any visible means of support. Comets come and comets go (die). Stars flame out over aeons of time, yet the heavens do not fall. Seasons continue year after year and spring **always** comes after the symbolic death that occurs in Capricorn when winter is at its harshest. The seasons of our lives come and go on earth. All cycles and their rhythms move inexorably forward. Why not we after this incarnation? Should the rhythm of the Universe be interrupted only by women and men? I don't think so. That's not the way it is built!

> *A bitch,* **with style knows** *she is a spiritual being having an earthly experience.*
>
> —Vikki Ashley

Rebirth is the process of remaking your Self psychologically and physically and is also the process of returning to earth after a previous sojourn here in another body, called reincarnation. Returning to earth time and time again until we finally perfect our souls in the knowledge of every aspect of life, we can safely conclude that we are students in this schoolhouse called Earth. Such a process permits each soul to eventually reach the plateau of unity with the Godhead (the *Permanent Health Department* of the Universe) and to accept that he and she are microcosms of the macrocosm. Earth *is* the plane of manifestation and demonstration. There may be other planes out there that have manifest life, **but we don't live there. We live here!** We can, if we are open minded and ready to "see," and "hear," learn how to exercise our powers and energy *right here on earth!* It is this joyous experience and eventual understanding that leads a **bitch** to become a **bitch,** *with style* right here on earth! The prospect of doing it again looms large in the decision to grow and make significant contributions to her Self and to others, with love, accountability and knowledge of who she really is.

On the other hand, death of the old Self and creation of a new Self, a New You, right here on earth is what the **bitch,** *with style* is all about and that takes place in the "now".

11. *Transformation* is a pulling of the covers, a peeling of the onion to reveal the form of a new person. Transformation means new and different from the inside and on the outside as well with all types of cosmetic surgery available! Our bodies are, after all, our own and can be lasered, shaped, changed according to our own perception of our Selfs. What this outward makeover does *not* do is change the internal soul energy of the person who has been cosmeticized. An internal transformation is an act of love, desire and will on the part of the **bitch,** *with style;* an external transformation is as well, but of a different degree. Such an internal change may occur in personality (our mask) or character (how we value our Selfs and reflect that new value in our behavior) or as a result of a spiritual journey entered into consciously. Transformation means "amping up" the internal light that shines through one's eyes and comes out of every pore, self-expressing a new internal understanding. A transformation may *feel* like a cosmetic makeover only it occurs on the *inside* and is *hardly* cosmetic. It's fundamental, spiritual and permanent! It's a soul thing.

12. ***Resurrection*** occurs each and every day we wake up and open our eyes. In the dark of the night we "die" to the world. Our bodies continue, however, to do their involuntary work and to expend energy in the service of our resurrection the following morning. And as we close our eyes, we expect to continue living. Yet, I had a friend in New Orleans who lay down one night with his wife to sleep. When she woke early in the morning, she discovered he was dead. She heard nothing. He made no moves or sounds. He just died in his sleep. Frankly, we should all be so fortunate in our transitions, but it was traumatic, nonetheless, for her. I, as an example, have put forth a contract with the Universe about my own transition. I want to drop dead on a tarmac *going somewhere* at 130+ years of age! There is so much to do here and so much to learn that I feel as though I have just been born—only this time I'm awake and bring my knowledge and understanding *with* me.

Keep in mind that there are statements in the bible and in other literature that say there is no earthly reason we can't live to at least 144 years old! Think about *that!* It would certainly require that we live our lives differently and have a lot more information on health: spiritual, mental, emotional and physical. Don't you agree?

Did Jesus, the Christ really rise from the dead? If you consider that Jesus, the Christ was by the time of his resurrection, the perfect man; if you consider that Jesus, the Christ represents God's idea of man and woman ***in expression;*** if you consider that He represents the **I Am** identity in each of us; then I believe He did indeed rise from the dead. This is so because each of us can, through the exercise of our consciousness and acceptance of the energy of our souls, be directed by our thoughts, words and deeds. We can rise from the deadness of ignorance, error and pain into enlightenment, with love. We can indeed metaphorically emulate (equal or excel) the process of resurrection if we understand that we are the microcosm of the macrocosm. Christ said him Self as recorded in John 14:26-27: "*But the Counselor, the Holy Spirit, whom the Father will send in my name will teach you all things and will remind you of everything I have said to you. Peace I leave with you; my peace I give to you. I do* *not give to you as the world gives. Do not let your hearts be troubled and do not be afraid."*

Who is this Counselor, the Holy Spirit Christ refers to? It is the "I Am in Action" who is **you** moving forward on the strength of your thoughts, words and deeds, *expecting* your visions to materialize because you have indeed combined your thoughts with your emotions (desire) and focused your intention, attention and energy on what you desire. It is **you** acting "as if" what you envision *already exists!* You are "walking into" whatever it is you have thought, decided, perceived as *your* reality and have created in your mind! So, have no fear of the future and its results and do not worry (let your heart be troubled). In this curriculum, there is ***no room for doubt or worry*** because they interfere with the proper functioning of the electrical and chemical systems of your mind, emotions and body. You must have **faith:** A **F**antastic **A**dventure **I**n **T**rusting **H**er!

As a **bitch,** *with style* opens her eyes and "sees" with new understanding, she knows the difference this information will make in her perception of her Self. She knows that error, ignorance and pain lurk in the shadows of her perception ready to grab her consciousness and pull her into the abyss of ignorance once again if she lets them. To avoid such a regression, each of us must practice, practice, practice the application of this new learning every moment of every day. The object is to expand your mind, your environment and your world to *know* more about what is possible and to "mine" the potential in your life. Your transformation and resurrection will consciously create a New You.

These are the very important elements that will flow through every aspect of this book and its curriculum for living that I share with you. Included will be relevant parts of my own story and dusty march on the loose gravel path of life to **BITCHHood**. Where relevant, I will reinforce my own learning. We're walking this path together here. So, if any of the information is difficult for you, then it is time for you to "*seek,* and ye shall find; *ask* and ye shall receive; *knock* and it shall be opened to you." Go out and talk to people, "go to school in other people's heads" (call them up and ask them questions), go to seminars, etc. and look into dictionaries and reference books. I've done my best to invoke what I consider the three steps to clarity for purposes of teaching what I call the *CTI Principle:* **C**ommunicate, **T**ranslate and **I**ntegrate. I hope this book evokes interest in pursuing further reading and learning. There is an eclectic and extensive bibliography in the **Bitch's Book Bag**. Do not let a concept or phrase throw you. Look it up. This is not a cook book. It is an evocative, inspirational statement of my views on the power of women and the spiritual development of that power through an understanding of their spiritual/energy roots. I am sure I have overlooked and even possibly left out some relevant fact in specific cases. I ask that you take the bull by the horns and go after the information. This book is intended to light the path to new and exciting knowledge that has very practical uses in be-coming a **bitch**, *with style*.

BITCHHood 101:
Self-Discovery: I *Am*, Therefore I AM.

Information and knowledge will lead to more *wisdom* and *power.* Notice, I did *not* say power and wisdom, for wisdom *always* precedes the effective use of power and power *always* comes from within the individual, no matter how it manifests in the outside world. People who are out of control, *project* negative energy and "power" *into* the environment. People who are in control in their centers, *radiate* positive energy *into* the environment. They do not lose energy, but gather and synergize positive energy for continual use in their endeavors

The wise use of energy must begin with acceptance of spirituality, which translates to energy and vitality which equal life. Each **individual** (which we become only after we grow beyond the **personality)** must become unified (holistic) in the integration of *masculine and feminine energies.* The **bitch**, *with style* becomes conscious of how these energies function, uses them consciously 24 hours a day and eventually, because of daily use, becomes a *conscious competent* as she makes this process her own.

Remember: energy follows your thoughts and **intention.** **Intention** leads to **Attention,** which provides the **energy** for establishing specific goals which lead to results. Becoming a **bitch** *with style* requires learning from those of us who are now the teachers and who are anxious to share the process with people of all ages.

Because of power imbalances in society, men are losing out because of an unconscious desire *not* to appear "feminine." If they read this book and understand the science of *be-ing*, they will get over that fear and begin to consciously use their feminine energy in their daily lives.

Women, as a matter of fact, are not focusing enough on *their* use of masculine energy. Each gender is imbalanced in their use of energy and it is past time for them to **both** integrate their masculine and feminine energies to achieve their spiritual and material goals in life.

This book focuses on women because it is past time for more effective use of their ***masculine energy*** which is needed to balance out their overuse of the feminine. Men with open minds who read this book will benefit from their recognition of the importance of integrating *their* feminine energies into their consciousness on a daily basis and in all situations in life.

Actually, this knowledge and its use is millennia old, but it has always been the province of the kings, leaders, priests, soothsayers and other patriarchal figures running individual societies and the world. There was a time, however, when there were goddesses who also had this knowledge and who used it. They were displaced in their power by males who decided eventually to eliminate the impact of goddesses, and then women, by controlling their lives. Examples abound, but I find the following instructive and devastating: enclosing their private parts in chastity belts, burning them at the stake as witches (I contend the Inquisitor Priest always screwed the wise woman the night before the burning), rewriting legislation and inheritance laws to undermine their wealth and administration of their wealth, sending them to nunneries when their husbands died, using the bright women as consorts and mistresses without social contract or legal portfolio and, ultimately, maintaining control over progeny by opposing legal birth control and abortion. Though the latter are "legal" in America, there are those who are still fighting a battle against the forces of the enlightened. They will not win because of the wave of feminine power and energy entering the Universe that will overwhelm the negativity and control they seek, still, to impose on women.

I have often said in lectures that the **bitches, *with style*** of the 13th Century—dynamic women who had *knowledge of* matters of the spirit, use of herbs, and inner understandings—were threatening to the hierarchy of the Church, and they had the power to *use* the information in the service of their families, friends and neighbors. Yet, the burnings at the stake of these women reinforced the rocky road of women with special knowledge and powers thus demonstrating the misogynistic behavior and fear of female power expressed by the Church fathers about the knowledge these women possessed. They deliberately stamped out the power of the goddesses formally in their dogmas, replacing the idea of goddesses with the virgin Mary, mother of Jesus. The church could not hope to bring families (which included women) into its folds without some type of supportive female deity to round out the image of God the Father and Jesus, the Christ as the Son. Two male energies can create nothing. The Church fathers knew that. So, enter Mary, the mother of Jesus, to round out the energies required for creation and to ameliorate the public's need for a female deity.

Mary represents not only the feminine aspect of our human nature (Mary, from the root word *mare*, which means "sea," "water" and translates into "emotions.") She is the symbol of emotion! Mary is often called "Stella Maris,"—Star of the Sea!

Words are the most potent weapon used against women's individuality and independence. Yes. Words. Language drives behavior, and words and the tone with which they are spoken determine the intensity or ease of the energy flow in any interaction. The powers of the word and the knowledge of the flow of universal energy have always been available to a select few (including churchmen) who used these words to imprint on the minds of men **and** women the policies and interpretations *they* wanted to impart in order to control the social environment and the rules of engagement between the sexes. These "words" did, indeed, change the vibrations around women and their understanding of who they were, what they were supposed to do and be and why they were put on this earth. Repeated often enough without any outside corroboration and isolated from the vault of knowledge possessed by the priests, women their Selfs came to believe what was being said about them ostensibly without giving up hope in their souls that they would one day be treated as part of the human race and not just breeding animals and house cleaners.

The most powerful words used to subjugate women were contained in the bible. Bear in mind, though, there were no feminine priests and no feminine scholars in the hierarchy of the Church for centuries—none even now that have official recognition and serve in Rome on the staff of the Pope. But the interpretations were done by men who had alternative agendas . . . power over people and the intentional restriction of knowledge in order to maintain that power.

Were they successful with this strategy? Yes. Definitely. For thousands of years they were successful. But times they are a-changin' and their strategy, some of which lingers in the hearts and minds of some very fundamental people and organizations, is outmoded, outdated, and outgunned by the abilities and determination of **bitches, *with style.*** You'll see!

The Beginning of the Cirriculum

"What's so *bad* about being a *bitch?* I asked my Self. It's obvious the term is used by men *and* women to denote women who are forceful, often abrasive, but most usually those who have a mind of their own and don't go along with "the program" whatever that is. It's even used on TV these days *without impunity.* It has entered the language and doesn't even cause a cough or raised eyebrow. It was a bit disconcerting to go to a movie with my grandchildren last year—one of those Home-Alone-Type movies with a smart-mouth kid—and listen to this kid call his father's girlfriend a bitch. Besides being obnoxious, the girlfriend wasn't going along with this kid's program, so she was a "bitch." It doesn't take a smart pig to get *that* point! So the term *bitch* is indeed part of our language and is usually meant in negative terms.

I use **bitch** (Being In Total Control of Her Self) to express in positive terms a word not usually considered positive and to **bring new energy and understanding to the *use* of the term.** I've been called a **bitch** (and probably still am) by people who find me intimidating. I am a direct and sensitive communicator and tend to go to the bottom line in discussions. I really do have a built-in crap detector and I find bullshit offensive when layered on in the service of undermining my intelligence, regardless of its source. As I indicated in the introduction, I was called a **bitch** every time I showed up at the hospital when my son was near death. I could see it in the eyes of the nurses, residents, and even the doctors. Let there be no misunderstanding here, I would have taken on the whole world to help Alan obtain the highest standard of care and medical assistance he needed *once he told me he wanted to live.* I was a **bitch**, there is no doubt. But I was a **bitch**, *with style.*

Stories To Tell

Women, in my experience, are called **bitches** all of the time on television and in movies for being the "other woman" or for doing something someone (man **or** woman) doesn't like. The term **bitch** springs readily to the lips of individuals who see their Selfs as having "power over" you when you decide to do something contrary to their wishes or to their designs. Because of sexual harassment laws and growing awareness, this is not so readily apparent in the workplace, but while it may not be said, it is often thought and therefore comes out in behavior anyway.

How many times have we heard *"Who do you think you are, bitch?"* It was a favorite question asked me by my first husband. The answer rarely mattered. I was doing or saying something that displeased him. Unfortunately, he was physical at times and I eventually removed my energy from this relationship, under threat of being killed, and started anew . . . with three children to support. The question really is: why was I *in that* relationship in the first place? Well, I was just a naive, bright-but-dumb-about-life woman. Yes. I found the answer. Yes. I changed my life by consciously deciding to remain single for 18 years after my divorce in 1968! Then I married again—this time, the **bitch** married the right man. Even then it wasn't a cakewalk. But by this time I *was* a **bitch** *with style* and still growing!.

Superbitch

"Do you think you're some superbitch or somethin'?" That question was directed to me in 1976 when I was in a position of authority as a consultant to the Housing Authority of Houston, TX. My response, flippant to be sure, was: "Would you define that for me?" The point was, in this instance, I had the upper hand and I was requesting something from this man. He didn't like responding to me **in my position of authori-**

ty. So the best he could do was call me a superbitch. His definition, by the way, just dug the hole deeper for him. "Yeah. You think you're so uppity or better than me, right?" Wrong. Still, the issues were not mine to solve. His own low self-esteem was showing. What I **could** do, and **did** do, was show him the value of accomplishing what I was requesting and how it would demonstrate his own competency, which was in question as a manager. I "showed" him by walking him through the plan for the organization and "telling" him I did not believe the plan could be carried out effectively without his knowledge, expertise and cooperation. I "told" him I needed his support and counsel as well since I readily admitted I was not a subject matter expert but I was in charge of the overall strategy and process. I asked him to agree to a two-week "working relationship" during which time the two of us met daily and went over *his* issues and challenges and allowed me to offer suggestions for both of us coming to solutions that we (a) agreed to and (b) worked in the new organizational environment.

Over time this individual, who described him Self as a Texas Redneck, whom I had to work with, among others, for over a year, became one of my greatest admirers and supporters, but the road was full of potholes! He continued to call me *superbitch*, but toward the end, he'd smile and call me "*Ms. Superbitch.*" That was OK by me because I *knew* what that represented *for him*—I had won both his confidence and his admiration. To him, that appellation was a great compliment. I thought so, too.

Many women would be threatened by this approach and by the use of that name. Today, *some* might even consider it a form of harassment. But a **bitch *with* style** will not. Her sense of self is internal and a *name* will *not* set her off. I was fully aware of the total situation and conscious of the importance of this man to the assignment I had contracted to complete. Why would I allow a word to get in my way if I had the power to turn the situation around? At least I had to make the effort. And that's the important point.

A **bitch,** *with style* refuses to accept limits on what she can *be* and *do.* Her spirit and mind don't accept limits. Yet she is often caught in the vise of society that insists that limits be real for everyone. Such illogical (to a **bitch**) thinking becomes a source of great stress and emotional strain for individuals whose consciousness and soul *know* better and who want to break the surly bonds of mind and soar—somewhere.

Running Away and Growing Up

I have always been a precocious child—from birth. I walked early, talked early, wrote early, knew my ABCs very early and read books early. And could I count? You bet! At the same time, I was like any other little girl who wanted to have fun, but I *thought* having fun was talking with adults! My dad was a college professor and the people who would stop by our apartment were associated with him in that profession. They thought it was "cute" to see one so young behaving "like a grownup," so they fueled my tendency to talkativeness and to inquiry. I was very curious. My father and mother's friends indulged my curiosity and answered my questions. Establishing communications with adults was a strong base for my learning and I used it without shame!

But, there has always been a "feeling" in me that there was something else "out there" as I peered through the slats of the third-floor porch of the apartment building on Church Street in Xenia, Ohio. I always wanted to "go away." I just didn't want to be there. And, so, one day I took my 18-month old brother, (I was two years and five months old!) and ran away from home!!! We didn't get very far, of course. Only two blocks, which for youngsters of our age, was pretty far. And considering we had to cross a busy street to do *that!* Rheva Gilmore, a friend of my mother's, saw us and asked if Mom knew where we were. Of course she didn't and I told her the truth. She calmly took my hand, I took Ronnie's, and walked us back to the apartment. My mother was frantic but relieved when she saw us. She didn't spank me but I got a definite "talking to." I later heard both my mother and father sharing this episode with some of their friends and they all had a good laugh about it.

By the time I was five, I was shopping for the family because my mother was tied down with four children and my father was busy teaching and working a second job to take care of the bills. I would go to the local Krogers in Mr. Johnson's taxi. I had a small purse with a list of groceries, note to the manager with a postdated check with a blank to be filled out when the groceries were tallied, and money for the cab. I was barely tall enough to push the cart, but the manager also thought I was "cute" and had no trouble responding to my calls for help when I couldn't reach something or needed advice. Shy, I was not!

The manager would help load the cab with the groceries. I would sit in the back seat (my feet did not touch the floor, but I felt so grown!) and we would head home to the third-floor apartment. Mr. Johnson always carried the groceries up to the apartment. He would say, "Run along, now. I'll take care of this."

The symbolism of both events is not lost on me. My grownness extended to shopping for a family of six but when I returned home and there were no adults with whom to interact, I was just "one of the kids." Something was wrong with this picture.

I remember that run-away event vividly to this day and smile as I write about it. Seems I *always* wanted to run away from home and "get out of there." I finally did it in 1957, all the way to San Diego which was as far away as I could figure a way to get to under the circumstances. Besides, I had to help my husband get a job before we could leave town. So I did, through my job in the alumni office of a small college. I set it up and made sure he did all the things necessary to ensure our getaway. I remember the sigh of relief as I saw Xenia in the rear view mirror of our car, filled to the gills with two babies, one two and a half and the other just 13 months old! I had done it. I ran away from home with my children! Oh, yes, and a husband!

The Soul—Defined and Explained

The soul is the holographic designation for **each** human being that can **never** be separated from the Universal Energy Field or the Godhead. We use the term God because as lowly, puny humans, we find it hard to accept our Selfs as being the powerful units of divinity we really are. So we have manufactured a third person "out there" called God, Allah, Jehovah, Yahweh, whatever, so that our fellow human beings will not mistaken us for maniacs! If this person "out there" somewhere is the cause and we are the effect, then we truly have someone else to blame for whatever happens to us. Right? Well, y'all, wrong! The joke really is on each of us if that is what we think. In the end, the truth is: I Am the God of My Universe. No one else is responsible for the choices or the decisions I make. In order to acquit my Self well with this information, I have to do some *work* and expend some *mental and emotional energy*! To do this work well, I have to accept a few truths about my holographic Self:

Truths About My Self

1. **My thoughts control my life.**
2. **My decisions determine my destiny.**
3. **My perception of reality *is* my reality until new information changes *my* perception.**
4. **I create my own reality. I make it what I *truly* want.**
5. **I Am *never* late for my appointment with destiny.**

The soul is the Human Energy Field (HEF) or the Aura that surrounds each and every thing on earth. This soul is a hologram of the entire Universe and allows each personality to function on the earth in whatever culture we chose this time around. This personality we try on in each incarnation has one purpose and one purpose alone— to integrate with the *individuality* of the soul who is having the experience *as* that personality! In due (do) time, when we awake from the dark night of the soul, the earthly journey's experiences move us ever closer to the integration of the personality *with* the individuality to form that union with the One and to move into the light of knowledge of who we *really* are: God. As we progress in this journey, then, we begin to "amp up" our six light bodies contained in the aura and that work hand in glove with our chakra system (the energy wheels that keep all of this energy moving *in* each of us in relation to our auras and in relation to the flow of information required for each cell to do its work in maintaining our physical body). I have said more than once that the physical body is the "Temple of Solomon," our "home," and the vehicle for our earthly purpose which is to answer the question "Who am I?" It is the "ship" that sails the earthly seas of emotion and encounters the calm as well as the chaotic flow of the weather of life on the "outside." But, the "ship" is steered by the internal mechanisms contained in our soul/aura, the pilot house of our physical Self and the *real* Self, the ***internal*** Self.

The Soul's Components

1. The Mind

The mental energy atoms that make it possible for the brain to accept and process information to and from the soul's vehicle—the body. This information has more than one way of entering the physical vehicle, including via electrical signals to the brain as well as to the "emotional brain" called the Solar Plexus, among others. Our thoughts are **the** beams of light—trillions of them—in our auric body that generate the "sparks" that connect to the vibrational energies of our emotions and are transmitted to our marvelous processing station called the brain. It then distributes the energy as appropriate for the functioning of every aspect of those billions of cells, miles and miles of veins and arteries and gazillion capillaries, and all of that blood as well as the various fluids, most importantly the spinal and lymph fluids in our body. Whew! What a job and what a magnificent orchestration of electrochemicalmagnetic particles and waves required to keep each of us alive and functioning.

2. Emotions

The fuel that is essential to the movement of the person. Emotion is the primal energy that allows each of us to *know* something is **real** to us. It is energy essential to the functioning of the mind and is the spiritual companion of the mind. This energy can be harnessed and focused in the interest of the soul's purpose. It is also the big gun for healing the ills and woes of the mind and the body. Without emotion, nothing is real to the mind, soul or the body. So, those people who believe they should repress their emotions have it all wrong. They should control their emotions consciously and focus them in the service of their purpose and establishing who they are. Repress them? No way. Each and every time you repress what you truly feel, you are setting in motion negative energy that has to come out somewhere in *you*. It usually finds a way to corrupt your inner organs, blood system, gastrointestinal system (why do we sell so much Maalox?) and/or most especially your mental functions.

3. Spirit

Undifferentiated energy—the Unified Energy Field (UEF) that physicists *know* exists and which they use. The UEF is power, living energy, animated force, inner essence. The UEF is the essence of Life. And we carry that animating force around and in us all of the time. The UEF does *not* arise from the physical. To the contrary, the physical comes from the UEF.

A quick refresher regarding electricity. You and I have never seen electricity. I know this to be true because it can't be seen—it is *invisible*. Yet you and I use it every day since its discovery by Ben Franklin and his kite. Does it exist? Yes. How do we know it exists? By the results we obtain. Can something that is invisible be *real*? Of course it can. I just refreshed your memory about electricity. Just take a look at the computer (all sizes, including my palmtop!!), fax machine, telephone, microwave, coffee pots, etc., etc., etc., and all the other gizmos we "plug in" every day of our lives. Are *they* real? Well, I guess so, because I use them everyday and I get results.

So, then, what's this bullshit we all tell our Selves, scientists included, about things we can't see *not* being real. Wake up, people! We **bitches** know that this is the God we all talk about and we each are part of that energy so each of us is God as well. One part of a hologram carries the complete "picture" of the whole and is a "whole" unto itself. So it is with human beings and everything on this earth.

Guess what, y'all. *You and I are God.* Hello?

4. Akashic Records

The soul records *everything* we have ever done no matter in which life it was done. It is, therefore, *our* Akashic Record. And that's the only record we want to read. Those among us who are psychics and seers can read everyone else's and that's all right, too. We have that capacity if we but develop it. But for now, y'all, it's our own aura and record that counts.

Another Way of Looking at This

All things in this creation exist within you, and all things in you exist in creation; there is no border between you and the closest things, and there is no distance between you and the farthest things, and all things, from the lower to the loftiest, from the smallest to the greatest, are within you as equal things. In one atom are found all the elements of the earth, in one motion of the mind are found the motions of all the laws of existence, in one drop of water are found the secrets of all the endless oceans, in one aspect of *you* are found all the aspects of *existence* . . . [Thus] Your life has no end, and you shall live forevermore."

—*Kahlil Gibran*

STEP TWO

I Have What It Takes!

There is always another way of looking at this.
There is another way of looking at the world.[1]

All a'glitter! An evening on the town in New Orleans—1997

BITCHHood 201
Self-Love: I *Have*, Therefore I Am.

ove is so misunderstood. Yet it is so explainable when you know what it is: **a type of focused emotion,** energy that is available to all and is used for all types of purposes in our society, including but not limited to thinking, creativity, sex, climbing mountains, painting, water skiing, writing, sculpting, picking up garbage, and even killing people. **It is energy!** Neutral and impartial energy to be directed by the individual toward whatever he or she wants to do or obtain. This energy gives a **bitch,** *with style* the get-up-and-go she needs to *choose* to walk the loose gravel path of growth and change when she decides upon **BITCHHood.** When she decides to build a foundation for knowing Self, this will provide her with information on her **S**trengths, **W**eaknesses, **O**pportunities and **T**hreats (her **SWOTS**). The **SWOT** process provides a mechanism for knowing your behavior, values and perceptions (the way you take in and use data). With this knowledge, a **bitch,** *with style* is able to communicate and interact with understanding. This is so because she is coming from a center core of knowledge, confidence, courage and power—hers!

> **Love is focused emotion.**
> —Vikki Ashley

Be-coming a **bitch,** *with style* is a grand design for your life. It is a state of mind, a thought about your Self in your mind—held in silence and with desire (which is *laser-beam intentionality*) and recorded on the universal template of your subconscious. You never have to share your thoughts with anyone unless you want to or when you are ready. You can also change your thoughts and ideas anytime for any reason, as you so choose. It's *your* mind, *your* thoughts, and you have dominion over them—*at all times . . .* unless you are in a state of weakness that is diagnosed as a mental illness. A **bitch,** *with style* controls her own reality through her perception until new information

> *My perception of reality* **is my** *reality until new information changes* **my** *perception.*
> —Vikki Ashley

changes her perception. The point, then, is to carefully choose the information you use in your life to support your thoughts, beliefs and values because it is recorded in your subconscious and follows your intentions and desires and will surface in your behavior . . . nonverbally, to be sure, and verbally for those who have "ears to hear."

What we think about all the time eventually appears in our life. How many times have you heard: "We are what we think." "What we think, we are." "As a man thinketh in his heart, so is he." (*Proverbs, 23:7*) "Heart" in this usage refers to the emotions and therefore refers to the necessity of combining thought with desire and feeling if one is to achieve any result.

Reflections on Information, Dreams and Visions

Early in life I thought intently about being rich and able to travel the world. I wanted to experience adventures in some exotic place. I wanted to be a powerful person who is recognized for her contributions. I wanted a floor-length mink coat and hat, beautiful clothes and good-looking shoes. I wanted to live in a big house and drive a big car. I remember even indulging my Self and "seeing" me in a long beautiful red dress with a white mink coat being taken somewhere in a chauffeur-driven limousine. The limousine was white. I pictured and imagined a business some day that would have my name on it. This was the "stuff" of childhood fantasy, to be sure. I didn't use fancy words; I just continued to keep that as a running picture show in the back of my mind. I focused on the material things I wanted and thought I needed. It was a wonderful diversion from the reality of my life.

My love of books fueled my vivid imagination. I traveled in my mind every day. I would wonder, sometimes out loud, about the world "out there." I would dream of ocean voyages and flying in airplanes. *How* I would do all this never occurred to me. I was totally unaware that I was programming my subconscious to "see" those images as *real* and it was working even then to ensure that those intensely held fantasies would someday come true—unless I changed my mind. Of course, I didn't.

I mentioned earlier how curious a child I was. I was also a questioner. When I spoke with adults, I always asked questions that otherwise would have been considered impertinent had I not been so interesting and "cute" to adults. Lo! and behold, they *always* answered my questions. I don't remember ever being turned down. What I was doing, of course, was "interviewing" people and practicing for what would become a major tool in my psychological and management consulting career. The art of asking questions became my hallmark and is to this day. Then, though, I was relentless in pursuit of information and knowledge, which I

> *An* **infoholic** *is a person who just wants to* **know** *as well as know* **how.**
> —Vikki Ashley

absorbed like a sponge. I was an *infoholic*—a person who just wants to *know*. In addition, however, I also wanted to know *how* to *use* this knowledge and information. One of my life's passions has been to "make things work or build things people say can't be done." The *infoholic* in me just loves the challenge. In time I became what I refer to my Self as: *a mental architect*. As a teenager I did not know this term, or any even close, but I was building in my mind the world I wanted to live in personally.

I found my Self perplexed by adults who did not want to provide "straight" answers but who always obscured information in their responses or "went around Robin Hood's barn" to finally get to a conclusion. Today I find this only slightly more irritating than an inconvenient sneeze. There was a time, though, in my late 20s, when I was grossly insulted by such approaches. Mentally I would be saying "hurry up, hurry up, get to the point, get to the point." On occasion, I would even *say* to the other person, "Would you *mind* getting to the point?"

My mother was prudish about sex and never spoke to me about any of life's necessary processes; not even before I got married. She just never "got to the point."

When I was four, my parents took me, my brother Ron and sister Irene to visit our grandparents, Dad's brother Carl and my Aunt Gerri. I remember taking a bath in a galvanized tub in the kitchen and discovering my vagina. I asked my mother what that hole was and she said "Shhh!" And shut me up.

Grandma Henry said "Nice girls don't talk about *that.*" I then piped up and asked Aunt Gerri the same question and she looked at Mother and Grandma and said with a smile, "That's your *pussy*, honey." She liked to shock Mom and Grandma and never lost a chance to be both interesting and profane. She was already my best friend, having spent one year in Xenia, Ohio with us while she attended college at Wilberforce University. (It just didn't work for her. I think she partied a little too much.) Nevertheless, that's what it was for the rest of my growing up years until I found out in my conversations with Ms. Martha Clark what it's real name was: my vagina! I guess, given the nature of error and ignorance and given my Mother's talent for hiding things and never getting to the point, I was lucky to find out at twelve!

When I started my period, I pointed out to my mother that my panties were being stained with blood. What should I do about it? She unlocked her famous (among us children who wondered what was behind *that door)* bedroom closet and brought out a box of Kotex. "You'll need these once a month. Let me know when you see a dripping and I'll make sure you get them. They fit on that belt, there." Of course, I struggled with these instructions but finally got the job done. It felt sort of warm and interesting and thus began my womanhood. No muss; no fuss; no information, either. By then our family had *twelve* children. Count 'em! You'd think I'd get a lot more information from my mother than I did. At the same time, I was still doing shopping for the family, was the only baby sitter, and was getting straight A's in school. But I was not entitled to information about my own body from my own mother!

One day Mom left her keys on her dresser when she ran an errand and left me in charge. I saw them and couldn't contain my curiosity. I wanted to know what she had in that closet that had to be under lock and key. Breathing hard, I opened the door. There were piles of clothes and in one corner, stacks of magazines in another. I picked up one and looked at the cover: *True Confessions. True Romance.* I sat down with a *True Romance* and began to read. Wow! I thought. This stuff is *interesting.* It was interesting, but it was also very sad. I leafed through the magazine pile swiftly and thought it funny they were under lock and key. Today, I understand. I empathize, now. Then, it was a puzzlement. Why would she hide something like a magazine?

In spite of my mother's reluctance to verbalize details of matters important to life and growing up, I found a way to invent the necessity for learning about my body by inventing biology reports for school that became my ticket to the "locked room" at our city library. There, in the quiet of the life sciences reading room and under the vigilant eyes of the librarian, I read about the body, sex, babies, penises—the whole nine yards—and took copious notes. I found it amusing that St. Brigid didn't even have a biology course in its curriculum. Today I find that hard to believe, but it was so. An arrangement was finally made with Xenia High School to allow us "Catholic school" kids to attend life sciences and physics courses. Occupied as I was with Latin, music and French as electives, I only took advantage of this arrangement my senior year. I took physics.

On the matter of life, though, there was Martha Clark, a neighbor at least 30 years my senior when I was 11 years old, who was my reading buddy. We exchanged paper backs and I often sat on her porch at her feet and listened to stories of her life. They were always instructive, sometimes hilarious and had a deep impact on my thinking. She shared with me the fact that she had made a living as a prostitute before deciding to leave that world and "settle down" with Earl. She told me that had been many years prior to our meeting, as if it would have *mattered* to me. My parents? Well, that's another matter. I never told them this side of our friendship story.

When I was 14, the same year I got my first peek at Mom's *True Romance* and *True Confessions,* Martha told me she thought it was time for me to stop playing baseball with the boys because my body was developing very nicely and even though I was considered "one of the boys" then, the next day I might find my Self in trouble with one of those boys sexually and not know how I got there. "Remember to always look out for your Self. Never trust a man to protect or take care of you.

You will *always* be disappointed. Look out for and take care of your Self. Someday you may meet a man who will appreciate you for who you are and then it will be all right to be in a relationship with a man who respects you and you him." She also reminded me never to let a man physically abuse me. "Run like hell from that type of guy," she said. Funny, I don't ever remember Martha talking about love except in the context of loving your Self. I would later wonder if she knew something I didn't about love. **Many** years later I found out she knew a **lot** about love. That it starts with loving Self and then spreads abroad. Just like the Nazarene said. "Thou shalt Love thy neighbor *as thy Self.*" But at 14, I just tucked her words away in my heart for safekeeping. They *felt* right. I just didn't know *how* right at the time, especially that part about "run like hell" when a man physically abuses you.

> *"Thou shalt Love thy neighbor as thy Self."*
> — Mathew 19:19

The journey into acceptance of Self and love of Self has taken me over 40 years. How about your journey? Where are you on this loose gravel path of life? Take a minute to reflect on that question, take a deep breath, and let's continue. It takes a lot of practice, this business of living, and it never ends. Oh, well, "Life is like playing a violin solo in public and learning the instrument as one goes on," said Samuel Butler, the English poet. I agree. I played second violin in the Pius X orchestra at Manhattenville. So I personally related to Butler's comment!

Love, Love, Love

Everywhere you turn you see images designed to provoke interest between the genders and to support the "idea" of "love." Music, art, books, buildings (Taj Mahal), flowers, you name it. Calvin Klein ads. Other seductive visualizations. All created in the name of love, of money, sales, fame, whatever.

Love is *the* energy that drives us, we think, to passion, tender devotion, affection, all of the wonderful words we use on Valentine's Day and Wedding Days to express our Selfs and share our Selfs with someone else. It's the energy that takes care of the homeless; serves dinners to the hungry on Easter, Thanksgiving and Christmas. It's the energy that encourages people to fly to Honduras to help restore some form of order and help people after a hurricane, collects medical supplies for clinics in Africa, gives up a kidney for a child, and gives clean blood for operations and blood banks. This is definitely a form of love of neighbor, there is no doubt. And it is also part of doing unto others as you would have others do unto you. It's being a good and caring citizen. Every **bitch, *with style*** says to her Self, after her prayer of thanks and affirmations, "There but for the grace of God go I."

But Jesus said *"thou shalt Love thy neighbor **as** thy Self."* Remember? We hardheaded human beings didn't *hear* that. We kept on truckin'—backwards! It is not surprising that we got it all wrong. We were taught to travel backwards where love *and* our neighbor are concerned. Everyone, including my parents—and I'll bet yours, too—taught me to put everyone in the universe, including "missions" in far away places I'd never heard of, *before* me. "Don't be selfish," was a constant refrain when I wanted something for my Self. Did that happen to you, too? Or some of you, at least? I have always wondered how a message so clear as Christ's message got so twisted around and screwed up. ***He meant what he said and said what he meant—seven times!.*** You'd think we'd have "got" it by now. So, why didn't we?

Well, try the desire of those in Church and other authority positions to diminish individual knowledge and power so that people (the thundering herd) would more easily come under their control and do what they wanted. You know, churches, governments, social organizations, etc.

Try greed—greed for power, money and influence, temporal goodies that have tempted men from the beginning of time. Try arrogance, the type of disregard for "regular" people that is still rampant all over the world and denies countries and people their rights and individual liberties. But that's not *our* problem. *We* are *our* problem.

Self-knowledge is a pearl of great price and to grow into a **bitch** (a **B**eing **I**n **T**otal **C**ontrol of **H**erself) is to be willing to pay the great price. Self-love is knowledge applied to *your* daily life. Wherever *you* are on the scale of self-love, I want you to just keep on pushing the envelope by reminding your Self day and night: *I love me just the way I AM.* It doesn't matter what your condition is, it is important that you *start now* to say *I love me just the way I AM.*

In due (do) time your cup will flow over with more love than you need and you can give the overflow away to others. Your cup will stay half-full not half-empty for the rest of your life. But you have to start, *now,* to say it and *know* it to be true for you. The thought takes some getting used to, I know, because the tapes that play in our sub-conscious minds have to be *consciously with desire* reprogrammed. However, no thoughtless and lackadaisical approach will get this job done, believe me. To be a **bitch** *with style,* this statement, as part of your daily "getting up and getting ready" routine, is *essential.*

A **Bitch *With Style*** Defines Love

I have determined that **love is focused emotion.** It is the **intensity of thought integrated with the intensity of desire** and focused on a person, place, thing or nature in general. It is the fuel that drives our desire and creates the movement of our intentions to whatever we need, want or don't want in our lives. *Emotion* is gen-erated from our auric field connected to inner Self via the Solar Plexus, heart and pineal gland and fuels our nervous system in such a way as to produce feeling states, e.g., excitement, distress, happiness, sadness, love, hate, fear, or anger. The external manifestation of these feeling states is called *affect,* and the pervasive and sustained emo-tional state is a *mood, as in* good mood or bad mood or a malaise.

So, if **love** is **focused emotion,** what, then, is hate? It, too, is **focused emotion.** As are *fear, anger, distress, excitement, enthusiasm, joy, happiness, sadness.* **It is all the same** and is part of the "reality" we all encounter in our lives without knowing the *underlying idea.* The *underlying idea* is the Principle of Polarity, which I go into at some length in Step Seven when I share with you the natural laws of the universe, which include the Principle of Polarity. Suffice it to say that the only difference between *love* and *hate* is the degree of emphasis/focus directed toward someone or something at any given time. **Love** and **hate** are *really* the same energy—identical in *nature* but different in *degree*. So that, when you understand *this*, you will come to know and understand that one pole of energy, **love**, *builds and supports* (Is anabolic) while the other end of the pole, **hate**, destroys and inhibits (Is catabolic).

> *It isn't love that puts people together; it's* **attraction.** *It isn't love that keeps people together; its* **commitment.**
>
> —Vikki Ashley

Our concept of love is greatly diminished by the way we utilize it in social terms. The truth is, you or I can love *many* people. Nothing stands in our way of being able to handle this energy and direct it toward *many* people. This should come as no surprise. What is surprising, though, is the way men and women misconstrue the term and use it as some type of "magic" for a relationship defined by "social" terms instead of spiritual and universal terms. That's where the train begins to come off the rails. It isn't love that puts people together; it's *attraction*. It isn't love that keeps people together; its *commitment*. Love, if it exists between people at all, is a "renewable resource" and can come and go according to the energy levels of the individuals involved. Love will grow, however, just as surely as it will die based on the *intentions* of the individuals and on the *attention* given to the third entity, *the relationship itself*.

Love, like any energy must be **directed.** Therefore, it must become an intentional focus, which makes it a force—like a laser beam, on the part of any person **using** the energy. Our behavior, values and perceptions of the world will be decidedly different when and if we understand that we use our energy to obtain what we need and want. When we want food, we focus on obtaining food (our emotion/energy is directed toward obtaining food). *That* is a way to love Self and others—by feeding Self and others. Too much of a good thing, though, leads to obesity, illness and in many cases, death. So the point is to *balance* out the use of energy—no matter *how* we use it. All overbalances in our lives create negativity and chaos. Not all directed energy creates **hate**, however. **Hate** is focused and directed emotion that is *intended* to harm someone else or one's Self. Self-hatred is absolutely real and works the same way it works when directed outwardly. It inhibits and destroys the person who is expending the energy negatively. But that person has a choice and is exercising it by polarizing on the negative side of the energy.

> **Energy is purely neutral and works 100% of the time to produce results when used consciously.**
> —Vikki Ashley

Growth will occur when that individual directs his or her energy toward the positive pole of love as a result of *conscious choice.* That occurs when crisis, chaos and significant emotional events (SEEs) jolt them into a new perception of their Selfs and therefore a new reality paradigm. Until then, however, hate will poison that person's internal system and take its toll in illness, chronic dis-ease and even death.

Energy is purely neutral and works 100% of the time to produce results when used consciously. Even unconsciously, energy is holding us together and working its magic in our bodies until we can wake up and direct its use for our own development. It *is* everywhere and every one of us is an emotional being walking around with our own individual energy fields (called auras, biofields, electromagnetic fields) but not each and every one of us is *conscious of it or aware of its powerful results when focused!*

This energy called emotion *can* be scattered, contained (as in repressed) or focused. Let me call your attention to the fact that **anything repressed will find a way to be expressed.** That expression may take the form of nonverbal expression that others see as well as negative expressions of anger and fear or negative chemical and electrical reactions in the brain and body.

> **Anything repressed will find a way to be expressed.**
> —Vikki Ashley

Love as focused emotion is what makes men and women lose their sense of balance and make rash decisions leading to often disastrous consequences. **Love as focused emotion** is what makes men and women lay down their lives for a cause. **Love as focused emotion** is the underlying energy used to attract lovers to each other. **Love as focused emotion** is the connection we **feel** to an item that beckons us depart with our resources to obtain it. It is the connection that permits one to "enter" another's space, literally, when projected by thoughts. That is why love is *seen* as magical, but it's not, it's scientific! To focus we have to think. Thoughts are "things" that are pure energy. When directed and focused emotions are directed by powerful thoughts, you have an "atomic" situation and you know how powerful *those* energies are. We have the same "atomic" resources at our command used by scientists who built the atom bomb! A **bitch,** *with style* will learn how to use all the resources within her command. *Knowledge of how to use these emotions and direct them is power.* If you don't have the information, you can't obtain the knowledge. If you don't have the knowledge, you **won't** be able to consciously and effectively *use* this power and gain the experience that results.

Use of the energy of **love** begins with Self. This notion is **not** the way religions and society have **focused** its use, as I have established. In the context of this book, however, having what it takes means that you know how to use this **love as focused emotion.** As you gain confidence in your Self, you will no longer *need* religion or churches to provide reassurances of your spirituality. You will be in a position to **be** the *love* that you now know how to use, the *energy* you now know how to focus, and the *person* you truly know you are. Priests, ministers and rabbis are teachers and nothing more.

> *In a state of wholeness we act; we* **do not** *react!*
> —Vikki Ashley

They are not intermediaries between you and the Almighty. They can't be because God is within *you.* They, therefore, should be charged with the process of directing you in the *unlocking* of the powers of the spirit rather than the *depression* of these powers to keep the size of their congregations growing and fiscally healthy.

I am not in any way opposed to those who need to engage in the community, camaraderie and education churches represent. What I am opposed to is the misuse of clerical authority. Priests, ministers and rabbis *know* that the processes of religion need redirection, change and, in some cases, "elimination" because they are not only out of step with the times, they are out of step with the *intention* of their founders and their scriptures. I do believe some theological leaders *know* what must be done but are in fear of doing the things that make a difference in the lives of their community members. After all, it may even be true that some of them *don't know* the truth their Selfs and are groping in this dark night of the soul for their own answers. If so, they must meet their fears and open their minds to new ideas. They must march through the Red Sea of confusion to the other shore of enlightenment. And they must take their communities with them!

Each of us **bitches, *with*** or ***without style*** are at different places on the loose gravel path of life and growth and each of us needs varying types of supports along the way and at different times. Churches, priests, ministers and rabbis may not be where we want to be right now.

The **bitch, *with style*** will apply her talents, values, and knowledge to set her *own* spiritual banquet table and learn how to invite the participation of the Masters of the universe to sit down with her and share their knowledge at her Roundtable of the Mind.

Love is so misunderstood in its *essence*. And yet **love,** like other emotions, is absolutely explainable as you have seen. **It is focused emotion** that "drives" our choices when we are conscious, including when we are "conscious" of a sexual encounter about to occur. When we are "unconscious" with regard to our motives, our subconscious permits us to indiscriminately *react* to people, things and situations **without thought.** *Unthinking reactions* are usually the meat and potatoes of life until we each in our own way get a "wakeup call" that sets us on an individual journey into wholeness, which is a state of complete health. In a state of wholeness we act; we do *not* react!

Revelations on Love

On June 7, 1998 at 7:57 A.M., I put my fingers on the keys of my computer to enter a revelation that was so powerful it rocked me in my soul! I was in my den in my favorite chair for thinking, reading, meditating and just be-ing. I had put out my request to the Universe years ago to tell me how to *describe* love. Everything I read tells me what love *does*. It never tells me what love *is*, really! So this was the morning of my revelation and confirmation.

This particular morning I was reading James A. Decker's *Magnificent Decision*. I was on page 18 when the information began to come through to me. I grabbed a pen and wrote down this formula:

"Love is **focused emotion**. Whatever you **intend** to do and **do**, you pay **attention to**. This paying **attention to = desire** which grows into **concentration (focused energy)**
   Intention + attention + desire = focused energy."

I then ran upstairs to my computer and continued:

Love is emotion/energy that is focused on anything one wants. Love comes about through **intention** that becomes **attention** that is paid to the person or objects of one's focus. In its manifestation, the process is **detached**.

Example:

When a boy meets a girl and they **feel** that spark between them, they begin to believe they are "falling **in** love." This is the beginning of the emotional **connection** that can lead to a variety of actions and behaviors. If they **act** on their emotions/feelings and begin to declare their **intentions** toward one another, they then begin to pay **attention** to one another. Paying **attention** is a form of **concentration** (laser-like **energy focused** on a specific object—in this case, a person) until that **concentration** brings about a **burning desire** to be together.

How is *this* accomplished?

Well, when young, it is accomplished by **coupling** (like the electrical outlet—one must plug in the appliance in order to connect to the electricity.) **Danny DoRight** *is the* "plug," the masculine "spark" and *Daisy Dodo,* the electrical outlet or receptacle is the feminine "power" the "plug" has to connect with. No power, no connection, no energy! No spark, no connection, no energy. They both are essential to the flow of that electrical energy.

In anatomical terms, the "plug" is the phallus, the penis—the human spark plug and the electrical outlet

Electrical Plug (Masuline Energy)
The "Spark" that needs a "place"
to receive it (Femine Energy),
THEN Energy flows!

that holds the connecting power lines is the vagina, the **yoni**. You can picture and imagine what is going on here since you, like I, have had this coupling experience Lord knows how many times! This is the long and the short of it. But, oh boy! This is **only** the beginning. The process of coupling and the results—well, that's where the "fun" starts.

And it is "fun" for one or two times until the reality of what might happen sets in and then the fear begins. Especially for the girls and women. Men often think of coupling or fucking, to put it precisely, as a man's dart game—your goal is to hit the bull's-eye and make it stick! that's *it!* Y'all! No more; no less. The phallus "rises" to the occasion because of the heat and energy of the emotions. The only **intention** was to score that bull's-eye. The **attention** paid to the girl or woman was for the purpose of setting up the strike. The **concentration** was on getting her panties off or down far enough to "get it in." getting into position to **make** the strike. The **burning desire** is to *feel* that release when the egg goes hunting for that sperm and time is suspended. "Bull's-eye! Ohmigod. I think I have just died and gone to heaven" is the mental note he makes when finished and is laying there for that furtive, perhaps peaceful, and certainly detached moment in time.

And what about *her?*

Daisy Dodo here is thinking about—you guessed it—*love!* What does *she* know about love? What does she *know? Period.* Not much, I can tell you, but she is emotionally wired and intellectually imprinted by her social and religious teachings to expect such a coupling to carry intimations of love. And she **believes** that shit! OK, so what does that mean in the end. For her? If she's not careful and if she falls for that line of bullshit that "it doesn't feel good if you have a condom on" which seems to be the consensus of males, and if she pretends she is different from other girls and women in the human race (which is her perception of reality in this fogged-up state), and if she is already pretty naive and not well informed on the rudiments of **BITCHHood**, she can expect several things:

1. Utter disappointment because he really didn't *give* a fuck; he just liked *to* fuck.
2. He is a carrier of a sexually transmitted disease and, guess what?
3. He is an HIV carrier and did not communicate this to *her!*
4. He is handsome, tall, smooth talking (you bet) and he said he *loved* **it**, not *her*. *But she didn't hear that! She heard "her."*
5. An answer to a reality check by asking her Self: "What am I telling my Self about what is going on?" A lie, perhaps?
6. She got lucky. He really does *like* her and wants to date her some more. Anyone taking bets why?

So ask your Self. "What were they doing?" Answer: Exchanging energy. Nothing more; nothing less. That's right. *Exchanging energy.* Energy is neutral and carries **no** emotional loading unless put there by the parties involved. They were **"having sex"** with one another, the consequences of which could be enormous in its results and they were *sleepwalking!!!! Unconscious!!!* Not at all awake to the event taking place. They were *allowing* their Selfs to be unconscious victims of their raging hormones. ***Their choices!***

So, what's the point? They had an **experience!** And that's what life is made of: ***experiences—unconscious and conscious experiences.*** Daisy and David must keep walking on that loose gravel path in this valley of the shadow of death until or if they come to the point of enlightenment due to chaos, crisis or significant emotional events (SEEs). Remember, y'all. Love is a *detached* energy. It is we who focus it and provide its meaning for each of us.

If Daisy Dodo and Danny DoRight wake up!, they will get to cross the Red Sea! Let's hope. No! *Don't* stay tuned!

The critical question regarding love is this: "How will I *use* this energy?"

Choices, Choices, Choices!

A **bitch** *with style* accepts all her behavior as having originated from her own choices, *regardless of the consequences.* If consequences appear as acts outside her locus of control, she willingly, though depending on the circumstances, sometimes emotionally, is responsible for her **attitude** in that or any other situation. Your **attitude,** of course, is a reflection of your beliefs and values which we psychologists often call "hidden motivators or internal stimuli." Your **attitude,** when reflective of your *true* Self, supports your beliefs and values. Otherwise, if you are "unconscious, not awake and driven more by habits and thoughts accepted in your mind from others," your **attitude** will surely show your mental state, emotion or mood as a reflection of *that* position as well.

> *A **bitch, with** style knows she is responsible for creating her own reality at all times.*
> —Vikki Ashley

One of the hallmarks of a **bitch,** *with style* is that she **knows** she is responsible for creating her own reality at **all** times. That reality can and does include love as well as all other emotions. With every other act, true **love** must be, finally, *an act of consciousness,* starting with Self. Such intentionality may appear to the reader as manipulative and contrived. Trust me. It isn't. It is simply another type of "habit of growth" that one decides to identify with, relate to, and reinforce over time in one's life. The **bitch,** *with style* is always confronted with a myriad of choices on her platter of life. She *must* choose and stand with her choices until she decides to change them.

> *Information is the antidote for ignorance.*
> —Vikki Ashley

Of course, you're still a **bitch** until you put your own individual stamp on your life and add *"with style."*

Information is the antidote for ignorance. So why are so many people asleep?

People are asleep because to be " awake" is to be accountable and responsible for Self. People are asleep because to be awake is to be a seeker of information and knowledge, to ask questions, seek answers, and analyze information. Then, to "decide" takes energy, discernment, and the capability to discriminate. Why are so many people asleep? Because it is so *easy* to be ignorant, blame others, be irresponsible and believe others owe you something, usually for nothing. It doesn't take a rocket scientist in today's world to figure out why this paradigm of behavior is rampant in society. And, let me add, at **all** levels of society. Lazy is easy. Payback is a **bitch!** Responsibility is difficult. Payback is wonderful. You *do* reap what you sow! What goes around *does* come around. Many people live a superficial life as protection against the work that is required to be one's

> *You **do** reap what you sow! What goes around **does** come around.*
> —Vikki Ashley

own person and to take responsibility. What does it take? To be pushed over the psychological cliff? To be cornered in the cul-de-sac of your own behavioral and values-based world of your own making can be the "wake-up call" that makes the difference just before you reach the new off ramp on the Interstate of life!

Kids and Responsibility

It doesn't feel so hot to just walk around and let things happen **to** me so I can blame someone else *for* it. Even as a kid, though it was sometimes hard to do, I would take responsibility for whatever I did because, as the oldest of twelve, I couldn't find anyone else to blame. I was the leader of the pack, for good or ill. So, it turns out the younger children would turn around and blame me for "letting" things happen to them. Growing up was a lesson in responsibility that was to stand me in good stead but it wasn't exactly easy to be the top of the heap, "Mama's little helper," Daddy's "surrogate wife regarding errands, shopping, etc." and still be "just" one of the kids. They made it hard on me by telling my parents that I "made" them do all manner of things when I was babysitting. Of course, they lied. So it goes with siblings!

But, as adults, when they didn't have me to blame any more, most of them weren't ready for responsibility of any type. Some have grown into it by the grace of God and some haven't. It is no longer **my** responsibility to oversee their choices. Thank, God! Do I have compassion for those more unfortunate than I? Yes, I do. Do I help them out when appropriate? Yes, I have, but not in every instance. It has taken time, but I have found out you can't throw help at other people's challenges when they refuse to change their perception of *their* reality. Better they take the bull by the horns and learn the hard way. That's how they got to that point in their lives in the first place by avoiding responsibility for their own behavior. Besides, people in trouble don't really want the help of successful people. They want to exploit what they perceive as *your* good fortune without taking responsibility for how they got into trouble their Selfs. That's a no-win situation, and a **bitch, with style** learns not to contribute to the delay of another person's reality check or spiritual growth.

The Devil Made Me Do It!

I used to laugh heartily when Flip Wilson said "the devil made me do it." Then, as time passed, and my powers of perception grew, it seemed to me that there was a one-to-one translation of that phrase into the lives of people around me. I used to hear my dad talking about how he couldn't do things because of *someone else* standing in his way, or a classmate would say that her brother *made* her do something she didn't want to do. Or, I would say that my father made me do something I really didn't want to do, like take a letter with a postdated check to one of his creditors. Or, a nun at school would say that the Pope had decreed what we *could* or *could not* do in situations related to morals, like read books on the *Index* or not use birth control, or . . . .

Since when, I would think, are these people, including me, not able to open their mouths and disagree or say "no?" Since when does a person **make** you do *anything* you don't want to do, either consciously or unconsciously? Since when does a man sitting on a throne in ceremonial robes **decree** what I can or cannot do with my life? Since when? In each of these instances and in the spirit of Pogo, "we have met the enemy (in this case the 'devil') and it is us." So, "since when" really refers to the moment I make other people the "regulators" of my life and "agree" with *their* thoughts instead of *my own.* "Since when" refers to my acquiescence to higher authority when I either believe or suspect that authority will do me harm. "Since when" refers to my choice to be lazy in pursuing information and not using it for my development and growth. "Since when" refers to when I make someone else's *reality* my own even when I don't want to! I have already noted that "your perception of reality *is* your reality until new information changes *your* perception." Memorize this rule. It will make a huge difference in how *you process information and use it.*

Since the "devil" is us, seeking new information opens up new avenues of *thought* and provides the ammunition to use against others whose position "worries" your soul and makes you internally uneasy. You must simply be willing to take responsibility for your Self and pay the price for that *decision.*

ASHLEY MAXIM

My perception of reality *is* my reality until new information changes *my* perception

---

The desire for self-responsibility is **not** natural to us as human beings. Self-survival is. Self-responsibility is developed behavior and ultimately occurs in the service of spiritual growth based on decisions made usually during chaos, crises and significant emotional events (SEEs).

We relate to others in our environment and consider that the "other" person fulfills us as individuals. Nothing could be further from the truth. Society has led all of us, **bitches** included, to believe we have a missing piece out there that can *only* be filled by someone besides our Self. That's one of the pieces imbedded in our collective unconscious that must be reprogrammed (see Step Seven). Our attraction to others is built in, but we don't truly understand how to turn this to our personal, individual advantage and growth. That is part of the journey of self-acceptance we all must take to achieve understanding of our **individuality** (true Self, spiritual Self, soul Self, the God within) which goes beyond our **personality** (our mask, projection, public self, ego).   This journey involves embracing self-esteem, self-worth and a sense of high self-value. All **bitches, *with style*** have high self-esteem, high self-worth and *strong values.*

What is Self-Esteem?

Some years ago, the state of California organized a Task Force to Promote Self-Esteem, a unique undertaking for a state government. This task force sought to bring the *idea* of self-esteem to everyone in the state and especially to school children. Self-esteem is a critical idea for individual development and success. It has the benefit of giving an individual a feeling of self-worth and value that expresses it's Self in everything one does. It is an emotionally based sense of confidence that leads a **bitch, *with style*** to **say to** her Self "I AM somebody!" and *know* it is **true!** To her, at that moment, she's the only one that counts in her universe.

This step is titled "I Have What It Takes" because part of the development of a **bitch** and especially a **bitch *with style*** is the development of high self-esteem. Self-esteem is an essential ingredient for those who are healthy. A **bitch, *with style*** knows that self-esteem is based in the health of the individual. It is specifically related to the mental state of the individual and is shaped by internal factors that reinforce a sense of self-respect and self-efficacy.

Nathaniel Branden reports that *"Self-efficacy* means confidence in the functioning of my mind, in my ability to think, understand, learn, choose, and make decisions, confident in my ability to understand the facts of reality that fall within the sphere of my interests and needs; self-trust, self-reliance.

"Self-respect means assurance of my value; an affirmative attitude toward my right to live and to be happy; comfort in appropriately asserting my thoughts, wants, and needs and the feeling that joy and fulfillment are my natural birthright."

Branden lists six pillars of self-esteem and I like them all and added a seventh of my own:

1. Living consciously
2. Self-Acceptance
3. Self-Responsibility
4. Self-Assertiveness
5. Living Purposefully
6. Personal Integrity [2]
7. **Love thy Self!** *(I added this one.)*

Psychiatrist and author Carl Jung once said, 'We need not pretend to understand the world only by intellect; we apprehend it just as much by *feeling.*" Self-esteem is at the core of all you think, say, do and *feel.* Self-esteem affects all seven areas of your life: *Spiritual, Social, Mental, Physical, Financial, Family* and *Career.* You can observe self-esteem in the behavior you and others display on a moment-to-moment basis. Please be aware that your self-esteem is always fluctuating; it is always in process; it is intangible and it is recognized in your behavior. The result is, you may *feel* very respectful one moment, and be in the pits the next. This is an emotional roller coaster that can continue well into later years until you stabilize your life by (1) knowing who you are, (2) practicing who you are and (3) sharing who you are with everyone you meet. This integration of **SpiritMindBodyEmotions (SMEB)** is the *underlying idea* behind being whole (unified). Being whole is impossible without Self-love, Self-knowledge, Self-esteem and Self-acceptance.

William G. McGrane II: " . . . Self-Esteem is the bottom line for the future, for family and business relationships. When you live by self-image, you are guaranteed pain because you base your life on comparison and value judging. When you have self-esteem, which is the self-respect you *feel* for *your Self,* then you have 'freedom.' It does not matter if you are young or old or somewhere in between; we all have inside *feelings.* No one can know what you are *feeling* inside unless you let them know . . . "

McGrane's self-esteem principles have five pillars:

1. Release Value Judging.
2. Evaluate: accept reality of situations, actions, people, events.
3. Inner Knower: accept and affirm a higher power—a perfect guide.

4. Accept total responsibility for everything you think, do, say and feel.

5. TUA—Total Unconditional Acceptance[3]

Bill McGrane II was a friend and colleague. His later years were totally dedicated to making Cincinnati, Ohio the Self-Esteem Capital of the World. He certainly made a magnificent contribution to all those who knew him, me included. His legacy is being carried on by his son, a friend as well, Bill McGrane III. I mention Bill II because he represented a human being who sought to walk his talk and like the rest of us, slipped off the loose gravel path now and then, but his compass was "right on" with his dreams and though he left some matters unfinished, he left living legacies of hundreds of individuals whose lives he touched and changed because he walked the earth and shared his story. Not bad for 66 years this time around. Bill transitioned at 5:30 A.M. on October 14, 1991, the day after my birthday.

I went to the annual Scholars Conference in 1991 one month before his death. He held this conference every year for former students of his psycholinguistic course and it was the first time I had attended since my psycholinguistic experience. I told him then he looked "yellowish" to me. He smiled and assured me he was OK. In one sense he was. He was prepared for his movement forward. His was a conscious trip to another plane of existence and he had declared that he wanted people to celebrate after the tears were shed. I admired him for this. His passing was appropriately celebrated like the graduation ceremony it indeed was. A party was held and a good time was had by all. Smiles were evident through the tears, I am told. I was unable to attend his celebration. I felt his loss and miss him tremendously. But I know where to find him when I need him. Life goes on.

A celebration is what I want when I transition: a big party celebrating my arrival at a new beginning! My will specifically requests that everyone wear bright colors, especially red, purple, white and royal blue. There will be music, dancing, memorials and remembrances by my friends, colleagues and family. What a deal!

He Knew What He Wanted

When I helped my son Alan plan his posttransition memorial celebration, which was held on January 29, 1991 at 11:00 A.M. in San Diego, seven days after his transition on January 22, I found it a healing process and an act of love on both our parts. He directed me in the handling of all his high-priced stereo equipment and CDs as I sat by his side and played his assistant while he did the recording and wrote each name of each artist and the piece being played on the cassette index. He wasn't very strong at the time, but I noticed how much energy he gained from the music. I handed him each of the CDs he requested and listened to the music as he played through each one of the pieces. He happily determined the music and the order in which he wanted it played and *then* recorded the tape we played at his memorial. He told me he wanted the occasion to be a celebration and rejected a traditional funeral. He also said he wanted his ashes scattered off the coast of La Jolla, California. He got everything he wanted. This is a precious memory for this **bitch *with* style** and I know he remembers it with love and smiles as well.

Here is the music he selected in the order it was played:

Somewhere	Barbra Streisand
Too Shy to Say	Stevie Wonder
Celebrate Me Home	Kenny Loggins
Give Me Time	Minnie Ripperton
Return to Forever	Minnie Ripperton
Celebrate New Life	The Winans

Beautiful program, isn't it? Beautiful selections! Every time I hear any of this music I am reminded of his desire to have his presence on this earth *and* his transition celebrated. I thank him for that lesson and for the strength it conveyed to me at the time of his leaving. *He had what it takes!* He had great *self-esteem*; he *knew* what he was worth, spiritually, to him Self, to me and to all those who loved him. He was a teacher, a friend *and* a son. It doesn't get much better than that.

Such an approach to death eases the pain a bit and helps remind one that there is another dimension that represents a new beginning for the deceased. Such thinking is growing, I believe, and in due (do) time will be normal and accepted as a way to handle what is now usually such a sad occasion.

Possessions

Possessions are those things we have in our life that "matter" to us. Some examples are property of all types (homes, antiques, art, jewelry), all manner of material things; and money, values, talents, non-material things but nonetheless real and important. Among the many things we can own (possess), *values* represent, perhaps, the most important of all because they are based on our individual beliefs.

In my value system, health is my most important possession. Bar none. Health, for me, is far out in front of anything that is in second place, like money and other resources of exchange. I can only fulfill *my* contract with the Universe to "drop dead" at 130+ on a tarmac *going* somewhere if I remain healthy each and every day! I desire wealth as well because the more I have the more I can use for my own purposes, many of which are philanthropic. Still, though, I am already a **rich bitch** at this stage of my life and I express my gratitude each and every day as I communicate with the Universe. (See my daily affirmation, page 444.) I am clear about what I need (nothing material) and what I want (more knowledge spiritually). My health represents the opportunity to demonstrate the integration of *SpiritMindEmotionsBody (SMEB)* in my own life. "I am my own experiment," I tell Bob. He laughs when I say that, but he knows it is true. I have been applying various alternative and complementary methods in support of my own health for over thirty-five years. My studies and work in psychology and clinical hypnotherapy have provided me with an academic and research framework for pursuit of my interests.

My Mental Possessions

I *know* that my *thoughts* determine *my* health and "state of mind." My values sustain me and help determine my attitude toward life, people, places and things. These values are *my* intangible possessions that find expression in my body through my behavior, perception and attitudes. This is true of you as well, whether you know it or not.

The **focused emotion (feelings)** I have defined as **love** determine our visible behavior toward Self and others. How? If every time you do something good, wonderful or even timely, if you silently give your Self an "attagirl" and pat your Self psychologically on the back, you are reinforcing your own self-esteem and programming your subconscious to accept that feeling of love for Self so crucial to be-ing. When you do something that isn't so great, make a mistake or make a colossal blunder,

> **Health is my most important possession.**
> —Vikki Ashley

then program your subconscious to cancel this mistake (it's like clearing a file on your computer's hard drive) and keep in mind the statement at the beginning of this Step: *There is **always** another way of looking at this.*"[4] *Always!* Tell your Self you are grateful for the information and experience the mistake has brought you. Thank your Self for being open to the lesson and move on. *Don't look back.* Resolve to do something different if presented with a similar set of circumstances. Remember this: You can change your mind about *anything* at *any time* and move on! Just remember to laugh as you go, because in many ways, in "playing" the game of life, the joke's on us. *Really!* In the end, what looks hard is really easy when you *know* what to do. The key is simply practice, practice, practice. (Use **The Bitch *With Style* Tool Kit**: the order form is in the **Bitch's Book Bag** at the end of this book.)

The behavior of **conscious** people is situation specific. Their consciousness (awakeness!) determines where they are going to put their energies and focus to accomplish their goals. Conscious people can do this because they have knowledge of their own core behavior, tendencies, emotions, values, and perceptions. They have made the effort to *know* their Selfs. Such awareness does not mean that people change **their Selfs** to meet specific occasions. What it means for a **bitch *with style*** is that each individual who has chosen to walk the loose gravel path of growth and change decides to take Step One to discover and **know her Self**. Armed with the information about Strengths, Weaknesses, Opportunities, Threats, **(SWOTs)** emotions, perceptions and how to use her energy, she is able to **communicate** and **interact** with anyone because she is coming from a core of knowledge, courage, confidence and power. She is adaptable with regard to each specific function and occasion while coming from a place of **knowingness** within her.

Duality In People

Let me put to rest right now the idea that we are different people at home, different people at work and a different people socially. No way is that possible. It *appears* that we are two people because we *react* to people and environments differently. What a **bitch, *with style*** does is come from her center. She *acts;* she doesn't *react.* She strives to be conscious and aware 100% of the time in order to direct her energy (and thus her behavior) to *specific situations* and *many different people.* I find it fascinating to hear people talk about being "one person at home, another person at work, and yet another socially." Setting aside individuals with multiple-personality disorder and legitimately diagnosed cases of schizophrenia, that type of "schizoid-appearing" behavior is based on a misunderstanding of how individuals respond to and react to environments and people. With knowledge of one's own **S**trengths, **W**eaknesses, **O**pportunities and **T**hreats (**SWOTs**), individuals no long "feel" out of control and mentally scattered. They no longer *react* to people and environments but take them in stride according to their own individual style and ability to read other's behavior. They have found the means to "pull it all together." Sound easy? It's not, but neither is it as hard as one might think once a decision is made to take control of your own life. It *does* require learning and practice. To be in control of *you* is the object. That will not occur without effort, information and the application of people-reading skills and knowledge. I will provide a means to help you build this foundation upon which the *real you* can function regardless of environment, people and challenges directed your way. That method is mentioned in Step Five and detailed in Step Nine.

In many instances, those "someone else's" in control of your life are the church, your organization and boss, your boyfriend, girlfriend, spouse, best friend, colleague. Just about anyone can be "in control" when **you do not know your own mind or make your own choices.** How many people do you know who are in this situation? I know many, though as I interact with them, I positively reinforce that they create their own reality and ask them what they intend to do about the situation, and when?

Marrying Your Head and Your Gut

I have an Ashleyism that I always share with my clients or with executives and managers when talking about the decision-making process: *Marry your head and your gut and let your head make your decisions.* The point is to integrate your mind and your emotions and **then** go to your mind for your final response. Put another way, listen to your gut (guided by your subconscious) and then consciously choose, recognizing your responsibility for the consequences of that choice.

ASHLEYISM

Marry your head and your gut
and let your head make your decisions.

Self-Knowledge and Relationship.

The idea of relationship, including marriage, is not for two people to become "as one" which is silly and impossible anyway, but really refers to the marriage of your masculine and feminine energies integrated **consciously** by you as a whole person! Surprised, aren't you? Don't be. It's critical to being a **bitch,** *with style.*

Actual physical marriage, in order to replicate this holistic integration, actually causes the marriage of two people to become three! A whole person joining another whole person (whether living together or joined by legal certification—religious or civil) together form another union. That union becomes the third entity, a relationship—to be considered, nurtured, cared for, experienced, released, and consummated. I have always wondered, mathematically, how two people can each be *half* a person in marriage and then make the relationship one! It flies in the face of the *underlying idea* of the Trinity (Father, Son, and Holy Spirit), three in one—three wholes in one.   The process of developing physical reality (the triangle is the first physical symbol that can be formed from straight lines) is *three-sided* and is crucial to physical architecture, as are also the square and the circle. The mind has *three* parts: subconscious, conscious and superconscious.   The whole idea of "two or more gathered together in my name, there also am I," infers a type of power to be gained by two or more asking for *anything* in Christ's name and getting it.   There is another way of looking at this: that it is synergistic as is nature and it puts another face on marriage which will be covered in depth in Step Seven.   Marriages that work are those between *equals* and those between *individuals* who understand that they *stand alone* and bring to the marriage something of value that makes the whole greater than the sum of its parts (synergy).

The **bitch *with style*** describes her Self as a spiritual being having an earthly experience. Talk is cheap, to be sure, but that really is the essence of a **Being In Total Control of Herself**. She accepts the physical reality of being a lower form of **energy**, called matter or physical ***body***, while at the same time being a spiritual being called a ***soul*** who is having a unique adventure and experience that will contribute to it's growth and her human understanding that *all matter is energy vibrating at a slower rate than spirit!* Can she prove it? Only by results and by seeing her own auric field. (See Step Twelve) She uses her thoughts to control her life. They are energy. She learns how to walk her talk through self-knowledge, self-respect, self-esteem and accepts that self-love and self-responsibility are part of her true birthright.

Each individual is totally responsibl*e for her Self* and her own search for answers. She *must* learn to walk on her own two feet and make her own decisions. All of this information is laying the foundation for answers to the question "Who am I?" and for the marriage of masculine and feminine energies with knowledge of her soul for use in becoming a fully healthy individual.

As for marriage in the future (sanctified or not or socially accepted or not), it will be the conscious decision of two individuals who have decided to join with each other for another type of experience and to bring into existence a **relationship** to which each pledge their energies to keep it whole, living, committed, and conscious. Honest communications and feedback will be central to the power of the relationship. Such a relationship will not be based simply on gender, but on soul-felt knowledge of what love truly is . . . **focused emotion** directed to any and all in the Universe and reserved for those to whom we make commitments for a walk together on the loose gravel path of life.

Love, then, knows *no* gender distinction in the human sense. Two men or two women can love each other as intently and spiritually as any man and woman can. Love is energy (focused emotion) and is 100% neutral. It works regardless of your gender, and is just as powerful and holy when the intention is true. It's a soul thing.

Become very clear on the distinction between values, attitudes, material possessions, and resources, because once you give your Self the name, **bitch,** you then develop, gather and bring into your life those resources necessary to bring that name into power

Be very sure you understand what you are asking for when you ask for it. Being a **bitch,** *with style* requires that your possessions serve and please you and that you **own** them lightly and with detachment. They do not **own** you. Every material possession in your life, including your body, is expendable. They can be burned up, blown away, destroyed by bombing, tornadoes, hurricanes, and earthquakes. And in every instance, if you survive, your strong desire for creative expression will rebuild and replace, most likely with something better, every single thing you *supposedly* lost. Your soul, however, is with you forever and cannot be replaced. *It always was and always will be.* Your body, which is the soul's vehicle of earthly self-expression will also be replaced at the appropriate time.

Stay tuned.

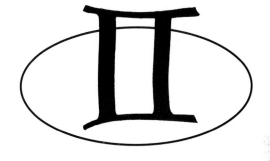

STEP THREE

I Am A Thinker,
Teacher and Learner!

Deep within you is everything that is perfect,
ready to radiate through you and out into the world.

Dr. Vikki's ceremonial walk across the stage eighteen years
after receiving her PhD from The Union Institute!
Dr. Robert Conley, Presiding
October 25, 1993

BITCHHood 301
Self-Knowledge: I *Think*, Therefore I Am.

Self-love is the open door to self-knowledge. The **bitch, *with style*** pursues her development out of an appreciation for her Self and the "need to know" more about who she *really* is. So you think you know? Have *you* got *another* thought coming! Wait until you find out what it takes to actually put a foundation of knowledge under you and to walk into the world *every day* with confidence *because you know who you really are!* ***Think of it:*** No more slippin' and slidin' around issues of which you've been afraid. No more looking in the mirror and flinching at the image staring back at you. No more telling "little white lies" to cover up *anything*. No more low self-esteem. No more kissing butt to get what you want from *anyone*. No more worrying about who loves you, baby! You know who loves *you. You do!* The Universe does and always will.

> **Self-love is the open door to self-knowledge**
> —Vikki Ashley

The trip down Lovers' Lane with your Self is a **bitch!** The world of the inner Self is so rich with images, myths, archetypes, dreams, fantasies, and, yes, new perceptions of a new reality that puts into play the New You. Love of Self is the energy driving you down the Lovers' Lane of your mind. It's a leisurely stroll. No need to hurry. You've got all the time you need to do what you want and no one can take your destiny from you. No one.

Keep recalling the **Ashley Maxims** of the **BITCHHood** curriculum:

1. Your thoughts control your life.
2. Your decisions determine your destiny.
3. Your perception of reality *is* your reality until new information changes *your* perception.
4. You create your own reality. Make it what you *truly* want.
5. You are *never* late for your appointment with destiny.

A **bitch, *with style*** never has to compete with anyone because she understand the rules of the universal road. She may not always be able to articulate what her purpose is, but she does understand she is walking toward it and will "arrive there" at the appointed time. She knows in her *soul* that, if she does her part moment to moment and day by day, ***she will not be late for her appointment with destiny.*** What a comfort to know this to be true.

> **A bitch, with style *is the Master Architect of her destiny.***
> —Vikki Ashley

A **bitch**, *with style* understands that her blueprint for life (her agreement with the Universe this time around) is hers and hers alone. She is the Master Architect of her destiny. So she arrives here hardwired to function as a human being carrying a number of programs (software) that can be mentally manipulated at some time in her life when her knowledge permits. Only *she* can alter these spiritual programs by thought, word and deed through her growth in self-knowledge and by the use of the tools available in the **Bitches Tool Kit** and many other sources. (See the order form in the **Bitch's Book Bag**.)

There really is no such thing as "unalterable destiny." I am not using the term destiny to mean fated or predetermined, though that is a synonym, as well as are other words. Here, I am talking about *purpose*, your final port in the stormy trip of living. The thing you will be remembered for, whatever it is. In a sense, your destiny *is* your destination. But it is *not* fated. Your lessons based on your life blueprint (your prebirth agreement with the Universe) are designed to move you forward in knowledge and afford you the choices with which *you* decide your destiny.

Every step of the way involves choice. You can decide every moment of your life what it is you want to do with your Self. Funny thing, though. You *cannot*, repeat, *cannot*, decide *any one else's destiny*, no matter how hard you try or how much you want to interfere with another person' exercise of his or her will. Think about that for a minute. On an individual basis, you actually have **no** power over *anyone*. An individual *allows* you to do what you do to him or her. They are choosing (consciously or unconsciously—usually the latter) to *allow* you to interfere in their lives. The problem is, they don't know it or don't want to confront whatever is standing in the way of their walking on their own two feet! Or, they know it and are too lazy to think for their Selfs. The bottom line here is that *other people let you do what you do to them.* When they are tired of "putting up" with it, in due (do) time, they **do** something about it—usually in anger and always as a reaction.

A **bitch,** *with style* acts. She does not react. She does not "put up with" anything she doesn't want in her life—after she learns *who she is* and *what* she wants. In other words, she gains self-knowledge and builds that strong foundation of self-understanding.

Building Your Own Community

In our day-to-day world we encounter stress, chaos, pleasure, joy, distress, anger, love and a lot of duality. The ability to discriminate, make choices and reconcile all of the polarities take their toll. Facing such choices happens at all ages. In the preteen years ("I want to be a dancer; Mom wants me to be a doctor."), teen years ("I don't know what I want to do or be"), college (Do I use drugs, smoke, drink, or not?), marriage (I've lost my Self!), single life (What's this rat race *for* anyway?, the divorced years (men just fuck up your life), after fifty, sixty or seventy, during widowhood (Where's the meaning in my life? What's it all been for *anyway?*).

> *It appears to me that 99.9% of all families are dysfunctional and unstable.*
> —Vikki Ashley

Such familiar refrains establish that somewhere for all of us there are sometimes unintended consequences for our choices and we only "see" these consequences after the fact when hindsight is always 20/20! The blurred dimension of daily living requires an extraordinary effort to awake to the morning light much less the scutty, slimy, murk and mire of "seeing" real reality! Ugh!

It's not all *that* bad. After all, we all start our lives in a world of instability, the family unit! Another shock to the system, because "everyone" says the family is supposed to be the stable unit of society. I have only one thing to say: show me one—a stable family unit, I mean. It appears to me that 99.9% of all families are dysfunctional and unstable. Why wouldn't they be? Based on the unrealistic expectations people have of their Selfs, the lack of knowledge about their higher potential and purpose (Do they teach this in elementary/high school or college? Not yet!) and no way to express their individuality except through rebellion of some sort. So, why wouldn't parental leadership be unstable? *Instability is the norm **not** the exception.* All the pious platitudes and speeches on the floor of the House and Senate in Washington, D.C. *will not change the facts.* The very congressmen and senators talking about the importance of the family unit are their Selfs usually the very reason their family units are unstable. All this malarkey about two parent families being the only way to go for stability for children is also not true. Religion and other social entities like schools, colleges, and universities don't contribute to the stabilization of the family unit because, in truth, the "family unit" is a mythical ideal that has been chased throughout history, especially western history, as *the way it is supposed to be.* Well, wake up, people, and know what **bitches, *with style*** already know: It just isn't true what they say about family units. There may be exceptions here and there, but the truth is:

1.   Men and women "mate" for reasons having nothing to do with creating the ideal family unit. Raging hormones coupled with good looks, muscles and butts in the right place, and beautiful faces, hair, etc., etc. not to mention, "Man, is she good in bed! Wow.!" are among them. Most are too young and unknowledgeable about life to think about anything but their next fuck or roll in the hay, smiling at each other, holding hands in public so everyone will know they "belong" to each other and going home throwing their clothes on the floor and hopping in bed. Even young people raised in church and told that they should be looking for something different get caught up in the emotional juggernaut called "relationship" without knowing what it truly means to *first* be an individual or a conscious and awake Self. How long does *this* euphoria last? Until the wife has to pick up all the clothes on the floor, wash them, etc. and until the routine of living begins to take its

toll on two originally well-intentioned (for the most part) young people. Well . . . how long did *your* euphoria last?

2.   Children usually "happen." The idea of "thinking" about having children, about *how* you want to rear them, what *values* you want to impart, whether or not *religion* will play a part in their upbringing and if so, which one; the notion of *both* parents having a part in the rearing and the whole idea of each parent having *some time to him Self* or *her Self* as a regular part of the schedule of living so they can refresh and expand their spirits is **not** what is going on out here, folks. Some people do it. ***Most people don't.***

3.   If you can't answer the question "Who am I" or speak to your own **S**trengths, **W**eaknesses, **O**pportunities and **T**hreats **(SWOTs) before** you marry, what makes you think you're going to do it **after** you marry? I call this a case of the "blind leading the blind." Is it possible for two people to "wake up" together. Yes, it is *possible*. What usually happens, though, is one wakes up, grows up and then leaves the other. And rightly so. Energies have changed. Clashes of minds create continuing chaos. If there is love, understanding, and the will and desire to *be* together, there is something with which to work. And *work* it is! Nevertheless, such work is both warranted and often rewarding if both parties choose it. Still, it is so much more difficult to do *in* a marriage with children, job, daily living requirements, etc., but it *is* doable.

4.   "The children at all costs" is not a reason for having a traditional family unit. When family strife escalates and when one parent is cruel, there is *no* family unit. That is an assemblage of people held together by a social contract that is no longer worth the paper it is written on.

5.   A real family is one where the energies mix harmoniously with only occasional disagreements that are not angry escalations of unfettered emotions. This type of family does not have to be distinguished by blood but is *almost always* a family put together *by choice*. In other words, there are other ways to define family and community to sustain and

support individuals (including children) who have no true family units worth expending energy to maintain.

6.   All children have tales to tell about family members who act badly in all manner of circumstances, or family secrets that they were told to keep secret (they never do), or "Did you know about Aunt Alice and that trip she took to Colorado? Well, she had a baby and gave it up for adoption!" "No!" "Yes!" I say, "so what?" So, what? is when the child shows up at her mother's door 21 years later looking for a relationship with the birth mother who gave her up. So, now, what do you do? Should have done the right thing 21 years ago and either aborted or stayed home and faced the music. This is a case of doing what the *parents* wanted done to save the family face. Just like Dorian Gray's portrait, the family plays "let's pretend" while underneath, the ugly cancer of lying and coverup spread through the minds and souls of every member of the group.

One must have compassion, understanding and tolerance for everyone attempting to develop the mythical family unit. Knowledge is lacking about each entity that could make a difference in how they put their "family team" together. I often smile when consulting with companies and assisting them in their team building. How ironic, I think, that we are here doing this in the market place when we should also be doing this in these people's homes as well!

Well, team building can and should be done in the home. Information about who each member is can be used to develop better family relations. The **bitch,** *with style* will lead the way.

The family unit that really counts is the "family of one," the *individual person.* Each person who knows Self, who takes care of Self, and who *first marries Self* is a much better candidate for social marriage if he or she chooses to go there. More on this in Step Seven. It is critical to understand that each of us is made up of two energies—masculine (active and aggressive) and feminine (passive and supportive and developmental) that are to be used by the mind consciously to help us become internally balanced and thus integrated in **SpiritMind EmotionsBody (SMEB)**. Men **and** women each have both these energies and the **bitch,** *with style* consciously *uses both.*

Right Here In River City

Hello, Vikki? Hi, this is Bee! (Crying) I've got a problem and I need your help."

This telephone call from one of my sisters began her odyssey supported by my complicity and cover for the agony she was enduring. She was pregnant and my father had threatened to kill her. At the very least, he told her he was going to put her out of the house and all that kind of stuff. Sounded familiar to me, since I had endured a similar fate. Only, in my case, he *did,* throw me out of the house and I went to live with my first husband's mother until we got married.

But this time, Bee asked me to be her cover for the nine months it would take for her to deliver the baby and give it up for adoption. She'd write letters and send them to me to post from San Diego. We'd talk and stay in touch, but I helped her out during a time of her need. The irony is, we pulled it off. The whole family thought she was in San Diego visiting me and going to college. Only this year, 1998, did *she*, not I, tell our brothers and sisters about her ordeal and how I helped her through it.

September 30, 1998 my second oldest brother died in San Diego of cardiac arrest. He had had complications due to emphysema, asthma and cardiac problems for years. He was an alcoholic and had been warned by his doctor that continual drinking would jeopardize his life. At a family reunion a year ago he told me he only took a nip "every now and then."

We buried my brother on October 6 in a very good looking navy blue suit from the thrift store, a brand new shirt and tie and put him away with honors in the Dayton Veterans Cemetery—all paid for by three of his siblings. He had nothing to his name.

When my father threw him out of the house and told him never to return to Xenia, Ohio, he did so on the heels of a story that said he had made a young lady pregnant. He told my brother never to "darken his door." Well, he didn't. He darkened mine in San Diego when he would come there for shore leave after he joined the Navy (and that was after he had served as an army paratrooper). He'd call me from jail . . . drunk. I'd go and bail him out and bring him home to dry out.

This went on for about three years. Finally, he called one night. Same song, same station. I told him "NO. I will not come and get you out of jail now or ever again. As far as I am concerned, you can rot in jail until you decide not to go there any more." I hung up the phone. I didn't hear from him for years. Next time I saw him he was sober and broke. He asked me for $25. I gave it to him. And walked away.

It was good to see him at the family reunion in 1997 because he seemed to be straightening out his life. He called me a month before his death, just to chat and "check in." He had extra time on a new phone card and was making the rounds of all the family. We had a good chat and I told him that I love him and would see him at the next reunion. He always ended his phone calls with "Over and out." "Well, Corky, over and out to you, too."

He did no harm to anyone but his Self. He lived alone and he died alone. That was *his* blueprint. He was *his* architect. He has a son, I learned at the funeral. Hope I meet him some day.

See what I mean? Family "stuff." We've all got to deal with it, but we don't have to "carry" someone else's baggage. We can help but we can't control other people's lives. We can learn and apply what we learn to our own experiences.

Actions Speak Louder Than Words

Grow. Teach. Learn. Experience. Gather new information. Bring new energy into your environment. Haven't you wanted to know more about you, art, building ships, flying planes and helicopters, watching the stars?

Don't you have any curiosity about:

- life
- your body
- herbs
- aromatherapy
- astrology
- numerology

- reflexology
- massage
- Chinese medicine
- acupuncture
- acupressure
- comparative religion?

Why not:

- Get a manicure and pedicure on a regular basis.
- Volunteer.
- Audition for a role in amateur theater.
- Take photography lessons and use your camera more effectively.
- Go fishing.
- Take in the latest show at the art museum.
- Wander around the aquarium and people watch.
- Go to lunch with a friend on the spur of the moment.
- Change your pace.
- Go to a movie. Alone.
- Play hooky on a Saturday or Sunday and stay gone all day.

Give your Self a challenge around your own needs and wants. Put your Self in the center of your circle and see how it feels. Ask your Self how your self-esteem is these days. If it's high, do something totally new and different—for you.

- Do something different.
- Get out of your rut.
- Stop being predictable.
- Imagine a new version of you: new hair cut, makeup, clothes.
- Make it happen!

Answer these questions:

1. Do you believe you have a *right* to do what you want to do?
2. Do you believe you have an *obligation* to know who you are?

3. Do you believe you can make choices and decisions that will change your life?

4. Do you believe that you create your own reality and can make it what you truly want?

If you answered "yes" to all of those questions, your foot is on the path of health. If you answered "no" to any one of those questions, your health is questionable. Remember, *health* is the integration of spiritual, mental, emotional and physical energies. Which one is missing for you?

Picture and imagine your Self in a multicolored bubble floating outside and going up into the atmosphere. Picture and imagine your Self *outside* the issues of your day-to-day life in order to bring some balance, perspective and stimulating energies into your life. You become more conscious of your options as a person who has a right to individual happiness and individual choices when you realize you have the power to picture and imagine anything you want. When you wake up, and you will, begin to listen to the "still small voice within" that speaks so loudly to your soul. Let that "still, small voice" make a difference in your life. It is, after all, your own God voice and it belongs to *you*.

The Most Important Person in the World

> **You,** *dear* **bitch,** *are the most important person in the world.*
> —Vikki Ashley

You, dear **bitch**, are the most important person in the world. This is so because you are all you have regardless of whom you share your Self with. Wasn't it Andy Warhol who talked about 15 minutes of fame? Well, how lucky some people are to get a minute of time on *their own clock* because that's how little time they truly spend appreciating their Selfs and who they are. It is an enormous challenge to engage in focused emotion called love of Self. It's downright frightening to most of us because of the guilt we feel at being so, so, well, OK, say it, narcissistic and selfish as opposed to self-sacrificing. Well, damn! You got it out! Let's talk about that.

Before you can engage effectively and without hostility toward another person or group, you are **required** to have self-acceptance and self-love before there can be any hope of self-esteem. You must have self-respect before the seeds of self-esteem can be sewn into the furrows of your heart. *The way to eliminate resentment in your life is to find a way to fill your cup first so that you can share what you have with others and still have some left for your Self.* Nourish and water that seed of self-love until it flowers into confidence, self-assertion , commitment to your right to exist, firm self-knowledge of **S**trengths, **W**eaknesses, **O**pportunities and **T**hreats (**SWOTs**) and an iron-clad understanding that you do not have to live up to *anyone's* expectations *but your own.*

To many people, this is a terrifying responsibility. To be a **bitch,** *with style* means their life is truly in their **own** hands. It means that mother and father and other authority figures cannot be counted on as protectors nor can they be blamed as enforcers. It means you are responsible for your own existence—and for generating your own sense of security. You have to *surrender your fear* of "have not" to a higher power that guarantees abundance according to your determination. If you will not stand up for your own right to exist—*your* right to belong to your Self—how can you experience a sense of personal dignity? Personal dignity cannot be conferred on you. You must wear it proudly from the *inside, knowing who you are!*

> *Personal dignity cannot be conferred on you. You must wear it proudly from the* **inside, knowing who you are!**
>
> —Vikki Ashley

Keep in mind always that when you lay down this body you have used during this incarnation, and it is embalmed and put in a coffin or put on a wooden block to be cremated, ask your Self who else will be joining you there—by choice. If your answer is "no one," then be sure to give "no one" or anyone else in *this life* control over *any* aspect of your life. Say to your Self: I know there is no one out there who will jump in my coffin or urn with me when **my** time to transition comes. So there is no one to whom I must give my life except me. So, I am in charge of my life totally, since I am a **bitch,** *with style.*

Be clear on this point: No one will die *for* you or me though some may die *with* you and me. **No one** will be able to make me healthy, cure me of disease or even show me how to cure my Self **unless** they have begun to understand that there is an inner and outer world for me and for everyone else in the universe and that our thoughts control our lives.

Some of us focus on the outer world exclusively to the detriment of the inner. The **bitch,** however, seeks peace and harmony by consciously bringing *balance* into her world. She knows that there is a world of cause and effect, love and hate, hot and cold, birth and death; and that those dualities represent choices of simply degrees of the same energy. We are free to think or not think, expand our consciousness or maintain *status quo*, move toward new perceptions and information or retreat from knowledge, self- and otherwise. The **bitch,** *with style* knows that self-responsibility and integrity are never automatic; they always represent an achievement, and a big one at that. Such achievement comes from dedication to teaching (sharing), learning and growth.

> **We always teach what we need to learn or have learned. Always!**
> —Vikki Ashley

We always teach what **we** need to learn or have learned. Always! That is what I'm doing through this book and the others I will write, as well as through speeches, seminars and media opportunities. At this stage in my life, I've just got to tell "it" because the news is too good to keep secret! As you already know, I've been getting ready for *this* moment in time ever since *my* beginning.

It Takes Time to Tango

New insights require time to consume. Adrienne Ashley, in **The Zodiac: A Pattern for Meditation** says something quite profound and right on the mark for a **bitch,** *with style.* "It does not happen all at once; but when instability has exhausted itself, there comes the first fleeting intuitive impression that there is a higher, more enduring pattern for life. This point marks, perhaps, the most crucial period in the progress of the human spirit, for it is **the** moment when the aspirant takes hold of the power to contact and work with his own soul. In whatever incarnation it occurs, **from that moment on,** in spite of regressions and digressions, **soul (individuality) and personality go on together.**" The duality, (Individuality + Personality) becomes consciously *integrated* into the **bitch,** *with style* pattern of life. This is when the **bitch,** *with style* is born, regardless of age, culture, race, religion, national origin or station in life It's a soul thing!

River City II

My father used to call me "Mouth Almighty." Actually, my Aunt Gerri gave me the name early on and it "stuck" throughout my preteen years. I would always find a way to insert my Self in adult conversations. Truth be told, I found talking with children my age very uninteresting. I was never ugly or inappropriately assertive, but it was clear I was growing into a person to be reckoned with from the time I was two years old! But then, something strange kept occurring simultaneously with this entertainment act. When I freely presented my ideas to my parents (not in conversation with other adults around), I was dismissed. My thoughts, wants and even needs were never listened to by my parents. I remember thinking they didn't care about what I *really* thought. I was just some kind of entertainment for their friends. After they left, they just closed me out.

One day when I was about three, I told my mother, "Grandma is going to die." My mother said "What? What do you mean? What grandma are you talking about?" "Grandma Snell," I said again, this time insistently, my aunt reports. "You don't know what you're saying," my mother said. "I don't ever want to hear you say a thing like that again, do you hear? *What do you mean?*" She huffed off indignantly and dismissed my warning entirely.

One week later, my mother received a telephone call. Grandma Snell had died. Exactly one more week to the day, Grandpa Snell died, also. It was a traumatic time for my family. Mother and her brother and three sisters were devastated. When the funeral was over, my mother shook her finger in my face and threatened me with bodily harm if I ever opened my mouth and said *anything* like that *ever* again. I had never been so threatened and I took it seriously. All of a sudden I wasn't so "cute." She effectively shut down what might have grown into a real spiritual talent had she known how to work with me. But she didn't know and neither did anyone else. That event changed the climate around my "talking" and I think it forever changed my relationship with my mother. She viewed me as some strange little kid who happened to be born into the family. Mind you, I grew up to be the chief baby sitter, shopper and continued my conversations with visitors, but a chill had fallen on my relationship with my mother, and it was never to lift, not even before her death.

I now think I scared her half to death and she looked upon me thereafter as a strange person invading her already inse-cure space. I was walking evidence of her sexual indiscretion with my father to begin with. When he was angry he talked about how he *had* to marry her and both of them were reminded of this every time they looked at *me*. Now, I had thrown some real crazy family stuff into the game and my rela-tionship with my mother became much more tenuous. My father took it in stride. He didn't "believe in that stuff" anyway and he wasn't home when it happened. My mother and Aunt Gerri were the only witnesses to the event and I am grateful to my Aunt for sustaining the memory in order to later share it in detail with me.

What about those men and women who have lost their intuitive voices to the power of fear, theirs or someone else's, like my mother's fear. Fear is only **F**alse **E**xpectations **A**ppearing **R**eal, but not if you are without knowledge and understanding due to error, ignorance and even pain. Now, if someone has a gun to your head and you are being told to do something you don't want to do—well, you have to decide how much you want to remain in your current body and what the odds are under those conditions. I can't speculate about this, nor can anyone. But it would seem to me that if you are not afraid of death, your behavior will reflect that in some way that will allow you to escape what appears to be an inevitable fate. If you felt like a lowly worm and of no worth, chances are . . . .

On the other hand, my childhood religion (Catholicism) taught me that *other* people, even people in Asia that I didn't know about at the time, were more important than I. I was always being asked to give up some of my babysitting money (meager as it was) to help the babies or people somewhere else. The term "selfish" was freely tossed about by the nuns, as we scrambled to have contests room by room to see how much money we could collect "for them." These nuns were not into self-esteem, self-assertiveness, self-efficacy, Self—nothing! They were into strict obedience and no fooling! Still, I usually found a way to get my point across, even though my "mouth" got me in lots of trouble with the nuns. I would be sent to the church next door to do acts of contrition and say ten Our Fathers and ten Hail Mary's for my mouthiness. Usually at 30-minute clips. Great way to relax and day dream. But this behavior had its ominous side and I felt its blow when I least expected it and certainly when I least wanted it—just before I graduated from high school.

The Robber Baron

One month before graduating from high school, Sister Isabella called me to her office. "Aren't you excited about going to Manhattanville and the Pius X School of Music?" "Yes, of course, Sister." "Don't you feel fortunate to have this opportunity. After all, things like this don't happen here at St. Brigid very often and we're so proud of you." "Well, thank you, Sister." "Now, my dear, something has come up that I am sure you will want to support. Michael Gorman has an opportunity to go to the naval academy and I believe Congressman Van Deerlin will recommend him, but we want to make sure. I would like to make Michael the Validictorian and Summa Cum Laude and you the Salutatorian and Magna Cum Laude. I know you're first in this class, but you're already taken care of with a full four-year scholarship. I know you won't be selfish in this matter, will you?" "*What!* I shouted at her. *What* are you **saying**? No. I will *not* give up what I earned. His grades are high enough to go to the academy. He doesn't need to take my honor. I *earned* it. I want it and I *won't* give it up." Crying, I ran out of her office, scooped up my books, still crying and walked out of school and directly home. That one-mile walk should have calmed me down, but by the time I arrived at 416 Columbus Avenue, I was smoking!

"Mom, Mom, guess what Sister Isabella wants to do? She wants to take away my academic honors and give the first place in the class to Michael Gorman so it will look good on his record when Congressman Van Deerlin recommends him for a commission. I won't stand for it." Crying I asked my mother what she thought. She looked at me, solemnly, and told me that Sister Isabella had already called her on the phone and explained what she wanted to do. "Why can't you see how selfish this is," MY MOTHER said. "How can you be so selfish when God has been so good to you? You're all set and this won't make any difference to your future at all. So why not do it?" "I won't, I won't. You don't understand. This is what I worked for. This is my place in the class. How can you support her robbing me of what is my just due? How *can* you?" I looked at my mother in utter disbelief, turned and walked out the door. "Come back here," mother called. I kept on walking. I know who I can talk to. I walked all the way back to school and went to see Father Schumacher, my champion, friend and supporter. I didn't know where else to go.

After hearing my story, he looked at me and said the words I shall never forget: "You know I would do anything in the world for you. But I have absolutely nothing to do or say with how Sister Isabella runs the school. She can do whatever she wants to in the end and there is nothing I can do or say to stop her." I looked in his eyes and felt his pain. I told him I knew he would change things if he could. I thanked him for his time and left. My walk home was very slow. I knew that by then my father was at home. He was and his position was the same as my mother's. He saw me as selfish and always thinking of my Self. He said things I never knew he thought about: how I wanted to be the center of attention and was always taking center stage away from other people. "Why not let Michael have center stage for once," he said. "You're set. Stop being so selfish."

I was summoned the next day to Sister Isabella's office and I had to bring my parents. There, in front of my face and hers,

I heard both my parents not only tell her she was right, but they admonished me again for my selfish attitude. True to my nickname as Mouth Almighty, I took my last shot: "This is my honor. I earned it by getting all A's. Michael is stealing this honor from me with Sister Isabella's help and support. It's highway robbery, and you're *all* wrong," I shouted, crying. "Quiet, child," said Sister Isabella. "I will not be quiet. I hope the whole school knows how you stole my honor from me and *gave* it to Michael Gorman," I said with my voice rising loudly. I turned, stomped out of the office, crying as though my heart would break, barely able to see the steps to the door. I walked home slowly, climbed into bed in the small office my father had finally allowed me to use for some privacy from that herd of people, (I'm 17 for God's sake!) and cried my Self to sleep. I did not eat that night nor did I speak to either of my parents for the next week. I mumbled and did just what had to be done. I did not want to be in their presence nor did I want to do anything more for them. I had been used, abused and thrown away. I had been dismissed and undermined by the very people I had worked so hard to support all my life. I had nothing left to say to them.

Well, I somehow got through graduation. Michael Gorman was nervous when he gave his speech as the #1 graduate in the class. Everyone knew about what had happened. It was ugly. But then, some people thought it was OK because he was a man and would have to support a family. A commission from the Naval Academy and a career in the navy would be much more important socially than my budding music career. So, you see, even then, some individuals were willing to write off a female who was competent and had earned her place for a man who had not.

I spent the summer of 1951 making clothes and getting ready to "get out" of Xenia. Anxious to see the big lights of New York, I allowed my vision of the future to hold down my pain and anger. I went to college and had a wonderful first semester. I started smoking (in self-defense since all the girls smoked) and when I returned home for Christmas with my

Dean's list honor, I learned that Michael Gorman had been told to leave the academy. He could not, I was told, respond well to discipline. He lasted six weeks! Six weeks! So much for God being good to *me* and *my* selfishness. I didn't know it then, but the law of cause and effect works constantly. What goes around comes around. You reap what you sow. Truly!

The seeds of this book were planted deep in my soul after this event. They would be watered and nurtured by events throughout my life. In the case of Sr. Isabella, I never felt victimized. I felt robbed. I was angry and had no power to redress the wrong that was done to me, not even through the parish priest. She was a law unto her Self and she was using her power abusively and capriciously.

With reinforcement at home for these same doctrinaire principles as expounded by the Church, I had to struggle to find my true voice, my individuality, my very soul throughout my school years. Entertainment is one thing. Authenticity another. What happened to "Love thy neighbor **as thy Self?**" Buried under the loose gravel path of life, hiding the truth of who I am. Regardless of the rules and regardless of anyone else's point of view, I determined long before I fell to my hormones in my early 20s that I would find a way to make a difference in *my* world. I just didn't know *how* or *when* at the time I made that vow.

A Little Light Music

A **bitch,** *with style has* to laugh at her Self to keep from crying. Life, even in its serious moment, can be absolutely so hilarious it's ludicrous. Some of the best humor is the fun I have had laughing at my Self and I urge all of you to take this advice seriously. I didn't always feel that way. In fact, I grew up way too serious except when in my Mouth-Almighty entertainment mode. I have learned, however, as a significant part of my learning to de-stress in times of tension, that laughter loosens me up faster than anything except deep breathing. Deep breathing is my 150% sure shot to handle stress but laughter accelerates my energy flow and warms my blood. It opens up my head and gives me such a good feeling.

Let's laugh together.

- The only reason some people are lost in thought is that they're total strangers there.
- The problem with most people who reach their wits' end is that it doesn't take them long to get there.
- An inventor is a crackpot who becomes a genius when her ideas catch on.
- The most unexpected injury most people suffer nowadays is being struck by an idea.
- Most people are like rivers: there's usually more activity at the mouth than at the source.
- People on ego trips should do others a favor and buy one-way tickets.
- An egomaniac is a person who always opens her mouth and puts her feats in it.
- Ever notice how everyone wants to go to heaven, but no one wants to die?
- What most women look for in a beau is someone who's tall, dark, and has some . . . in other words, a man who's fiscally fit.
- A wise girl is the one who gets taken out, not taken in.
- Two's company, three's the result.[1]

These one-liners should afford you a chuckle or two and you may find a few others. I think it is wonderful to read a joke book occasionally, watch funny movies, and take a smile break. Good for the heart and soul. Good for me. Gets that love flowing! Keeps my internal chemical factory and electrical power plant handling their jobs without cluttering up any of "the works."

Who am I?

The **bitch,** *with style* must begin to build her own foundation on solid ground. The formal **P³ Baseline and Growth Package**, which identifies behavior and emotions, values and perceptions—the most critical elements in understanding people is mentioned in Step Five and outlined in detail in Step Nine. If you wish to complete the self-assessment instruments and receive your own **P³ Baseline and Growth Report**, the forms for completion are contained in the **Bitch's Book Bag.**

All work that I do with organizations *and* idividuals begins with this package. For psychological and hypnotherapy clients, this package shortens the time required to zero in on issues, challenges and **SWOTs**. For executive and management clients, these data provide the most effective foundation for building teams and a harmonious workplace I have yet encountered. To build functional work enviroments, cultures *and* teams, it is *essential* that this type of foundation be laid. Most businesses and organizations do not take the time to do this up-front work and preparation and thus build foundations on sand instead of rock. I submit that they therefore continue to throw billions down rat holes in the name of human development, training, team building and benchmarking. They talk about **benchmarking** their organizations against **best practices** before they have a **baseline** against which to do such **benchmarking**. Amazing, indeed. It's their money and they can throw it away if they want to. My question is, why should they want to deprive stockholders as well as employees, managers and executives of money they could put to better use *if they but knew the alternative?*

I would put all of these executives and managers into the **BITCHHood** curriculum!

Qualities To Be Developed in BITCHHood 301

Including but not limited to:
1. Communications skills
2. Vision and direction
3. Flexibility
4. Depth
5. Understanding
6. Serenity
7. Soul knowledge and contact
8. Learning *from* experience
9. Ability to *unplug* from inharmonious energy fields

Bitch, *With Style* Characteristics

1. Healthy
2. Conscious, Alert
3. Energetic, Spiritual
4. Courageous
5. Responsible
6. Independent
7. Warm
8. Cooperative
9. Caring
10. Youthful—totally unrelated to calendar age
11. Dynamic
12. Inventive

Potential Potholes and Weaknesses

1. Fear
2. Value judging
3. Scattered energy
4. Lack of focus
5. Overemotional
6. Overcommitment
7. Unable to keep her own counsel
8. Tentative in decision making
9. Mistrust of intuition
10. Following other people's suggestions without question
11. **Not** marrying her head and gut and letting *her* head make the decisions
12. Loss of faith in her Self

BITCHHood 301 provides information on **self-development** that permits one to determine, interpret and evaluate his/her relationship to the phenomenal world. Choices have to be made in a chaotic world. The decisions you make about your choices determine the direction of your destiny.

The **Fourth Step to BITCHHood** is about the psychological and spiritual roots and emotions, required to develop the New You.

PART TWO

Roots, Wings and
Creative Self-Expression

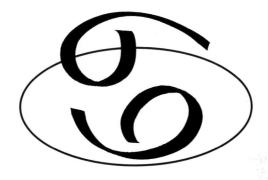

STEP FOUR

I Have Roots and Wings!

*My perception of reality **is** my reality
until new information changes **my** perception.*

Bob and Vikki at the Kam's Fund Gala, New Orleans—1996

BITCHHood 401
Self-Development: I *Feel*, Therefore I Am.

Every function of the body is a microcosm of the functions of nature. Nature **absorbs** the elements, **assimilates** them into her flora, fauna, earth, minerals, water, and then **eliminates** them through various acts of destruction, e.g., hurricanes, tornadoes, earthquakes, tsunamis, locusts, ants, etc.

The **bitch,** *with style* seeks information and knowledge through experience (called wisdom) and she **absorbs** the elements mentally and emotionally; she **assimilates** them by using the information in various aspects of her life as in the use of nutritional knowledge to begin a regimen that will lead to proper nutrition, exercise and, above all, rest and sleep so the body can maintain and renew it's Self. She **eliminates** and discards those pieces of information and experience that **do not fit** with her life and the path she has chosen. This includes people, material things, groups, jobs, whatever.

The human body does exactly what I just described at the physical level. The body **absorbs** whatever I put into it, including poisons and toxins contained in foods and drinks. It **assimilates** what it can based on the electrical and chemical formulae that run the body and **provides** the nutrients for the bloodstream, muscles and tissues. All of the matter taken into my body goes **somewhere** for good or ill. The system **digests** the food and prepares what it does not need to be expelled. This expellation is known as **elimination,** which is the dumping of our body wastes through sweating, defecation, urination and on occasion vomiting.

It is amazing to me that this correlation is so exact. The nature of each process is the same differing only in degree but **not** in complexity.

Our minds go through a similar process, but let's stick with the body and its functions first. As a means of establishing the foundation for **BITCHHood 401,** it is essential to know how you basically function as a microcosm of the macrocosm. The body is our spiritual vessel, our home, our "Temple of Solomon," that we must **learn** how to care for and use in order to develop our health and spiritual powers. These spiritual powers are based on our knowledge and use of energy. Energy is matter *and* light, the same in nature but different in degree. Einstein said it best: **E=mc²**. Recall that he talked about "riding on a light beam?" Well, in a sense, he did that to obtain his answers. Riding on a light beam is so real that its surreal. It's amazing he thought of it. We do, each of us, constitute a light beam in the Universe. When light (us) releases energy (thought, color, sound, words) in the form of heat, we are then functioning as a human power plant. Energy represents movement that gets things done. In a word, work. It can change form, as from heat into light and light into heat, but it cannot be *created or destroyed*. ***That's right: Energy cannot be created or destroyed. It simply IS!*** Now to all of you out there, doesn't that sound like a description given in Sunday school about God? It does to me, too. (See page 145.)

> *Matter is energy, spirit is energy, matter is spirit . . . the same in nature, but different in degree*
> —Vikki Ashley

Each of us, through the physical body, is a miniature Universe. Our job therefore (yours **and** mine) is to become conscious (awake!) of this magnificent piece of dirt in which we live because it is evident that matter **is** energy, spirit **is** energy and **therefore** matter **is** spirit. Matter and spirit are the same in *nature*, but different in *degree*—meaning matter is the densest form of energy/spirit, but spirit nonetheless!

BITCHHood 401 is about *building* the appropriate knowledge base about our body, its functions, its correlations and its templates of power. In fact, learning about our body is a form of nurturing Self. Put another way, this learning is a form of "mothering" our Selfs and watering that seed in our hearts. We are watering, fertilizing, pulling weeds and pruning where necessary so that the final product will stand tall, firm and beautiful as it walks in the sun. That final product is *you*. Mothering her Self is a **bitch, *with style's*** way of expressing unconditional love for her Self, of being in touch with her feelings and intuition in order to make her body (her home) secure and safe.

This course will dwell on self-development which speaks to our sense of security. Emotion is the fuel of life and is critical to this sense of security. What you don't *feel* doesn't exist . . . for you. Once I *feel*, I make anything that I direct my emotion toward *my own*. My body (my home) is moved by my thoughts and emotions to *choose* the life I have. Where I am today is where I am *supposed* to be, otherwise I'd be somewhere else! So, when I know better, I will choose to do better. For now, this is the *plane* and this is the *place* of manifestation. I ask that we respect our soul foundations and feelings and pay attention to the intuitive messages received in our solar plexus, through which our emotions flow into to our physical bodies among other openings. With this critical physical messenger available to alert us to our true feelings, we can then go to our roots to Self develop. Our roots are psychological as well as social. Physical roots can be a ranch out in Texas in the South Forty, a small bungalow in Maine, a townhouse in the French Quarter in New Orleans, a penthouse in New York, a hut in New Guinea, a paper shack on the banks of the Tijuana River and an igloo in the North Pole. Those are "roots" in the social sense and provide us with an earthly connection that lets us know from whence we came.

Psychological roots are a different matter. These roots are "soul stuff" and come from our blueprints brought with us when we arrived wailing, bloody and wrinkled as we drew our our first breath, and entered the human race. Where did we connect psychologically? Initially with our mothers, of course. The soul connection was also initially with our mothers, but it would not be long before others would enter that field of energy to love, support, antagonize or challenge us for our own spiritual good, whether we believe it or not.

The soul and mind are one and the same and are **not** the brain. The soul/mind is the electromagnetic field surrounding our bodies that is intricately and totally connected to the universal grid "out there in the Universe." It carries electrical messages that holds all of these molecules together including you and me, animals, plants, minerals, planets—everything! We are biopsychoneuroelectrochemoimmuno-logical (whew!) creatures held together in a electromagnetic pattern that has built-in intelligence via the soul/mind. I'm going to reduce that long word to **BPNECI** and make up a phrase to help us remember: **Bitches Produce Nature's Energy Connections Ideally.** And we do because our emotional reserves are more deep and visible than men's. We are going to dig further into our psychological ground to determine the source of our energies and then "*name* them, *claim*

> **Name** *them,* **claim** *them,* **reframe** *them and then* **proclaim** *them to the world!* **What?** *Our Source and Our Energies.*
>
> —Vikki Ashley

them, *reframe* them and then *proclaim* them to the world! With this firm foundation of knowledge about self-development, emotions and the body, we will look forward to putting that psychological foundation under our whole being by using the P³ **Baseline and Growth Package** of self-assessment instruments mentioned in Step Five and detailed in Step Nine. These roots will give flight to our creativity and imaginative thoughts about our lives. These data will help us "put on" our psychological and spiritual wings. This New You Review tool will yield more self-love, workplace confidence, less stress and distress in body and mind, more competency, mental clarity, wisdom and insight than you can imagine. You will earn your wings and soar, safe in the understanding of who you are and confident in the guidance and support of your Master Architect as you build your body eternal.

Knowledge for Nurturing Roots

The picture of a woman on page 141 shows where chakras (energy wheels and power centers) are placed in the body. They reside in what is called the etheric body, a twin body to our physical body. It is like a topiary frame around which greenery grows into a variety of forms, like elephants, horses, reindeer, etc. You've seen them in the plazas and atria of very large and glass-laden skyscrapers, or on the green at the racetrack in front of the clubhouse, or on people's lawns for Christmas—all shiny with thousands of Italian white lights. Well, it's sort of like that with our etheric body and all the other five subtle bodies that inhabit our space. We can't see them, but they're there.

These subtle energy bodies are reflective of the various dimensions of space, or planes. It's not a secret that there are various dimensions of space. These are planes of higher and higher frequencies and vibrations that are out of the reach of ordinary people. Since humans are microcosms of the macrocosm, it should not surprise you that sages and wise women have discussed our auric egg that surrounds us for millennia. This information may be researched through the extensive literature that exists on the subject, but following is a recap that will provide the barest minimum for your understanding.

We have seven subtle energy bodies that constitute the sum total of our auric egg or electromagnetic field surrounding our body. They have names: *physical,* the earthly vehicle, our temple and home; *etheric,* often described as our physical body's twin. This is the subtle energy body to which our chakras are attached. Next is the *astral,* the emotional body that is so essential to our projection of energy and to its expression. This body is the one that "holds" us to the earth after death, sometimes, because of our emotional attachments to people, places, things. Next, *mental,* an energy body of a higher frequency and range than the astral, but still not the highest level of which we are capable of vibrating. It is beyond scientific measurement but it does exist, I assure you, because the Universe does *not* play dice with its units and if there are seven chakras, there are seven corresponding planes and bodies with which to function.

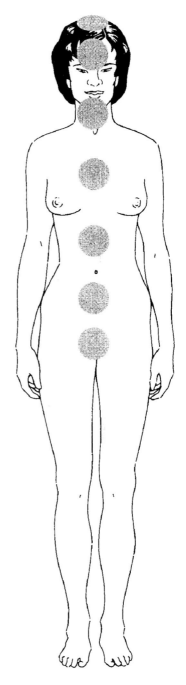

Woman with Chakras

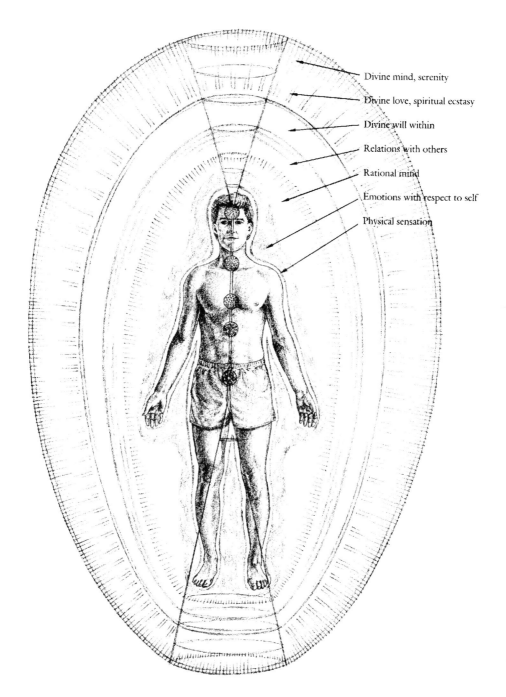

Divine mind, serenity

Divine love, spiritual ecstasy

Divine will within

Relations with others

Rational mind

Emotions with respect to self

Physical sensation

Seven Levels of Auric Envelope Each Person posseses=The Soul [1]

Next, *buddhic,* the energy of this body promotes wisdom, universal love and humanitarian deeds for soul-mind growth. It works down the superconscious mind to the pineal gland and reaches the human psychically through intuition and inspirational thought. Next, *spiritual,* the body of universal will and self-realization. Here one experiences total love and unity with the One. Finally, the *causal* body, sometimes called *the Monad,* or the Higher Self is our connection to all that is and holds the light that no human being can see with physical eyes—only spiritual eyes. The soul-mind that surrounds the physical body and is said to extend out to as much as eight feet in some individuals of great consciousness. But eight feet or one, these bodies interrelate, permeate our physical sheath and hold us together whether we want to believe it or not.

Frankly, belief is not required here. The laws of physics and the Hermetic natural laws which I discuss further along are ground-floor study groups for all of you who aspire to complete the curriculum for **BITCHHood.** As we move toward more sophisticated methods of handling energy and health in the new Millennia, we will have many ways to prove the existence of this energy field around everything in the universe. Today we have biofeedback, aura imagery cameras and other sophisticated methods that generally go under the term kirlian photography, invented by Semyon and Valentina Kirlian in Russia. The camera provides a method for the conversion of nonelectric properties of an object into electrical properties which are captured on film by means of high-voltage spark discharges.

You will see some of my own aura imagery in Step Twelve beginning on page 424 to illustrate various aspects of this book. I urge you to pay attention to this process, for I predict that some day in the not-too-distant future, doctors, mental health professionals, policemen, employment offices and others will use this technology to determine not only the state of our health, but during an interview or diagnostic workup, the state of our minds as well. Who knows? Liars will not be able to change the color of their auras (soul-minds) to reflect words that are not truthful. The colors will show that the words are **not** truthful just as sound technology is used today to determine whether someone on TV or in a courtroom is telling the truth. I predict aura imaging, however, will be far more effective.

The Learning Ground

Seeking information is a lot easier than absorbing it. You're lucky there are no written exams for the **BITCHHood** curriculum. Nor is there an open-book exam. No, Ma'am. There is only one exam for **BITCHHood** courses and it can be repeated in a phrase I shared with you earlier" **Go and Grow."** This is an *experiential* curriculum. You can't walk it if you only talk it. The manifestation of this curriculum will be in your eyes, your pores, your very Be-ing. You are not the only one who will know if you're using the information from *this* curriculum. The whole world (at least that part *you* live in) will know.

To "grow" your New You, nurture yourself, put down psychological roots, dig further into the dirt of your soul and weed out that crab grass of ignorance that is threatening to choke off your lifeline. Know thy Self. Establish a "home," for your **bitch** within your mind and, over time, be confident to share her with the world as each course calls for application and action. Then, with a firm foundation, giving flight to creative imagination about your life— stare into the mirror and look into your own eyes and say, "All right, **bitch,** it's time to fly!" Step out your door and off the mental cliff of uncertainty and spread your wings! Take the New You *anywhere.* Spread your wings in the workplace, funplace, churchplace and homeplace. Eliminate distress from your mind and body, identify your competencies with confidence, don't hide your light under a bushel or in the backrooms of office buildings and cloakrooms of Congress. Take your public image, newly restyled, redressed and redone (liposuction and all) and *walk your talk, baby.* And, with apologies to *no one* for exercising your god-given right to use your knowledge in the exercise of **bitch power!** Remember, though, that the hallmarks of being a **bitch, *with style* are love, understanding, compassion, tolerance and acceptance of people *where they are.*** It is always essential to keep in mind the words of the Master: "Do unto others as you would have others do unto you." It's just another way of saying you reap what you sow. You do, and a **bitch, *with style*** will *always* remember *that!*

Roots
THE MIND

The part of our Self that contains our "thinking" mechanism, "perception," and our "emotions" is the mind. The mind is an organized field of energy which exists in invisible dimensions. It is an invisible source of intelligence that permeates every cell of our body. It is an ethereal vibrational frequency that contains an individual's akashic records and present belief system, also called the subconscious mind and the soul-mind. It is also the soul that we are taught "always was and always will be." Remember that statement from Sunday school? Or the Baltimore Catechism? Well, the soul your teacher was discussing is the electromagnetic energy field or aura around our bodies and is the seat of our subconscious, conscious and superconscious **mind.** The Mind/Soul/Aura is the Mother Board. When it is no longer functioning, the soul (The **I** of you) has left the body and you are considered "dead."

The Brain

Before you read this, review the section on The Soul, on page 73.

The brain is physical and housed in the head and, together with the spine, forms the Central Nervous System (see page 240). The physical brain is the transmitter, receiver and circuit breaker of our body. It processes the electrical and chemical signals required for our systems to function. It is like the Central Processing Unit of our computers, but it is **not** the Mother Board, but the source of the executive functions that process the body. Information comes into the brain via vibrations (electrical energy signals—trillions of them) and goes out of the brain into the Universe. So the brain is truly not only a generator of electrical and magnetic energy but a transmitter/receiver and circuit breaker as well.

Nerve cells in the brain communicate with each other electro-chemically through a microsopic gap between them called "synapses." Lipofuscin, or age spots, are indicators that we are moving in the direction of senility or dementia, some medical scientists believe. The brown, slimy lipofuscin apparently presents, alters or slows the communications through the brain's synapses. A deficiency of important nutrients has been correlated with substantial increases of lipofuscin. Apparently, alohol increases lipofuscin and it is well known that *heavy* drinking over many years destroys brain cells. Alcohol also takes zinc from your body and zinc is important for numerous functions of your body. Men should be especially concerned about maintaining high zinc levels since it is very important for the sex drive and lack of it *may* cause severe prostate problems.

The point here is not to go into great detail about the necessity for nutrients through food, vitamins and minerals plus water, but to point out their importance through a few examples. You must pay more attention to these matters in order to spiritually, physically, mentally and emotionally maintain *your* health.

It is estimated that the brain uses almost 40% of the total energy produced by the body. Its primary fuel is glucose. Chromium is important for brain function because it helps regulate the production of glucose. And then there is magnesium, important, even some say critical, for heart functions. If you have a heart attack or stroke, the sooner you get magnesium into your system the better your chances of survival!

Magnesium is also involved in the production of glucose. Some scientists believe this mineral is essential to the function of enzymes used by the nervous system. It is a critcal mineral for osteoporosis and the skeletal system. Often depressed individuals show magnesium deficiencies. It has been reported that animals given magnesium deficent diets slept very poorly and developed mental disorders. That is not to say people will, but it is worth noting since many of our pharmacological medications have been developed on the basis of animal studies and are now being used by humans.

Human bodies will not metabolize magnesium without pyridoxine (Vitamin B-6) being present (which is said to improve memory) and pyridoxine is necessary for the metabolization of another important nutrient, zinc. Some scientists report that women who take birth control pills are usually deficient in pyridoxine because the pill forces it out of their systems. Pyridoxine is a key factor in red blood cell regeneration, amino acid/protein metabolism, and carbohydrate use. It is a primary immune system stimulant, supports all aspects of nerve health, including carpal tunnel syndrome, and is a key to anti-aging.

About free radicals, those scavengers that are like electric sparks—when they hit brain cells, they either damage the cells, thereby reducing their functions, or destroy them completely. Antioxidants (like Vitamin E, pycnogenal) are essential to eliminate the effects of free radicals and destroy *them*. It is also important to know that *Gotu Kola* is a brain and nervous system restorative and *Ginkgo Biloba* protects the cells against damage from free radicals and is supposed to reduce blood cell clumping which leads to congestive heart disease. Ginkgo causes an increase in acetylcholine levels and therefore the ability to better transmit body *electrical* impulses. The point is, various nutrients like minerals and vitamins are absolutely essential for the healthy functioning of the body and are *dependent on each other* for optimum effect. Our bodies are highly integrated and *everything* in and about the body interacts and works with myriad of other parts, organs and systems.

I take more than a handful of vitamins and minerals everyday. I also suggest you read further on this matter of nutrients and your health by starting with Linda Rector Page's **Healthy Healing.**[2]

I intend to write more about these matters relating to nutrition and lifestyle in my next book. For now, just be aware that *you* are responsible to learn more about all of this.

One of the first things to know about your brain is that it can be physically regenerated. It has three major divisions: the *brain stem,* the *cerebellum* and the *cerebrum.*

The **brain stem** sits atop your spinal column and is the first part of your brain to be formed in the womb. It is also one of the first brain types to evolve over 280 million years ago in the reptiles who were the first animals to walk the earth—they had *only* a brain stem. That's where the term "reptilian brain" come from is often used as a term for the human brain. The brain stems functions are: relay information from the senses and control such things as breathing and heartbeat. It does not *think or feel.*

The **cerebellum** lies just behind the brain stem and helps your body move. It governs coordination of the muscles and holds some *memory* for movement. Athletes have very well-developed cerebellums. Good athletes also have good *kinesthetic memory* or muscle memory which helps them to remember complex movements. As we

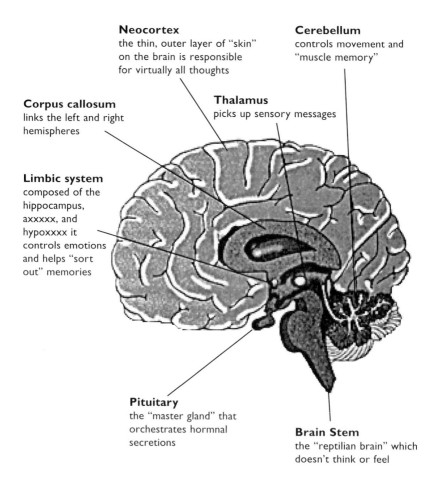

Neocortex
the thin, outer layer of "skin"
on the brain is responsible
for virtually all thoughts

Cerebellum
controls movement and
"muscle memory"

Corpus callosum
links the left and right
hemispheres

Thalamus
picks up sensory messages

Limbic system
composed of the
hippocampus,
axxxxx, and
hypoxxxx it
controls emotions
and helps "sort
out" memories

Pituitary
the "master gland" that
orchestrates hormnal
secretions

Brain Stem
the "reptilian brain" which
doesn't think or feel

age and mature, the cerebellum is gradually trained to improve its functions. Yoga is a good regimen for testing body muscle memory! Over time, your body *does* remember the movements.

The **cerebrum** is the most recent part of our brain and is often called the "mammalian brain." It is the most complex division and is usually what people refer to when they say "brain." It looks like two halves of a walnut joined together to form a sphere. It is covered with a thin layer called the *neocortex*—which neurologists call the *thinking brain* and which they refer to as "you." I don't agree with this assessment and have already indicated my view of where the mind is. *That* is where *you* are.

CHAKRAS	ENDOCRINE SYSTEM	(With Hindu Names and meanings)
Crown 7	Pineal	Upper brain. Right eye.
Violet	Sahasrara	Spirituality
Brow 6	Pituitary	Lower brain. Left eye. Ears.
		Note, Central nervous system (CNS)
		(brain and spinal cord).
Indigo	Ajna	Mind, intuition, insight, wisdom
Throat 5	Thyroid	Bronchial and vocal apparatus. Lungs.
		Alimentary Canal.
Blue	Vishuddha	Will, self-expression, speaking up for
		yourself
Heart 4	Thymus	Heart. Blood. Vagus nerve. Circulatory
		system.
Green	Anahata	Love, forgiveness, compassion,
		relationship
Solar		
Plexus 3	Adrenals	Spinal column. Kidneys.
Yellow	Manipura	Ego, personality, self-esteem, intuition,
		personal power
Sacral 2	Pancreas	Stomach. Liver. Gall bladder.
Orange	Svadishthana	Sexuality, work and physical desire
Root 1	Gonads	Ovaries. Testes. Reproductive system.
Red	Muladhara	The material world, the kingdom, fear

On page 148 is an illustration of the brain that will help you understand where the "parts" are located.

Now, I am a psychologist, not a neuroscientist, so I cannot be considered an expert on the brain.

I do, however, take issue with the idea that a thin layer covering the brain is the essence of me. How can that be, I asked my Self. It doesn't make sense that the "**I**" who can "stand aside and witness" (**SAW**) everything, is the same "**I**" "within" this thin layer of the brain. Furthermore, it doesn't make sense to me that the processing function and the creative function occur in the same place. Example: I create in my mind and send electrical signals to my brain; these signals are cap-

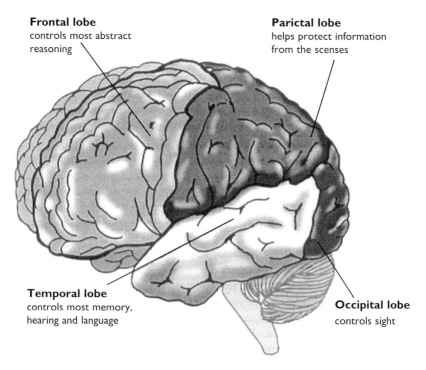

Frontal lobe
controls most abstract
reasoning

Parictal lobe
helps protect information
from the scenses

Temporal lobe
controls most memory,
hearing and language

Occipital lobe
controls sight

tured in the neocortex and processed via the vast network of nerves and neurons that constitute various brain structures and take on specific ways of transmitting nerve messages. The brain is thus processing the messages, eliminating redundant messages and directing electrical and chemical traffic via the adult network of 100 billion neurons capable of a body movement. I believe, however, that thought, perception, and emotion are functions of the mind/soul/aura, *not* the brain.

It's important to note that many of the mechanisms of human brain development remain secret even though increased research endeavors to unlock those secrets and will, in due (do) time.

I predict this research will not reach its ultimate promise until the spirit/energy is made a full partner with the body and until the mind/soul/aura is integrated into the process and given its place of honor in research laboratories.

The illustration above is one more view of the brain that will complete the physical understanding of its dimensions.

The Endocrine System

The **endocrine system** is the automatic defense mechanism of the body under the leadership of the pituitary and pineal glands. This system connects physical matter (people) to the subtler realms of the universe, to the "ethereal" aspects of our nature and essence. Physically, the Endocrine System generates the chemical messengers within our body called hormones, whose function is to keep the body's chemistry in balance. These "ductless" glands introduce their secretions *directly* into the bloodstream and are carried to other parts of the body whose functions they *regulate and control.* This is a master system within the body but it must work with many other systems to maintain life. There are 119 references in **Stedman's Medical Dictionary** to systems in the human body with other subsystems listed as well. Some are cross references to one another, but my mind was boggled with the variety of systems that affect our body's functions. And all are important. I then looked at the pictures of our veins, arteries, and nerves! Wow! What a study we are in intricacy! What a powerful advertisement we are for the work of the Master Architect, whoever *she* is!

With each thought we think, I believe the body secretes these hormones for good or for ill. Thoughts that support a positive mental attitude secrete a different chemical substance than thoughts that are negative. Positive thoughts of *love, peace, harmony, success, achievement, pleasantness, beauty* provide the basis for keeping the body working with the on-going **life** process or, through negative thinking and continually holding negative thoughts of *anger, doubt* and *anxiety*, with the ongoing **death** process.

We **bitches** know about out-of-control hormones, don't we? Your memories dredge up those early years when hormones were just beginning to make them Selfs known as your reproductive system was waking up to its possibilities as a carrier of potential life, and your pubic hair began to appear, and when Johnny smiled at you, your vagina got wet even though you had no idea why. Remember? That was all happening because your hormones were telling your body "It's time, y'all, to fire up the engines and separate this nice young **bitch a-borning** from her senses." That's around age eleven and twelve in my time, but I understand it's happening as early as age eight now. Whew!

And then, when you've begun to be attracted intensely to that guy in French class in the tenth grade and you want a date with him, your adrenals pump you up to a high pitch and create an emotional overload that literally sometimes make you ill. What's happening is your thoughts and your desire for that guy in French class have come together and you've just *got* to go out with him! Got the picture?

Well, you finally do, and in some—but not all—cases, when that guy in French class starts to hug and kiss on you (we used to call that petting, and I guess young people still do), your legs go to jelly and you succumb to his hands in your panties. When you realize you like what you feel, you wake up and start crying "don't do that." Next time, you may not "wake up" but may just let it all happen. OK, so what do you think is driving your behavior and obtaining consent for actions that don't match either your mom and pop's admonitions or your religious and social teachings? Guess what, **little bitch?** **You were just subjected to the power of the hormones in your body as was he** and the results may not be what you either expected or thought they *should* be. "Hello in there." (I'm speaking to your mind.) Where did you go? *That* is the million-dollar question?

Now you're 50, having night sweats, hot flashes, your menses have slowed down, you're overweight, the kids are out of the house, your husband is not very exciting to be with, you gave up regular sex 20 years ago, but every now and then you can work yourself up for a night of revelry. But, oh, these problems with menopause (the name until recently we dared not speak in public—just like God of old). So now this is where *you* have to decide whether or not you're going to have HRT (hormone replacement therapy) and get one type of cancer or *not* have HRT and get another type of cancer. Of course, your doctor can't advise you what to do because he or she doesn't have enough information *either* and you are *not a statistical average* so the research studies **don't apply to you!** You are reading all the new literature on natural hormone creams with herbal and natural ingredients (whatever *that* means) *and* you've been told to read all the ingredients on food and drugs, and now *herbs* for God's sake, to determine what hormones are the most important and are at the head of the line of ingredients on the label. *Then* you have to read about them and find out just what they *do*. *"Shit. I'm going to drink wild yam tea!"*

You can see why **BITCHHood 401** is a required course and I suggest you be ready, willing and fully prepared to go to your dictionaries, books on myth, Joseph Campbell audio tapes, Bill Moyer's videos and books contained in the bibliography in the **Bitch's Book Bag** in Part Five. This is where you can also order the **The Bitch's Tool Kit**.

As you continue to read, have your pen in hand, make notes in the margin, pursue further information and don't say "I don't understand." Don't be embarrassed to read this chapter and any other again and again, if necessary. It's important, in the end, for *you* to *get it*. You have no one to please and no grades to obtain. Remember that the **bitchhood** curriculum is about *"Go and Grow."* It's experiential. What you're learning here is the simple stuff, an overview, not intended to exhaust any aspect of these areas of information, but to whet your mental appetite for much more. Your understanding of this system is essential to building a foundation for your own health. That's the key. Now, take a look at your Endocrine System and see how it has nerve endings in your hands, ankles and the bottoms of your Feet! No wonder your legs turned to jelly when you were in the tenth grade with that guy from French class! What was his name? (Chuckle.)

What this shows is that there is another way of looking at and working with the body and that is called reflexology. We all like to have our feet rubbed, don't we? Bet you weren't aware how important that really is!

You are **not** your body however, but you must live in and work *with* your body in order to survive. Remember: *you are a spiritual essence having a physical experience*. That spiritual experience won't be worth much or last long if you disregard your temple! The sooner you become familiar with your powers, which will manifest in your mind then in your body **as soon as you understand the code**, well, then, the sooner you will bring yourself to health. Don't you want to hurry yourself along this loose gravel path of development? All **bitches,** *with style* do.

You will notice that all the chakras in the picture on page 158 are listed and identified by color, organs and systems and properly placed. This type of information is "out there" daily and in the most interesting places, like mass market magazines and now on television shows of all types, including news and magazine programs (**Dateline;**

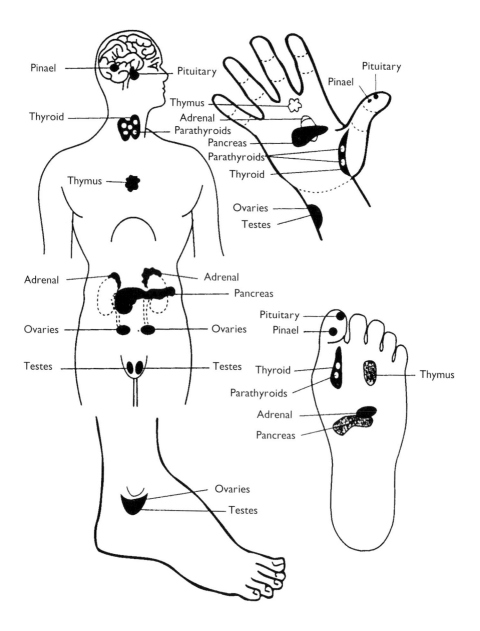

Body Reflexology, 10
Integration of Endocrine System: Body, Hands, Feet and Ankles

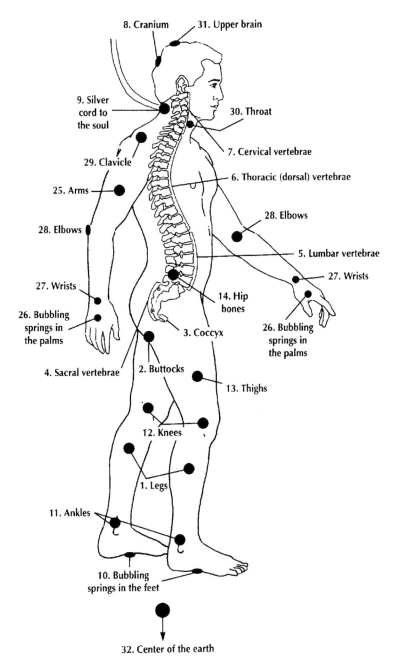

Energy Centers Connected to Body Meridians
These centers relay and reinforce energy flowing toward organs and the nervous systems.

The Today Show, for example) There **is** movement in the universe and individuals **are** searching for that "something extra" that defines them. Media everywhere are "latching" on to this growing wave in the population toward taking care of individual health. Notice the energy centers in your body that relay and reinforce energy flowing toward organs and the nervous systems. See illustration on page 155.

BITCHHood 401 is about defining your roots and placing these data squarely in the hands of the universe (God to some people. Mohammed to others. Jehovah to yet others, and **YOU,** according to me.) You are, in the context of **BITCHHood,** defined as **I Am That I AM.** You are the only person in the universe that can use that term and make it **real.** Example: **I am Vikki Ashley.** Not Oprah Winfrey, Marsha Clark, Barbara Walters, or Diane Sawyer. No. I am that **I am.** When others are asked their names, invariable they say "My name is . . . ." **Promise me you will stop doing that**! At least at this stage of **bitch** development, **own** your own name **or change it if you don't like it or want its energy in your life.** As a matter of fact, I **did** change my name but how and why I did so I'll divulge in Step Seven! When I did this, however, my parents were furious. They felt I was denying my roots, but I explained to them it was part of **my** spiritual development and the energy associated with my other name did not work for me at that time in my life. They weren't buying *any* of it. But the energy was wrong *for me.* More on this later.

The point is, your parents give you your original name. It's no surprise that *some* parents might be offended if you change it. So, if you like your name and want to keep it for whatever reason, begin today to answer the question "What's your name?" with the answer: **I am** and then state your name—whatever one you **own** for yourself. (I am Jane Jones.) Your name is the most powerful identifier you will ever have. It is your "energy connection" to the world "out there" whether written or spoken and those vibrations connect or don't connect in ways that will always let you know whether or not you're in the "right space" with someone else (this occurs on the phone, as well). It's not the first thing people see when they look at you, but your name is usually the first interchange with others who do not know you. Right? So change the way you **use** your nominal energy! The **bitch** *with style* carries the name **she** *wants* with the energy vibrations that match where her spirit and mind are focused at a particular time in her life. We are, of course, very familiar with how actors change their names in order to provide a different energy and connection with the public. If you're born with a name that "works" then keep it. Only, when asked "What's your name?" answer "I am Sue Barnes." Not, "My name is . . . " Got that? Do it and see what a difference it makes in you.

Now let's look at how your **chakra** energies **integrate** with your endocrine system. A chakra is an energy "wheel, " psychic centers, or power centers in the body that are active at all times, whether we are conscious of them or not. Energy moves through the chakras to produce different psychic states. Modern biological science explains this as the chemical changes produced by the **endocrine glands**, ductless glands whose secretions mix into the body's bloodstream directly and instantaneously.

Integration of Chakras with the Endocrine System

The chakras are sometimes referred to as the playground of the elements—fire, earth, air, water and ether. Westerners do not include ether as an element, but Easterners do, and I include it here because of the importance of ether as the unified energy field that carries the electromagnetic impulses that hold this Universe together. Ether comes from the Latin *aether* and the Greek *aither* and in their root forms mean to *kindle and to burn!* So, our etheric body is our spiritual body and is also the "energy body" surrounding and interpenetrating our physical body—the electromagnetic auric field!

The ether is a "substance"—invisible to be sure—that makes utilization of electricity possible. After all, *something* out there makes it possible to transmit information electrically and capture in light fixtures a substance absolutely critical to our existence. Yet, absolutely *no one **has ever seen it!!!*** We use computers, fax machines, telephones and never question *how* information can go from our desk to a desk in Europe in seconds! Amazing, isn't it? Not that it happens, but that the average person doesn't question *how* it happens!

OK, class. If anyone in here has seen electricity, raise your hand? "No, darlin', put your hand down." You've only seen the *results* of electricity, like when the light bulbs go on when you flip the switch.

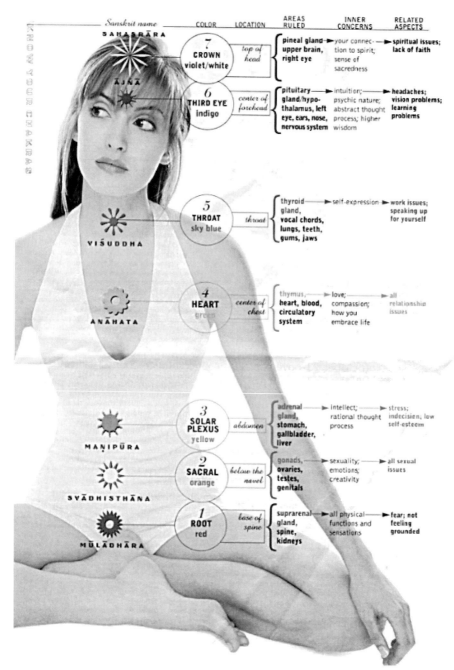

Sanskrit name	COLOR	LOCATION	AREAS RULED	INNER CONCERNS	RELATED ASPECTS
SAHASRĀRA	**7** **CROWN** violet/white	top of head	pineal gland, upper brain, right eye	your connection to spirit; sense of sacredness	spiritual issues; lack of faith
ĀJÑĀ	**6** **THIRD EYE** indigo	center of forehead	pituitary gland/hypothalamus, left eye, ears, nose, nervous system	intuition; psychic nature; abstract thought process; higher wisdom	headaches; vision problems; learning problems
VIŚUDDHA	**5** **THROAT** sky blue	throat	thyroid gland, vocal chords, lungs, teeth, gums, jaws	self-expression	work issues; speaking up for yourself
ANĀHATA	**4** **HEART** green	center of chest	thymus, heart, blood, circulatory system	love; compassion; how you embrace life	all relationship issues
MAṆIPŪRA	**3** **SOLAR PLEXUS** yellow	abdomen	adrenal gland, stomach, gallbladder, liver	intellect; rational thought process	stress; indecision; low self-esteem
SVĀDHISTHĀNA	**2** **SACRAL** orange	below the navel	gonads, ovaries, testes, genitals	sexuality; emotions; creativity	all sexual issues
MŪLĀDHĀRA	**1** **ROOT** red	base of spine	suprarenal gland, spine, kidneys	all physical functions and sensations	fear; not feeling grounded

"Do you give Good Vibes!", Mademoiselle, Nov. 1995.

Or, the computer works when you turn it on. Or, you open your eyes when your body's bicircadian rhythms are working right. Or when your synapses in your brain work because the electrical signals are 'firing' accurately and in rhythm." Pretty **bitchin'** stuff when you get right down to it, isn't it?

As for the Endocrine System, it, too, works because of this mysterious ether and electricity that we can't see. I can see how the chakras, connected as they are to each of the endocrine glands work in concert with them. I can also see how low energy and negative thoughts can slow down the turning of the wheels of force and energy and slow down the movement of the hormones in our body. I can see how we "burn out" and can't handle life when our energy circuits "blow". Only because the brain has the capacity to function as a circuit

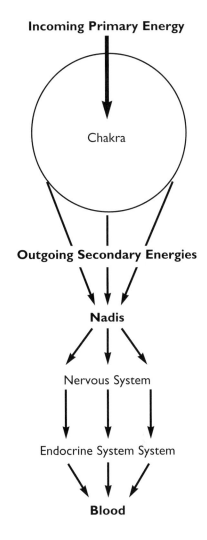

How Chakra Energy Flows in the Body

breaker do we not literally "blow our brains out" in some of life's circumstances. Then again, sadly, some people do *just* that.

The **bitch**, *with style* has her work cut out for her: how will she use her integrated energies to become her highest and best Self? Read on.

The roots of your development lie in your knowledge of your connections to your own inner power and your willingness to pursue information to change your own perceptions of reality! Review and learn from this information about your seven "invisible" bodies, your Endocrine System, your chakras and how they affect *your* body.

These whirling vortices of energy are high frequency energy systems that connect our anatomy and all its parts to the Universal scheme. Look again at how the Endocrine System is connected throughout the body and how the hands, bottoms of your feet and the ankles can be utilized to reduce tension, blockage and pain in the principal organs of the body.

Notice that the pancreas is a unique organ that has three sections: a body, head and a tail. So here we have the 3 in 1 (the trinity) repeated in an organ of great importance in the body. The pancreas contains cells having both exocrine and endocrine functions. The two principle hormones of the pancreas are insulin and glucagon. The endocrine part of the pancreas, consisting of the islets of Langerhans, produces and secretes insulin (from beta cells) directly into the bloodstream, glucagon (from alpha cells) and somatostatin (from delta cells); some islets contain PP (or F) cells that secrete pancreatic polypeptide. The exocrine part, consisting of secretory units, produces and secretes into the duodenum a pancreatic juice, which contains enzymes essential to protein digestion. (**Dorland's** *Illustrated* **Medical Dictionary.**)

With all the billions being spent on dieting and all the information about eating nutritiously and healthily, you know very well that you are *not* to eat a lot of refined sugar (no more chocolate chip cookies unless made sugar free and fat free!) And no more sugar producing carbohydrates unless they occur naturally as in vegetables and fruits. (Forget those baked potatoes, **bitches.** Even without butter, sour cream and cheese, those insides are like eating *pure* sugar! Say the Sugar Busters!) Oh, well . . . Diabetics are very familiar with the importance of the pancreas since their's is not functioning effectively and they must take insulin injections to maintain life. There are some new alternative treatments that are leading to better health for diabetics, including but not limited to nutritional adjustments in diet and herbal remedies. There are some new herbs being tested from Africa that I am told have the potential not only to control but to perhaps cure diabetes. That, should it happen, will be only one of the miracles in health awaiting us in the new Millennia.

The **endocrine system** is full of information **and** mystery. I'm not going to crack each and every seal in this first book. But I want to pursue more information about the **pineal gland** located in the crown of the head. It has always fascinated me because every time I ask a medical doctor friend what it's there for, I get a very unclear answer. We do know that it controls the action of light upon and within the body and is reduced in the body as we mature, impacting our circadian rhythms. I know that I use melatonin, which is the hormone secreted by the pineal gland, which helps my body handle long overseas trips and to adjust to jet lag without missing a beat. It works! What can I say? If not overdone, I understand taking it helps in the reduction of insomnia. Might be worth looking into, but check it out thoroughly first.

What else does it do? Well, I believe this little "pine cone" gland is the instrument that plugs us into the higher energies of the universe. I can just see a docking connection with other higher frequency "bodies" surrounding each of us that assists in our elevation to more powerful frequencies as we open up our minds and hearts to this magnificent universe of knowledge. For now, though, it is often described as the controller for the Third Eye or Brow Chakra/Ajna and works in concert with the body's master gland—the pituitary, controller of our growth and metabolism. The pineal is seen by some spiritually minded writers as the master gland of the etheric body, masculine **and** positive (balanced) in polarity. Or consider this: the pineal is an antenna that transmutes cosmic energy into electrical energy for the brain to use, mingling it with conscious and subconscious activity and emotional energy, sending it along to the pituitary gland and the nervous systems to be used by the body.

Since I believe the Master Architect put everything in the body for a purpose, I also believe that the pineal gland's day has *not yet come* with regard to our recognition of its full functions. As we **bitches** become more awake and enlightened, its benefits to us individually will be demonstrated through our use of higher energies in our day-to-day living, e.g., clairaudience, clairsentience, telepathy and other psychic talents. We **all** have these abilities. They aren't awake in most of us at the present time. But in due (do) time we will enjoy their fruits as we continue with the curriculum of **BITCHHood** into the next course.

In the meantime, let us continue our journey to BITCHHood, setting down **roots** of spiritual, emotional, mental and physical information, and begin our walk toward managing our psychological, emotional, mental and spiritual **wings.** These **wings** I am referring to relate to the our creative self-expression.

Another Way to Look at This

Physicians, psychologists, psychiatrists, counselors, social workers and others who work with individuals as collaborators in their developing healthy minds are taking money under false pretenses if they refuse to acknowledge the spiritual dimension of human **Be**-ings.

In order to aspire to **BITCHHood,** I had to learn about those "feelings" inside me that wouldn't go away until I faced my Self and looked in the mirror of truth. There is an audible release of anxiety and tension when I "let go" of any issue that has been "bugging" me. I feel my inner Self relax and I know I have relieved the tension and restored balance—for the moment—to my Self.

Wings

I have known all my life that there was something missing in me. I am a seeker and sooner or later I knew I would **find** what I was seeking. I just wish someone in my youth could have showed me the way to become a **B**eing **I**n **T**otal **C**ontrol of **H**erself sooner rather than later. I wish someone could have guided me in the use of my mind to obtain what I desired. I wish someone had shown me how to develop and maintain a **healthy** body, one that would carry me many years over the long road ahead. Don't I sound just like an ignorant, uninformed **bitch** who sings that song all day long "just a wishin' and a hopin'" with nothin'—do you hear me—nothin' to back it up in the form of right action based on knowledge?

No one was there with **this** specific kind of information. There were some people who encouraged me and gave me a very secure notion about self-worth: Father Alphonse Schumacher, now transitioned, recognized this precocious child's earnest desire to "be somebody" and he encouraged my talent (musical and academic) and saw to it that I put it to good use playing the organ and piano at church and school. He paid me out of his own pocket and made sure I was given every opportunity to spread my cultural wings early. His housekeeper, Miss King, took me to the opera held at the zoo each summer in Cincinnati, Ohio and my heart soared with the possibilities that invaded my imagination as a result of the excitement of La Boheme, Carmen, Aida, The Magic Flute, Il Pagliacci. I was all of seven years old! Don't you *know* this **little bitch** was soaring. I count my acquisition of **mental wings** from the moment I heard the singer playing Carmen open her mouth and heard those glorious tones! The excitation began when the conductor raised his baton and I heard the first notes of the orchestra. It was my first live performance of any kind. Even today, when Bob and I attend the LSU basketball or football games, or we take a week end and fly to New York for live performances of current plays, I sit in rapt anticipation for that first sound of the orchestra or the horns at the basketball games when the first notes of "Hold That Tiger" blare forth, or especially when the drum major takes that first step to the beat of the drums at the football games. Wow! It still gives me chills to think about it! I often joke with Bob after the LSU band has completed the opening ceremonies by saying, "OK, we can go home now." That's how tied into the energy of music I still am. The only reason I am willing to drive to Baton Rouge for an hour and a half and sit in those hard seats is to see that drum major step off to the beat of the drum and hear those horns address every area of the stadium. Energy, folks. Energy!

Am I so different? Is there someone else out there like me? Does your soul leap at odd moments in time, too? Well, then, you are experiencing what I call the **wings phenomenon.** It's that **something extra** that makes your emotions well up in your chest and almost, or even sometimes actually, makes you cry with excitement and happiness!

Wagner's magnificent soaring music has this same effect on me. Also, the "Regina Coeli" from the opera **Cavelleria Rusticana** by Mascagni **always** makes me cry, no matter where I am when I hear it. When I hear certain Christmas music, especially "The First Noel," "Angels We Have Heard on High," "The Hallelujah Chorus" I cry. Always. "Panis Angelicus," "O Holy Night," "O Divine Redeemer," and the "Hallelujah Chorus" from Handel's **Messiah** count as cloud busters in my life, especially since Alan's death. Christmas is our favorite time of the year and he, from the time of twelve, always trimmed every Christmas tree for the family. I am still using his ornaments each Christmas and they hang and sway on the tree in memory of his love and the beauty and music he brought into my life and that of his siblings and friends.

There are more examples, but my **emotions** instantly erupt in waves throughout my body and my mind and I cannot still this eruption. I can only cooperate with its movement and "feeling tone" until it eventually is released. Afterward I feel physically and mentally "lifted." This **bitch *with* style** acknowledges the power of directed and focused emotion and the benefits of enjoying it through music.

Of all the arts, esotericists acknowledge noble music to be the highest expression of spirit. Issuing direct from the godhead, every human soul on the path from "clod to God" is a song sung by the Master Musician. We are made of the very substance of divine harmony. Those who have ears to hear may listen to this harmony; and some may transcribe, in immortal music, the likeness of God in man.

In this fourth step to **BITCHHood**, it is, as I have mentioned more than once, important to have roots and a strong sense of who you are, what your values are, how you relate to the world around you and where your true **home** really lies. It is also a time to find a place to live in the world that reflects, to the extent your resources permit, the kind of energy and environment you personally need and want. I know, everyone is talking about **feng shui**. 'Feng' signifies wind and 'shui' signifies water. Air, astrologically, indicates expression and relationship. Water, of course, is feeling, emotion and power. That ties in with the integration of spirit, body, mind and emotion. Still, there is no single meaning of this expression, but some talk about the "feel" of a place; others about good or bad luck, but essentially it about the art of placing things to utilize the earth's natural forces and balance of *yin* and *yang* to achieve good energy or *qi*, (chee) which renders health and vitality. In other words, getting the best balance and flow of energy for you **in** your space. This is not the place for detailed discussion, but it integrates with and fits into everything being said about steps to **BITCHHood.** I know you get the point. Why **wouldn't** you want to **feel** good in your physical home and enjoy looking around at the supporting environment that creates balance in your mind? Check out the books and seek more information. There is really no counterpart to **feng shui** in Western culture. Astrology has some elements but good **feng shui** is achieved through a combination of common sense and good taste (characteristics of a **bitch,** *with style*) in the conception of space, placement of furniture and best use of structure. Excellent living conditions contribute to **good health**, which often leads to success and prosperity.[3, 4]

Bear in mind that getting into **feng shui** will require you to become familiar with the five elements (water, wood, fire, earth and metal. Westerners and most of the world have four: fire, earth, air and water) and the *I Ching*, the Chinese Book of Changes. Let me insert several passages from the James Legge translation that will reinforce the direction a **bitch** must walk and the growing understanding and wisdom she must acquire while "feeling" for her true Self.

> *If the form of heaven is contemplated,*
> *the changes of time can be discovered.*
> *If the forms of men are contemplated,*
> *one can shape the world.*
>
> —I Ching

"The basis of the *I Ching* is in the belief that 'the future develops in accordance with fixed laws, according to calculable numbers. If these numbers are known, future events can be calculated with perfect certainty.'

"The concept of strict numerical values relating to what we believe is an infinite universe may seem strange to many, but it must be remembered that the *I Ching* forms itself around the idea of **change**. The Chinese concept of change is never one-dimensional movement but more accurately a 'cycle.'

"The mathematical ideas implied by a cyclic theory of alternating forms are widely known in Western science, beginning early in our civilization with Pythagorus . . . the main doctrine (is) of successive destruction and reconstruction (an idea basic to the *I Ching* . . . It is believed by some that Einstein's cosmogenic theories may also be interpreted cyclically. There is . . . an enormous amount of testimony to the periodic character in all phenomena . . . (See Step Seven and the Hermetic Laws of Nature.)

"The *I Ching*'s concept of change applies to simple organic forms of life as well as human activity. This attitude that simple forms are governed by the same laws as man, by the **law of change from which there is no escape,** was highly developed in early Chinese philosophy.

"Change is thought to be active in all human groupings as well as in the individual's life. Thus it **embodies and cradles the 'soul' of the mass and the 'spirit' of the time.** Helmut Wilhelm writes in his **Eight Lectures on the I Ching** that the 'universality of its power (i.e., Change) includes all levels in all dimensions; every seed that is planted grows and matures within its scope.'

"Western science's initial biological view of the world seemed unaware of this idea. But modern science has recently turned its attention to such interdependent functions in living organisms, out of which have grown the new disciplines of ecology and ethology."

"Human beings do seem to have an inner dynamic toward change. Alfred Adler calls it a goal-seeking quality in the human 'soul' that is continually 'attempting to map, plan and direct its future toward a goal of security.' In Chinese philosophy such dynamic inner development or change is not an immutable fate, or determinism, inflicted from without, but rather a sign showing the direction that decisions take.' It is the awareness of this directing flow of internal development that allows the *I Ching* to be an effective oracle. The *I Ching* would not say this dynamic flow of life is a law which **must** be followed (as do many occult, religious, and metaphysical systems); that one is forced to obey by a watchful or vengeful God; but rather that it is a guideline which indicates the '**flow of events.**' This idea complements man's unique capacity for self-reflection and encourages him to perceive future trends through *sensitive identification with universal principles and rational investigation of him Self . . . '* **To stand in the stream of this development is a datum of nature, to recognize it and follow it is responsibility and free choice . . . It is in constant change and growth alone that life can be grasped at all."** (Emphases added.)[5]

Ah! More work to do. **Feng Shui!?** Color coordinate my room? Move my bed around? Oh, well . . . guess I'll have to move! More information to seek. If we choose.

The search for your **Self** and for the **Bitch** within you is the most important journey you have before you. Just consider all the different types of information that eventually flow into the same stream making the mighty River of Truth a part of your perception! You are fortunate to be open to new information and to be getting it! The results and applications will take different forms for each because by now you must be sensing that each of us, though part of a grand design, is a

> *The search for your **Self** and for the **Bitch** within you is the most important journey you have before you.*
> —Vikki Ashley

unique individual. Each of us is either **asleep**, a **bitch a-borning, a bitch,** *with style* or a **bitch** *with style*! Which are you? Which do you want to Be-come?

Hey, **bitch,** it's up to *you.*

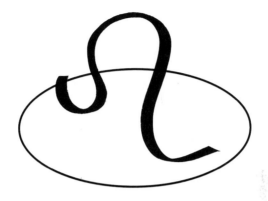

STEP FIVE

I Am A Creative, Self-Expressive Individual!

You create your own reality.
*Make it what you **truly** want!*

Vikki going "local" at Manuel's Cafe—Final Four—San Antonio—1997

BITCHHood 501
Self-Expression: I *Create*, Therefore I Am.

Our roots provide us with the knowledge to accept the I AM of our souls. Our wings indicate the promise and potential we all have to acknowledge our own power to soar in joy and accomplishment. With this support and promise, a **bitch,** *with style* steps out on the loose gravel path of life to explore her personal foundations in a creative way. She *thinks* she knows who she is. She *believes* she knows what her values are and she understands how she *sees* her own reality.

> *"It's not about* **them.** *It's about* **you.** *Always come from within, based on knowledge, and you will never be shaken from your foundations or roots."*
> —Vikki Ashley

But when put to the test to answer the question **Who am I?** she falters as she opens her mouth.

This very tentative movement may lead to an entrapment of her own making. She thinks about how she wants to be viewed by those around her. What *is* my image in the world? she thinks. What will I, in fact, say about my Self that lets everyone "out there" know who I truly am?

What *is* my impact on my environment? "Wow," she says to her Self, "This is **show time!** I want to put my best foot forward. How am I going to do this?"

Inside, she is a bit frightened. She has turned the searchlight of reality on her external environment. She recognizes the importance of what she says, the tentativeness of her preparation and the nature of her risk. This **bitch,** *with style* knows her statement will be seriously evaluated and she must be able to handle the feedback she will receive from those impacted by her thoughts, words and deeds. She looks in the mirror to practice her definition of **Who am I?** She "hears" a small voice say, "It's not about *them*. It's about *you*. Always come from within, based on knowledge, and you will never be shaken from your foundations or roots."

This **bitch,** *with style* is on the road toward **individualization,** that point in life when she takes control of her own self-expression and accepts the feedback and information from the environment as important to her choices about who she *really* is and whether or not she *knows* who that person is. "But where did that *voice* come from?" she wondered. "There's no one here but me!"

The Foundation of Individuality

Following is an introduction to one way the **bitch,** *with style is* going to build her foundation of knowledge to answer **Who am I?** Furthermore, the material will be enhanced in Step Nine of the **BITCHHood** Curriculum. For now, though, let me share an introduction to the most sophisticated, effective and relevant package of self-assessment instruments I have ever used.

This book, remember, is sharing with you the **BITCHHood** Curriculum so that you can *use* every part of it as you so choose.

I have been a management consultant and psychologist for over thirty years. For the last 15 years, I have worked with clients in business and nonprofit organizations using three self-assessment instruments which I now call the **P³ Baseline and Growth Package**[1] or the **17-Minute Miracle.** This material has been researched, validated and is in use all over the world. I have found that no other instruments have such dramatic **and accurate** results for such a short **time** (17 minutes) investment in completing them. Included in this package are the following instruments that will build a baseline to help you answer your **Who am I?** question.

The Building Blocks of The Foundation

The P³ Baseline and Growth Package:[2]	Time to Complete	About
1. Style Analysis Profile (SAP)	7 min.	Your perception of your behavior
2. Personal Interests, Attitudes & Values (PIAV)	5 min.	Values and attitudes

3. The Work Environment (TWE)   5 min.   Behavioral requirements for your position if you were hiring someone to take your place.

                        Total   17 min.

More data will be shared on this material in Step Nine.

Once you invest the **17 minutes** it takes to complete these instruments, you will receive a multiple-sectioned report based on **your** input and perception of **you, as you see you!** Not, I repeat, not as anyone else in the universe sees you. The honesty with which you appraise your Self is the soul of this process. This is an essential **step** along the road to **SWOTing** your Self and **using** these data for growth, development and evaluation. Remember this: you cannot know where you're going and how you are doing if you don't know where **you are right now. You cannot "benchmark" if you haven't "baselined." You cannot evaluate later if you haven't "baselined"!** To build a house that will stand against time and the elements, one must build a strong, deep foundation on rock, not on sand. This package is the rock. Mine the treasure that is *you*. The "map" to *you* is the **P³ Baseline and Growth Package.**

> *You cannot "benchmark" if you haven't "baselined." You cannot evaluate later if you haven't "baselined!"*
> —Vikki Ashley

Your **Bitch's Book Bag (B³),** which you find at the end of this book with all manner of information and data in it, will include not only the means to complete the instruments but the information that will tell you more about other resources, if you choose to read it.

For now, just keep in mind that the **bitch,** *with style* is consciously building the Temple of Solomon, her **home.** The baseline/foundation is her beginning **in consciousness.** It is an ideal way to reinforce her growing, and sometimes tentative, self-expression and a perfect way to communicate individual self-expression that is expanding.

This package is for men and women. It is for everyone who has a desire to answer the question **Who am I?**

Life Is A Numbers Game

Meanwhile, a small integration here with the science of numerology,[3] the study of numbers. Numerology is applied to the selection of time for each of the above instruments. It was based on my experience with hundreds of clients coupled with my knowledge of numbers and what they represent. There are those of you who may not understand or subscribe to the science of numbers. But those of you who do will understand what follows. All others will have to tag along with an open mind.

Seventeen (17-minutes to complete) is a carefully chosen number. It resonates positively with the energies of men and women who take the **P³ Baseline and Growth Package**. Why? Because they have put their Selfs in an energy field of learning about who they are. This timing resonates with their ability to complete the instruments in or before the time allowed.

The ancients saw numbers as a philosophical reduction of principles that explained the life process, the source of all things. Symbols with meaning. Pythagoras saw numbers as the 17 equaling eight (1+7=8). One is the number of unity/one/the Universe (we are growing toward a unity that will make us each whole) and 7 is the magical number that indicates, "it is finished," "the **pattern** has been laid." "The work is done." Eight is the number of manifestation.

Five minutes to complete the PIAV. Five is the number of man, the creator, the person who is self-expressing. Dusty Bunker, a numerologist, identifies five as the keystone in the Arch of Life because it is the central number in the cosmic blueprint represented by the numbers one through nine. She says:

> "The symbol of Five is the pentagram whose five points are a stylized replica of wo/man with her/his arms outstretched . . . It was used by Pythagoreans and other philosophers in their ceremonies. It represents the five senses with which the human being is endowed: see, hear,

touch, smell, and taste. Five always has been recognized as **the pivotal point in cycles** when a change in the physical will occur. The most elementary change in the physical is **when the soul enters and leaves the body—birth and death.**

"Five is the quickening. In early cultures it generally was accepted that the soul did not enter the fetus until the fifth month of pregnancy, therefore the fetus could be aborted prior to this time without spiritual retribution.

"Prior to 1869 the Catholic Church's Doctrine of Passive Conception concurred with this belief and again, abortion prior to the fifth month was not considered a crime.

"Before the fifth month, the fetus was a form, number four, without the life breath, the soul, that entered through the Five. This idea was prevalent throughout many cultures at that time."

More about numbers later and how the energy they express through their symbolism relates to each of us on our journey to wholeness and health.

What has proven to be behaviorally and emotionally important is that the **P³ Baseline and Growth Package** can be used to evaluate your conscious progress with your own behavior around the four factors used to describe behavior. I have not met a person who could not complete this package in **17 minutes!** The results will truly astound you. (See the **Bitch's Book Bag** at the end of this book.)

Create your own reality through information

To create your own reality is to use all of you consciously: *Spirit MindEmotionsBody (SMEB).* It is to determine your level of energy for people, things, opportunities and threats. It is to take all of the ingredients you have, and bake your own cake! Once you have the baseline and your **SWOTs,** you will be more open to other cultural inputs. These individuals, however, may have an awakening as a result of **chaos** in their personal or business lives (mergers, downsizing, layoffs, firings, etc.), **crises** (strokes, heart attacks, *e-coli*, hepatitis C, multiple sclerosis, car accident—you name it, or **significant emotional events (SEEs).** These "moments in time" have reoriented many hard-nosed, disinterested, and dissatisfied individuals and turned them into seekers, explorers of the mind, and eventually **individuals** on their loose gravel paths of development toward a higher knowledge, understanding and eventual "knowingness" about who they are. Each of us is on our own path, walking it in our own time, doing our own thing (which is what being a **bitch,** *with style* is all about) and paying our own price tags.

The eight ingredients offered here for your information are part of the formula for understanding that you are a *spiritual be-ing, having an earthly experience!* The ingredients for your cake may have some additional pieces, but these constitute the basics for baking your cake of life for you and each of us from a Hindu/tantric perspective. My respect for this information is deep. It resonates with truths within me with which I cannot disagree. I **know** that this information has been sustained over time because it resonates at a deeper and higher level within mankind and will continue to do so. Indian and Hindu medicine and philosophy have given us centuries of information. Seek and you shall find.[4]

1. Mind	(Manas)	**5.** Air	(Vayu)
2. Intellect	(Buddhi)	**6.** Fire	(Agni)
3. Ego/Identification	(Ahamkara)	**7.** Water	(Apah)
4. Space/ether	(Akasha)	**8.** Earth	(Prithvi)

This information combines with data that are also centuries old, even before Christ, on the elements of the earth. The five elements (fire, earth, air, water and ether) form three **doshas,** or basic humors in the body)

1. Wind (from the air elements) (Vayu)—Sanguine
2. Bile (from the fire elements) (Pitta)—Choleric
3. Mucos (from a combination of water and earth elements)—combines melancholic and phlegmatic humors (see next page)

In the West, we refer to the humors, originally explained by Hippocrates and Galen, centuries before Christ, as the four main fluids of the human body:

1. Choleric	(Yellow bile)	D	Fire	(Hot-blooded/hot tempered)
2. Sanguine	(Blood)	I	Water	(Thick-blooded)
3. Phlegmatic	(Phlegm)	S	Air	(Thin-blooded)
4. Melancholicic	(Black Bile)	C	Earth	(Cold-blooded)

There are also three **gunas**, or qualities, that operate through the three **doshas:**

1. Equanimity, lightness (Sattva)
2. Passion (Rajas)
3. Sloth, darkness (Tamas)

As you are beginning to surmise, *as in the macrocosm, so in the microcosm; as above, so below.*

These eight ingredients noted above are known as **mula prakriti.** They are linked into a network by **vayu prana**, which operates through particular **nadi's** (from Sanskrit root *nad* meaning movement). In the Rigveda, the most ancient Hindu scripture, *nadi* means "stream."[5] The concept of nadis is based on the understanding that they are channels; any channel through which anything flows is a nadi. Included in this concept of nadis are:

1. Acupuncture meridians
2. Streams of the cardiovascular system
3. Lymphatic system streams
4. Nerves
5. Muscles
6. Arteries
7. Veins
8. The manovahini, *or* manovaha *(*the channel of mind*)*
9. *Chittavaha—the* channel of *chitta*, or being.

Thus nadi can be translated as "vessel," "channel," "cord," "tube," or "duct."

There are two types of nadis, according to the foregoing:

- Subtle—invisible channels of subtle energy
- Gross—channels of subtle energy **visible** as cords, vessels or tubes

"This explanation gives a clear indication that nadis are not only nerves, but all kinds of channels, and this is the reason that the tern **nerve** is not used for nadis in the texts of the Ayurveda, ancient Indian medicine. In tantric tradition, the universe if made of two things, **matter** (with attributes—*saguna)* and **energy** (without attributes—*nirguna).*

" . . . matter is the vehicle of energy and energy is considered to be conscious. This consciousness, when it becomes manifest, **finds a vehicle for itself**, which is **mind, or *manas.***

Consciousness is fourfold:

1.	Mind	Manas
2.	Intellect	Buddhi
3.	Identification (Is-ness)	Ahamkara
4.	Being	Chitta

In physical form, this **consciousness** exists in five *koshas,* or sheaths, and operates **through** the physical body, the best vehicle for expression: These sheaths are:

1.	Matter	Annamayi Kosha
2.	Vital Air	Pranamayi Kosha
3.	Mind	Manomayi Kosha
4.	Knowledge	Vijnanamayi Kosha
5.	Bliss	Anadamayi Kosha

Ayurvedic medicine is best done when integrated with spiritual principles as expressed by Deepak Chopra, and yet there is room for other perspectives that integrate from more than one place. We will see later how these integrate with numerology, astrology, the Tree of Life in this process of gathering **information** for your own development.[6]

Study the information and the growing connections between the chakras, the use of your mind, your growing awareness that everything means **everything** is connected, regardless of language, culture, alphabets, symbols, archetypes. It makes being an individual a very difficult assignment, but become one we must if we are to develop into **bitches** *with style.*

Review the following diagram and think of it as a schematic of more than your head. It represents the arena of connection to a universe that bring you the power to decide for your Self what you want in life. It is a connection, a transformer, a transmitter and receiver station. The brain and spinal cord constitute the Central Nervous System. This system is wondrous by any standard, but there is so much more to it and its connections throughout the body. (See page 240.)

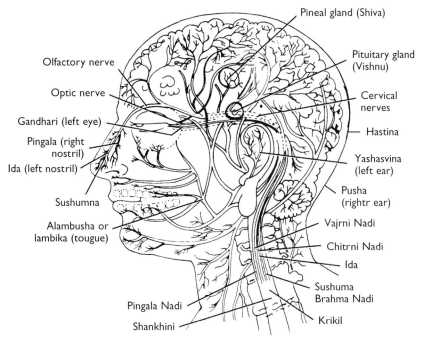

Major nadis in the head.

Notice the major nadis in the head (see definition of nadi, above). Nadis are linked with the chakras. The central canal, Sushumna, plays a vital role in yogic and tantric practices. Chakras are centers of interchange between physical and psychological energy within the physical dimension, and prana is the force that links the physical with the mental and the mental with the spiritual . . . The physical, the mental and the spiritual **are the same** and work together on all levels. Some of the gross nadis, such as physical nerves, veins and arteries are known in modern medical science. But, as all nadis do not take a physical form, nor are visible in character, it is impossible to locate them, observe them, or trace their pathway through less subtle means. Subtle nadis are of two kinds: (1) conduits of pranic force and (2) conduits of mental force and generally run together. They are connected, it is postulated, with sensory nerves of the autonomic nervous system. Yoga nadis and nerves of the autonomic nervous system work together in the same way the psyche works with physiology.

Let me call attention to the Pineal Gland (Shiva) and the Pituitary Gland (Vishnu). More on them later, but they are part of the Endocrine System noted in Step Four, page 151. The function of the pituitary gland, which is attached to the *hypothalamus*, is that it releases many hormones which carry signals to all the other glands, stimulating their operations. The pituitary is often called the **master control gland** because it is so important to growth and control of the body's metabolic rates.

Rothenberg defines the **thyroid gland**, a large endocrine gland situated at the base of the neck, as consisting of two lobes, one on each side of the *trachea*, connected by an isthmus. Under the influence of *thyroid-stimulating hormone (TSH)*, released from the *interior pituitary gland* (there's the connection), the **thyroid** secretes the hormone **thyroxin** into the bloodstream; it is **essential** for normal growth and development in children and normal *metabolic rates* in adults . . . . (Emphasis added.)[7] It is so important that its relationship to the pineal gland has always intrigued me. I am certain there is a connection and I will discuss this in Step Nine.

I want you to look at the pituitary gland, first, and let your mind take in the shape of this important vessel in the endocrine system.

Next, let me share with you a vision of the pineal gland. Look

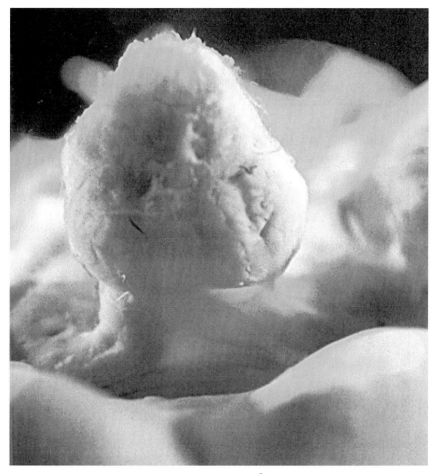

The Pineal Gland[8]

at the shape of this vessel, and keep in mind that physicians do not understand the function of this gland in our bodies. Einstein said that God doesn't play dice. I agree. I say that God (Energy, The Universe, however you believe) is the The Supreme Energizer (not that pink bunny rabbit!) who has geometrized the whole universe, so there is nothing in the body (which can be looked at as geometric, and it **is)** that has no purpose. Nothing. So, picture and imagine a pine-cone shaped instrument that is used a lot in our technologically advanced world? Picture and imagine a pine-cone shaped instrument that has sexual connotations? Can you picture and imagine . . . .

what? Do it! Picture and imagine. What comes to mind? The pyramids—Energy Sources for the Universe.

Ponder this image of Minerva, the Greek goddess that we know today by her Roman name Pallas Athena. In astrology, Pallas Athena is an asteroid that transits the birth chart first (360 degrees in just under five years). She marks the place in the birth chart a deeper inner knowing and understanding can develop. As she transits other planets and angles, she allows the energies to be combined and refined, giving us the opportunities to unlock the flow of ideas that may be just below the surface. Ideas "spring forth" at an unbelievable rate just as she was born (sprang forth) from the head of the Greek god Zeus who became Jupiter.[9] Her sacred animal was the owl (wisdom) and her sacred tree was the olive. (What oil is now popular **and** healthy for use in our bodies?) Her head shows the energy fields of the **pineal** and **pituitary glands**, blending them to form the **third** or **spiritual eye.** Allow your Self to picture and imagine what this means!

Definition of pineal gland: A gland situated centrally in the brain which was once thought to be the seat of the soul. The pineal gland is known to be involved in the hormonal changes which signal the onset of puberty, and some recent research has indicated that it may also be involved in **diurnal** and **seasonal** hormonal variation, although the precise functioning of the gland is far from being known.[10]

Dorland: 1. Pertaining to the pineal body. 2. Shaped like a pine cone. That's it. Under **pinealocyte:** the principal cell of the pineal body, being an epithelioid cell with pale-staining cytoplasm, prominent nucleoli, and large nuclei that are often irregularly infolded or lobulated; cords of these cells make up the body of the pineal body. Called also *chief cell* and *pineal cell*. See also *interstitial cells* under *cell*. (Emphasis added)[11]

Stedman: 1. Shaped like a pine cone. Syn piniform. 2. Pertaining to the pineal body.

Pinealocyte: A cell of the pineal body with long processes ending in bulbous expansions. Pinealocytes receive a direct innervation from **sympathetic neurons** that form recognizable synapses. The club-shaped endings of pinealocyte processes terminate in perivascular spaces surrounding capillaries. Syn. chief cell of corpus pineale, parenchymatour cell of corpus pineale Emphasis added.).[12]

The Goddess—Pallas Athena/Minerva [13]

Harre and Lamb: A small brain structure (weight approximately 150 mg) lying along the quadrigeminate groove between the superior colliculi. The gland was first described in the third century BC by Alexandrian anatomists who believed it was a sphincter which regulated the **flow of thought**. According to Descartes (1596-1650) the gland was the site of the Arational mind". In fish and amphibia, the pineal cells have an **eye-like, light sensitive function**. The function of the **pineal gland** in higher vertebrates, including man, **has not been established unequivocally**, though it clearly has an endocrine role, probably related to **gonadal function**. The nerve supply to the **pineal gland** consists of postganglionic sympathetic fibers. Part of the input to the **pineal gland** consists of postganglionic sympathetic fibers. Part of the input to the **pineal gland** via these fibers originates from the hypothalamic suprachiasmatic nucleus which is believed to be a biological "clock." The **pineal gland** contains, and probably secretes, a number of biologically active compounds. These are mainly small peptides and biogenic amines, among which the serotonin-derivative **melatonin** has been most extensively studied. The activity of the **pineal enzymes**, e.g., those involved in **melatonin** synthesis, is dependent on the **light-dark cycle**. (Emphasis added.)[14]

I Wonder Why God Did This?

As you read the definitions, wonder what the pineal is *really* for. No suitable definition exists and Harre and Lamb provide the best definition of function while also giving us the information on melatonin, which has been manufactured and is in use (some might say it is all the rage) for better sleep, elimination of jet lag and regulation of one's sleep cycle. The other definitions are mostly descriptive, and only Stedman's is very descriptive within the context of **pinealocyte.** So it is interesting that the most recent medical reference works used by medical students and faculty decline to speculate about what the pineal is and what its function is in the body. That leaves room for the development, at least, of an hypothesis by me.

I believe the pineal gland is very important to growth and development at the energy level. Be sure that God designed the pineal gland with a purpose. Make no mistake. As Einstein said, "God does not play dice."[15] People do. They make **choices** from a universe of local and nonlocal connections. An integrated web of possibilities and potential all part of the universal energy field.

Continuing the integration processes of varying ways to look at symbols for creative self-expression, the Governor Vessel Meridian in acupuncture has some correspondence with the Sushumna (Brahma nadi), the central canal, which is the cerebrospinal system of the human body and controls the body's functioning. In this meridian, the energy flow starts at the tip of the coccyx (root chakra), ascends the spine, reaches a point at the top of the head, and then courses down along the meridian line to a point just below the navel.

There are fourteen principal nadis. Of these, Ida, Pingala and Sushumna are considered the most important; all nadis are subordinate to the Sushumna. (Refer back to page 179.) Prana (travels through Sushumna from the pelvic plexus to the hollow space between the two hemispheres of the brain, which is situated in the interior of the cerebrospinal axis. Muladhara Chakra (the root chakra) is the meeting place of the three main nadis (Ida, Pingala, and Sushumna) and is known as Yukta Triveni (combined three streams).

A Bitch's Curiosity: Continuing the Journey Into Enlightenment

By now you may be getting the idea that creative self-expression is truly a "bitch." Well, it **is**. There is no easy way out or any easy answers to growth. I'm still learning about all of this and fully expect to be growing when I finally transition at 130+ years! So don't be discouraged. There's more to this and your own individuality will reflect the state of your thinking. The use of your power will reflect the confidence of your understanding and knowing. The choice is yours. You can sit on the curbside anytime you want. You can choose not to go further.

Now, think of the times in your life when conformity "felt" easier than expressing your own point of view, pursuing "questionable" information, and going to "those funny meetings." There are also times when being silent was, and is, required. That, too, is "self expressing" in a discriminating way—making choices based on your conscious awareness. This takes experience, feedback, observation and intuition. There is no substitute for **knowing who you are** because that is the only way you will have a chance to walk your talk **as an individual,** not as a **personality.** A **bitch** *with style* is about nothing if not creative self-expressing and sharing her love. How? Through the use of her:

1. body—by keeping it physically purified and healthy.
2. mind—in putting her ideas out on paper in concrete terms.
3. spirit—in being an **inspiration—NOT** a role model—to others.
4. voice—in putting her energy out through song, speech, debate.
6. body—in "nurturing and growing" the seed that becomes a child.
7. vagina (yoni)—in the birth of children.
5. sexual energy with self and others.
8. breasts—in suckling the young and her lover(s).
9. love—in relating to her Self and others.
10. spirit (energy)—by walking on her own two feet and maintaining her spiritual health—knowing who she **really** is: a *spirit having an earthly experience.*
11. soul—by doing what she must for her Self (filling her cup first and then sharing it with others and maintaining her mental and emotional health.
12. hands—in their artistic and craft-oriented products.

Self-Expression

I found self-expression in three areas: **leadership, communications** (speaking, writing and sewing) and **music** (piano and organ). Looking back on my development, I am confident that playing the organ at church became a ritual that allowed me to "what if" my life and daydream about using my talent to someday be somebody and "get out of Dodge," otherwise known as Xenia, Ohio. It made all of the family issues that confronted me doable.

Did I know about chakras when I was 14? Of course not. Did I know about biology? I wasn't sure what a cerebrospinal system was, let alone knew that I **had** one. I knew only what I was able to "peek" into in the library when I lied about having biology assignments. Truth is, I never took a biology course in high school. We didn't have the support for an instructor or lab space. I filled my extra course time with Latin, French and music. I am still consumed with enthusiasm as I research my work through medical books and through **A.D.A.M.** on my computer. It's clear to me now I could have done anything I wanted to do but being a medical doctor at that time in my life seemed beyond my horizon. Totally. I knew two doctors and I didn't like either of them. One of them was rumored to be a womanizer, though I am told he was a "pretty good" doctor. The other was a religious zealot whose medical practice was filtered through the precepts and canons of the Catholic Church. No inspiration there!

There were times when my breasts were developing and when I was becoming aware of boys as other than playmates and noticing that sometimes their pants would bulge in front at the oddest times that I speculated about life and what this all meant to me. For years I saw my Self dead-ended in a town I clearly didn't like with a family I felt out-of-phase with and daydreaming about music, physics and going away to college. Still, I was very mentally discontented with what I was learning morally **and** intellectually. Everything seemed to be designed to stagnate and rot, but I never gave up my dreams. In spite of everything, I kept thinking about what was happening in my life and in my wildest dreams. I just **knew** there was more to life than what I was experiencing.

My early life was filtered through a Roman litmus test before it had any "reality." Everything was filtered through the veil of faith. If you had it, you did what The Church said do and thought what The Church said think. If not, you were a heathen, agnostic or worse. Even being a cheer leader for the basketball team was ruined by wearing long, below-the-knee uniforms that inhibited action and flexibility! Didn't want to show "anything," did we?

The Baltimore Catechism never "felt" right to me. Too much dogma and not **any** discussion. When the nuns "talked" in religion class, they would clearly answer questions with "Because The Church, or the Pope, or the catechism said so." At a young age, I would verbally and intentionally dispute the catechism and the nuns. There is no doubt I walked around with bundled up emotions and a busy mind through high school. I always had a long list of "whys" that were either unanswerable or not answered to my satisfaction. Since reading was one of my favorite pastimes, I made a vow early in life to seek **satisfactory (to me)** answers to **my** questions through questioning and read books by *anyone*.

Why, I asked, were we unable to read other bibles or go to other churches?

The Pope said I couldn't because I would be risking my faith and be enticed to become a member of another religion. The Catholic Church was the source of the only true religion. So therefore, I could not read other materials that would contradict what I was learning in school and in church.

Why were some books on a list called the Index and why were we told you couldn't read them under pain of mortal sin?

Because these books were morally corrupt and The Church (some priests in some department of the Vatican over in Rome) had read these books and determined that the material was harmful to me as an individual and as a child of God. If I read the books I would have to confess a mortal sin. Did I want to deliberately and with intention **commit a mortal sin?** (Is this brain washing, or what?) Did I find and read some books on the Index? You bet. I read **Tropic of Cancer** and **Lady Chatterly's Lover.** Enjoyed them both.

Why does The Church disapprove of birth control? We already have too many children in our family . . . 12!

Children are gifts from God. You must take as many as God sends you. Birth control is a way of thwarting the will of God, so it is a **mortal sin.** The only reason men and women marry is to make a home for the precious gifts of love God

sends them. Sex for pleasure is not permitted because pleasure was not the intended use of this miracle; only the birth of
children. Now, there is one exception: it's called the rhythm
method. You count your days each month and make sure you
avoid having any sex prior to and immediately after you ovu-
late. If your period is irregular, well . . . this system won't work
for you. That's the only permissible way birth control is toler-
ated and then only for good reasons. In addition, using artificial means to avert pregnancy is a **mortal sin.** Further, you
know abortion is **absolutely** forbidden under any and all circumstances. No exceptions! Not even for incest or rape.
None whatsoever!

And those twelve children?

Your family is very blessed. Right! Your parents have
twelve opportunities to possibly give The Church a vocation.
Isn't that wonderful? Where there's a will, there's a way. God
will provide for your family. He always takes care of those who
do His will and follow His commandments. (Don't forget the
Pope! And Canon Law!)

**Why must my skirt be twelve
inches off the floor. I'm too short for
that length?**

Young ladies must never show their
knees and thighs. You must be modest and
not use your body in an inviting way. Let
the Blessed Mother be your model (cov-
ered from head to foot—another time, another era, another
culture). You must make sure you don't look like you want to
participate in sexually inviting relationships. In fact, you should
never wear shorts, except in gym or to play tennis, and a skirt
would be more appropriate, to your knees. (No mention of
boys and their "sexually inviting" ways.)

> *Evolution is
> always forward
> motion.*
> —Vikki Ashley

**Why was I born into this religion, this family, at
this time?**

Strange question, easy answer. I chose it for my soul's
development. When I reincarnated, it was necessary for me to
chose a situation that would test everything my soul ever

thought it knew and then some. I could sense I was on some type of path without knowing what that path was. The Universe kept putting wonderful people in my way to teach me lessons and to love me in spite of circumstances. Father Schumacher; Miss King, who took me to the opera; Martha Clark, the reformed prostitute; Geraldine Jester, my aunt and surrogate mother; Carl Henry, an uncle who understood I needed "watering" and "nurturing" and someone to give me money when I was in college "just because." Mother O'Gorman who taught me how to incorporate wonderful ideas into my literary pretensions. MaryBeth, Norma, Angie—roommates at Manhattanville in New York so far removed from the corn fields of Ohio as to be on the moon. All made a difference as I self-expressed, developed, learned, failed, and moved forward in a herky-jerky motion.

> **The mind knows only what lies near the heart![16]**

A **bitch,** *with style-a-borning* makes do with what she has, knowing in her soul that is **not** all there is, yet understanding she has to keep on walkin' since, in spite of appearances, evolution is **always** forward motion! As she **learns** through the combination of knowledge and experience, she understands what she must do and how she must move ahead. Well, perhaps.

Why is life the way it is?

The mind knows only what lies near the heart![16]

STEP SIX

Health Is My Highest Value!

*My perception of reality **is** my reality*
*until new information changes **my** perception.*[1]

Peace at the seaside—Vikki at Gulf Shores, AL—1997

Bitchhood 601
Self-Integration: I *Choose*, Therefore I Am.

I "invented" a process I have used in my work for over twenty years called "threading the needle." Many of you reading this book have probably never threaded a needle or even sewn on a button, repaired a seam rip or patched **anything.** However, as a former seamstress, I made everything I wore and threading a needle is significant to me.

In order to thread through the needle, there has to be a thread catcher that gathers up the fibers (amazing how many strands exist in a very thin thread!) or put spit on the ends until the fibers stick together enough to put the singular-appearing thread through the eye of the needle! Now, this all seems easy to the uninitiated, but let me assure you appearances are deceiving, as is the case in life. When I thought of "threading the needle" as a framework for my work, it became clear that in life I had to thread the needle in order to focus and concentrate my energy to accomplish my "work." As I began using this process with task groups, growth groups, teams (as in team building), I noticed how easily this framework worked with people as the processes we were engaged in proceeded.

BITCHHood 601, the sixth step, is threading the needle, pulling the many threads of a single strand of thread through the eye of the needle of life. Threading the needle of life to calibrate the understanding of the concept that **all is one!** Once you "get it," you've "got it!" **Doing** it is the real challenge. The beginning of the **doing** is the acceptance that all of the information I am sharing with you has a bottom line: your decision/choice to take control of your life. Every stinkin' bit of it. And to follow through on your curiosity and desire **to know,** beginning with the baseline of "know thy Self."

Choice is the very **essence** of **BITCHHood.** It is the power to use your energy through your thoughts, words and deeds to turn matter into energy and energy into matter. Choice is likewise the very **essence** of health. In every aspect of health, you are in charge and must make the decisions that lead to **your** ultimate sense of "health." There is no health care professional, including medical doctors, psychologists, licensed professional counselors, chiropractors, nurses, etc., who is in charge of your health. Besides, none of them can cure you. Only your body can heal itself after whatever interventions occur to assist you along your path to health, if that is your choice. When you are advised to do **anything** that sets your solar plexus (I call it your "belly button") off, **stop** and then listen to your innate response and do nothing until you are able to make an informed choice. Never let a doctor tell you what you **must** do without getting a second, or sometimes even a third, opinion. The only exception would be a genuine medical emergency that must be taken care of **now, this minute!** Otherwise, take charge, ask questions, be curious and maintain your own integrity about what is right for you. We are chemically, psychologically and physiologically different from everyone else. Your "personal note" belongs to no one else, even when you are in harmony with other people, you are still your own individual Self. Remember this because a **bitch,** *with style* is sure of this very fact!

Energy Centers (Chakras) and Their Integration With Other Processes

I have already introduced the chakras and their various representations because these energy centers and the endocrine system represent the keys to physical/biological and psychological health. The endocrine system , governed by the chakras, controls the seven major systems of the physical body and is responsible for the correct functioning of the entire organism, producing both physiological and psychological effects. (Refer to Step Four.)

Those seven major body systems (among many others) are:
1. Central Nervous System*
2. Cardiovascular System
3. Autonomic Nervous System**
4. Endocrine System
5. Genital or Reproductive System.
6. Immune System
7. Limbic System

*The entire nerve apparatus, **composed of a central part, the brain and spinal cord, and a peripheral part**, the cranial and spinal nerves, autonomic ganglia and plexuses.[2]

That part of the nervous system which represents the motor innervation of smooth muscle, cardiac muscle and gland cells. Consists of two physiologically and anatomically distinct, mutually antagonistic components: the **sympathetic and parasympathetic parts. See Step Seven, page 240.

The importance to health of the endocrine system cannot be overestimated. Alice A. Bailey calls it "a replica in miniature of the septenary constitution of the universe and the medium of expression and the instrument of contact for the seven ray forces, the seven spirits before the Throne of God. A round this at-present-unrecognized truth the **medicine** and the **healing methods** of the future civilization will be built."[3] The terms "seven ray forces" and "seven spirits" refer to the seven major energy centers in our etheric bodies—the chakras.

Remember, a **bitch,** *with style* must have information in order to make choices and if one is a **B**eing **I**n **T**otal **C**ontrol of **H**erself, the highest value she adopts is this:

"I am a healthy person. My energy (spirit), mind, emotions and body are working together in perfect harmony. Consequently, I have everything I need to achieve my highest goals."

This affirmation is an important aspect of continually "talking to" my Self about what I desire and expect to take place in my life, including my lifestyle which must reflect this idea as well. Becoming more informed about my body's functions, learning about the importance of all of its aspects, especially the seven major body systems, learning how to activate, **at will**, my own electromagnetic systems to maintain an environment of healing in my body are part of my work. More on the methodology later, but there are four processes a **bitch,** *with style* understands are required to initiate, consolidate and maintain health: **relaxation, focused attention, focused intention** and the **acceptance of her desires as already accomplished.**

Lest you think I am overdoing my emphasis on **information**, let me remind you that the body is nothing if not a series of intelligent systems that are fed information constantly by a variety of messengers: chemical, mineral, mental, emotional and physical (as in food and water). Our cells are. Information is the gut (center) of all systems and good communications (information that connects and is usable) is the bottom line process to delivery of a healthy individual at all four levels: spiritually, mentally, emotionally and physically. **Always remember what I just said and never weary of asking, for when you ask, you receive** as promised by the Great One called Jesus the Christ.

In a variety of ways, all "wisdom-of-the-ages" materials have defined health, calling it by many words such as harmony, balance, integration, and peace. For a **bitch,** *with style* to do her best work and provide her best service in whatever arena she has chosen, learning to be a totally healthy person is her most important task, one she does with full knowledge and acceptance of the fact that it is **her** responsibility and no one else's.

A **bitch,** *with style*'s state of health will be totally reflected in every aspect of her life, including her performance in her personal, professional, home and social functions. The use of energy to maintain health, must, like all other functions of an individual who is growing, be based on consciousness and being aware (i.e., Awake!!!). The baseline for health is the use of information and knowledge in every area of life. She is a seeker and a "user" in the best sense of that word. To sum up: **If you are healthy, if your body is in balance, if you know who you are and make choices in accordance with that perception of your reality, then you are a bitch,** *with style.*

The Seven-Second Syndrome (S³)

As indicated in Step Five in the brief discussion on numerology, seven sets the pattern of anything. It is the number of the Christ, who set the pattern for all humanity. So, in seven seconds, when you meet **anyone**, the pattern of your interaction is set. I have, therefore, taken a concept that is very apt for the subject of health and integrated it with the **Seven-Second Syndrome (S³).** When you meet someone for the first time, something happens that you can *feel*—for those who are psychic or highly intuitive, they can "see" the integration of the auric fields. For those who are insensitive and unaware, it carries no meaning of great importance. But let me demonstrate what I mean.

There are people who meet and instantly take to one another.

You've met people like that and so have I. It's like the song in South Pacific says: "Some enchanted evening, you will see a stranger across the crowded room and somehow you know, you know even then, . . . " Well, you know lots of things, but one of them is that there is a "drawing" power that will bring you together across that crowded room. That power is energy, highly magnetic and electric **when you tune in to someone.**

"Tuning in" is a talent—a wonderful intuitive capability that all of us have but not all use and develop. A **bitch,** *with style* develops and uses this talent. In fact, she *relies* on it to serve as her guidance system. And it does.

So, the **Seven Second Syndrome (S³)** helps you to "tune in" immediately to the nature of the encounter. The material you will learn as a result of putting the **P³ Baseline and Growth Package** under your feet as a foundation will enable you to present your Self well *and* understand and relate to others in the most effective and least hostile way. There are certain ways to use this data that will support and reinforce the learning that goes with the **Seven Second Syndrome (S³).**

On that note, let me share this concept I converted to **S³**— **WITMA-WIGO** and it means **W**hat **I** **T**ell **M**yself **A**bout **W**hat **I**s **G**oing **O**n. I believe Hemingway called his **Seven Second Syndrome (S³)** talent his crap detector. It's much more than that. What I tell my Self about what is going on is crucial to my survival. It's the difference between life and death in many cases—like in war, or when confronted with some type of danger. There is no time for intellectualizing. One has to move or, put another way, go with one's gut! You know, internally as a result of all the work you are doing in this **BITCHHood** curriculum, what the truth is for you, but you do not often, or in some cases ever, acknowledge the "what-I-**know**" part of that statement.

What you work with in your daily life until you wake up (if you *are* awake) is what you have stored in your subconscious mind. This may not be your conscious reality at all but your **perception** of what happened or what you know, which is **your** reality until new information changes **your** reality. That is why family members, especially children, often have divergent viewpoints about experiences they both participated in but remember differently. This is why hus-

band's and wives differ on just about anything. They do not understand how to communicate their individual reality without putting
down the other person or saying that the other person is wrong?

One of the first questions to be addressed to another person
with whom we are differing is: "What is **your** reality about this situation?" Then **listen** to what is being said. With this capacity to **listen**
and **hear**, new hooks provide the next step in communicating that
eliminates, for the most part, the hostile energy between individuals.
Not always, of course, because learning to communicate in this way is
not rewarded by society nor is it the stock in trade of education,
though it should be. *Listening* and *hearing* must be given more serious application, however, if individuals are to learn to control stress in
their lives and bring more balance and harmony to bear on day-to-day
relationships. In other words, to be more healthy! This is so because
we allow other people's issues to invade our minds and emotions
without knowing how to turn the situation around. From hence-
forth, make one of your key opening questions for anyone you are in
disagreement with, "Well, then, what is **your** realty about this situation?" Then *listen* and *hear. You will "hear" where your next "hook"
should go in order to carry the conversation into a more balanced and
less hostile arena. I guarantee it.*

What are the keys to communicating my perception of reality?

My perception, then, directly influences what I carry internally
in my subconscious and my subconscious then influences the way I
perceive my experiences. I view the subconscious as the psychological equivalent of the Universe. It is, in my judgment, the *Akashic
Record* of our lives recorded in the subconscious of *each* of us. .
Akasha comes from the Sanskrit that means "primary substance" out
of which all things are formed. The subconscious mind as the *Akashic
Record* of each life stores everything—absolutely everything that has
ever happened to us in this or any previous life. It is the willing servant who is totally nondiscriminating in her service. She does what
she is told—no more; no less. She is nonjudgmental, totally unat-
tached to emotional content, absolutely unrelenting in the truth of
what she records and doesn't give a whit what you think about your

record.   In today's parlance, the subconscious is analogous to my computer's hard drive. Whatever I put on it, well . . . that's what's there. No judgments pertain to any of it. **GIGO**—garbage in, garbage out. **LILO.** Love in, love out. **SISO.** Secrets in, secrets out, in due (do) time.

I must either make a conscious decision to change my program on the hard drive of my soul and thus put new programming on it, or I must live with the struggle that ensues when my subconscious and conscious **do not agree!** That struggle between my *SpiritMind-EmotionsBody (SMEB)* (my individuality which a **bitch**, *with style* is developing) and my personality (which is the mask the public sees and relates to (my projection) before I become integrated and whole— this struggle is relentless and without concern for class, age, race, sex, religion or any of those superficial aspects of humans in which we place so much stock.

What results from that struggle? Why **stress, y'all!** Actually, it isn't stress that results but varying levels of **distress**. Distress? So why do we persist in calling it stress? Habit. Poor definitions. Reinforcement. It is very hard to change the public's mind about the use of words, but I can tell you for sure everyone has heard of stress. Enter **distress** as a major player in the health of each of us. Distress defines the pain, worry and suffering leading to probably most of the severe illnesses in our society today. Review the following definitions and note the inclusion of biological and neurological terminology.

According to Hans Selye, *stress is a process.* The process is that which describes the way in which people realize and identify their problems, how they react to them and attempt to cope with them, and the "cost" of doing so. Situations involving high demand and high constraint, but involving poor problem-solving resources or low support are perceived and reported as aversive or problematic, and are often associated with the sort of changes in behavior and in physio-logical states which have been diagnostic of stress. The term "stress" is thus to be treated as an economic descriptor of a particular prob-lem-oriented process.

The psychological definition also identifies "stress" as a process, which in fact it is. Your mind and body have a buildup of events that bring you to the threshold of energy that is scattered and not man-ageable for whatever reason. Attempts to "cope" with the life events that have accumulated run the gamut from crying, talking to your best friend, seeing a counselor, staying home in a state of depression, suicide, wrecking the car, making a novena, praying in church before Mary or Jesus or St. Jude or whomever. All of these efforts are done to seek relief from the buildup of the tight chest, thumping temples, throbbing top of the head, fatigue, buckling knees, anger at others, and unrestrained tears when spoken to, to name some. You can form your own opinions, but I thoroughly understand how individuals suffer pain, anxiety and depression when out of balance and harmony in their mind, body and spirit. This is, in my way of thinking, distress.

"Selye's theory states that any prolonged stress can cause physiologic changes which result in physical disorder. Each of us, it is theorized, has a "shock organ" that is genetically vulnerable to stress: some of us are **cardiac reactors, gastric reactors, skin reactors.** Individuals who are chronically anxious or depressed have a greater vulnerability to physical and/or psychosomatic (physical condition aggravated by psychological factors) **dis-ease.**

Hans Selye described the general adaptation syndrome (GAS), as the sum of all nonspecific systemic reactions of the body that follow prolonged stress. The **hypothalamic-pituitary-adrenal** axis is affected with excess secretion of cortisol producing structural damage to various organ systems. George Engel postulated that in the stressed state, functional changes occur in all neuroregulatory mechanism that depress the body's homeostatic mechanisms, leaving the body vulnerable to infection and other disorders.

"**Neurophysiologic pathways** thought to mediate stress reactions include the cerebral cortex, limbis system, hypothalamus, adrenal medulla, and sympathetic and parasympathetic nervous systems. Neuromessengers include such hormones as cortisol, thyroxin and epinephrine.[4]

The integration of "stress" and its results on the body, especially the neurologic pathways and endocrine system **are** important to my health and yours. There is no need to know all there is about these systems, but to understand that we do not function **outside** our minds and bodies! We function **within** and the results appear **outside.**

So, **What I Tell Myself About—What Is Going On (WITMA-WIGO)** turns out to be critical. Why? Because that **is** what's going on!!!. **For me.** Is it real? Absolutely! **For me.** In this process of

WITMA-WIGO, which applies to each of us, there is an understanding of me by me that leads to internal harmony and peace. If the world is falling apart around me and if I am not responding to "that world out there" as others think I should, several things may be happening that bear scrutiny, analysis and response. I may be unable to face new information that will change my reality. I may have to challenge everyone else's notions in favor of my own perception of reality. I may be diagnosed as mentally incapacitated and, depending on circumstances, be happy to be there!

So, what are the keys to communicating my perception of reality?

1. I understand that what I communicate is true for me at the time I communicate it.
2. I remain open to new information.
3. I am aware of and recognize when other perceptions conflict with mine and create dissonance and hostile energy.
4. I stand by my own perceptions of my reality based on my values and desires for my Self.
5. I make decisions in concert with others so long as those decision do no harm to me spiritually, mentally, emotionally and physically.
6. I have the courage to withdraw my energy from relationships that no longer support where I am in my life. Such relationships are toxic to my true perception of me. My true perception of me (**Know Thy Self**) is the most important understanding I will ever have. I will not permit anyone else to trample on my spirit.
7. I live my life according to my knowledge of Self and values, with the courage to communicate that perception of my reality to anyone for any reason under any circumstances. I must love me *first* and *foremost* if I am to love anyone else and I must express that love openly and with vigor and enthusiasm.
8. I live from the world "within" (thoughts, emotions and imagery) that makes the world "without" manifest. The world "within" is the **only** creative power and everything I find in my world of self-expression has been created by me in the inner world of my mind—consciously or unconsciously.

ASHLEY MAXIM

I create my own reality. I make it what I truly want[5]

Pat Muller, in an article "Practical Harmlessness and Right Speech" introduced **WITMA-WIGO** and puts forth the premise that our "feelings are not caused by external events or other people but rather are the result of our unconscious evaluation of the gap between our desires and the perceived reality of our life.[6] How true. This **bitch,** *with style* understands that feelings are indeed internal and *knows* how crucial feelings (emotions) are to the growth of all aspects of my life. Remember, **Love is focused emotion!**

Moving forward

In **BITCHHood 101**, I define **love as focused emotion.** I **know** that is the case, and as we move forward in our information gathering and in the integration of knowledge from multiple disciplines, philosophies and cultures, it is even more important to remember that definition.

Another Look At Chakras

Take a close look at the back view of the chakras on the next page. The chakras **are** operating in the etheric body, one of the bodies that interpenetrates the physical body. This etheric body is that part of our auric field closest to our physical body. Earlier I introduced the various "fields" or bodies we have around us as part of the framework of understanding I am sharing in this book. (See page 142.) For now, it is important that you begin to understand that the information being provided by reviewing these figures is designed to demonstrate sources of knowledge affecting your use of energy in your *SpiritMindEmotionsBody (SMEB).* The goal is your understanding of the "integration of the universe" as it relates to such mundane effects as the energy presented for your use.

Following that is the side view of the spinal column with the chakras shown to the left. Notice how these energy wheels relate to

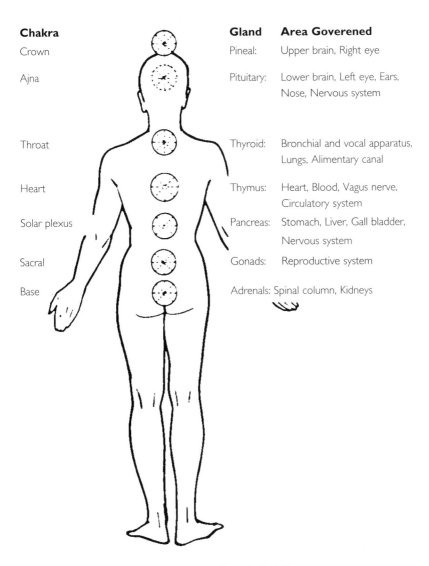

Chakra	Gland	Area Goverened
Crown	Pineal:	Upper brain, Right eye
Ajna	Pituitary:	Lower brain, Left eye, Ears, Nose, Nervous system
Throat	Thyroid:	Bronchial and vocal apparatus, Lungs, Alimentary canal
Heart	Thymus:	Heart, Blood, Vagus nerve, Circulatory system
Solar plexus	Pancreas:	Stomach, Liver, Gall bladder, Nervous system
Sacral	Gonads:	Reproductive system
Base	Adrenals:	Spinal column, Kidneys

The seven major spinal chakras.

your brain, spinal column and root chakra. In the brain, the top chakra relates to the **pineal gland** at the crown. Next down is the chakra related to the **pituitary gland,** next in descending order, the **throat chakra,** the **heart chakra,** the **solar plexus chakra,** the **sacral chakra** and the **root chakra.** Note the insertions within the lotuses and keep in mind that these symbols tie in with numerology (gematria of the Kabbalah):

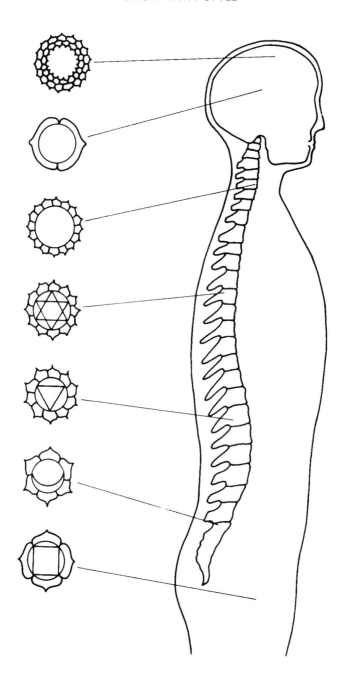

Position of the chakras as viewed from the side of the body.

Chakra Symbols And Their Meaning

CHAKRA 1—Root
Lotus Leaves 4
Color—Red

Red causes densification of the descending forces of life and manifestation in the womb of our mother. Four provides earthly orientation: north south, east and west.

The ultimate goal, units of matter with spirit (God/Energy)

Inserted Symbol— Square

Numerological Meaning of the Symbol—The second perfect form that can be constructed with straight lines. The first is the triangle. Symbolic of the ancient sacred formula for Divinity. Stands for the four elements: fire, water, air and earth which the Kabbalah said were the four stages of creation as represented by the four parts of the name Job-He-Va.-He, a form of the verb "to be." Spirit (fire/Job) acts upon creative substance (water/He) which is given mental form through thought (air/Va.) and finalized in matter (earth/He) . . . . In spirit reside the ideas, the animating yet formless forces behind creation The square is the pattern for the building blocks of the material world and four expresses earthly connections: four winds, four corners of the earth, etc.[7]

This chakra identifies us all as one, one as all. It is about "root support," our foundations in the material world as well as our foundations in the psychological world.

CHAKRA 2—Sacral
Lotus Leaves 6

The sacral chakra provides the images which can now create a further instrument of creation, the body.

Color—Orange

Represents the joy of Eros and causes the idea to take hold of the energies with the intention to create. Orange is a combination of red and yellow. Red typifies the personality; yellow the mentality.[8]

Six rules the balance of opposites, the cooperation of male and female.

Inserted Symbol— Circle

Numerological Meaning of the Symbol—Zero—Not a number. It represents Spirit, the Source, the "I am that I am." It has no reference within the realm of the three-dimensional experience. Form exists *within* it, but it can exist *without* form. In the material world, Zero operates beside one of the nine digits as a symbol of recycling from one set of numbers (or awarenesses) to the next, e.g., 10, 20, 30. etc. Its geometrical counterpart is the circle which has no beginning and no end, representing infinity and Divinity.[9]

The integration of masculine and feminine energies creates new forms, including progeny. Identifies source of sexuality, work, and physical desire. Asks that we honor one another and accept the equality that presents itself in the act of creation.

CHAKRA 3—Solar Plexus
Lotus Petals 10=1
1 is the number of the beginning and means action, outbreaking of self, individuality, the soul coming forth in its essence, the seed of life.
Color—Yellow
Yellow is high intelligence and wisdom and represents the transformation of spirit into matter.

Inserted Symbol— Triangle, Pointing Downward

Numerological Meaning of the Symbol— The triangle is considered the first perfect form because it is the first that can be constructed with straight lines. It has long been a religious symbol of the trinity, the three parts of Divinity that is the moving creative force behind manifestation. The triangle also represents the three parts of the self—body, mind and soul. (Mind includes emotion) In some ancient societies is also recognized as the trinity of the Goddess in her three forms—Virgin, Mother, Crone. The triangle was the Egyptian hieroglyphic symbol for woman. In the Greek alphabet, the symbol for delta is the triangle, signifying "the Holy Door, vulva of the all-mother-Demeter (Mother Delta) known in astrology as Ceres, goddess who nurtures and provides the grain for food. The downward-pointing triangle, as in this chakra, represents the female genital area.

Very appropriate for the power center of the body, especially in relation to the emotions, fight or flight and very much tied to love, which is *focused emotion*. Honor one Self. Establish a strong sense of self-esteem and recognize the role of the *personality* but only as the polarity for the *individuality*. The power is in the two becoming one.

CHAKRA 4—Heart
Lotus Petals 12=3

> 12 indicates time: cycle of the year, the zodiac, the 12 stages of man.

> 3 is the number of Spirit (energy/fire) manifestation, multiplication and growth. In 3 the pairs of opposites (polarity) are united and harmonized.

Color—Green

Green is the color of balance and health.

**Inserted Symbol— Star of David,
also called Hexagram**

Numerological Meaning of the Symbol— Two interlaced equilateral triangles—one apex pointing up and one apex pointing down, making a six-pointed star, called the Star of David or

David's shield. Represents the Law of Polarity, male and female, fire and water, God and man, spirit and matter. This symbol was adopted by the Jews in the seventeenth century as an official symbol. The original source predates Judaism and was the Great Yantra, which represents the union of the sexes. The triangle that points downward symbolizes the Female Primordial Image or Yoni Yantra, which was before the Universe was. In infinite time, the Goddess conceived within her triangle the bindu and brought forth the upward pointing triangle, the male, the lingam (penis) or "the fire." The symbol represents the eternal union of Goddess and God.[10]

The lower triangle has long been recognized as the element water, the upper triangle as fire. The hexagram was eventually de-sexed because of puritanical influences. Its message is verbally transmitted in the third sentence of the Bible describing the beginning of creation. "And the Spirit of God moved upon the face of the waters." Fire, or spirit—the male—moved "within" the face of the waters—the female—the cosmic womb, to bring about physical manifestation.

CHAKRA 5—Throat

Lotus Petals 16=7

Color—Blue

Soothing, spiritual, peace and love, a blending of knowledge and understanding which is wisdom. It is the color of infinity and creates an experience of space. Helps to penetrate the mysterious depths of life's mysteries through communications, sound vibrations, speech.

16 is the double of 8 which represents manifestation. Eight also represents infinity (on its side).

7 is the magic number indicating rest, "it is finished." 7 is the bridge for the Superconscious to perceive the material world.

Inserted Symbol — Circle, Cube

Numerological Meaning of the Symbol— The throat with a circle is the beginning of the higher chakras. It represents the will and self-expression. The circle is clear to represent the transformation of lower energy from the three lower chakras into higher (spiritual) energy and the conscious recognition of the power of sound, which represents "the Word." Sound, color, numbers— all are energy vibrating at varying levels and speeds.

7 sets the pattern. *Thought precedes reality.* You, your family, your home, your job and your city were thought before they became realities and that is why seven precedes eight. Seven is the promise of things to come represented by the rainbow with its seven colors. Seven is a complete cycle in the sense that it symbolizes the cosmic blueprint that precedes manifestation.

Eight is manifestation, physical reality is the result of the first six steps in the cosmic blueprint energized by *thought* in the seventh step. So, manifestation is the result of energized thought . . . God spoke the word and it was done (see Genesis). The throat permits us to "speak the word" and it is done according to how we speak.

- Four represents the *idea* of form in the blueprint.
- In eight, the idea of form "takes form" in the physical world.

Eight gathers all the ideas generated through the cosmic blueprint and gives birth to them in the material. The seven days of creation are the pattern leading to the physical plane of eight.

In eight we begin to understand that all pairs of opposites (opposite forms of expression) are effects of a single cause from the One. Eight is the physical embodiment of the previous principles of the cosmic blueprint One through Seven.

Physical embodiment or the eight is symbolized by the cube. Salt crystallizes in cubes; we are called the "salt of the earth." Salt was considered the most material of the minerals used by alchemists. Here on earth, in the *physical body* which is *the cube*, the stone of the Mason's work in the temple (our body) not built by human hands, the Ego (personality) has taken on the most material of all cloaks.

The cube is associated with the number 26 which adds to 8 for several reasons: The four stages (elements of creation) which produce the material world, the cube, are found in the sacred trapezoid and its name Job-He-Va.-He, with its values of 10-5-6-5. These four numbers add to 26. A cube is constructed of 6 planes, 12 lines, 8 points, for a total of 26.

CHAKRA 6—Brow

Lotus Petals 2

Color—Indigo (Navy Blue)

Indigo is about insight, intuition, imagination, peace of mind, wisdom (the blending of knowledge, understanding and perception) beyond duality.

Indigo is also the color of the deep silence of the vast spaces of the heavens. Because of the depth of this color, it is difficult to see with the outer eye. We must open the inner eye and experience images of life before they become manifest on the physical plane. Indigo represents the curtain that veils us from the light of the true spirit. When we are ready, this curtain is gently dissolved, revealing the light of the spirit and the purpose behind creation.[11]

Inserted Symbol—Circle

Numerological Meaning of the Symbol—Two is the number of petals assigned to the brow chakra. The symbolism represents duality, two definite aspects which function as opposites, both vital to the function of the whole: negative and positive polarity. Science states that for every action there is an equal and opposite reaction. Occult science teaches that when any force begins to work in the Universe, another force opposed to it arises at the same moment. When the One moved out, it caused the opposite reaction, a moving in or the law of attraction. At that moment, duality was born—the polarity of opposites that underlies all manifestation: day and night, up and down, good and evil etc. Two is the mirror of illumination where the Self sees and knows it's Self through reflection of its opposite. There would be no "short" unless there were a "long," against which to measure it. There would be no "cold" without "hot." Two collects and assimilates. It is the gestation period.

Duality is calling for Integration or choice, the latter giving each part of the duality energy to express. Integration allows the polarities to unify, recognizing that each pole is simply another aspect in degree of the other. Point: matter is the same substance as spirit (energy), simply a lower vibration.

Hot is simply the upper end of the thermometer from cold. The understanding is that we make much more of difference than we should, but *only through knowing difference can we make a choice and stick with it.* Discrimination is required to know which choice works for you *individually* and that *knowing* comes with *information* and *experience.*

CHAKRA 7—Crown
Lotus Petals 1000=1
Color—Violet

Zero (the circle) represents the Spirit, the Source, the "I am that I am." In the world of form (matter) zero operates beside one of the nine digits as a symbol of recycling from one set of numbers (or awareness) to the next, e.g., 10, 20, 30, etc.. Metaphysically, zeros permit repetition and represent the promise of eternal life, infinity, the continuum of life's energy, reincarnation. Zero is Divinity, cosmic awareness, the universe, the cosmic egg. It has absolute freedom from any kind of limitation. If you add unlimited zeros to a digit, in this case 1, you still get 1 but an expanded "idea of 1. A higher vibration.

Inserted Symbol—Circle

Numerological Meaning of the Symbol— The crown chakra identifies the beginning of the mental-spiritual stage in our development. In yoga, the crown chakra is seen as the abode of the highest consciousness. It is situated above the head. The 1000-petalled lotus represents eternity, which has no ending. In this center, consciousness, matter and energy unite. It represents growth of the individual spiritually, mentally, emotionally and physically. This union provides supreme knowledge and allows the individual to pass beyond life and death.[12]

This ability to grow to the point of being able to "pass beyond life and death" is to see life in cycles and know that it is a continuum and not to see death as "the end." Each individual has many "little deaths" along the loose gravel path of growth and can advance at an individual pace as consciousness is awakened. Little deaths include changing one's vision of oneself; moving beyond one's birth culture and home and making a new home with "new family" not of one's blood; coming through a cloud of mental illness to a new understanding of health; divorce is a "little death" designed to transform and "resurrect" the parties to new possibilities.

Through the energy and information received through the pineal gland, human beings are able to continue to grow "beyond" their Selfs and to know that here in this life, in this time, in this day, it is not only possible but is very likely that a full understanding of the potential represented by human beings will be rewarded with the ability to control one's life and the outcome of that life *knowing* it continues in another dimension, which the 1000-petalled lotus represents.

The power to know and use these powers is what a **bitch, *with style*** considers her goal and, indeed, her *obligation*, so she can share what she has learned with others.

I have been working for years on a chart designed to integrate anatomy, the chakra systems, numerology (gematria), astrology, minerals, etc. There is some disagreement among writers and philosophers about a number of items, principally color and the correspondence with chakras and numerology and some differences about the seven rays and the chakras and body areas. By and large, I have found that what I know and can support through research is probably correct **for me.** I use Alice Bailey's writings as a great source of infor-

INTEGRATION OF INFORMATION—A PERCEPTION CHECK [13]

Chakra	Gland	Area Governed	Planet Ray Tone Exoteric	Color	# of Petals
1. Root/Base Muladhara	Adrenals Vitality	Spinal column. Kidneys	Mars 4 do=c	Red	4
2. Sacral Svadisthana	Gonads/Ovaries Enthusiasm	Reproductive System	Sun 7 re=d	Orange	6
3. Solar Plexus Manipura	Pancreas Confidence Power	Stomach, Liver, Gall Bladder, Nervous System	Mercury 6 mi=e	Yellow	10
4. Heart Anahata	Thymus Love	Heart, Blood, Vagus Nerve, Circulatory System.	Saturn 2 fa=f	Green	12
5. Throat Vishuddha	Thyroid Creativity	Bronchial and vocal apparatus, Lungs	Jupiter 3 sol=g	Blue	16
6. Ajna/Brow	Pituitary Knowledge	Lower brain, Left eye, Ears, Nose, Nervous System	Venus 5 la=a	Indigo	2
7. Crown Sahasrara	Pineal Unity/Oneness	Upper brain. Right eye	Pluto 1 ti=b	Violet	1000 (1)
Soul/Energy		Subconscious/Memory	Pluto/Moon White		
Mind/Energy Spirit/Energy Body/Matter/ Energy		Higher Consciousness First Cause	Moon/Uranus/Mercury Sun/Neptune/Venus	Silver Gold	
			Earth Black		

mation and recognize that she has fostered interpretations based on the level of growth and knowledge of the aspirant wishing "to know." As with the alchemists of old, formulae often had one ingredient left out so that people of negative intent could not use said formulae to do harm. It was their thinking that those seeking information would continue the search until they found their missing piece of the puzzle. And so it has been from the beginning of time and continues to this day. **You must search for your "missing piece."**

My desire has been to integrate all of the areas of life in a chart that clarifies the relationships of each to the other. Included are behavior, emotions, psychological preferences, chakras, numerology (Gematria), color, sound, the elements, the key chemicals, etc. I also have noted those body areas that correspond to or are influenced by these "universal codes." The point is: learning about the energies and correspondences may make a difference in **your** health some day.

As you review these figures and charts, the path to **BITCHHood** requires you to develop **your** mind, seek information for **your Self,** be able to **discriminate** through **your** choices and ultimately develop **wisdom** within **your Self!** It can be fun, exasperating and utterly frustrating. But never dull!

I expect disagreements and discussions. That's what makes information so important. There are still some missing pieces for me, I am sure, but I expect to fill out, massage and change some aspects of this work as I grow. It represents what I know at this moment in time, and I want to share it to reinforce how important each and every piece of information is, no matter how esoteric, out of your current field of interest, etc.,

All is connected. All matters. Who cares? Well, I hope you will. Your growth and your health depend on it.

YANG/YIN BODY ENERGIES AND RELATED BODY ORGANS [14]

Yang—Right Side Large Intestine, Stomach, Triple Warmer, Small Intestine, Gallbladder, Urinary bladder

Yin—Left Side   Lungs, Spleen and Pancreas, Circulation, Sex, Heart, Liver, Kidneys

There will be more discussion of astrological **information** later, but it is obvious to any **bitch, *with style*** that there **is** an amazing correspondence among and between data bases arising from various belief systems and cultural philosophies. The **Yin/Yang** symbol of feminine (yin) and masculine (yang) energy is the very heart of the universe and its functioning. (See page 228.) There is absolutely **nothing** in the universe that does not function on a combination of masculine and feminine energy. Think for a moment how your lights work. They are attached to a plug that is the **male** plug that is inserted (got that word, inserted? The plug is like a penis, right?) into the **female receptacle** in the wall (the receptacle is like the vagina, right?) and the lights come on (just like when the penis (**lingam** in Hindu) meets the vagina (**yoni**), right? So, is sex basic to the universe for all creation? No. Gender is. Connection is. And therein lies a differing perspective. Masculine and feminine energy has nothing to do with sex. Sex has everything to do with the **use** of your masculine and feminine energy. Love has nothing to do with sex. Sex has everything to do with procreation. Emotion has nothing to do with sex. Emotion has everything to do with love and desire. Sex has everything to do with connecting—creating "juice" that makes one feel alive—for the moment, for whatever the reason.

We call this connecting "relationship." But is it? Is emotion always involved in connecting? Often if not always. Does emotion create a reality that is often mistaken for love? Definitely. What, then, is going on with the desire to connect that we call emotion that is often miscalled love? We are either focusing or dispersing our energy in a way that makes a difference in our lives. It creates a momentary spark like a lightening strike. But, if it's a direct hit, it does just as much damage physically as a bolt hitting a tree and then does incredible damage to the mind and emotions of those expecting that "hit" to make a difference in day-to-day living.

Do you think that teen-age sex is focused or scattered emotion? Think about it. Is sex being used as a substitute for real love? Is it a temporary safe harbor for ragged emotions and minds too unfocused to understand that they are creating their own reality and **not** making it what they truly want? How many of us have been *there*? I have. And I paid the price. Until I woke up and noticed that love didn't

matter to my ex-husband. Only sex mattered. And only for the time
it took to ejaculate and roll over. We never "connected" after that
first blush of excitement when he returned from Korea and, I now
know why I allowed him to take "control" of my emotions as I let my
body go forward on autopilot. After all, he was the first and only.
Why wasn't this love? As I defined it.

   I will continue this tale when we arrive at Step Eight of **BITCH-
hood.** Meanwhile, note that the following chart again provides information that is designed to reinforce the notion that life at all levels is
somehow moving in circuits embedded in our etheric body's spinal column: *spirit (energy), mental, emotional* and *physical (SMEB)!*

   As you review this chart, over and over, through the months and
years, you will come to understand how much the whole world in
every aspect is totally integrated. The codes imbedded in various
types of information, whether you **believe** in them or not or even
understand them, should not be dismissed. When I first began my
journey into wholeness, I would get totally exasperated because I did-
n't understand a concept, or a piece of information, or didn't have the
right reference book, or whatever. Still, I kept digging and I would
silently ask my Inner Knower to find the data for me. I would then
forget it and move on. Shortly thereafter I would find the information in a book I picked up and "just happened" to turn to the right
page, or I would see something in a magazine that is right on the
point, or I'd be talking to a friend who just happened to bring up the
area of my interest, or more interestingly, I would be in a bookstore
and the damn book would just jump off the shelf, fall to my feet, or
push itself toward my hands. Always, always, always, the information
I was looking for was contained therein. It still happens to this day.

THE ELEMENTS AND THEIR CORRESPONDENCES

Signs of Zodiac, Body Humors, 4 Functions of the 4 Behaviors & Dimensions, Chemical Psyche—MBTI,[15] Emotions—DISC[16]

Element	Zodiac Signs	Body Humor	MBTI	DISC / Chemical / Emotion	Focus	Dimensions
Fire	Aries, Leo, Sagittarius	Choleric — Red*	Intuition (N) (Judgment) (Introvert)	Dominant (D) (Extrovert) — Oxygen (O)	Problems and Challenges	Anger/short fuse — Hi D Active; Slow to anger/long fuse — Lo D Passive
Water	Cancer, Scorpio, Pisces	Sanguine — Yellow*	Feeling (Perception) (Extrovert)	Influencing (I) (Extrovert) — Nitrogen (N); Trust/Optimistic; Distrust/Pessimistic	People and Contacts	Hi I Enthusiatic; Lo I Suspicious
Air	Gemini, Libra, Aquarius	Phlegmatic/ Lymphatic — Green*	Sensing (Judgment) (Extrovert)	Steadiness (S) (Introvert) — Hydrogen (H); Unemotional; Emotional	Pace and Consistency	Hi S Slow to change; Lo S Flexible
Earth	Taurus, Virgo, Capricorn	Melancholic* — Blue*	Thinking (Perception) (Introvert)	Compliance (C) (Introvert) — Carbon (C); Fear; Challenging/Independent	Procedures and Consistency	Hi C Adheres to Rules/ Do it right first time. Lo C Rule Breaker/ Careless with details

*These are author designations.

PART THREE

Relationships, Sex, Death and
Rebirth, Transformation

STEP SEVEN

The Duality of Life
and the Crux of Relationship

*Let us make man in **our** image, in **our** likeness . . .*
*So God created man in **his** own image,*
in the image of God he created him,
male** and **female** he created **them.
(Genesis 1:26-27)

Bob and Vikki "glittering" together—1997

Bitchhood 701
Self-Marriage: We *Are*, Therefore I Am.

The reality of anything is the underlying *idea*. Our true relationship to anything or anyone in the manifest world is this: "Thought is the formative power of the mind."[1]   When one spiritualizes thoughts (gives energy to them, or, put another way, "loves" them through focused emotion) one is lifted to a level of conscious reality and unity that are more important than any external riches or moral law dogmas!

It is stated in *Genesis* that God created man in **his** own image, but also said that he decided (Let us) to make man in **our** image, in **our** likeness, and **then** "created" him, **male** and **female,** he created **them**— they put forth a puzzle that is important to our view of who we are. Really! It is a puzzle to people and has been very misinterpreted.

How do **I** know?

Well, after over thirty years of research and going through an integration process of the materials available in all forms of philosophical and metaphysical thinking, I am convinced this passage is a critical one that identifies the **Yin** and **Yang** of all creation, including each of us as *individuals* and is a plausible paradigm for relationship. I am also convinced that marriage is one of the processes that this passage refers to but is not the "marriage" we all consider social marriage. It represents, in my view, the ***marriage to one's Self,*** an essential principle required to develop *the person who is whole* and an essential principle required to answer the question "Who am I?" It is critical to love thy Self before you love your neighbor! The problem with this is that we have inoculated our Selfs against this approach for the benefit of the church *and* the state. The integration ***in each of us*** of the masculine and feminine energy principles (what should be our *first* marriage) makes us each whole (one) with a dual nature. Our masculine active energy is outgoing and radiating (Yang/masculine) and our passive energy is introverted and conserving (Yin/feminine) and these provide each of us with the basic understanding required to *become* the **I** in the **I Am That I Am.**

Keep in mind that using this knowledge has absolutely nothing to do with age. It happens to each of us *in due (do) time,* as I continue to say, and according to the time line we each agreed upon before we were born into this incarnation. And the "do" in that phrase relates to the action phase of the trilogy of results known as *thought, words and action!* My correspondence for those three phrases, called the Holy Trinity in most religions, is as follows:

Thought (Generation)	Father	Superconscious	Spirit
Word (Vibration)	Son	Conscious	Mind (Mental & Emotional Energy)
Action (Manifestation)	Holy Spirit	Subconscious	Body

Let me reiterate that I view the Bible as one of the most powerful psychological tomes ever written and I also view it as a personal handbook for individuals to develop their spiritual powers and from whence they learn the "code" and how it applies to each of us. The stories throughout the book are there to allow us to *know* that every kind of good and evil that could possibly have been imagined, when the New Testament was written long after Christ's death, is *still* part of the human story. The purpose of this reassurance, as I'm sure the Church fathers knew when they directed that the doctrine of reincarnation be taken out of its pages by the Church, was the desire of Christ to *demonstrate (take action)* how men and women were to become the true powers they were always intended to be. And to *do* as He had done while on earth, including the resurrection and ascension, metaphors about our growth into our higher selves. He intended this process of resurrection and ascension to happen *in* us *without the crucifixion occurring over and over again.*

The Catholic Church fathers, however, wanted more; they wanted power to have and to hold and they knew that they must eliminate certain ways of thinking and certain doctrines in order to obtain it. They understood clearly then, as they do now, that the object is to "get and hold" or in another sense, "marry" the minds of men and women to the Church and her doctrines. This occurs in *all* religions, no matter what the church or doctrine. When you have the minds of men and women, you *have* the men and women. That's why *ideas* are so powerful and why we see dictatorial nations and leaders eliminating the press as their first acts of office. Isolate people and keep them ignorant . . . the original sin, right?

A decree was adopted at the Second Council of Constantinople in 553 that stated:

"Whosoever shall support the mythical doctrine of the pre-existence of the soul and the subsequent wonderful opinion of its return, let him be anathema."

"Nothing can be canceled by official decree unless its existence is first acknowledged. The Second Council of Constantinople, in reducing acceptance of reincarnation to a heretical belief, robbed man of the very hope that inspires him to do his best, and, at the same time, made possible the escalation of man's inhumanity to man."[2]

It's clear that reincarnation was part of the early Christian church since it wasn't declared anathema (condemned) until the sixth century A.D. And yet, the references continued through the New Testament. Look them up: *Matthew 17:10-13; Luke, 1:17; James 5:17-20, John 9:1-3, Revelations 3:12.*

Sybil Leek indicates that she can find no reference in the Bible condemning reincarnation or even warning against it. But, the Bible warns that "whatsoever a man soweth, that shall he also reap." Yet, there are instances where this does not appear to be true if you consider *just* one life. Nonetheless, it has worked its way into our language: "What goes around, comes around" and "You reap what you sow." In this life or the next.

I am not asking you to believe in reincarnation if you don't; what I *am* suggesting is an open mind to the possibility. All of the Eastern world and many in our Western world already believe, so it *is time* to consider that *deja vu* does not occur in a vacuum. Consider the phrase, "Don't I *know* you from somewhere?" to someone you've never seen in this life before, and "I've seen you *some place b*efore, but I can't recall where," take on new meaning with this understanding.

First, be clear. Duality and relationship are absolutely essential to life, *this* life. The Chinese Taoists follow The Great Principle of Yin and Yang and the laws of nature as the guiding light on "the Way" to spiritual liberation. This Great Principle has the advantage of simplifying and unifying the understanding of *all* things. Basically, it holds that "*all objects or phenomena in the universe can be understood as lim-*

itless pairs of opposites—yin and yang—which interact according to the following principles:[3]

- **The source of *yin* and *yang*, and therefore all dualities, is that which is unified and unchanging.**
- **The *yang* principle is active while the *yin* is passive, yet nothing is purely *yin* or purely *yang*.**

"The *yin-yang* symbol shows *yin* within the *yang* as the dark eye in the white fish, and conversely *yang* is shown to be contained in *yin* by the white eye of the dark fish.

The symbol below shows the integration of the *yin-yang* symbol with the signs of the Zodiac. Another reminder to the reader that when seeking "new-to-us" knowledge, keep in mind how there is *nothing new under the sun.* And everything is ultimately related to everything else.

Pritchford points out that even though *yin* and *yang* specify change and separation, their source is permanent. "The Great Ultimate is Unmoved" according to Shao Yung, the 11th Century philosopher. The Bible expresses this idea in the phrase, "I *am* the Lord; I change not." (Malachai 3:6). The rest of that quote is: "there-

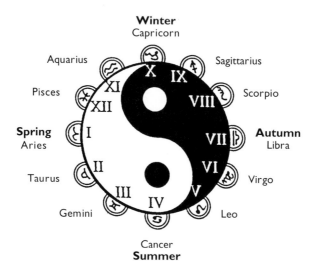

Yin/Yang Symbol with Astrological Signs

fore ye sons of Jacob are not consumed." Translation: The law does not change and Jacob represents the mental consciousness of higher understanding within all of us, according to the *Metaphysical Bible Dictionary (MBD.)* "Jacob also represents an idea of the **I AM** identity through which the faculties of the mind receive their original inspirations. Jacob (The **I AM***)* had twelve sons to each of whom he blessed, or inspired, with his spiritual wisdom."[4]

The twelve sons are the astrological signs of the Zodiac. Those signs provide insights into every aspect of one's life when utilized by a practitioner who knows how to "read" one's astrological chart. Remember that this is just another source of information you can use or not use. But you will not have a choice if you don't take the time to find out about *that* information. So, **bitch**, the next time someone asks you, "What's your sign?" think before imparting that information.

I tell people that one of the enduring traits of a **bitch** *with style* is her insatiable curiosity and her desire to *know.* That desire helps her to maintain an open mind and to have the personal courage to really "seek," "look," and "find" out who she is and use that information for changes in her own life . . . regardless how difficult it is to confront one's shadow. Astrology is very useful to those who *want* to know. If you're a skeptic or don't *want* to know, then don't use it. Don't knock it, however, for others. There is something profound to the saying, "Don't knock it until you use it."

As you are seeking information, spending time in review of spiritual literature, self-help literature, and any philosophic text where the word *Lord* may appear, translate every instance of the word *Lord* into the word *law* and begin to understand that what **I am** suggesting here is that the natural laws of the Universe are really the *"underlying idea"*

> ***Thought + Word + Action = Result** Is the same as **Energy + E-motion (energy in motion) + Conscious Use—in due (do) time = Manifestation.***
> —Vikki Ashley

behind *all* creation. As we proceed, keep in mind **the whole creation process** is about *Thought (Energy)* + *Word (Emotion 'energy in motion')* + *Action (Conscious Use—in due (do) time)* =

Manifestation (Results). Albert Einstein changed the thinking of the whole scientific world when he published this *"underlying idea"*—E = mc² (Energy = Mass X The speed of light Squared! Keep in mind that "in due (do) time" is up to the Universe. You have *already* done the work in *your* mind and put the vibration (energy in motion—e-motion) into the Universal Energy Field. It's a done deal.

I suggest that we take into our individual minds this understanding: **I am a microcosm, exactly, of the macrocosm and *that* is the miracle of my *being here!!!* I am energy, mass and light**. I *know* this to be true. Once I know *this*, I am no longer victimized by outer circumstances or people and I must take *full responsibility for who I am, what I do, and how I live (create) my life, totally!* That responsibility extends to any biological offspring as well and it is my job to instill values and knowledge that will provide this kind of inner strength and courage to young people early in life. **Society and its organizations will not cooperate in this endeavor. It is too threatening now, but in due (do) time . . .** There are people, institutions and organizations who are on this wave length and will continue to grow in strength and numbers. A **bitch *with style* knows *and decides*** to walk this path consciously, for consciousness and energy do, in fact and in deed, create the nature of reality.

Next, since my basic premise is that energy and consciousness create the nature of reality, I believe strongly that what I have to say about **our** creation held true **then** as recorded in Genesis and is true **today.**

What Does This All *Mean?*

Let us make man in our image, in our likeness . . .

This means there is not only a *Father God* but a *Mother God* too. It's clear, isn't it, that it takes *both* energies to create, and our job here on earth is to create, beginning with our Selfs, our lives, our work, our children (artistic, musical, architectural, etc., as well as biological). We are, after all, divine creatures created in the likeness and image of God. All religions believe this, so I have always wanted to know the *"underlying idea."* I didn't learn it from the nuns in grade school, high school or even in college. I have decided they didn't even know but were sharing what had been poured into their heads. All well and good if you're not curious and just *settle, but* a **bitch with style** *is* curious and she does not settle! She finds out because she *wants* to know. She always opens Pandora's box!

As I said, we *are* divine beings. Ours is not a road to discovery, though it seems that way day-by-day. We already *are!* Our earth is the place of *creation (and destruction)*—taking things and making them into entirely new objects with entirely new functions. And guess what? That means *you* as well! We can recreate our Selfs as many times as we deem necessary *in this lifetime.* But first, we must have a foundation from which to make those changes.

We give the name "discovery" to new things because we have not been taught that we are "creating," according to the natural laws of the Universe, but that is what we are doing. Along the way we make discoveries and unearth new information, like the name Jacob (meaning **I AM**). It's how we put it together that reflects the creative powers we possess.

> *So God created man in his own image,*
> *in the image of God he created him . . .*

Here we are told that we are a unified whole. **His** own image is clear. It was repeated to make sure we "get it." So, what does this mean, to be created in the image of God? It means we are little versions of God and have everything God has in our make-up. That's what it *means!*

The word *image* is key here. It has at least 28 synonyms:
Reflection, counterpart, **double**, representation, form, appearance, similitude, show, **perception**, **likeness**, portrait, picture, figure, effigy, photograph, **copy**, imitation, **resemblance**, status, drawing, facsimile, counterpart, **duplication**, model, **pattern**, impression, illustration, **reproduction**.[5]
Webster's New World Dictionary also includes **vision, replica "spittin' image", dead ringer, chip off the old block, thought and memory.**

I have highlighted the ones I believe support my interpretation. I particularly like the "chip off the old block" concept because it allows me to propose that we are a bioelectromagnetic chip off the Universal Hologrammatic Block, otherwise known as the Unified Energy Field of the physicists. At any rate, by now all of us who have credit cards know what a hologram is, but let me explain a bit further to make my point:

A **hologram** is a photographic plate containing the record of the interference **pattern** produced by means of holography. **Holograph** means written entirely in the handwriting of the person under whose name it appears. **n.** a holograph document, letter, etc. Finally, **holography** is a lensless, photographic method that uses laser **light** to produce three-dimensional **images** by splitting the laser beam into two beams and recording on a photographic plate the minute interference patterns made by the reference light waves reflected directly from a mirror and the waves modulated when simultaneously reflected from the subject: the virtual image can be reconstructed by shining laser light, white light, etc., through the developed film.[6]

The roots are Greek *holos,* whole + *graphein,* to write.

Before I'm through here, I might as well add *write* to this listing of synonyms:

Record, compose, pen, scrawl, inscribe, draft, draw, engross.[7]

I admit that when I saw "engrossed" I was spurred on, to wit:

Absorbed, busy, engaged, taken up, monopolized, fascinated, rapt, captivated, filled up, enamored, bewitched.[8]

It seems this last set of synonyms throws a very clarifying light on this whole *image* business, don't you think? It had never occurred to me that *write* would be so "right on" with regard to describing God as "engrossed" but that is absolutely the case with regard to *Genesis.* It seems to me to be describing my new definition of love: Focused emotion (or energy in motion). The Intelligence we *call* God was, indeed, busy with the creation of His own likeness, but because He was in his Absoluteness unable to experience everything "out there," He created us as Gods to do it and find a way to express our God Self in the bargain. What a deal, don't you think? I was absolutely bowled over with excitement when this thought came to *me*. It makes so much sense.

I've heard the following items since I was a tiny tot:

1. God is All.
2. God is everywhere, everything, and in every place.
3. God made you in His image and likeness (never got explained).
4. Love is everywhere. (never got explained).
5. God *knows* everything you think, see, hear and do. (Ooo!)
6. God is within you. (Really? How?)
7. Your soul always was, is and always will be. (How? Don't ask. Just accept.)

My question has always been: "If any one or all of the above statements is true, then I *must be* God, but how is that so?" No one could explain. No priest, nun or preacher ever had an explanation I could accept. I long ago discarded as propaganda the Baltimore Catechism. And "The Pope said so," has never had any place in my thinking.

I had to seek and find my own answers and I am sharing those with you now.

So, literally to "write whole" means to produce entirely in the handwriting of the person under whose name it appears. In our case, the name is the name of God, and we are the hologram that appears entirely in His handwriting; in other words, in His image.

Any tiny piece of the hologram contains the pattern of the whole. As we *do* with regard to our cells and genetic patterns. Any *piece* of us is truly *all* of us. Medicine is beginning to understand that message as is being demonstrated by Energy Medicine, the use of magnetic energy, not just for imaging (i.e., MRIs) but the use of magnets directly on the body, the effects of which I will explain in a later chapter. Nikken magnets changed my life and that of my spouse. The impact on us as images of the divine who are holographic in nature is even being demonstrated right now by Dr. Joseph Vacanti of

Children's Hospital in Boston. He says there are so many people who need organ transplants that won't get them—50,000. Of these 50,000, four thousand are likely to die before they get them. Instead of replacing a faltering organ with one harvested from someone else why not take a few healthy cells from the sick person and grow him or her a new one? Such an organ would probably work better since the body is less likely to reject tissue made of its own genetic material. This is not science fiction. It is Dr. Vacanti, his brothers, Drs. Martin and Charles, who could, *Life Magazine* noted, go down in history as the Wright Brothers of tissue engineering. Martin is a pathologist at the University of Massachusetts and his brother Charles heads the Center for Tissue Engineering at the Center in Worcester. They are working on tissue engineered jawbones, ears, noses, you name it. See the footnote for other remarkable thresholds of medicine.[9]

What makes the difference? These doctors are being their divine creative Selfs. They are on to the holographic nature of our bodies, and are rewriting, engrossing their Selfs in something new! The medical textbooks about what is not only possible but most probable in our lifetime are being rewritten as I write. Therefore, we will live to see livers from individual cells, and other organs engineered (created); arms, legs and digits replaced; and nerves rejuvenated.

Others are also doing wonderful and magnificent things in medicine that will include integrating alternative and complementary processes with the contemporary allopathic methods and drugs. In fact, I predict the drug industry is going to change its tune and come up with more plant-oriented and natural products that will not only reduce side effects, but will, in many cases with the patient's involvement mentally, *cure* diseases that currently baffle us. Diabetes is one of those headed for the cure. I predict cancer will also be one of those diseases that will be cured without the harmful side effects now encountered and will be *prevented* by more competent use of the mind, information and the boundless energy of the Universe. This journey has just begun, and it is so thrilling and exciting to be living at this time in the history of the world.

Is it so far fetched, then, to propose that it is time our interpretation of some of the verities of the universe ought to change with the times as well? I am talking about some of the outmoded dogma that churches and religions preach. You should be thinking, about now, that priests and preachers, nuns and brothers *may* not be so necessary any more. After all, once you recognize *who* you are and claim your power and take back your energy for focused use in the service of your growth and development and *then* in the service of humanity, you clearly might enjoy them as part of a social scene, but there won't be much use for them from a doctrinaire or dogmatic point of view. None at all. We are our own priests, as I hope I am laying the groundwork to prove. We are also our own saviors and our own Gods. Each and every one of us. Churches currently serve as places where we integrate our energy with that of others who believe as we do. We are entranced by song (whether gospel or Gregorian chant), stimulated by lessons of life (some not so accurate but biblically acceptable) and we are hypnotized (though we don't know it) by the tonality and energy of the preacher or priest and the smell of incense and sound of music. We put our conscious mind aside and wallow in the arms of the church for one or two hours. Then we go home to whatever we left and go on about our business until a crisis, chaos, or a significant emotional event (**SEEs**) *wakes* us up and gives us an opportunity to **choose** a different way of looking at things. And then we must consciously **act** by **doing something** about whatever created our crisis.

When we take hold of our lives, we may still seek religious and spiritual community but we will seek a new kind of thinking and a new kind of organization. We will not support traditional religious venues.

The whole point of being God is that there are no limitations and no second or third parties placing limitations on our minds. **We do *that!*** Not the Universe! So . . .

. . . *male and female he created* them.

Men and women (them) were each created both male and female. Yes. *Both male and female. This is one of the most important facts to be learned from the new interpretation of this line in Genesis.* We *each individually* have these powers of *masculine* and *feminine* energy and this is reflected in our holographic construction by the Greater Intelligence that created the Universe.

We women and men have been handicapped by decisions made eons ago by church "fathers" who decided

1. we should not know the truth about who we are (divine beings, Gods),
2. women must be made to "serve" men for the replenishment of the earth (be a baby/race carrier), and
3. women are the source of man's greatest weakness, sex, therefore, she should pay the price for being the temptress as well as the mother, and
4. a woman should be subject to the husband.

Society has made some strides away from this antediluvian thinking, but not much at the spiritual level. That is why society cannot be expected to make this shift. It must come from *individuals **because that is how they were created—as individuals.***

Evidence of Our BioPsychoElectroMagnetic Duality

For years now, I have described the nervous systems of the body as the electrical streets that carry all the information and messages for the coordination and integration of our bodily functions. I have also been describing the endocrine system as the system of chemical highways that ensure the information and messages get to the right organs and tissues and don't somehow go where they don't belong. The beauty and majesty of the organization and functions of the human body have preoccupied my thoughts for years. However, I could never figure out why I didn't "buy" the primacy of the brain as the center that was the initiating center of thoughts and everything required to run the mechanistic body. It finally "dawned" on me after years of reading, seminaring and research, that the brain is a critical part of the information process. The brain is a transformer, a transmitter, a circuit breaker, but **not** a generator. It **processes** information (critical to be sure) and it provides the template for all of the functions for the brain. But **it does not originate** any of the information used to handle all of the body's elaborate, intricate and mysterious functions. So if not the brain, from whence does it come?

I do believe that all of that information comes from the electrical biofield—the aura—surrounding the body and that this electrical biofield is the soul of the individual. The Universal grids "out there" are the equivalent to our current cellular grids that we use for telephones. People, though not acknowledged as such, are part of the Unified Energy Field and its holographic and cellular properties. Information is *everywhere*. **Thoughts** are generated in this area and stored in the memory function as appropriate and always stored on the hard drive of the subconscious. The memory function, in my view, "lives" off the subconscious and therefore accounts for the loss of short-term memory in people who have advanced senile dementia and Alzheimer's. Various possibilities have destroyed their brains ability to handle the short term information while their long-term data, which comes from the subconscious, seems to be, for many of them, right at hand as if it were only yesterday.

Of course, depression, dementia, Alzheimer's and other mental challenges appear to me to be evidence of places for souls to hide who have decided to no longer face up to issues and problems that they have been unwilling to face. *Of course*, this results in physical debility, including chemical imbalances, loss of memory, loss of contact with loved ones—all part of their decision to *let go of responsibility for their actions* and *let things drift along* until they close their eyes in transition to the "other side." In some of these challenges there is the notion of "getting even" with people in their lives—often a husband or wife who "stands" by them and becomes ill with the burden of care giving. It's getting worse as our country ages and these disabilities appear more often in our friends and relatives. It's too late for those who have decided to "escape" into another world. It's not too late for prevention and use of new thinking to make escape unnecessary.

Following are examples of attributes and examples of *yin/yang* pairs based on the Chinese system, though most are by now fully integrated into our Western way of thinking. Such considerations were part of the thinking of the original writers of the Bible when they wrote the document we all revere, in code. It has been left to generations upon generations to seek keys to answer the "mystery" of life and to ensure that the mechanistic and scientific view of "biology and chemistry as destiny" does not continue to hold sway in our contemporary thinking. It's time for scientists to admit to the "something" they cannot explain!

Otto Loewi who shared a Nobel Prize with Henry Dale in 1936 for the method of conveyance of messages by chemicals (later to be called neurotransmitters) finally said "the life sciences contain spiritual values which can never be explained by the material attitude of present-day science."[10] I am sure some scientists "think" this way but are afraid to speak out for fear of being ridiculed or damaging their careers. It *will* happen. And in our lifetimes. In fact, I predict that physics will be the science that corroborates the existence of God as a Universal Intelligence called Energy/Spirit/Ether and we are the intelligent holographic lights of that godhead!

I defy a scientist to *explain* the beauty of a Mozart sonata or the proud majesty of a Liszt piece that stirs our *souls,* and in the case of the songs I love, make me *cry! Mechanistic? **I am sure not.** Spiritual? What else?*

Still, it is the all-inclusive Mind that we *directly* experience that is the ultimate condition of health. And health is the conscious integration of spiritual, mental, emotional and physical energies.

We are a triad *and* a quad. We are body, mind and spirit as well as fire (energy/ether), earth (body/physical), air (mind) and water (emotions) In our bodies, the *image* of God (energy) reflects itself in our physical Selfs. Everything in our physical bodies is dual (masculine and feminine) except for key organs, the endocrine gland system and the chakras. The individual aspects of our being are what make each of us unique because of our use of information and knowledge that maintains the health of these individual units of the body.

Furthermore, Ross Harvey postulated that we each have a personalized time mechanism that identifies our metaphysical metabolism burn rate. This fascinating thought leads to his point that each of us hit major life events according *to our own individual schedules and "burn rate."* Calculated over our lifetime, whether a long or short one, this **individualized** energy rate inevitably determines our transition (death) into another dimension.[11]

I find this thinking very appropriate since "death" is one of the Western world's last taboos and must be addressed to get "beyond" fear of living life fully one moment at a time, one day at a time. In

YANG	YIN
Mind	Body
Doing	Being
Electrical	Magnetic
Repulse	Attract
Focused Mind	Quiet, Serene Mind
Light	Dark
Time	Space
Sun	Moon
Day	Night
Life	Death
Construction	Destruction
Expand	Contract
Specific	General
Yes	No
Spirit	Matter
Active	Passive
Masculine	Feminine
Heaven	Earth
Function	Substance
Positive	Negative
Logical	Intuitive
Angry, impatient	Fearful, insecure
Aggressive	Timid
Outside	Inside
Heat	Cold
Energy of the body	Blood, body fluids, tissues
Excess and acute	Deficiency and chronic
Exterior and superficial	Interior and deep imbalances
Imbalance	Balance
Expansion	Contraction
Warming	Cooling
Sweet, Pungent	Salty, bitter,. Sour
Energizing	Builds blood and fluids
Ascending energy	Descending energy

due (do) time, we will each understand that there is **only** this "moment in time."

Think, finally, of the nervous systems, which I have named the "state highways of the body" as, in contemporary terms, the "Interstate Highway Systems of the body" that carry information and messages from our "major cities" and key "hubs" (like our Endocrine System) to every part of our anatomy. Let me share a description (See box at left.) that I believe sets up in brief, general terms the functions for the Central Nervous System, Peripheral Nervous System and Sympathetic and Parasympathetic, in language anyone can understand.[12] It also helps one to understand how critical each system described below is to the information processing that maintains the body of each human.

Spinal Cord and Nerves. The central nervous system (CNS) consists of the brain and spinal cord. The brain sends nerve signals to specific parts of the body through peripheral nerves, known as the peripheral nervous system (PNS). Peripheral nerves in the cervical region serve the neck and arms; those in the thoracic region serve the trunk; those in the lumbar region serve the legs, and those in the sacral region serve the bowels and bladder. The PNS consists of the somatic nervous system which connects voluntary skeletal muscles with cells specialized to respond to sensations such as touch and pain. The autonomic nervous system is made of neurons connecting the CNS with internal organs. It is divided into the sympathetic nervous system which mobiles energy and resources during times of stress and arousal, and the parasympathetic nervous system, which conserves energy and resources during relaxed states.[12]

The Central Nervous System has *two* parts: the brain and the spinal cord. The spinal cord is *the* transcoastal super highway, the very critical carrier system for the total body. The Peripheral Nervous System (which carries messages in and out of the brain and spinal cord) is made up of two parts: the Autonomic Nervous System and the Somatic Nervous System. Brain, cord and nerves appear first in vertebrates; animals below that level do not have them. The Autonomic Nervous System has *two* parts, the sympathetic and the parasympathetic nervous systems. The systems act **alone and in concert** with all aspects of our physical Selfs. The autonomic nervous system existed among lower animal forms long before conscious control existed—it is the oldest and most primitive part of the nervous system's structure.

What Do These Systems Do?

They are further proof of the duality of our natures and the masculine/feminine dichotomy that is so prevalent in Nature. I will refer you to an anatomy book, a medical dictionary or the excellent book by Sherwin Nuland, **The Wisdom of The Body.** But I can tell you this for certain, the Sympathetic Nervous System constitutes a *Yang* energy (masculine) and the Parasympathetic Nervous System is the *Yin energy (feminine)*. They are integrated, however, in their functions as follows on page 242.

Dr. Nuland and I don't agree on the *source* of thought (he says the brain; I say the auric field) nor does he accept any spiritual explanation for the miracle of the body though he accepts the "mystery" of it all. I say the brain is the processor of the data received from the mind/soul/auric field and that the nerves are the recipients of the stimuli/impulses that the brain transmits after it is received from the mind/soul/auric field. It's not a point to argue. It is simply a disagreement and will probably remain so. It is not my intention to go into this aspect of the body deeply but to point out the miraculous coordination of its dual functions by using the most significant source of our information and messages (nerves—and only one part at that).

Nevertheless, it is clear that the autonomic nervous system, the most primitive part of our physical Selfs is a dual **and** integrated system, just as each person is (whether male or female). This type of duality and integration go on throughout the body and throughout the Universe.

Pay attention to this part of *who you really are*! It will give you command over your life and revise, eventually, the relationship between individuals and our nation's health care practitioners, especially medical doctors.

So, it is possible, then, to "see" why I have come up with *another way of looking at* this very basic passage from Genesis and how it all turns on one's interpretation of "the truth." BITCHHood 701 lays the foundation for acceptance of each of us as **divine beings** whose

General Plan of the Autonomic Nervous System, Indicating the Actions Governed by Sympathetic and Parasympathetic Impulses[13]

+ = Masculine/*Yang* and B = Feminine/*Yin*

Sympathetic Nerves		Parasympathetic Nerves	
Dilates Pupil	+	Contracts Pupil	B
Inhibits secretion	B	Stimulates secretion of lacrimal and salivary glands	+
Accelerates heart rate	+	Slows heart rate	B
Increases force of cardiac contraction	+		
Constricts most blood vessels	B		
Dilates bronchi	+	Constricts bronchi	B
Inhibits activity	B	Stimulates gastric and pancreatic activity	+
Stimulates glucose release Stimulates adrenal	+	Stimulates gall bladder	+
Secretion	+	Stimulates GI motility and secretion	+
Inhibits activity	B		
Relaxes bladder	+	Contracts bladder	B
Inhibits genitals	B	Stimulates genitals	+

*first marriage (**FM**)* and *first responsibility (**FR**)* is to her Self (him Self, too!) and to growth, development and the conscious use of our creative power and self-expression. That *first marriage (**FM**)* is acceptance of the dual nature of each man and woman on this earth while at the same time being **one** with the creator (each of us) in our triune nature: ***spirit, mind (includes metal and emotional) and body (SMEB).*** Note: Keep remembering that ***Mind*** is a "two-in-one" equation that leads to 3, synergy and creativity. What a difference it makes in each life to *know* you are a being of light (thoughts information and knowledge) and a being of love (emotion), and manifestation (body).

My formula for establishing the true relationship foundation utilizing this information for growth is this:

FM +FR+Knowledge Applied (KA) = Health in S+M+E-B.
H (SMEB) = Life Lived Fully (LLF) as a Bitch With Style (BWS)

Put another way:

$$FM+FR+KA = H(SMEB)$$
$$H(SMEB) = LLF$$
$$LLF=BWS$$

This formula works. I guarantee it!

Can you picture and imagine for a second what such an approach to living would mean to the development of social contracts, i.e., relationships and/or marriage in the external world? For one thing, individuals would marry individuals and you would have synergy (1+1=3) and not the currently established wisdom of two people becoming one—that formula is ½ +½ =1. I didn't know each of us was a half! By now you are aware that this reference is not to the social contract but to the individual body and that is to be interpreted in terms of the mental unification (become one) of our feminine and masculine energy. (Two shall become one. Got that? Makes sense if you keep an open mind.)

This approach to relationship would do two things immediately:

1. Cut the divorce rate because people would marry *much* later, if at all, and if they do, their consciousness and energy levels would contribute to a more selective and informed choice of mate, thus making for potentially more harmonious matches.

2. Reduce the need for others' approval because of the growing security *within* each person and their desire and commitment to **know thy Self** and **love thy Self** *before* making stupid mistakes with others that reflect their projection of their own ignorance.

3. We are all electrical receivers and transmitters. We **are** the **body electric.**[1]

4. We all (male and female) have in our physical bodies masculine and feminine energy streams that are often characterized throughout history as "serpents, "the *kundalini* of the Hindus. Even the caduceus, the emblem of the medical profession has the "serpents" boldly wrapped around the staff of life (the spine). (See symbol on page 245.)

Wouldn't it be grand? It won't happen over night or even soon, but in due (do) time, it will come to pass. Some of us did learn and more *can* learn about how it is possible to become "one within" by using the tools in this book and attending meetings, seminars and lectures on these subjects. Use your car as a school house and listen to tapes and CD's. Read books. Fill your Mind with knowledge and then **use** it.

A Recapitulation

There has been a lot of data between each of those *Genesis* phrases. So let's remind our Selfs again of how this interpretation plays out at the beginning of a New Millennium, a time for sharing new ways of thinking.

So **God created man** *(generic) in* **his** *own image,
in the image of God he created* **him, . . .**
*God has already indicated that he was both masculine and
feminine energy (male and female) in his opening statement,
so now he makes it clear once again by identifying "man" as
an individual and saying he was created in his own image
(God's masculine and feminine energy—Father-Mother God),
and for emphasis he repeated it one more time to underscore
the individuality of this duality.* **And then,** *he finished off the
idea with* **"male and female** *he created* **them."** *So that is*
four *times he emphasized this thought. Four times! His last
emphasis reinforces that the duality* **(male and female)**
(them) *was created* **in man** *(meaning man and woman).*

As I pursued my life engaged in self-expression and lived through the experiences I had *chosen*, I also searched continually for understanding and enlightenment. I have always been an insatiable reader and listener. I noticed however, how my interests veered most often toward leadership, business, management **and** anything esoteric, astrological and spiritual. The combination has always seemed appropriate and I now know why. Leadership, management and business subjects and programs rely heavily on esoteric knowledge though few people "talk" about it or acknowledge that fact. But, it is *so—just follow stocks and bonds for a year and watch the rhythm, polarity and cycles.* Pay attention as well to the language used to describe the movements, etc., of the markets. Accident? I don't think so.

Along the way it was clear to me that there is a power and unity in the universe that is both amazing **and** methodical. Otherwise, why do planets stay in the sky? And why do flowers, vegetables and trees grow and die, and some "resurrect" their Selfs each year? Why? Why?

The beginning of it all is that the Universe, by **any** name, is the **ether surrounding us all. Everywhere** we are, it is! Everywhere we go, it goes. That clear space outside your home and inside your home is **it!** The Big E of the Einsteinian equation $E = mc^2$—**Energy = Mass X the speed of Light squared.** *All is in motion.* All is in vibration, All is from the same source. That is true. So what's that got to do with you and the most important relationship you will ever have? Everything! It has to do with Understanding the following "realities:"

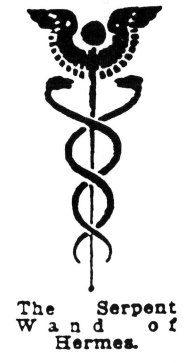

The   Serpent Wand   of Hermes.

The Caduceus
Represents the spine encircled by the two major nervous systems, The Central Nervous System and the Autonomic Nervous System.

The Natural Laws—In The Seven Hermetic Principles[14]

I asked you earlier to replace the word *Lord* with the word *Law*, let me share with you the following laws of Nature that will **never** change.

I. THE PRINCIPLE OF MENTALISM

The *ALL is* **Mind;** The Universe is Mental.

"Mind (as well as metals and elements) may be transmuted from state to state; degree to degree; condition to condition; pole to pole; vibration to vibration. True Hermetic transmutation is a Mental Art."

"Under, and back of the Universe of Time, Space and Change, is ever to be found The Substantial Reality—the Fundamental Truth."

"Substance" means "that which underlies all outward manifestations. Under and behind all outward appearances or manifestations, there must always be a Substantial Reality. This is the Law."

"THAT which is the Fundamental Truth—the Substantial Reality—is beyond true naming, but the Wise Men/Women call it THE ALL."

"In its Essence, THE ALL is UNKNOWABLE.'

"But, the report of Reason must be hospitably received, and treated with respect.

"The principles of Truth are Seven; he (she) who knows these, understandingly, possesses the Magic Key before whose touch, all of the Doors of the Temple fly open."

"Matter cannot manifest Life or Mind, and as Life and Mind are manifested in the Universe, THE ALL cannot be matter, for *nothing rises higher than its own source*—nothing is ever manifested in an effect that is not in the cause—nothing is evolved as a consequent that is not involved as antecedent. Matter is merely "interrupted energy or force," that is, energy or force at a low rate of vibration."

"Death is not real, even in the relative sense—it is but Birth to a new life, and you shall go on, and on, and on, to higher and still higher planes of life, for aeons upon aeons of time.

"You are dwelling in the Infinite Mind of THE ALL, and your possibilities and opportunities are infinite, both in time and space. At the end of the grand cycle of aeons, when The ALL shall draw back into itself all of its creations, you will go gladly, for you will then be able to know the Whole Truth of being At One with THE ALL. And in the meantime, rest calm and serene—you are safe and protected by the infinite power of the FATHER-MOTHER MIND."

"The Universe is Mental—held in the Mind of THE ALL." And the all is Spirit! Spirit is energy. Matter is energy. Spirit and matter are one. Spirit and matter are energy. Consciousness and energy create the nature of reality!

2. THE PRINCIPLE OF CORRESPONDENCE

"As above, so below; as below, so above."

"The Universe may be divided into three great classes of phenomena known as the Three Great Planes. I. The Great Physical Plane. II. The Great Mental Plane. III. The Great Spiritual Plane. A plane is not a place nor an ordinary dimension of space and is yet more than a state or condition."

"The Great Physical Plane" has Seven Minor Planes:

1. The Plane of Matter (A)—Solids, liquids, gases.
2. The Plane of Matter (B)—Radiant matter
3. The Plane of Matter (C)—Subtle and tenuous
4. The Plane of Ethereal Substance—Medium of transmission of waves of energy such as light, heat, electricity
5. The Plane of Energy (A)—Seven subplanes of Light, heat, electricity, magnetism, Attraction (gravity, cohesion, chemical affinity) and two others not classified but used for scientific experiments.
6. The Plane of Energy (B)—Seven subplanes of Nature's finer forces used manifestation of mental phenomena.
7. The Plane of Energy (C)—Divine Power—bearing many of the characteristics of "life" but not recognized by the minds of men (women) of ordinary development.

"The Great Mental Plane" has Seven Minor Planes which have Seven Subplanes each:

1. The Plane of Mineral Mind
2. The Plane of Elemental Mind (A)
3. The Plane of Plant Mind
4. The Plane of Elemental Mind (B)
5. The Plane of Animal Mind
6. The Plane of Elemental Mind (C)
7. The Plane of Human Mind

The above elementary planes bear the same relation to the planes of mineral, plant, animal and human mentality and Life that the black keys on the piano do the white keys. The white keys are sufficient to produce music, but there are certain scales, melodies and harmonies in which the black keys play their part, and in which their presence is necessary.

The Great Spirtual Plane. What shall we say? It is difficult to explain these higher states of Being, Life and Mind to minds as yet unable to grasp the higher subdivisions of the Plane of Human Mind. How is light described to a man born blind? How sugar, to a man who has never tasted anything sweet? How harmony, to one born deaf? Difficult, but we must do it regardless.

The Seven Minor Planes of the Great Spiritual Plane (each minor plane also having seven subdivisions) comprise Beings possessing Life, Mind and Form as far above that of the man and woman of today as the latter is above the earthworm, mineral or even certain forms of Energy and Matter. The Life of these Beings so far transcends ours that we cannot *think* of the details in the same way. They appear to be clothed in pure energy—pure light beings.

On the Seven Minor Planes of the Great Spiritual Plane, we have Angels, archangels, Masters, Adepts, the great hierarchies of the Angelic Hosts and above them all, "The Gods," so high in the scale of Being as to only be called "Divine." An yet, they take the greates interest in the affairs of the Universe and of Man. These unseen divinities extend their influence freely and powerfully in the process of Evolution and Cosmic Progress. Their occasional intervention and assistance in human affairs have led to the many legends, beliefs, religions and traditions of the race—past and present. They have superimposed their *knowledge* and *power* upon the world, again and again, all under the Universal Laws of **The ALL, ALL IS MIND.** Their plane, however, is below that of **Absolute Spirit.**

Absolute Spirit as used by the Hermeticists means "living Power," "Animated Force," "Inner Essence," "Essence of Life." It must *not* be confused with the meanings commonly associated with "religious, ecclesiastical, spiritual, ethereal, holy, etc., etc." To those who *know*, the word **Spirit** is used in the sense of "The Animating Principle," carrying with it the idea of *Power, Living Energy, Mystic Force,* ect. This *power*, this *animating force* is neutral and may be employed for good as well as evil ends in accordance with the **Principles of Polarity**, a fact recognized by the majority of religions in their conceptions of Satan, Beelzebub, the Devil, Lucifer, Fallen Angel, etc. So the *energy* and *animating spirit* impacts the world based on the *intention* of the user of that energy and the *attention and desire* paid to the vision of the holder of the *intention.* The results will be whatever they are according to this *intention.*

Should anyone *misuse* these high spiritual powers their fate is litteraly *in their hands.* As the swing of the pendulum of **Rhythm** will inevitably swing them back to the furthest extreme of material existence from which point they must retrace their steps toward Spirit and toward consciousness and enlightenment along the weary rounds of the loose gravel on The Path until they *get it*! They carry with them the torture of a lingering memory of the heights from which they fell owing to their misuse of their spiritual powers and the harm or evil their actions wrought. Put another way, what goes around *does* indeed come around. Each of us reaps what we sow—*not* what the other person does. *That* is *their* challenge.

Even so, each soul will be provided an opportunity to return and they will make the choice to do so in order to perfect their capacity to *know who they are* and use thier powers for the good of their Selfs and all mankind . . . if they so choose.

This information should provide pause for the *thinking bitch*. After all, she is in control of *her* powers to *think, choose, perceive, create* and *act.* Every word out of *her* mouth sends vibrations into the

Universe. Will they be thoughtful, humorous, honest and interesting, or will they be words that diminish her spirit and identify her as one of the walking unconscious on this earth?

Such "reality" is embodied in the **Principle of Correspondence,** which embodies the truth "As Above so Below, as Below, so Above." This principle is of universal application and manifestation on the material, mental and spiritual planes of the Universe. It is a Universal Law and is one of the most important mental instruments by which women pry inside the obstacles which hide the Unknown from view by reasoning intelligently from the Known to the Unknown.

All of the Seven Hermetic Principles are in full operation on **all** of the many planes, physical, mental and spiritual. The **Principle of Mental Substance** applies to **all** the planes for all are held in the **Mind of The ALL.** The **Principle of Correspondence** manifests in **all** for there is a correspondence, harmony and agreement between the several planes. The **Principle of Vibration** manifests on **all** planes; in fact, the very differences that make the planes arise come from Vibration. The **Principle of Polarity** manifests on each plane, the extremes of the Poles being apparently opposite and contradictory but of the **same** nature. The **Princile of Rhythm** manifests on each plane, the movement of the phenomena having its *ebb and flow,* rise and flow, incoming and outgoing. The **Principle of Cause and Effect** manifests on each plane, every effect having its cause and every cause having its effect. The **Principle of Gender** manifests on each plane, the **Creative Energy** being always manifest and operating along the lines of its **Masculine and Feminine Aspects.**

"As Above so Below; as Below so Above. As Without so Within; as is Great, so is Small. All is All." This centuries-old Hermetic axiom embodies one of the great principles of Universal phenomena, the **Principle of Correspondence.**

3. THE PRINCIPLE OF VIBRATION

"Nothing rests; everything moves; everything vibrates."

"'Not only is everything in constant movement and vibration, but the 'differences' between the various manifestations of the universal power are due entirely to the varying rate and mode of vibrations. Not only this, but even THE ALL, in itself, manifests a constant vibration of such an infinite degree of intensity and rapid motion that it may be practically considered at rest. . . . Even on the physical plane, a rapidly moving object (such as a revolving wheel) seems to be at rest.

"Modern science has proven that all that we call Matter and Energy are but 'modes of vibratory motion." Some thinkers hold that the phenomena of Mind are likewise modes of vibration or motion. (Thoughts *are* things!)"

"In the first place, science teaches that all matter manifests, in some degree, the vibrations arising from temperature or heat. Be an object cold or hot—both being but degrees of the same things—it manifests certain heat vibrations and in that sense is in motion and vibration. Then all particles of matter are in circular movement from electrons to suns. The planets revolve around suns and many of them turn on their axes. The suns move around greater central points and these. . . move around still greater and so on, ad infinitum.

"Light, Heat, Magnetism and Electricity are but forms of vibratory motion connected in some way with, and probably emanating from, the Ether. The Universal Ether is postulated to be but a higher manifestation of that which is erroneously called matter—that is to say Matter at a higher degree of vibration is called "the Ethereal Substance," and serves as a medium of transmission of waves of vibratory energy—such as heat, light, electricity, magnetism, etc. Ether is also a connecting link between the forms of vibratory energy known as 'matter' on the one hand and 'Energy or Force' on the other. It also manifests a degree of vibration, in rate and mode, entirely its own.

"All manifestations of thought, emotion, reason, will or desire or any mental state or condition are accompanied by vibrations, a portion of which are thrown off and which tend to affect the minds of other persons by 'induction.' This is the principle which produces the phenomena of telepathy, mental influence, and other forms of action and power of mind over mind.

"Every thought, emotion, or mental state has its corresponding rate and mode of vibration.

By an effort of the will of the person, or of other persons, these mental states may be reproduced just as a musical tone may be reproduced by causing an instrument to vibrate at a certain rate—just as color may be reproduced in the same way. By a knowledge of the Principle of Vibration, as applied to Mental Phenomena, one may polarize his (her) mind at any degree he (she) wishes, thus gaining a perfect control over his (her) mental states, moods, etc. In the same way he (she) may affect the minds of others, producing the desired mental states in them.

4. THE PRINCIPLE OF POLARITY

"Everything is Dual; everything has poles; everything has its pair of opposites; like and unlike are the same; opposites are identical in nature but different in degree; extremes meet; all truths are but half-truths; all paradoxes may be reconciled."

"All manifested things have 'two sides;' 'two aspects;' 'two poles;' a 'pair of opposites,' with manifold degree between the extremes. This principle explains old paradoxes that have perplexed the mind of men (women)."

"The difference between things seemingly diametrically opposed to each other is merely a matter of degree."

'Spirit and Matter are but the two poles of the same thing, the intermediate planes being merely degrees of vibration. They show that THE ALL and THE MANY are the same, the difference being merely a matter of degree of Mental Manifestation.

"Thus the LAW and Laws are the two opposite poles of one thing. PRINCIPLE and Principles, Infinite Mind and finite minds.

"Things belonging to different classes cannot be transmuted into each other, but things of the same class may be changed, that is may have their polarity changed. Thus, Love never becomes East or West or Red or Violet, but it may and often does turn into Hate. Likewise, Hate may be transformed into Love, by changing its polarity. Courage may be transmuted into Fear and the reverse. Hard things may be rendered Soft. Dull things become Sharp. Hot things become Cold. The transmutation always occurs between things of the same kind but of different degrees . . . a Fearful man by raising his mental vibrations along the line of Fear-Courage can be filled with the highest degree of Courage and Fearlessness. . . . A Slothful man may change him Self into an active, energetic individual by polarizing along the lines of the desired quality. The change is not in the nature of the transmutation of one thing into another thing entirely different, but is merely a change of degree in the same things, a vastly important difference.

Another person may mentally influence others through Mental Induction—the communication of a certain mental state to another person so that his polarity in that class of mental states (if he or she so desires) can be changed. (Note: hypnotherapy, for example).

5. THE PRINCIPLE OF RHYTHM

"Everything flows, out and in; everything has its tides; all things rise and fall; the pendulum-swing manifests in everything; the measure of the swing to the right is the measure of the swing to the left; rhythm compensates."

"In everything there is manifested a measured motion; a to-and-from movement; a flow and inflow; a swing forward and backward; a pendulum-like movement; a tide-like ebb and flow; a high tide and a low tide; between the two poles these all manifest on the physical, mental and spiritual planes."

"Rhythm is closely connected to Polarity. Rhythm manifests between the two poles established by the Principle of Polarity. The pendulum swings to the extreme poles very rarely; in fact, it is difficult to establish the extreme polar opposites in the majority of cases. But the swing is ever 'towards' first one pole and then the other."

"There is always an action and reaction; an advance and a retreat; a rising and a sinking; manifested in all of the airs and phenomena of the Universe. Suns, worlds, men, animals plants, minerals forces, energy, mind and matter, yes, even Spirit manifests this Principle. The Principle manifests in the creation and destruction of worlds; in the rise and fall of nations; in the life history of all things and finally in the mental states of Man (Woman)."

"Beginning with the manifestations of Spirit—of THE ALL—it will be noticed that there is ever the Outpouring and the Indrawing; and the Outbreathing and the Inbreathing. Universes are created to reach their extreme low point of materiality and then begin their upward swing. Suns spring into being and then their height of power being reached, the process of retrogression begins, and after aeons they become dead masses of matter, awaiting another impulse which starts again their inner energies into activity and a new solar life cycle is begun.

"And thus it is with all the worlds; they are born, grow and die, only to be reborn.

'All things of shape and form swing from action to reaction; birth to death; from activity to inactivity—and then back again. Thus it is with all living things—they are born, grow and die and then are reborn. So it is with all great movements, philosophies, creeds, fashions, governments, nations and all else—birth, growth, maturity, decadence, death—and then new birth. Night follows day and day night. The swing of the pendulum is ever in evidence.

The Principle of Rhythm is well understood by modern science as a universal law as applied to material things. But the principle also applies to the mental activities of Man (Woman) and that accounts for the bewildering succession of moods, feelings and other annoying and perplexing changes we notice in our Selfs.

"A Hermetic Master or advanced student polarizes him Self (her Self) at the desired pole and by a process of "refusing" to participate in the backward swing of the pendulum or by denying its influence over him (her), stands firm in the polarized position and allows the mental pendulum to swing back along the unconscious plane. All individuals who have attained a degree of self-mastery accomplish and refuse to allow their moods and negative mental states to affect them. This is done by applying the Law of Neutralization.

An understanding of the working of this Principle will give one the key to the mastery of these rhythmic swings of feeling and enable him (her) to know him Self (her Self) better and to avoid being carried away by the inflows and outflows. The Will is superior to the conscious manifestation of this principle but the principle itself can never be destroyed. The pendulum ever swings but we may escape being carried along with it.

The Law of Compensation is that the swing in one direction determines the swing in the opposite direction or pole. The one balances or counterbalances the other. On the physical plane examples are: the tides follow this law. The seasons balance each other in the same way. One generally 'pays the price' of anything he (she) possesses or lacks.

If he has one thing, he lacks another—the balance is struck. No one can "keep his penny and have the bite of cake" at the same time. The things that one gains are always paid for by the things that one loses. The Law of Compensation is ever in operation, striving to balance and counterbalance, and always succeeding in time, even though several lives may be required for the return swing of the Pendulum of Rhythm.

6. THE PRINCIPLE OF CAUSE AND EFFECT

"Every Cause has its Effect; every Effect has its Cause; everything happens according to Law; Chance is but a name for Law not recognized; there are many planes of causation, but nothing escapes the Law."

Law pervades the Universe. Nothing happens by Chance. Chance is merely a term indicating cause existing but not recognized or perceived. Phenomena are continuous, without break or exception.

This principle underlies all scientific thought, ancient and modern and was enunciated by the Hermetic teachers in the earliest days.

There is no such thing as pure chance. Webster defines chance as: "A supposed agent or mode of activity other than a force; law or purpose; the operation or activity of such agent; the supposed effect of such a agent; a happening; fortuity; casualty; etc."

A little "consideration" will indicate that no such agent as "Chance" in the sense of something outside of Law—something outside of Cause and Effect—exists. How could there be something acting in the phenomenal universe independent of the laws, order and continuity of the latter? We can imagine nothing outside THE ALL being outside the LAW because THE ALL *is* the LAW in itself. There is no room in the universe for something outside of and independent of LAW. The existence of such a Something would render all Natural Laws ineffective and plunge the universe into chaotic disorder and lawlessness."

"There is a continuity between all events *precedent, consequent* and *subsequent*. There is a relation existing between everything that has gone before and everything that follows.

7. THE PRINCIPLE OF GENDER

"Gender is in everything; everything has its Masculine and Feminine Principle; Gender manifests on all planes."

"Gender" is derived from the Latin root that means "to beget; to procreate; to generate; to create and to produce." As used in the Hermetic sense, gender and sex are not the same. Sex refers to the physical distinction between male and female living things and is merely a manifestation of Gender on the Great Physical Plane of organic life.

"The office of Gender is solely that of creating, producing, generating, etc. and its manifestations are visible on every plane of phenomena.(Note: *Yin/Yang*)

There is a distinct manifestation of the Principle of Gender among the atoms, ions, electrons which constitute the basis of Matter. The formation of the atom, for example, is really due to the clustering of negative electrons around a positive one—the positive seeming to exert a certain influence upon the negative, causing the latter to assume certain combinations and thus "create" or "generate" an atom. This is in line with the most ancient Hermetic teaching which have always identified the Masculine principle of Gender with the "positive" and the Feminine with the "negative" poles of electricity.

The negative pole of the battery, for example, is really the pole in and by which the generation or production of new forms and energies is manifested. There is nothing "negative" about it. This is the Mother Principle of Electrical Phenomena and of the finest forms of matter as yet known to science. *This feminine energy is really the pole of activity. It actively seeks union with masculine energy, being urged in that direction by the natural impulse to create new forms of matter or energy. For example, feminine particles vibrate rapidly under the influence of the masculine energy and cycle rapidly around the latter. The result is the birth of a new atom. This new atom is really composed of a union of the masculine and feminine electrons but when the union is formed the atom is a separate thing, having certain properties but no longer manifesting the property of free electricity. The process of detachment or separation of the feminine electrons is called "ionization". The electrons are the most active workers in Nature's field.*

Arising from their unions or combinations manifest the varied phenomena of light, heat, electricity, magnetism, attraction, repulsion, chemical affinity and the reverse and similar phenomena. All this arises from the operation of the Principle of Gender on the Plane of Energy.

The part of the Masculine principle is that of directing a certain inherent energy toward the Feminine principle and thus starting into activity the creative processes. But the Feminine principle is the one always doing the active creative work and this is so on all planes. And yet, each principle is incapable of operative energy without the assistance of the other. In some forms of life, the two principles are combined in one organism. In fact, everything in the organic world manifests both genders. *There is always the Masculine present in the Feminine form and the Feminine present in the Masculine form.*

[Crystals are said to have a "sex" life (masculine and feminine energy) and the chips we have in computers bear this out. The tiniest part (hologram) reflects the capabilities of the whole. So very, very small crystals and minerals can carry the same or more information formerly thought only large ones could hold.]

The Principle of Gender is in constant operation in the field of inorganic matter and in the field of Energy or Force. Electricity is regarded as the "something" into which all other forms of energy seem to melt or dissolve." The "Electrical Theory of the Universe" is generally accepted. It follows that if we are able to discover in the phenomena of electricity—even at the root and source of its manifestations—a clear and unmistakable evidence of the presence of Gender and its activities we are justified in asking you to believe that science at last has offered proofs of the existence in all universal phenomena of that great Principle of Gender.

"Attraction and repulsion," of the atoms; chemical affinity; the "loves and hates" of the atomic particles; the attraction and cohesion between molecules of matter—all are manifestations of the Gender Principle. Gravity is another expression of the principle and operates in the direction of attracting the Masculine to the Feminine energies and vice versa. Submit all physical phenomena and you will see the principle in evidence.

8. THE PRINCIPLE OF MENTAL GENDER

The **"underlying idea"** of Gender on the Mental Plane is this:

"The Masculine principle of the Mind corresponds to the Objective Mind (**the Conscious Mind**). The Feminine principle corresponds to the Subjective Mind (**the Subconscious Mind**). [The third "entity" of the Mind is the **"Superconscious Mind"**—the Self within.]

The I AM, who is the Self within also contains the "I" and the "me". The "me" is that part of me known as the personality or the Self known to self and others. The mask is what I project into my environment. This "me" has feelings, tastes, likes, dislikes, habits peculiar ties, characteristics, needs, wants and values. All of this "me" is subject to the Principles of Rhythm, Compensation, and Polarity which take "me" from one extreme of feeling to another. This "me" has certain knowledge gathered together from many sources e.g., family, society, religion, government, etc., thus forming a part of this "me" of man. Some of us are conscious only of our bodies and physical appetites. This is where we "live." A writer has humorously said that "men (women) consist of three things: soul, body and clothes!" These "clothes conscious" people would lose their personality if divested of their clothing upon the occasion of a shipwreck.

As man (woman) rises on the scale of consciousness, however, s/he is able to disentangle the "me" from his idea of body and to think of the body as "belonging to" the mental part of him (her). The internal states are not identical with him Self but are simply "things" produced by some part of his mentality and existing within him—of him, in him but still "not" him Self. He is able to change his internal states of feelings by an effort of will and he can produce a feeling or state of an exactly opposite nature in the same way and yet the same "Me" exists. After a while he is able to set aside these various mental states, emotions, feelings, habits, qualities, characteristics and other personal mental belongings—set them aside in the "not Me."

After this laying aside process is accomplished, one will find him Self (her Self) in conscious possession of a "Self" which is the "I"— [the individual Self]. It reports to the consciousness as "Me"with latent powers of creation and generation of mental progeny of all sorts and kinds. Its powers of creative energy are felt to be enormous. It is conscious that it receives some form of energy from its "I" companion orelse from some other "I" [the Mind/Soul] and is able to bring into being its mental creations. There is Something that is able to will that the "Me" act, along certain creative lines and which is able to "stand aside and witness" (SAW) the mental creation as well as the operation of the "Me's"mental creation. This part of him Self (her Self) is his/her "I."

The "I" represents the aspect of Being; the "Me" the aspect of Becoming. *The "I" is the Masculine principle and the "Me" is the Feminine priciple at work.* These aspects of Mind—the Masculine and Feminine principles—considered in connection with mental and psychic phenomena give the **Master Key** to the still dimly lit regions of mental operation and manifestation. Mental Gender provides the *"underlying idea"* and truth to the whole field of psychology and disciplines utilizing mental influence. [Indeed, to communications in all of its phases and technological projections.]

Remember that the tendency of the Feminine energy is always in the direction of *receiving impressions* and the tendency of the Masculine energy is always in the direction of *giving out or expressing.* The Feminine principle has a much more varied field of operation than the Masculine principle. *Feminine energy conducts the work of generating new thoughts, concepts, ideas, including the work of the "Will" in its varied phases. Yet, without the active aid of the Will of the Masculine energy, the Feminine energy is apt to rest content with generating mental images which are the result of impressions received from outside instead of producing original mental creations.*

Persons who give continued attention and thought [focus] to a subject actively employ *both* of the mental principles—the Feminine in the work of active mental generation and the Masculine Will in the stimulation and energizing the creative portion of the Mind. The majority of people [men *and* women] employ the Masculine principle but only a few are not content to live according to the thoughts and ideas instilled into the "Me" *from* the "I" of other minds (family, school, society, religion, etc.)

An idea lodged in the mind of another person grows and develops and in time is regarded as the rightful mental offspring of the individual, whereas *in reality* it is like the cuckoo egg placed in the sparrow's net where it destroys the rightful offspring and makes itself at home [Read the section on *The Grand Inquisitor* in Fyodor Dostoyevsky's **The Brothers Karamazov.**]

[The object of knowledge is to use it for your *individual* growth, walk on your own two feet, think your *own* thoughts and once having done *that*, share it with others. First, however, you must *use* knowledge and *know* that it works.]

The object is for the Masculine and Feminine principles to coordinate and act harmoniously in conjunction with each other. Keep in mind that it is the *subconscious mind* that makes the impression on the *conscious mind* and that the *conscious mind* either *accepts, rejects* and/or *reprograms* the *subconscious mind* in accordance with his/her *"awakeness"* to the higher principles of natural law and understanding of his/her higher nature.

The energizing of the Feminine principle by the vibratory energy of the Masculine principle in accordance with universal laws of nature and the natural world affords countless analogies whereby the principle may be understood. Finally, the very creation of the Universe follows the same law and that in *all* creative manifestations upon the planes of the spiritual, mental and physical, there is *always* in operation the princple of Gender—*"As above so below, as below, so above. As without, so within; as is great, so is small. All is All."*

In this principle lies the *secret* of personal magnetism, personal influence, fascination, etc. As well as the phenomena generally classified under the name of Hypnotism [visualisation, guided imagery, the relaxation response, meditation, hypnotherapy]. This Principle of Mental Gender and Gender in general is also the *"underlying idea"* behind healing touch, reflexology, massage, accupuncture, accupressure, biofeedback, chiropractic and all of the healing arts, including medicine, but doctors are not *taught* about this *"underlying idea."*

I want to thank all of the ancients and the Hermeticists and others whose knowledge is now capable of use in a total framework that makes sense because of the technology that brings it all together via communications and its supporting media of all types.

This chapter is one of the most important in the book. It makes the case for why we have the power to change our lives and decide our destinies: *". . . in the image of God he created him,* **male and female** *he created* **them.** *(Genesis 1:26-27)*

Affirm daily the following:

ASHLEY MAXIMS

---

1. **My thoughts control my life.**
2. **My decisions decide my destiny.**
3. **My perception of reality *is* my reality until new information changes *my* perception.**
4. **I create my own reality . Make it what I *truly* want.**
5. **I am *never* late for my appointment with destiny.**

Let me share a biblical footnote that puts forth this *"underlying idea"* of universal reality in different but nontheless very strong form. This saying, too, has been misinterpreted in that its meaning in relation to you and I, the *individual,* and has been totally misused to give primacy to the race and society. But keep in mind that races of people and societies are made up of individuals!

Matthew 18; 18-19
I tell you the truth, whatever you bind on earth will be bound in heaven, and whatever you loose on earth will be loosed in heaven.

Again, I tell you that if two of you on earth agree about anything you ask for, it will be done for them by my Father in heaven. For where two or three come together in my name, there am I with them.

My explanations are in parentheses.

TRANSLATED:

I tell you the truth (*divine ideas, intuition, impulses and impressions),* whatever you bind on earth (*visualize as already done in your body/environment*) will be bound in heaven (*done/completed in my Mind)* and whatever you loose on earth (*let go of—like negatives in your life*) will be loosed in heaven (*let go in my Mind—repolarized to the positive*).

Again, I tell you that if two of you on earth agree about anything (*Your masculine and feminine energies work harmoniously and consciously together to bind what you desire. "Agree" refers to every aspect of your body's systems, all of which are ordered with the Principle of Gender in Mind! So to have Health, two or three of your critical internal organs must be working together—Heart, lungs, liver, pancreas, thyroid, pituitary, pineal, bladder,—if two or more of these aren't working **together**, then you're either on artificial support or you're dead!*) you ask for, it will be done for them by my Father (*Thoughts*) in heaven (*my Mind/Soul*). For where two or three come together in my name **[SpiritMindEmotionsBody (SMEB)]**, there am **I** with **them**. (**I** refers to the *individual* **God** Self, whose energy pervades all of the Universe and permeates every part of every aspect of the Universe. It also refers to each of us as microcosms. In the physical body, **them** refers to our nervous systems specifically and **all** of the organs and systems directed by them through the transmissions from the brain generally.

Think here of two or three being *anything* in the Universe. Remember that there can be **no** physical figure of *any kind* until **three** lines are put together and then you get the triangle! *You* as an individual with your own thoughts, ideas, wishes, desires, using your *masculine* and *feminine* energies (two energies) *in harmony with* your own mind to **create!** People, in community with one another, represent "one body" of thought, ideas, etc. and thus as "*one body* of people" correspond to what is intended in this passage—an *individual reference*. The message is for you and me as *individuals*. We then join with other **bitches** to make up a "community." Let her who has ears to hear, *hear*. Eyes to see, *see*.

And so *it is!*

STEP EIGHT

Sexuality, Death, Rebirth and Transformation

Desire creates power!

Vikki and Bob going Mardi Gras formal—1992

Bitchhood 801
Self-Creation: I *Desire*, Therefore I Am.

The Original Sin is Ignorance

Intolerance is ignorance. Ignorance is fear matured. I will share how those statements impacted my life in my journey into **BITCHHood**. Just remember this: Those who choose to be and remain ignorant are also hiding behind their fear of *knowing,* for *knowing* leads you to questions, new information, acceptance of responsibility, accountability and *growth!*

By now you understand that energy is simply energy and **all** energy is creative, even energy that is initially destructive, as in storms like hurricanes, tornados. Why? Destruction paves the way for new beginnings, physically, emotionally, mentally and spiritually. Energy simply **is,** doing what it does naturally. In women and men, however, that energy can be focused and directed. How it is consciously or unconsciously applied actually makes the difference in its use in our daily lives. Energy is used for many things, **including sex.** Sex is seen by most members of society as the most potent form of energy because it is displayed and talked about all of the time by most individuals who do not understand its role as "simply energy."

Let me briefly note the obsession of American media with the Clinton scandal, hardly an impeachable offense and hardly a surprise for any man in office or in power. The puritanical, "patented patriarchal prurient patoots" sitting in judgment of the President can dress the situation up in constitutional, moral and even religious terms if they want, but the bottom line is that they are seeking to steal the presidency in a bloodless coup while ignoring the people's desires because they know not many people will stand up and say that sex, no matter what form it takes or what is done, isn't a crime between consenting adults. It's simply directed energy used for a purpose, any purpose, and—in this case the pleasure of the President and Ms. Lewinsky. That this woman is responsible for her actions is absolutely obvious. That she was entranced with power and "getting her knee pads" is also obvious. That she was aware of the President's weakness and his proneness to sexual challenge is also obvious. That she was **effectively misused** by Linda Tripp, Kenneth Starr and the myriad others in the background of this obvious conspiracy is pretty clear to me, if not to the American public on the whole. It is a frightening thing to watch a bloodless coup attempt in a country purporting to be a democracy. We are watching the death of "supposed moral integrity" in leadership, **not** in the President alone, but in the congress and in the people who have decided sex is a high crime and misdemeanor. I could see this whole charade happening if the President had engaged in sex with an Iranian agent, or if he had done the things Ronald Reagan or John F. Kennedy did while in office, or even if he had personally engaged in espionage of some sort and gotten caught. But oral sex in the White House? Give me a break. High crime and misdemeanor? Not hardly!

I would say Bill Clinton has one hell of a healthy libido not surprising in a person of power, **and** I would say that he is also a highly integrated human being with his feminine and masculine energies nicely balanced and in *his* control. That is why he is so appealing to both men *and* women. He is strong when he must be; caring and sincerely nurturing when the situation calls for it. He is loving and not afraid to expound on his emotions on television. And yet, he is also human and full of all the strengths, weaknesses, fears and possibilities of all of us. He is everyman/everywoman and that is why I believe the "patented patriarchal prurient patoots" are afraid of his power. He is personally attractive and handsome, bright as hell and one of the finest politicians we've had. It is that very **energy** that he exudes that makes him **all** of these things. I have never spoken with him personally but his *use* of his energy is dynamic and palpable. Pay attention. Is he a human being? If so, he will make errors of judgment. He did. About sex and about other things as humans are prone to do. I consider the real high crime and misdemeanor the blatant attempt at a bloodless coup by the Republican Party.

To all those "patented patriarchal prurient patoots" I say, "what goes around comes around. You reap what you sow. It's the law."

In the end, it is the **conscious** use of this energy, focusing it where you want to achieve success, that makes the difference in those who make it and those who don't. Sexual energy is *raw power*. It is *desire* connected to *intent*. It is absolutely *neutral*. The moral statements occur as a result of the *intent and desire* of the individuals *using* the energy, or more to the point, afraid of its use.

This is the time of comeuppance for our nation with regard to what we consider character in our leaders. Books are written on leadership and students read about what it takes to be a leader. Yet, I have never read a strong exposition on the subject most important to leadership of any kind at any level: **Know thy Self** and be able to answer the question honestly, **Who am I?** and be willing to share that data *publicly*.

I have yet to meet a man over 40 who will honestly self-disclose on the subject of sex and who has not engaged in sex outside of marriage, or a relationship or whatever. Some sneak out on trips to prostitutes or pick up pretty young things at the bars of the hotels they stay in when they travel and do all manner of things, they think, are being done in secret. But you can hide from people "out there" but you can't hide from your own subconscious and sooner or later the doors to truth open and expose you for what you have done. That doesn't make you a bad person or even a horrible individual—just a dishonest, misguided individual who is seeking something outside that is *truly* inside. And those who do the finger pointing are those who have the most to hide and the most to fear from exposure and usually the most lively fantasies of things they wish they had done, and didn't.

The art of self-disclosure is the most cleansing, though often painful, experience one can have. It takes you out of the jail cell of your mind and reprograms your subconscious with regard to judging other people's morals and behavior. It takes you out of the power grips of people who like to "get something on you." and "hold something over your head." Self-knowledge and self-disclosure totally remove the sword of Damocles from over your head. People who have learned this lesson say "There but for the grace of God, go I, and *mean* it, because their power is in *their* hands.

Some of the most outstanding people I know would not be able to pass the "have-you-ever-fucked-someone-besides-your-wife-or-husband" test. Yes. Women are vulnerable here, too. After all, who are the men "doing it" with? Sheep? Are these people still outstanding in their persons? You bet! Do they still have the right to share their talents with their organizations and other people? You bet! Does it matter if that person does not pass "our" test of morality? Well, maybe it does if we're closed minded and afraid of the truth of our society and the people in it. The finger-pointing crowd will always be part of the "patented patriarchal prurient patoots" that want to say that we some-how live in an ideal world while all of us know there isn't an "ideal" for humanity. Each human being is a *unique individual* and each soul's blueprint is written just for him or her. So, tell me now, who are you or I to judge? Can I have permission to get into your psycholog-ical closet and "see" what's going on? Only if I'm your therapist, otherwise a resounding "no!". So how can a congressman on the Judiciary Committee know, much less say on TV that he knows what is in the President's head because he doesn't and he can't. How can a media anchor speculate on what's in a child's head who shoots up a school or a disgruntled employee who shoots up a post office? Can't be done but people make unwarranted attempts. These individuals lived their "troubles" in the depths of their minds and that's where it all takes place anyway. In such cases. What we see is the act in mani-festation, not the *act being formulated*. The pattern has already been set *in their minds*. The behavior reflects the state of that individuals' perceptions of their reality, not ours. And therein lies the difference. Who are we to judge?

Sigmund Freud delved deeply into this sexual energy and all psy-chologists and psychiatrists since him understand and are aware of the power of that energy called our *libido,* the term describing sexual desire and the energy derived from "primitive" impulses and raging hormones! In psychoanalysis, *libido* refers to the motive power of the sex life and, in Freudian terms, to psychic energy in general.[1]

On the other hand, back to **sex**—a most powerful use of this energy and more often than not misdirected. On the street and in uninformed as well as educated households it is termed "doing it," "fuckin'," "friggin'." "getting laid" "pussy pokin'," "making out" "screwin' and screwing" and probably a thousand other terms, depending on culture. *Feel* the load of those words! Amazing, isn't it. No wonder *language drives behavior!* Some of those words make you flinch. I can *feel* it. But there are other ways of looking at all of this. The attempt to categorize sex broadly and take it out of the realm of "creative energy use under the control of the individual" probably began with a scheme as far back as antiquity when the patri-archal system of power—those "patented patriarchal prurient patoots" began to notice that the mystery of bearing children was a power in women they didn't understand or have and so, feared. However, they sure loved "doing it" that eventually resulted in said pregnancy. So "doing it" became part of the "fun" of being male and the severe burden of being female. We are on our way out of this valley of death and the Millennium is a great turning point for feminine energy and its ascendance into the consciousness of both men and women. But let's not go there now.

In my early development as a **bitch, *with style* (bws)**, I can honestly say I was not taught **anything** about energy—**any** type of energy—and how to handle it in making the decisions that would ultimately direct my life. I have concluded that my parents, society, the church, government and business (though changing somewhat)—all conspire in their own ways to keep people, including moi, unconscious, infantilized and living in worry and doubt so that, for the most part, they will believe what the hear, do what they are told and generally fall into the cookie cutter of the world plan and fit into their slot without any questions asked. Or with little or no resistance. Ergo, the ultimate struggle is for each soul to eventually have a **breakdown** so that it can **break out** of its circle of control and experience a **breakthrough** of consciousness. Why? *To be in control of its own life!* In short, to *individually create its own reality* and *make it what it **truly** wants*. This is the road to **self-mastery** and it is a long, tough, potholed, narrow mountain road, believe me! But well worth the trek.

Psychologically it is so much easier to do what you're told and die early, to be reborn into the "round" to do it all again. But that is the route of the coward and he or she has to learn in one of those lives to face up to fear and reach down (in the gut/solar plexus) for courage. So, come on, let's some of us get it right this time, shall we? Or die in the process, which we are going to do *anyway!*

Circle of Life

I have concluded that the the four dominant uses of energy are for *health, wealth, love* and *perfect self-expression*. **Health**, my highest value, is the use of thought focused on supporting the miracle of the body and intentionally uniting with the universal life force, proper nutrition, exercise and use of vision and positive expectations; **wealth,** is the use of all the resources available to each of us based on our vision of our goals and future united again with the universal life force- including money but much, much more; **love** is focused emotion that energizes our desires, visions and goals and creates the power to **know** what is right for each of us individually, and **perfect self-expression** is the energy of creation that manifests through the vibrations generated when we focus our thoughts, intention, attention and actions, because *what we think is what we become and what we achieve.* "As a man thinketh, so is he in his heart," says the bible, and so *it is.* So, sex is **just** the use of energy for creating whatever we want in life, including another human life, **if we so desire.**

Churches, religions, counselors, psychologists and psychiatrists do understand how important this energy use is. They have been reluctant to share this information with you because to do so is to provide you with one of the most powerful keys to the kingdom, knowledge, which will permit you to heal all aspects of your own life and use this power as *you* see fit—for good or ill—according to *your* own definition and perspective. You reap what *you* sow and that is *your* responsibility. When you have this **key**—knowledge—you will then have a cup that is full to running over rather than one that is either empty or half full. You will be able to decide how to use *your* energy to help your Self and others and to make a difference in the world around *you. Or not.* Again, your responsibility, your accountability, your choice!

When you misuse this power of knowledge and place the key in the wrong-for-you doors, you will pay for your misuse now—in this life—or later, in the next. It is this **knowing** that makes reincarnation the next big collective consciousness breakthrough in the Western world. It is slowly becoming a part of the understanding of many individuals who are seekers on the path, but the churches are not opening up their vaults of knowledge actively because their dogmas will be subject to strict, scholarly criticism, attack and review as well as the mistrust of the populace. Changes in thinking will become mandatory not just a matter of choice if they wish to survive into the next millennium. The Eastern world already knows about reincarnation. Those souls reincarnated into this time understand for the most part *why* they are here. The Western world is still looking for its soul and has yet to accept what is very important in relating to their spiritual energy and spiritual life.

Contemporary society has individuals whose desire for structure and conformity to dogma continue to rob them of their ability to think for their Selfs. Some of those individuals are represented by what is commonly referred to as The Christian Right, or The Right-Wing Groups in our country who are essentially fundamentalists and who take the biblical "word of God" as *literal* rather than beautiful literature and symbolical codes designed to be unlocked in time by the minds of those who think outside the box.

The effort to unlock the code of the bible is so strong and so pervasive that outside the fundamental and Christian Right true believers, there are many groups and many religions that have differing perspectives on what the bible actually means and what its words say to us at the millennium. The bible is undoubtedly one of the most dynamic, personal, psychological manuals ever written.

Early Days and Original Sin (Ignorance)

My early experiences with regard to sex as sex began in junior high school when my curiosity got the better of me and I lied to the town librarian about having a biology exam. Would she please unlock the room in the library where "such books" were kept so I could complete my assignment?

Of course, I had no assignment but I spent a lot of time at that library doing papers, reading and taking out books. I **love** books and reading. I also love dispelling ignorance and at that young age I understood I was ignorant of a process that was producing babies under my nose every 11 to 14 months. I simply did not understand "why" and my mother was reluctant to discuss it then or even when I was about to marry, already pregnant!

When my menses began, I clearly remember going to the bathroom, seeing spotting and calling my mother. She immediately went to her closet (which stayed locked), got out a box of Kotex, handed me a brand-new belt and told me how to put this all together. Her admonitions about staying clean and being careful not to spot my clothes were all I heard. After all this, I put on a pair of shorts and went out to play baseball with the boys! So much for learning at my mother's knees. The library did a much better job and I did not let on how much I knew, but the time came for me to look for someone to talk to. In the small town of Xenia, Ohio that limited my choices because my sense was that most of the women my mother's age were just like her on the subject of sex (mute) or on the other side of the pendulum, barflies and prostitutes.

Let me say for the record that my earliest desire, when looking through the slots of our third-floor porch railings of our apartment at 326 E. Church Street, was to run away. Even then, I felt that the "energy" of this little town was inhospitable, negative and devastating to my spirit, though I would not have described it in those terms then. It always felt like I was in a foreign place. I finally "ran away" when I found a way to help my first husband get a teaching job in San Diego. A recent return to Xenia to bury a brother confirmed my view that the energy is deadening to the spirit, my spirit particularly. Perhaps it works for some people, but I bet, if individuals were honest, they'd say they felt trapped by their own lassitude, friends, families, etc., etc. Oh, well, I feel it every time I approach the outskirts of the town when driving in from the airport in Dayton or Columbus. Ugh! Glad to see family. (Yes, some of *them* feel the negative energy also.) Glad to go!

When I could no longer hold my questions inside, I sought out a neighbor "around the corner" with whom I exchanged magazines and books. I have thanked God many nights for Martha for she was blunt, direct, explicit and loving. She told me what I needed to know and much more. We often met at the end of the day and she ultimately told me "take care of your Self. Learn to provide your own needs as well as your wants. If a man comes into your life, be sure you are in a position to handle paying your own way if the relationship doesn't work out. And most young marriages don't." Why? I wondered out loud. "Because you don't know nothing about **real** life," she said. "It's hard out there and most men don't mean you any good. The only person you can really count on is your

Self. Then, when a man knows he can't control everything about your life, you've got a fighting chance."

Wise words from a wise woman. Her experience? Early in her life she had been a prostitute and by the time I knew her was happily settled down and married. My problem was the type of information I was getting from books did not match my education at our Catholic school. Back then (late 40's and early 50's) my inquisitive, assertive nature was considered "forward, fast and out of place." I can remember clearly being told by my father that I was "too mouthy and too inquisitive." He came from the school that taught children should be seen and not heard. I just wasn't buying any of that but I was careful to avoid his wrath and to make my Self useful. What else can you do when you are the oldest of twelve?

I do recall, however, a time when my mother went shopping and left five of us with a babysitter, a young man who lived next door. I was seven years old and I recall him suggesting I "swing" on a door while he held me and put his hand up and rubbed my panties. I was both scared and fascinated and I never told my mother. It also never happened again because I steered clear of him—and for good reason. It occurred to me that I was old enough to do what *he* did, which was nothing, so I suggested that I babysit on occasion. Mouthy me, I got my Self another job that I was never to relinquish until I went to college!

After my "education" about my menses in my many conversations with Martha, I began to realize that either my father or mother (or both) were not able to "take care" to avoid pregnancy. I didn't know which. I did, however, hear my father argue with my mom, shouting at her for believing "those god damn priests, who never had chick nor child and had everything done for them." My mother was a devout convert to the Catholic Church who **did** believe everything the priests told her, including what **they** said about having babies. They told her they were gifts from God and that God would find a way to take care of them. They also told her having sex with my father was her duty and refusing was a mortal sin! Can you **imagine** her believing **that?** She **believed**, and every year from 1934 to 1946 we welcomed another "gift" from God for which my father taught at a college by day and worked at night as an orderly in a hospital to just pay the rent and buy milk and food. I didn't yet know or understand that my mother wasn't so different from women throughout the world **before** they began to think for their Selfs and take their own lives into their own hands, the church be damned! I have always wondered how those "nonsexually experienced" priests knew so much about marital relations? Also, how someone who would never have to care for a child could tell **me** how to do so? Or, how someone who had supposedly never held, kissed or been sexually involved with a woman could tell anyone how to handle intimate, personal relationships? They either **know** or they *lie!*

A woman who is in charge of her own life would have had none of it. No one would tell her how to run her life on any level. It would be her responsibility and hers alone. But that is what becoming a **bitch,** *with style* leads to: **A being in total control of her Self!**

Moving Along

I knew then things were not "right" and that there was nothing I could do but help out and pull more than my load of responsibility. I really don't recall a loving feeling in my home. No one ever got a bicycle, or had a birthday party (perhaps a cake for dinner with the family and that was it), nor were friends very welcome at our home (we've got enough mouths to feed!). To this day I compulsively get out of bed and make it up almost immediately because the chaos that would have ensued in a house with all those bodies if that were not the case (three bedrooms with bunk beds and one bathroom) would have been unbelievable. I am quite certain my early rising habit took form because of these conditions. I figured out I would be able to get to the bathroom first and have some peace of mind and take a bath before anyone else woke up. I also read books under my cover with a flashlight after my bath until everyone else began to stir. It was the beginning of my strange "clock" rhythms that persist to this day. In my mind, however, it was a way to make do with my home situation over which I had no control. I knew then I could only control "my space," meager though it was on the bottom of a bunk bed in a room with two such beds. The boys' room also had two double-deckers. By the time the last four children were old enough to each have a bed, I was gone off to college on a music scholarship and my sisters were beginning to look for ways to "escape" as well.

Beliefs, Attitudes and Values

Beliefs are what we accept regarding the existence of an object or concept, most especially those objects and concepts instilled in our minds by our parents, church, schools, and society. **Attitudes** are our evaluations of those concepts and objects and our projection of our beliefs and values into our environment. **Values** are those standards or criteria for our behavior and actions that justify in our own minds why we do what we do. **Values** are those motivators that support our current moral judgments of our Selfs and others and even the basis for comparing our Selfs with others.

We adjust our beliefs, attitudes and values based on our experiences. Our experiences, however, come to us as a result of our *own* perceptions of reality. When we are stimulated by either an external or internal impulse, we immediately test it against our personal internal value system, which is made up of all those beliefs, concepts and objects established by family, society, religion , education and our peer group. You know, those *shoulds, have to's, cannots, ought to's, better nots, you'll be sorry's*—all those impositions that have taken residence in our minds. Then we decide on the basis of our evaluation to believe our experience if it is congruent with those beliefs, attitudes and values or not to believe our experience. When our belief and experience are congruent, we accept our experience. When our belief and experience are in conflict, either our belief must change or our experience must be denied. Therein lies the type of conflict that leads to excessive stress, anger, neurotic behavior, depression and for the more enlightened, trips to the counselor or therapist.

ParentSpeak: Rules of the Road

The "official" ignorance based on my family's beliefs, attitudes and values affected everyone in our household in a negative way. I was certainly so affected until my first true "ah ha! occurred in a confessional at age 20!

My father was always working: a spiffy dresser for teaching; work clothes for the hospital. We hardly ever saw him and when we did, he was always disciplining a child for mother, yelling at someone for something or fussing with her over just about anything. I was confident, as a child, that he stayed away from home because he just couldn't stand being in a house with all those bodies. Who could unless forced to? I learned later he also took some time occasionally with lovely ladies.

I am also confident my mother was quietly dying with all those responsibilities and her lack of education and training as well as lack of my father's presence and support mentally. She was a marvelous pianist and organist and could play absolutely anything "by ear." She figured out a way to buy a piano (on credit) and it certainly brightened up our days when she played and we sang. I now know that she soothed her soul in times of sorrow *and* joy by playing her piano, and, later, her organ.

My mother's playing provided me with my first experience with the musical vibrations lifting up the soul. I taught my Self how to read music and to play the piano. That led to "she might have some talent" and music lessons at school from Sister Rose Helene. It wasn't long before it was obvious to Sister that I *did* have musical talent and by my 13th birthday, I was playing the piano for school affairs. My next exciting musical experience was playing the organ at church (for which I was given breakfast and a few dollars a week by the priest of our parish, Father Schumacher—a wonderful person who understood life and *loved* me and my family).

Every time I turned on the organ and played the tunes I loved, including Gregorian chant, I felt my Self relax and feel better. I still didn't know why, but it didn't matter. Even today, every time I hear the song *Panis Angelicus* or *O God of Loveliness* (called Fairest Lord Jesus in the Catholic Church), I "fill up" inside and almost cry. The emotion of those songs creates another "place" and another plane for me. But I was still in the "state of original sin"—ignorant of the mysteries, the role of vibration, including sound (music), color and thought and of the inner life experiences that would transform my thinking and therefore my life some day.

As a result of our household's "official ignorance" and my mother's silence on the subject of sex, her beliefs and values based on what she was told by the Church in the person of our parish priests, we heard a constant recounting of the "thou shalt nots" and the "look-out for this behavior" in one form or another all the time. Our socialization (from both parents) went like this:

1. Stay away from boys (to the girls).
2. Stay away from girls (to the boys).
3. After the basketball game, come straight home (no stopping for cokes, etc.)
4. Don't smoke cigarettes. (Dad smoked until the day he died of lung cancer at 80 and Mom used to smoke, too)
5. You'd better not let anyone touch you.
6. Don't lie to us. (Of course we lied. Otherwise we would not have been able to have friends. Or do anything "normal" kids did.)
7. Be home by 10. (Dad at the door and turned the porch light on the minute our feet hit the steps.)
8. Good girls don't let boys touch them. (Where? What? How? What does that **mean?**)
9. Having sex is a mortal sin? (Who says so? The Church, of course.)
10. Don't touch your body "down there." (Masturbation is also a mortal sin and will make you crazy? What?)
11. I'll kill you if you ever bring a bastard into this house. (Dad)
12. Shut your mouth and don't talk back? (Just answer my question, **please?**)
13. You don't need to know how babies are born. You'll learn soon enough! (Mother. Dad was always mute

on these issues . . . until I came home from college pregnant, and then I was a slut, whore, ungrateful **bitch**, etc., etc. **and** he threw me out of the house. I disgraced him, lost a fully funded scholarship and laid up with my first husband after he returned from Korea. He was my first and only up 'til then. (I thought that was pretty remarkable since I was almost 20 years old!)

14. I will disown you as a daughter (or son) if you disgrace this family. (Disgrace was always code for getting knocked up or knocking up some girl.)

15. I put a roof over your head, food in your mouth and clothes on your back. Don't ask me to return the money you earned and I "borrowed." (I thought **parents** took on those responsibilities when they had children? Was I **supposed** to give **him** what little extra money I earned **because** he couldn't stop having babies? What was I missing?)

Now I *know* that **language drives behavior,** negative language drives negative behavior, all of it ending up in each child developing his/her own values based on fear and shoulds but also developing an enormous amount of curiosity about how life **really** works. Could it **really** be this bad? Any dum-dum knows that anything constantly railed against has just got to be something magnificent and wonderful. At least interesting, right? That's why adults appropriate it for their Selfs, right? Right! But for the uninformed, uninitiated, uneducated and the unknowing, it's all wrong and dreadfully so. The formula for happiness is nowhere to be found in what your parents tell you. I learned through experience that my life is *all inside me* and what I think about and tell my Self is what **my** life will become. *Without fail.* But first comes the clash of societal and family values vs individual experience. One moment in time, one day at a time. *Choices, choices, choices.* The *only* way to walk up the mountain!

Sex Is Dynamite!

Sex is a magnificent energy that should be looked upon with reverence and understanding because of its great power to change men and women's lives and because of its ultimate use in the act of all creation: art, music, architecture, sports, war, politics, and, yes, progeny. How many of us at puberty have a clue what sexual energy is for? *Not one of us.* We really *do* think it is for "getting it on" with someone because society has made it the forbidden fruit and hidden its power and majesty from all of us. We really *do* think it's just for making babies even though what leads up to *that* sure does feel good! Some of us do learn, though, that that's not *it*, honey, and it sure is a hell of a reality check!

The Hard Way

I was "tiger bait" the first time a good looking manchild paid attention to me. What I knew, however, was that I didn't want to get "killed" by my dad. He used to say to me and eventually all the girls, "I'll *kill* you if you get pregnant and embarrass me in the community!" Did I think he meant literally? Frankly, I wasn't so sure, he could be so fierce when he said it! So, boys were "out"—got that? O-U-T! The only manchild to eventually pass muster by my family and the nuns, when I was sixteen, was the son of a local businessman, who agreed to escort me to a basketball game (I was a cheerleader and a 16-year old junior). He was fascinated by my enthusiasm, ability to communicate and my athleticism. Soon he was calling to ask permission to take me to a movie now and then. Permission granted. Soon, we kissed and petted a bit, but nothing heavy and never got close to "real" sex. My father had threatened him, too, by telling Don he'd better never lay a hand on me. Honestly!

Finally, Don was drafted and went to Korea. I went to college. We wrote. After he returned, he came to New York and declared that he wanted me in his life. Would I have sex with him? Well, I had "kept" my Self a virgin just for him, so, of course. So, of course, I got pregnant. What did I know about birth control. I can't **believe** I was so dumb about my body! But I **was!!!!!** One thing led to another. I went to confession (still a guilty little Catholic girl!) at a church where the priest would not know my voice. I confessed my mortal sin of having sex with my boyfriend. The priest told me to stop having sex or leave the church. Upon a brief moment's reflection, I told him that I was going to leave the Church. And did. Then and there. That was my first conscious "ah, ha!" My first epiphany and wakeup call on beliefs and values. I walked out of that church, took a deep breath and walked into the future.

I married that local manchild, my first and only sex partner, and found out on my three-day honeymoon that he liked to drink and turned ugly when he did. I had never heard him curse and talk rough to me but he did so that first night of our marriage. I realize now I had chosen a classical misogynist. Then, I was in luv! Not love, luv!! Truthfully, it was downhill from there. I kept up my "front" until I was in danger of dying from the stress, cursing, physical and mental abuse and his running around. Turns out, I made a shitty choice. He wasn't a "good" man, but he sure could fuck! I *still* didn't know the difference between fucking and making love. I would, in due (do) time learn ... the hard way. How come someone so smart be so dumb? Talk about ignorance!!

I can look back on how I desperately sought an abortion when I missed my period that wintry month in 1954. In White Plains, New York that just wasn't going to happen. So, I did the next best thing, for me. I prayed that God would take this child from me and find a way to provide me with a start in life that would not include a baby I truly did not want. Certainly not under those conditions.

My emotional intentions and my attention to my prayer accelerated as the baby grew in me. Then something strange happened. My doctor, a good Catholic, told me he suspected I wasn't pregnant but was carrying around a tumor that was poisoning my system. "Then take it out," I said. He declined, on the basis it *could* be a fetus, but he couldn't be sure. "It should come on its own," he said. The bottom line of this ignorance was I became sicker and my body more toxic by the day. I was so swollen I could hardly walk. The baby finally was born dead August 27, 1954. How had it occurred? In a car accident during June of 1954, the umbilical cord wrapped around the baby's neck. Eventually, she died in my womb. I never saw her. She was buried while I was in the hospital. The doctor's words were: "Go home and get pregnant again. That will help you feel better about this." I did. And two babies later, it was clear my marriage was a wreck waiting to happen. I stayed on though. After all, no one in my family had **ever** gotten a divorce. "Grin and bear it" was the motto. So five years after my second child, my third arrived. I truly wanted them all, but I had made up my mind not to have more than three children no matter what. Twelve children in a household had ruined me for childbearing and I had stopped listening to priests when I left the confessional *and* the church on that "ah, ha" day six years before .

When I had my third child, I told my doctor it was time for tubes to be tied. Because of the problems I had with the first pregnancy and other health issues, including horrible varicose veins, he agreed. Imagine my surprise when I learned my husband would have to sign for my tubes to be tied after the delivery! Really! Paradise Valley Hospital in National City! A Seventh-Day Adventist hospital then, allowed doctors to harass me just before surgery in the interest of psychologically "giving me an opportunity to change my mind and not go through with the sterilization." I'll never forget the hurt and disgust that overwhelmed me when I learned that. Another example of how the patented patriarchal prurient patoots had control over women's bodies! My husband, dog that he was, decided to play hard ball and not agree until the very last minute. Then, as I was about to be rolled into surgery, three doctors came to the room with a form in their hands asking me whether or not I wanted to change my mind since I was such a young woman! Intimidation. Ignorance. "Suppose you want to have another child? Suppose you and your husband divorce and you marry again—wouldn't you want to be able to consider another child?" Suppose, suppose, suppose . . . My answer: "No, goddamit. Let's get on with it. This is **my** body not yours."

They "got on with it."

Sex Up Close and Personal
THE SPIRIT OF SHARING ANOTHER VIEW

Let's face it. The details of my life are worth a book by itself some day, but stay with me in this the picture I am sharing at this moment in time. Your beginnings, like mine, are important because they shape the direction of one's life—to a point, to the point of readiness. We carry with us *feelings* we have to *name* in order to *claim* in our lives. But *naming* and *claiming* take time. Moreover, to name and *claim* anything you have to be in the frame of mind I call the *"Be readies."* You have to *be ready* to call a spade a spade. You have to *be ready* to ask for what you expect to receive, *be ready* to seek for what you expect to find, *be ready* to knock on the doors you want to open to you and you have the handle on *your* side. You have to *be ready* to take hold of your soul and your spirit and tell them what you want for your Self. You have to *be ready* to experience life and know that experience is the cauldron of refinement for the soul. You have to *be ready* to go to that counselor, therapist, psychologist, psychiatrist, minister or priest. You have to *be ready* to accept change because the pain of what you *know* far exceeds the fear of the future you *don't* know. In a sense, you *"have to be ready to be ready."* Got that? And what gets you ready? Those old behemoths of change: *crisis, chaos, and significant emotional events (SEEs). The Trinity of Change.* Absolutely *nothing* will change in your life *until* **you are ready** to make the decision to take action. To put one foot in front of the other one moment at a time. And, as hardheaded as people are, it seems to *always* take one or more of the *Trinity of Change* to move our minds and therefore our butts. Ah, yes. You've got to *be ready* to *be ready!*

All this "getting-ready" experience is critical to growth. The decision you make to grow involves risk. Risks involve courage regardless of the outcome of the action and action is the **only** methodology that works. In fact, action is the vehicle and realm of what religion calls the Holy Spirit or the Holy Ghost, *always.* Thought (mind), Word (vibration/energy) and deed (action)—it's that action that the Holy Spirit is in charge of.

My experiences have led me to the following understanding and knowledge. I recognize some statements may be contentious to some people and that's all right. They may also be enlightening to others. They are intended to share my own experiences and to put this knowledge on the table of reality. These positions and values represent my own individual positions and may or may not be shared by others. Nevertheless, I don't believe they represent new thinking since there's nothing new under the sun. But I put them out there because a **bitch *with style*** (moi) has benefitted from them personally. So have others on whom I have had a positive impact **and** opened the door to enlightenment. The **Course in Miracles has a saying:** *There is another way of looking at this.(w, 50)* That is the spirit of whatever I have said or will say in my whole life. There *is* one other thing: I have found that, for me, the only impossible thing on the face of this earth is a closed mind! When I discover contentiousness, cynicism, overwhelming doubt and the desire to debate my point of view in a person I have met, I graciously find a way to bow out of that person's space and negative energy—and as soon as possible. Then, I don't put my Self into that person's space again. If I run into someone like that socially, I smile, say "hello" and move one. I don't even want to ask "how are you?" because truth is, I don't want to "hear" it. Should that person ever seek me out for a reason that is legitimate to his or her interests because I have something to offer, I will put my principles before him or her and tell them up front how I handle communications. They then have the right to get up and leave, no questions asked and *no hard feelings.* This is the way I have learned to keep *my* power in *me* so that it is not scattered about with people who don't need it or deserve it. Only this way is my cup always full to running over so that I can share with those of good will, energy and good intent.

In due (do) time, all of you **bitches, *with style*** will learn this lesson and this method as well. Count on it.

A Bitch With Style's Views On Sex
MASTURBATION

Teach children to love their Selfs, including their bodies. I remain shocked, still, at how many young children are taught to dislike their bodies and are told that touching is bad. I value the feel of my own hands on my body and I believe masturbation, a developmental process, assists children in learning how to respect the miracle that is their physical temple on this earth. It is our "house" of spirit and is housed in our soul. Would you not want to know more about the house you live in? If children know that masturbation is not evil and that touching their Selfs is a way to begin to know how to express expectations of potential in sexual relations, they will not begin the guilt-ridden behavior of seeing sex as titillating, dirty, smutty, secretive, evil, without pleasure, and only duty—well, you get the point. We are seeing as a nation a lot of **patented puritanical prurient patoots**—some of whom are female—who are voyeurs, sneakarounds, peekers, full-blown hypocrites masquerading as enlightened, self-righteous individuals driven, **they** say, by a high moral standard. **Theirs!**

There *is* another way to look at this, but they don't even want to take a peek! Or, have they been so indoctrinated to one way of thinking that they are literally *afraid* to step outside their boxes?

Touching and Oral Sex

I learned how to love and touch my Self when I was a mother with two children. My curiosity, one of my most enduring qualities, had always made me want to know more and experience more sexually. My life with my first husband had its moments (He loved to fuck! I was learning to love.) but, in my judgment, was sexually deficient and I did not know how to make it better **for me.** My husband was sexually oriented to intercourse but his far east experience had introduced him to oral sex and only when he was performing cunnilingus on me could I really "feel" good. A strange feeling, but wonderful. It led to my experimentation in masturbation because I wanted to know what more could **I** *feel* and what could **I** do for my Self to avoid his not-so-pleasant demands for my body. How many ways could I make my Self feel physically, mentally and emotionally good? I set out to find out, and did. After my divorce, it kept me in control of my life and my feelings.

It now makes my love life very satisfying in that my spouse has erectile dysfunction because of other physical problems and medication. No matter. I have always understood that one makes accommodations in relationships that work for them. This works for us. As part of our relationship, I have insisted on making an appointment for lovemaking and expressing the desire in this way: "I want to make love to you. How does Sunday, or Saturday,(or whatever day) look like for you?" I also insist on an appointment because it is an important event in my life to share my energy with Bob, and it *should* have a place and time like every other important thing in my life and his. We bathe and perfume our bodies and approach the event like the event will be our last and we want to make the most of it. I always have wonderful music playing in the background and my favorite is Rachmanioff's Piano Concerto No. 2 by Artur Rubenstein. I play it 90% of the time. It makes my soul soar as my energy rises to the occasion.

This approach is far more honest and open than having one or the other partner *insist* on each partner going to bed at the same time *on the chance* that sex *might* happen. After all, adults don't operate on the same clock and it's foolish for one or the other to "control" a spouse's sleep time or even evening time by displaying selfish, immature or even petulant behavior because of an unspoken but underlying possibility of "spontaneous" lovemaking! What nonsense.

When in this mood, I **know** and **feel** the intermingling of our energies. I feel my chakras pulsing and know that my whole body is working together to provide the energy for me to engage my spouse's spirit. My spouse **feels** the heat of my hands moving over his body and I **feel** his. He thrills to the climactic give and take of my mouth all over his body and I to his all over mine. We have found a way to turn something that could have destroyed our relationship into a thing of beauty. It makes me wonder why other women don't talk more about the benefits and possibilities of oral sex, not in a pornographic sense, as is usually the case, or in the Monica Lewinsky and Bill Clinton scandal—a personal but probably satisfying interregnum, but in the loving utilization of orifices (our mouths) meant to provide pleasure and intimacy of absolutely the highest order. One is never so close to the power of sexual energy (and to the power of the Universe) as in the feeling of one's partner rising to orgasm and the power of letting go in the sense of the *let-go-and-let-God* way not known in any other sexual act, not even intercourse for the man. I also find the oral sexual experience much more satisfying than intercourse; more sensual, pleasurable and more spiritual in my own soaring and letting go of everything for that heavenly moment when I am totally one with *everything*! In addition, I believe sexual pleasure takes place between one's ears, so the mental imagery and visioning I employ simply heighten everything I feel and make my experience with Bob exceptional every time. The most important thing, though, is that we are *intentionally* coming together, paying attention to each one according to each one's likes and desires, and taking our time sharing our energy and thoughts with one another under unhurried and serene circumstances. I rub his back with the Nikken magnets (the **Mag Boy** to be specific, which is dynamite). He often does the same for me. And, yes, there are all sorts of feelings, sounds and discussions! It's pretty amazing and I could not be happier. This joy has come to us over time, with communications and reassurances that life goes on and we must go with the flow and not be discouraged by small things like erectile dysfunction, stroke or Parkinson's Disease. That's just a test that's waiting for the testimony of bliss that comes with a willing and exciting partnership. That's really **l-o-v-e,** *focused emotion* and there's no doubt about it lasting over more than a moment. It accumulates and accumulates and, pretty soon, you're looking forward to those moments in time when you just touch, smile and kiss in public for no apparent reason—apparent to others, that is. So nice.

Birth Control and Physical Pleasure

When I was in college I learned from some of my classmates that petting and oral sex kept them "technical virgins" because it was *not* penetration and therefore not engaging in "sex." I was told oral sex is full of pleasure as well as a great birth control method. Yeah, right! Too bad I wasn't up to experimenting sooner! Turns out that oral sex is the world's finest birth control method and works every time. Too late for me to cash in on it, but even today, it's worth pursuing for young marrieds and even for those who are unmarried but sexually intimate with a mate. The matter of AIDS, sexually transmitted diseases, however, puts one on guard with regard to this type of intimacy. Got to know who you're dealing with to use this to greatest benefit. This is the time of AIDS and HIV and partners no matter who they are must use their knowledge (not ignorance) in determining who to have sexual relations with and how. Dying is no game to play for fun. However, the whole idea of masturbation and oral sex was anathema to religious zealots and still is because it puts the power of procreation on a level of intelligent choice not biological chance or emotional roulette. Condoms are in order whenever there is doubt and I predict there will someday be a condom for the mouth because of the times in which we live. Someone's probably applying for a patent for one as I write!

Abortion and Choice

This **bitch *with style*** is pro-choice. It would be very difficult to be a **bitch *with style*** and be any other way. It is my one issue that makes a difference for whom I vote and who I support financially. I believe a woman's body belongs to her and to her **alone. A decision to carry a child or not to carry a child is between her and her soul**. She may **choose** to include her spouse, her pastor, her doctor, her parents, anyone she wants, including the sperm bank. But she **must choose for her Self** and not be frightened or intimidated by pro-lifers or others who are mouthpieces for a time of terror that should be long since gone from the face of this earth.

Anti-abortion rights is the last frontier for the "patented patriarchal prurient patoots" and those forces of darkness who support them. Their spiritual and mental "property rights" over women are not only being eroded but are being rescinded by **bitches, *with style, knowledge and power.*** In other words, by wiser and sounder minds! These patented patriarchal prurient patoots have reached the line in the sand beyond which they cannot march. All women from the beginning of time have found ways to abort fetuses they do not want. Face it! It will be no different in the future. We must hold with the law of the land, Roe v. Wade, and understand the stakes—**they are still enormous.** However, **I do not believe the patented prurient patriarchal patoots will win.** It is time for women to step into the shoes of individuality and **think for their Selfs,** on *every* issue in their lives and the lives of this nation. The changes that will come about by women taking on the cloak of their individuality will in time be amazing to behold because the energy of the Universe is flowing in our direction. **But . . . Women must choose individually to make a difference in their lives and in the world.** And it won't be long before these **bitches, *with style*** will demonstrate their mental and, therefore, physical freedom from the tyranny of the church. Childbearing will be by choice and conscious communications of their *own* thoughts, words and deeds will radiate to all who would listen. The *functionaries of fear* should be *quaking* in their boots! Each of us is "walking into" her power! *Now!*

The Map of Change For The New Millennium

The New Millennium will be one of duality, but at a higher level than has existed in our times. The concept of choice for men and women will be uppermost in the mind of all those power brokers who are formulating policy

The Catholic Church and other fundamental religions, in my view and experience, are totally out of step with their understanding of the soul and when life begins and when a person—a human being—exists. The fetus is indeed living, organic matter. There is no doubt about that. But the appearance of a living organism in the womb does not, in fact, establish the tissue as a *human be-ing.* That reality begins when the ***soul enters the body of the fetus*** and it begins its journey on this earth as a ***breathing,*** individual—capable of "being" in the world—however that soul's contract has determined that it would "be" in its initial entrance. What about preemies? Their real role is to extend the role of science and healthcare and, in the process of survival **outside** the womb, to push the frontiers of medicine and pediatric care forward. The many who die have paid a price for "being" here that their souls agreed to in advance of their coming. Those who live have also shared their Selfs in a way that allows all of us to think differently about human possibilities and life outside the womb.

Those who object to abortion never seem to have an answer for spontaneous abortions or miscarriages, all of which constitute the *death of organic matter that is not ensouled.* It is also the case that if the patented patriarchal prurient patoots **really** believe what they say, the should also believe that **there are no exceptions to that belief.** Their argument is that abortion is murder. Well, then, if it's murder, it's murder, no ifs, ands, or buts. So what's this stuff about exceptions in the case of danger to the life of the mother, or in cases of rape or incest? Their arguments are totally inconsistent, based on their *ignorance* of the spiritual knowledge of the soul, and also based on their fears of losing their power over more than half the human race. "Keep that woman alive so she can conceive again and bring in one more voter!" Wrong, guys. That's not the way it *is.*

In the United States, and in other parts of the western world, it's time we begin the process of publicly dialoguing about the whole matter of reincarnation and its potential impact on our thinking and the future of the western world. It will indeed make a difference in how we view life and death. After all, if reincarnation does indeed occur, then there is no such thing as death *in reality.* Death is only giving up the physical vehicle we chose to learn life's lessons from this time around. Such thinking is not only the thinking of the majority of the world, but there is, in my opinion, a growing view in America that reincarnation is *real.*

The interest in death and rebirth (reincarnation) in the United States is growing. There is a man named James Van Praagh whose book **Talking to Heaven: A Medium's Messages of Life After Death (Dutton)** went from an initial printing of 8,500 to 600,000 copies in less than four months! The subject: Van Praagh talks to dead people! Brian Weiss, MD, has three books that recount his own experience with past lives and regression therapy. He went from a disbeliever to a believer and recounts how he made the journey in **Many Lives, Many Masters** and **Through Time Into Healing.** As a psychologist and clinical hypnotherapist, I too do regression therapy and have learned from training with Dr. Weiss. Sylvia Browne, the renowned psychic, appears as a regular guest on the Montel Williams Show and he tallies his highest viewer ratings on the days she is scheduled. Her books and tapes are selling very well. The reason: People are looking for information and some verification of what they *know* in their hearts and souls is true. This life on earth *isn't* the end.

My view is that those who know, *know.* Those who don't want to know, d*on't know.* Those who are open minded will move toward the light through many avenues and passages. Those who are closed minded will return again and again until they are willing to "see", "hear", and "be" one with the universal life force.

Death and Rebirth

Death is a subject I believe people should discuss openly and with more than the dread that currently infuses the subject. Children should be taught **not** to fear death but to understand it as a transition into another dimension of reality. It is a time in our lives when our soul (light body) leaves our physical body and returns it to the earth to be recycled and returned to its original state of "dust." That is one kind of death . . . the *main* kind.

There are other kinds of "death" that occur in each of our lives, the little deaths (*les petit morts*) that mark key transitions on our lives.

Deaths Along The Way

My first **"little death"** occurred the night my new husband turned on me in our hotel room and displayed a side of him I had never seen. I now know that it would have been visible to me if I could have "seen" but I was blinded by the emotional veil of "luv" and the fear of being alone in the world with a pregnancy I did not want, a life I considered in tatters, my dreams for the future ruined and my mind in a state of rebellion. I know that my "innocence and hope" were battered that night when I heard my husband tell me to "get out of that window and put something on." (no one could see me and the curtain was all but drawn) I grabbed a pajama top and jumped in bed, trembling at the ugliness of his voice.   Until then, "naked" had been the order of the day! I can tell you for certain that sex that night was not the emotional high I had hoped for nor was he the mate I *thought* I was marrying.

My **second death** occurred when my child was born dead and I realized I had to get out of or get on with the marriage. No one in my family had *ever* obtained a divorce and at that time I didn't want to be the first, so I chose to "get on" with it and get pregnant right away because that seemed the thing to do based on all of the "poor thing, lost her baby" sympathy coming my way. How could I tell *anyone* that I willed my first child to be dead and that the energy for that death did not change, even when I knew for sure she was not a tumor like that stupid doctor wanted me to believe. I could just picture the result of such an admission to *anyone*. I would have been ostracized as an "evil" woman and isolated even more than I was by my controlling, misogynistic husband who did not want me to even go to church, play the organ any more, talk to my friends in the choir or even go anywhere without him. I was in a mental, emotional and physical prison and we were living with his mother, whose understanding of my plight, I later learned, came from her own similar experience with my husband's father! But I was *dying* inside because of my own decision to stay in the marriage.

By a stroke of good luck, it became obvious after my two rapid pregnancies that I would have to work to supplement our income since my spouse could not seem to keep his father's store going. He just didn't *have* it—a business sense. So, the "what can you do to help" question came up as a way to help pay bills, keep food on the table and pay the rent. I suggested that I could go to work as a secretary and get a job at a nearby college. I did that with the wonderful child-care support of a neighbor and began what was to become the regeneration of my spirit and the return of hope. The man I worked for, Mr. Murray, recognized my abilities and, curmudgen that he was, came to care for and respect me as a person. He turned the office over to me to clean up 30 years of the previous secretary's neglect. I was on my way to feeling like I had the potential I once dreamed of. I did. It worked and I spent the next three years not only working to take care of business but to help put my husband through college. I think of it now and say to my Self, "Yuk! You idiot!" That was my generous and supportive nature working. Hallmarks of my persona to this day and now I know their place and its OK. Then I didn't. Not only that, I helped him get a job in San Diego upon graduation, packed up the car and two kids and moved across the country, as far away from Xenia as we could get! (Remember how I ran away from home at two-and-a-half? Well, I finally made it with my two kids; almost the same ages my brother and I were when I dragged him our two blocks to destiny!)

I was in the active mode of "making my marriage work no matter what." I just *knew* Don would change some day if **I** just made things right. At the same time I was beginning to read books about spiritual matters. I had already begun reading books like Napoleon Hill's **Think and Grow Rich,** which excited my mind and inspired me to set my goals. I was reading books on astrology, books by Ruth Montgomery, Edgar Cayce and Alice Baily. I was holding internal conversations with my Self assuring my beleaguered soul that someday I would be both independent and rich and would return to college and complete my education. I didn't know what I would become, ultimately, but my dream then was to be an attorney.

San Diego was clearly a city in which I was supposed to be. It was the cauldron that shaped my next round on the wheel of destiny and led to my **third death**. Once again, soon after arrival in San Diego, it was time for me to go out and supplement my first husband's teaching salary. I started as a temporary clerk typist at Convair San Diego and did such a good job I was asked to stay on though I was *very* pregnant! I was glad to do so because I was experiencing verbal and psychological abuse as well as physical abuse at home. My husband was a roaring alcoholic by then who could drink a fifth of whiskey at night, go to bed, be sober the next morning, and go to school.

How he did it I will never know, but he *did* it. During the evening when he was drinking, the children and I were subjected to all types of verbal abuse and, I, to slaps, shoves, and knock downs. On occasion, I attempted to fight back but was no match for his angry strength. I thought many times of the butcher knife but knew if I ever put it in my hand I would use it. Then what would my kids do without me?

I rationalized what was happening to me by attempting to figure out how to keep him from drinking. I would pour whiskey down the sink, toilet, in the yard. I was not a drinker at the time, but I even drank it as well. Less for him. Mistake!

My third child was born and I continued working. I *had* to. The abuse continued. In due (do) time I found my Self facing the ultimate reality: I had to do something to get away from this situation and put the children and me into a place away from the harm he represented, not just physically, but to my spirit and my soul. I felt I was being dragged into a sewer at a time in my life when mentally I was just beginning to believe that I was making a toehold for my Self in the world.

As a result of wage and sex discrimination which limited my opportunity for advancement (I made half the salary of the man I sat next to doing the same job and doing it better), I left Convair and applied for a job at the University of California, San Diego. That was a turning point in my life, a **rebirth.** I was hired to work with Dr. Herbert York, the new chancellor who was to direct the building of the new university. It was up to me to set up the office and make sure things ran smoothly by the time he returned in May of 1960. I was hired against all odds. Back in those days the criteria actually included age, no children, able to work long hours, etc. I so impressed June Saleebey, the recruiting officer of the university that she insisted, via the personnel director, Ruth Handley, that the chancellor meet me. This part of my life is worth much more treatment than this book can provide. Suffice it to say my horizons were opened wide and my fertile and sharp mind took in everything plus! It was an exciting adventure to be in the presence of outstanding minds, Nobel Prize winners, the state and country's political and governmental elite. It was just plain wonderful for my soul.

It was also the time of my life when I **knew** I would be able to get out of my marriage because I was making a good salary. I just hadn't figured out **how.** The **how** came when I finally confessed to Herb what was happening to me at home and why I had difficulties sometimes with being there. After he heard the story, he personally called his banker and cosigned a loan for me to get my divorce with. I went immediately to a lawyer and moved to make the break. It was neither easy nor pretty. My spouse did not honor a restraining order and had to be forcibly removed from our residence. His girl friend (oh, yes, he was a philanderer also, just like my father!) had helped him forge my signature to an income tax return and one-half the check I had hoped would help me over the hump of finding a place for the children and me never appeared.

I did not prosecute. Too much to do to survive. This was a very **"big little death"** in my life. For it forced me to not only look at what was happening to me but I had to **finally** take full responsibility for the mess I was in, the abuse I took, my unwillingness to call the police because of my *pride*, my own mouthiness that was the only weapon I had against his physical strength—except I just wouldn't shut up in an argument! I **had** to say something, didn't I? **Was I just supposed to lay down and take it? No way!**

My own sense of my Self up to that moment died. I knew I wasn't going to "take any shit any more from anybody!" Still, I was not able to get a clear picture in my head of who I was, what I wanted. I was enthralled to be back in higher education and I knew it would include *something* in that arena, but what? Would I always be the secretary, administrative assistant, assistant to the man on the top? Would I always be the caretaker? Always the "oldest of twelve" taking care of everyone but her Self?

I decided that I could not make those decisions or answer those questions without help. I sought out my first astrologer and opened up a whole new world of information that seemed to be made to order for me and my curious mind. In addition, there was information there with which I could make decisions, if I just chose to do so. What a mirror that first reading offered to my soul. I had to face the good, the bad and the ugly—not in the chart, but in my soul! I had never looked into my Self so deeply as I did that day I had my first reading and for months afterward. The session was taped and I listened to those tapes repeatedly until I "got it." I went to the bookstore, bought my first astrology books and, at night when the kids were asleep, I would read and read and read and look and look and look—at my chart! I would ask questions of my Self and hear my answers ringing in my ears. Some of those answers weren't too pretty to behold, so I would look at the chart and read more to determine if there were any answers in there for me to use. There weren't *any* answers, just information from which to formulate my own answers.

This "big little death" turned out to be a very, very big one! I took a good look at me and my situation. Finances were tough. I wanted the best for my children. Welfare or public support never was an option for me because I just would not consider them. I was seeking control of my own life not putting it back into the hands of someone else! I had just gone through *that!* I was determined to be father **and** mother and to make available all the things I wanted my children to have—that I never had growing up.

My ex-spouse never did pay child support or help with the children. My thinking at the time of the divorce in February, 1968 was that I would be able to be father **and** mother to my children and that we would all be better off without my ex-spouse involved in our lives, bringing in his negative energy, filthy mouth and alcoholic illness. And that's the first decision I made with my new knowledge ringing in my head. To make sure he had *nothing directly to do with the children's development*. I now believe I should have gone to court and made him pay the measly child support he was ordered to do. Truth is, by the time of our divorce, the court reduced what he should have been ordered to pay because my salary had by then surpassed his! Ironic, isn't it, how archaic laws were then! I later

Donald, Donna and Alan, Christmas 1988.

lost out on his retirement when his second wife, who was with him during his highest paying years, reaped the benefit of her years with him. By then, however, I was glad to be rid of anything to do with him.

MY CHILDREN AND ME: OUR COVENANTS

My plan of action included establishing values and behaviors for the children and me I believed would stand us *all* in good stead and handle the problem of being a single parent and being away from home at times when the children *were* at home without me or any other adult oversight:

1. Be responsible for what you think, feel and do.
2. Be prepared to pay the price of your own decisions.
3. I told the children that I would have to work hard to take care of us and could not be around to keep them from danger or even to monitor their day-to-day

behavior, so we had to go on an honor system and system of personal responsibility. I assured them we would make it but not without each of them working with me.

4. My oldest son was my helper. I leaned on him heavily to help with the other two. I had pangs of concern that he later (**much later)** would resent me because of all of the responsibility I placed on him as the oldest. We worked through it, but he did have strong feelings about it and rightfully so.

5. Sex was an open issue. Ask me anything. Read my books. Share the knowledge with your friends but make sure it's right.

6. You can put beer in the refrigerator and drink it at home, but none of your friends can drink in my home. (I'm sure that rule was violated, but not often. I didn't know about it, I can assure you.)

7. **Do not drink and drive ever. Remember those price tags for your decisions: YOU WILL PAY THEM!**

8. I love you with all my heart! Nothing you or anyone else can tell me about you that will ever change that. Never!

9. I will **always** be there for you, no matter what. Let me know the good and the bad. I want you to understand I am here for you, though you may not always like what I have to say, nor I agree with what you did.

10. Do not speak negatively of your father. That part of our life is over. Let's move on.

From the beginning, I exposed my children to the arts, theater, music (when in the womb and all the time thereafter.) They love the arts—all of them—and music, especially. Furthermore, whenever I could, I would travel with them in the car. Even across the country. I wanted them to grow up with an open mind and a very broad view of the world so they could choose how they wanted to spend their lives when *they* grew up.

I can remember leaving work, swinging by the bakery, driving to the Little League field, changing my dress shoes to sneakers and running onto the field in time to bring my goodies and watch my oldest son play ball! It happened a lot, but it happened. I had to make all sorts of accommodations in order to appear at events for my children. I did whatever it took. But I never put the source of my income in jeopardy and I explained as best I could when those occasions arose. Life was less than perfect, to be sure. But it was more good than not good. Looking back, I regret none of it. Would do it again. I am sure there are those who think single moms are, *de facto*, inadequate moms! Bullshit! Better *a* single mom than totally mentally crippled children, than the problems that would emotionally and psychologically damage children from the mental, emotional and physical inadequacies of **two** parents. Two parents are **not** better than one in *most* cases. Are you listening, Dr. Laura?

By 1968 I was reading widely everything I could get my hands on re growth, spirituality, energy, astrology, communications, management and leadership. I was inspired and impacted by books, books, books, cassette tapes and seminars and lectures! I was **reborn!** As **A Course in Miracles** says: "Rebirth is merely the dawning on your mind of what is already in it." (T, 86) I was hungry *and* thirsty for knowledge and I not only wanted it, I wanted to *use* it! And did.

TRANSFORMATION

I've read **The Power of Your Subconscious Mind** by Joseph Murphy so many times my personal copy is dog-eared and the cover has been taped back more than twice! Ditto for **Think and Grow Rich.** They held my mind until I could spread my wings further into the esoteric and exoteric literature of growth and development. Astrology became a mainstay regarding keeping on top of my energy although at the time I really did have a good grasp of what that was all about. I just *knew* the information in my natal, progressed and solar return charts told me how my energy was flowing, where it was flowing from and to and how I needed to handle this information to make a difference in my life.

If you had told me in 1968 when I made a decision to leave one university system for another that I would be walking down the road toward being an entrepreneur and independent consultant I would have laughed at you in absolute good humor because I had, by them, set my sights on being a university president. I *love* the academy though I am very aware of its shortcomings and high-stakes politics.

Little did I know that transformation was right around the corner in the guise of a very poorly chosen relationship with a younger man that rocked me to my socks. I was not open to a permanent relationship with anyone because I was too raw and wary from my experience with my first husband. To say I had no trust for the opposite sex would be mild. (I hadn't yet learned that the trust I had to have was trust in *me*!) What I *did* have was a desire to *be* with a man without *being* with a man, if you know what I mean. I didn't want to "do it" often but every now and then wouldn't be bad, I thought. But not at home!

I turned out to be a sucker for the deep-voiced patter of this guy who pursued me I now know because of my position and somewhat because of me but I was secondary to his plans for feathering his own nest and riding a gravy train I was getting ready (remember **the "Be readies?"**) to move out of the station! He could tell this train was going somewhere and he wanted to hitch a ride. He was very young and athletic and asked if he could meet the kids, and then when he worked his way into their sights, to stay over, and then, and then. He never moved in, but the situation became awkward when I discovered I wasn't the one and only and I wasn't even the most important female in his life. Whoa!

I had invested time in teaching him about management and leadership over a two-year period and then found my Self with him as a part of an exciting project I dreamed up, developed, obtained funding for and then put him into. I look back with utter disdain at my own craziness and, yes, ignorance, but I was determined to not notice how foolish and stupid I must have looked to people who really admired and respected **me**. They must have wondered what stage of life I was going through. Well, to be honest, I didn't know, my Self, what stage I was in, but I was consciously working on putting my Self together. One thing I **did** know is that I was *getting* ready to *be* ready!

What I learned from this encounter was that my young friend became a teacher for me in self-esteem, self-respect, self-worth, self-detachment *and* self-creation. My own self-esteem was not at its highest and I know I had called him into my life as a prop to teach me a lesson or two or three! I learned more than I bargained for. I got wonderful feedback about my capabilities, skills, political prowess and sensitivity and my projects. But, I also heard, "what are **you** doing with that gigolo?" A Washington colleague said directly: "You're too smart for this guy. Get rid of him."

My gigolo friend was ahead of me. While I used my contacts for work, he had used my contacts to get him a job in Washington. He left me. It was hard at the time because I finally worked my Self up to a way to tell him to leave me but he beat me to the punch!

I *did* cry but not because he left. I cried because of my own foolishness, lack of experience, and craziness. But what did he leave behind? My inner child had come out to play for the first time in my life of too-much responsibility. I had put on my first pair of blue jeans and gone go-carting with my children and friend. I found my funny bone and laughed a lot. I learned a great deal more about sex—some I liked and some I didn't, but I was no longer green as grass and his sexual prowess had been unbelievable and experimental. Yep! I had graduated from fucking to screwing. Not bad, either. Still didn't know shit about love.

I was embarrassed in my professional world, but I just had to get over it since I had done it to my Self! I sought counseling to avoid making an ass of my Self in the future. My counselor was this wonderful astrologer whom I consider a lovely, talented and insightful person. It did help that she was also a psychotherapist who used astrology to help her clients go deep into their Selfs.

At the time all this was happening, the planet Pluto was beginning its move to sextile my personal planets of Venus and Mars. What does *that* mean? Well, Pluto, the planet of power and self-mastery was providing energy for me to make deep and unalterable changes in my use of my resources (talent, money, brains) represented by Venus and my will and energy represented by Mars. Oh, yes, Mars also represents the emotion of anger which for me was raging.

I was *very* angry with me. Very determined to transform my life and do something about it that would make a difference to me and my children. My counselor told me that once I made this turn in the road, to stay healthy mentally, spiritually, emotionally and physically, *I could not look back!* The energy of Pluto rips off the covers and goes to the very bottom of your gut and gets rid of whatever is standing in your way—**if you are conscious and aware!** My consciousness was well aware of what I *had* to do and I was prepared to *do* it without looking back. I was finally *ready*, ready to consciously create the new me!

> *Faith—"a Fantastic Adventure In Trusting Her."*
> —Vikki Ashley

The Bible says *Whatsoever ye shall ask in prayer, believing, ye shall receive.* To believe is to have *faith* and accept something "as true" or to live in the state of *be-ing* it. It means to speak "as if" what you want has already happened. To use the *present tense* when you think of what you are asking for. For the second time in my life, this time fully conscious of what I was doing, I put all of my desire and emotion into affirming that I would have a professional position that would allow me to remain independent and yet make enough money to take even better care of my children and me. I was in debt and wanted out. I rested in the deep conviction that "it is done," and told my Self "health is mine." I passed on the idea of health to my subconscious mind to the point of conviction; then relaxed in the knowledge that it truly *was* already done. I told the apparent troublesome conditions of my life to "get out of my way." And to my soul in the quiet of the night, I whispered 'This, too, shall pass"[2]

And so it did. Thus began my own healing treatment and conscious use of my subconscious mind to get what I wanted. I was on the road to depth understanding. But, as is the case with growth, my transformation was just beginning.

My concern about where to go next did not last long. On my next assignment, I was appointed with great fanfare to an administrative post as director of affirmative action at a midwestern university. As I prepared to leave San Diego, I carried in my mind the following affirmation:

The infinite intelligence of my subconscious mind reveals to me everything I need to know at all times, everywhere.
(Murphy, p.131)

Step Nine to Bitchhood, Self-Improvement which leads to self-mastery will be a part of the process you are confronted with when you consciously seek the path of truth and wisdom. You've got to really *believe in your Self* in order to have the strength to walk on your own two feet into health. Keep the foregoing affirmation ever in your mind. It helped me survive a really intense and ugly experience at the midwestern university. At the same time, it brought me the source of one of my most exciting life experiences in a karmic connection that is still in my life.

Moving on down the path . . .

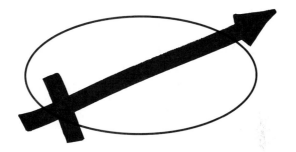

STEP NINE

I Am A Seeker Of Truth!

Ye shall know the truth
and the truth shall set you free.
(John 8:32)

Lost 50 pounds and lookin' good!—1997

Bitchhood 901
Self-Improvement: I *Seek*, Therefore I Am.

Lessons Of A Higher Order

I now know my thoughts always come true, but in 1972 "always" was not part of my mindset though I was getting better at affirming my right to wholeness, happiness and my own self-expression. I can tell you from personal experience that there is no response to your thoughts until desire (emotion) becomes part of the equation of your thinking and/or prayer. Napoleon Hill said that "dreams come true when desire transforms them into concrete action. Ask life for great gifts and you encourage life to deliver them to you." I With every inch of my being, I believe this and felt it to be true *then*.

My prayer for deliverance from my embarrassment **and** my situation in San Diego was answered. Today, I **know** it to be true that one need not worry. My dream was delivered to me as a result of an exciting project I developed between the San Diego State University and the public schools in guidance and counseling. A new opportunity opened up for me as an administrator in higher education. I moved my family to the midwest and we began our life in another time, in another space.

My reading, studying and mental development continued. I was stronger in my self-expression, mentally alert, and brought exceptional administrative skills to my job. The president recruited me personally as a consultant and then finally offered me a job. I was interested because of my respect for this man's ideas and his many books on leadership and management. I was absolutely charged with the whole idea of demonstrating the viability of affirmative action **and** the creativity and new ideas he said he wanted me to bring to this assignment.

I brought to the position a new process for the involvement of department chairmen, personnel, and the community and was thoroughly ready to go to work. I had to commute for six months to close out my program in San Diego. Traveling by air every week was tough on my body and my mind but I was learning how to handle stress through breathing, nutrition and exercise. Too bad American Airlines did not have a frequent flyer program then. I would still be flying free!

Staff and various people on campus were jealous of the contract I had with the president and began to complain. It didn't take much time for the pressure to mount that identified me as a person with too many privileges, never there, etc., etc. You know how it goes: the "How come *she* gets to . . . " syndrome began.

The president and I seemed to have the situation under control, I thought, and for two years I was part of the administrative circle academically and socially. I remember when I began to "feel" that something was changing. He was in the habit of asking me who I knew and I was at the time a popular speaker on the academic circuit and also had very good connections all over the country because of my former positions. I later learned that he was putting out negative information about me and poisoning the well of my reputation but this was not something apparent nor immediate. Nor did I know why this was happening. He was, I later learned, "isolating" me because he found me personally threatening and in many ways not willing to "stay in my place," wherever *that* was. I thought I was where I was supposed to be and doing what we had agreed I **would.**

While I am very sensitive to political waves, I hadn't picked up on the political details of *that* community in time to realize that a counter movement against my appointment had existed because a young woman (but older than I) thought she was going to get the job. The politics of the situation intruded on what became a job well done in preparing the university for its first visit from the Federal Government to go over the affirmative action plan. Imagine my surprise and dismay when I realized the plan that was being submitted was **not** the one I prepared. The truth was **not** going to be told and I was going to be the fall guy. Except that I knew the woman who was doing the audit from Washington and she and I had dinner the evening she finished. She told me of her findings. The president had refused to allow me to be present. I argued I should represent my own work, but he said he would personally handle it and now I know why. The figures and material she found were **not** what I had prepared. I was stunned. Surprised. Angry. Disappointed. I felt that I had been royally screwed, but for what purpose? What was wrong with telling the truth: that not enough minorities had *ever* been hired in this institution and those that had been were for the most part bootlickers and ass-kissers who did not want to endanger their jobs. Only I, I thought, would stand up for what was right, truthful, and in the interest of the program. That was *my* responsibility.

The results: the auditor returned and told the president she was aware of the deception and presented him with a copy of the **true** report which I had given her. Within two weeks she was told she would have to retire from her job in Chicago and was no longer to talk to me or to anyone at the university. Of course, we talked but it was clear the president's reach in Washington was much longer than mine and went into higher policy circles.

I sued and was told by everyone, "you can't win in this town. You should resign and go home or elsewhere." But I was determined. It was all rotten and I was determined to do something about it. You know: the truth's on my side kind of approach. What a rude awakening! I became *persona non grata* and my former "friends" did not want to be seen with me so as not to endanger *their* jobs. I was not paying enough attention to *my* home front and was having difficulty with my daughter and youngest son. My position was in danger and it was only a matter of time before I would be forced to resign or be fired. I made the mistake of getting a local lawyer who had a very fine reputation for winning civil rights cases, but it turned out he was on "the payroll," too and by the time I returned from his office the president knew everything I had said to him. I was offered a pittance to leave and refused. I was then offered an opportunity to go to Harvard to the law school but I felt at that point like that would be acting as an academic whore and I couldn't stomach the thought. I had done a lot to take care of me and my kids, but not that. And I determined with the gifts God had given me, I never would. So I said no, packed up my children and furniture and returned to San Diego.

BARGAINING DAYS

All the way home I could only replay the processes I had been through from the time I was a consultant, to my hiring, to my termination. What had I done wrong? It turned out it was not what I had done that *mattered*. My goal was personal integrity, telling the truth and getting my job done. I was willing to discuss the undiscussables and put things squarely on the table. I did it with finesse and charm, an occasional four-letter word and a clear understanding of what I was doing. Turns out I did not play the game. "You are *not* a team player," I was told. Lying about the condition of the university was necessary to save further scrutiny by the Federal Government and to ensure that the millions of federal dollars for research, medical care, fellowships, scholarships, would not be endangered. What was the sacrifice of one feisty, dynamic little lady, an outsider at that, for all of *that* greater good? Turns out I was dog food to them and they unceremoniously threw me to the dogs. I got to have my say before I left, but so what? I was not going to live life like a stinkin' pauper, kissing ass and losing my Self *ever* again. I had gone the be-good-and-shut-up route and I wasn't going there *ever* again. Remember this poem? Napoleon Hill referred to it in *Think and Grow Rich*.

> I bargained with Life for a penny,
> And Life would pay no more,
> However I begged at evening
> When I counted my scanty store.
>
> For Life is a just employer,
> He gives you what you ask,
> But once you have set the wages,
> Why, you must bear the task.

I worked for a menial's hire,
Only to learn, dismayed,
That any wage I had asked of Life,
Life would have willingly paid.

I later learned that one of my neighbors who was a striving administrative assistant in another college had entered into a Faustian pact with the president to "play the game," go to school on university time and get her PhD and *then* be in line for promotion. She wanted her PhD more than she cared about the truth of what she was doing. I have never seen or spoken to her since that day. I **have** forgiven her, however. Her *desire* to achieve her goal was far more focused than my desire to do my job truthfully. I did *not* focus on the politics of the situation nor did I even believe for one moment the leader of the university would stoop to such a low place. I have since learned about leadership and stooping! The energy my nemesis expended to fudge my numbers took a lot of concentration and effort. I knew then that what goes around comes around and that I would not have to do any more with the situation.

What *appeared* to be a diversion and a wrong turn on the loose gravel of my path was the moment in time and the place where I met my current husband. It would be ten years before that meeting bore fruit. And during the years after I left the university, we had no contact with one another.

It was time for me to regroup and consider how this whole experience contributed to my continuing self-mastery and transformation. But immediately and more importantly, how was I going to house and feed my children?

Reason and Logic

Some things in life just don't make sense using reason and logic. You have to use your intuition and your subconscious to *know* what is *really* going on. When your life seems to have hit bottom *again* and you are searching your soul for meaning, **starting** with reason and logic is a very good idea but it won't yield the answers you need. As you focus your thinking to answer these questions, you begin to get insights that would not have been triggered except for your honest feedback to your Self.

1. What do I really *want*?
2. Am I aware of all my options?
3. Which of these options appeals to me most? List the top five.
4. What are the probable consequences of each one? For each answer continue asking your Self . . . "and next?" " . . . and next?" " . . . and next?" until you've honestly gone as far as you can.
5. Am I telling *my Self* the truth?
6. What am I telling my Self about what is going on?
7. Does this *feel* right to me? Am I energized or drained by this feeling?
8. Am I afraid of something? What is it? (Meet your fear and continue *through* it.)
9. Is there anything in my way? If so, identify it.
10. Am I focused on *my* thing or someone else's thing?
11. Will I promise to take care of *me* and *my thing* first?
12. Will I only share my ideas with those who can advance *my thing* until I complete *my thing*?

Answer all these questions honestly, note those things you believe you have to eliminate as barriers, do that, and then move on and don't look back.

While answering these questions after my termination, several interesting things happened. It occurred to me that being a university administrator and professor wasn't really *my* thing. It was my father's thing. I had never faced that reality before. It had *never* come up inside me. That's what he wanted to do but never got beyond a department chairmanship. Was I really trying to out-do *him*? Could that be? Competition with my father? A true revelation because I finally faced that I truly wanted to do *better* than he had done in every possible way. That's how I truly *felt* but had never allowed my Self to think, much less utter, those words. What a relief!

I named it, claimed it, reframed it and sustained it. Yes, I wanted to do better than my parents and, more importantly, break the negative energy pattern of my life.

Was I afraid of anything? I honestly couldn't answer this question at first. After sitting with the question for a while however, it became very obvious to me that my old self-esteem problem had reared its ugly head. I had a dream of being independent and rich. Did I have the right stuff? Did I want to work for a penny or demand what I was really worth? Was I afraid my termination would stand in my way for future employment? Where and how could I capitalize on my strengths, compensate for my weaknesses and then make enough money to lead the type of life I dreamed about? Hell, I didn't honestly know what all my strengths and weaknesses *were* because in spite of all my training, I had never approached, full out, the question of all questions, **"Who am I?"** It was past time to find out and I went in search of my Self. I needed to know and I needed to work.

Riding The High Seas

I went to a search firm and went through all of its processes. In the end, I had a more enlightened view of my abilities and my shortcomings, but there was no self-assessment or testing that would have racheted up the data I was seeking. It did help, however. My next stop was my favorite astrologer. She made a tremendous difference and the information was far more specific than that received from the search firm. But the question, "Who am I?" remained unanswered in my gut. What was missing? I will tell you shortly and share how it can make a difference to you, as well.

The return to San Diego was painful. I had enough money to talk my way into an apartment and take care of us for one month! I requested my retirement funds from TIAA-CREF but had no idea when to expect them. I signed up for unemployment insurance and was told with a PhD, "Surely you can find work!" I said that, "surely I *could* but it will take time because of the nature of how universities and academic organizations recruit and hire." I explained to the intake clerk (and also educated her) that I look for work as a consultant by putting out proposals and networking with contacts. It was not the same way people go out and look in the classifieds, although some leads could be obtained there, too. I was in a city where I had connections. Surely she did not object to me doing what I do best and attempting to secure some compensation while also looking for a job, did she?

I was able to obtain a consulting job within eight weeks of my return. I checked in faithfully every week with the unemployment office. I looked around, talked to people in the line, and said silent prayers to the Universe like: "Please, God, **never** let me find my Self in this position again in life. **Please?"** My retirement check came August 23, 1975, right at the end of the eight-week ordeal (not much but it helped) and I **never** collected a weekly check from unemployment. The kicker is, however, the week before Christmas of 1975, all 8 checks came in the mail! Do you **believe** *that!!!!!* It was a great Christmas!

During those eight weeks of searching for a consulting gig, I spent early mornings reading, meditating and practicing using my subconscious to get what I wanted. I was opening up to a more spiritual approach to my life, my Self and my relationship with my children. It wasn't easy, though. I was nervous about being able to keep my promise to "take care of them" in the style *I* wanted. I could internally feel a shift in my perception toward the world. I decided to "go inside" and use the information I had learned to ask The Universe to take over my life and guide me to a better way. Back then I wasn't very specific because I still did not know what I really wanted to do. I wanted a reason, a purpose that would define my life.

IN DUE (DO) TIME!

In due (do) time is a phrase I use all the time to mean "action coming up." Just *know* there are *no* accidents in the Universe. Here's an example: A friend, Nan Powell, sought me out and asked me to join her on an assignment with the Navy to assist in the preparation of the men and ships for the coming involvement of women. Now **this** was up my alley. I had done some consulting with the Navy in 1974 before leaving the university. Now there was a chance to continue and **really** make a difference. The pay was good, there were travel privileges, PX privileges and I would have commander-level status because of my PhD. Looked like the Universe was on top of its job. I was thrilled.

What I noticed first was that my language was changing. I was seeking words to fit a more spiritual message into my work without ever using spiritual terminology. My attitude was much more confident (I **knew** I was not walking alone!). As I reviewed material for that assignment, I was pleased that I had begun the process of **consciously** saying what I mean and meaning what I say. It became obvious to me that my language made a huge difference in the behavior of those men I was training (there were **no** women). One of my favorite original sayings was and still is: **language drives behavior!** It does, believe me. The tension around discussing

> *Language drives behavior.*
> —Vikki Ashley

sex and race with Navy men was a challenge; I was up to it. I spent hours preparing and making sure I had dealt with the most important part of growth—**process, not content!** I assured the Captains in both San Diego and Pearl Harbor that, though we would agree on content, **the process belonged to me.** I obtained their commitment that no matter what, they would *not* interfere with **the process.** They could criticize the content, change it and do whatever they wanted, but **the process belonged to me.** What I meant by that was (and still is) that I was totally responsible for how **I:**

1. put the show together;
2. presented the content;
3. held the participants responsible for their **own** learning,
4. evaluated the process **with** the participants and
5. gave and received feedback.

My ground rules for the Navy program were as follows:

1. Leadership and communications are the Siamese twins of organization and change. All communications are important and breakdowns can be traced to

a *lack* of leadership and poor communications on whatever issue is being addressed. People are led; things and processes are managed and animals are "trained." People both lead and manage *their Selfs*. Remember **that!**

2. Respect for self demands respect for others. You *can* disagree without being disagreeable.

3. Find other words for four-letter words **except** when the meaning is *exactly* what you want to convey.

4. We all go through changes in a group from *dependent, interdependent* to *independent*. Pay attention and know where you are in the process. Leave your egos at the door!

5. No hidden agendas or behavior that smacks of undermining, lack of attention or movement toward disruption.

6. No stereotyping. People have names. Use them each time you address one another. When introducing an issue, accept responsibility for your position by saying, "My position on this issue is . . . " or "I want to share my view on this subject . . . " or "I disagree with this position because . . . " No nonspecific "they," "those people," "others say." Put names with behavior and do **not** pass on nonspecific "gossip."

7. You may always interrupt the process for a **Reality Check.** If you don't know where the process and content are going, it's your responsibility to say so. No one is to leave the seminar asking: "What did that mean?" Find out while you're there!

8. Always clarify what you say. Say what you mean and mean what you say. Feedback is not only important, it is *essential*. Communication is a two-way street. Listen and hear, then speak! Do it *now!*

9. Own your own position on anything (beliefs, attitudes, values, politics, whatever). You are responsible 100% for your *own* thoughts and behavior.

10. Be open to growth and model the new behavior out-side the seminar room. Learn to walk your new talk *everywhere*.

A strong principle that was said repeatedly by me is this: "Marry your head and your gut and let your head make the decisions." This means you **must** take into account your emo-tions as well as your thoughts—*always*. But you **must** learn to step back and let your head (mind) make the final decision.

As I was educating these Navy men, I was "talking" to my Self. It was the right time for the right work as I was developing my own style, process and confidence that would eventually pay my bills and lead me to my purpose.

> *"Marry your head and your gut and let your head make the decisions."*
> —Vikki Ashley

It was also apparent that this type of development could not be done with men only. Wives began to want to know what was happening to their husbands— good changes were occurring and there were noticeable lan-guage shifts. Next step was to do some evening events for the wives and pull them into the process.

REVELATION AND FAITH

I remember clearly stepping before the group of Navy men at HRMC in San Diego on that first day, standing there smiling at them before I began. I was nervous and, when speaking, I take whatever time I need to settle **me.** This also settles my audience and slows down the group energy as well as my own. I took deep breaths.

Mentally I was thanking the Universe for the success of the seminar (before it began) and for opening the minds of the men before me to what I had to say. I mentally finished with **Amen, and so it is!**

It worked. Like a charm!

There is no doubt this assignment was provided to bring home to me a way to be of service, have fun, have an impact and find my Self a stage for what I, by then, considered a part of my purpose: inspiring others to develop their Selfs and strive for goals beyond the mundane. I had found the language and a way to infuse my communications with energy that was spiritual, capable of being absorbed by anyone and not loaded with psychological terms that would have gone over their heads and eventually landed me on my butt with no contract and no impact.

I was asked to be the consultant to the Kitty Hawk aircraft carrier and to educate and develop their Human Resources staff in the "new approach" to team building. I was pleased to be asked and accepted the assignment. I'd always wanted to know more about these "floating communities" and now I would be working with the group. I designed the program from scratch; it went well and when they finished, I told them their exam would be participation at a higher education conference workshop being held in San Diego related to communications and human resource development. We were truly a sight that day. They were in their summer whites and I was dressed in a business suit. I felt like a proud parent. They were obviously the curiosity of the day. They did well. I was pleased. All passed!

The issue on the carrier had been the conflict and tension between the ship's company and the airdales (the guys that fly the planes). Bad blood between these guys could lead to accidents and all manner of problems on a ship that has to work without a hitch like a well-oiled machine. To show me what was at stake, I took a ride during a one-day exercise in the Pacific Ocean with the Admiral and watched every phase of the operations from the command center. I have only this to say: there has to be a very strong daredevil instinct in each of those young men (kids, really) because they had to be slightly insane to think they could land a moving plane onto a moving deck and not be killed. But they do it and do it well at great risk. I noticed that the ship's company was called on to support the human safety factor as well as take care of the planes that had to carry these men aloft. It was a very exciting and sobering day. Dinner with the airdales, the admiral and the executive officer proved to be even more exciting.

Meeting these individuals made me understand how much and how often we limit our possibilities. Why the hell **not** fly off and return to a moving deck? It looks risky but it's very doable to those who understand the risk, have trained for it and find it exciting. That's *life* for them. They were young, hard driving, hard drinking (some of them) and very dynamic individuals. A little "crazy?" Well . . . Yes! Those of us who need to take more informed risks in our lives should take a look at flying off and on the decks of life, which happens also to be a moving ship called Planet Earth!

The revelations I was having renewed my faith and belief in my Self. I **knew** this was not the end of the line for me. I was excited about my own business and continuing my consulting as well as my search for me and my perception of truth. This was a short stop along the way that led to a funny but disappointing end to my assignment with the ship.

Because of the successful work I had done with the HR group and its impact on the men, I was asked to do a research project with the ship that would leave San Diego and wind up in Subic Bay, The Phillipines. I would not ride the ship all the time. I would be on it some of the time (in the Admiral's quarters—with my own Marine guard) but would meet the ship at appointed places and times. Yes. I was up for this. To reinforce their appreciation for my work, I was made an honorary member of the air wing and received my own pair of wings. What a thrill!

The approvals made it all the way to the Chief of Naval Operations, Washington. They knew me by first initial and credentials. Somehow, though, a person in Pearl Harbor who knew me let slip that I was female and the admiral in charge of the Pacific said "No fucking female is going to ride **my** ship in the Pacific."

And so, the deal was killed. Too bad. I was ready to travel outside the US and to "fly" away to learn new things. But my wings were clipped.

My faith in me had been renewed. I had enjoyed my work in my home base. My travel was not too much, yet! I was growing, learning, sharing—essentially reframing my life. My business picked up through contacts made in the training and I found my Self doing more consulting in Washington, D.C. My methodologies were potent and working well.

Reality Check

Before I leave this seminal event in a **bitch, *with style's*** life, I want to share some of the feedback I received from these Navy men I was responsibe for:

1. Didn't want to come to this workshop. See its definitely beneficial to me and others I have to work with in the near future; feel very secure. Will trust the process and feel that risktaking will be for my benefit.
2. Struggling to marry emotions and mind. I am a philosopher and have my shit together. Means and ends are important to me.
3. Enjoying this. Have a refreshing feeling. Will undergo a better use of positive manipulation.
4. I like your style, but wonder if I can use it in my workshop. "Manipulation" is beginning to hit home. I'm comfortable with it.
5. Existing in two worlds. (Around skills—Marrying head and guts/integrate) Want a whole package out of this—a little more onboard today with what's going on. Having more contact with people in HRMC. Wish Team 1 was here.
6. I trust the process.
7. I am like a sponge—absorbing everything.
8. Learning a hell of a lot. I like the way you use manipulation. Like the way you handle emotion. Tying head and gut together.
9. Interest piqued. You have brought reality to this group by demonstrating **ability** and **responsibility.**
10. At a disadvantage because my training not at level of people in this room. I have a lot more to gain out of this week than almost anyone in this room.

11. Excitement; growing; discomfort but support from you. Marriage of head and gut—a direction I'm headed.

12. From the moment you mentioned manipulation, I felt good about it. I see a real person as one who can marry head **and** gut. Get some more people in this type of seminar.

13. I'm getting a lot out of this for me.

14. Was initially concerned because of negative feedback and power memo (before seminar), but am now on board. Did a 180°⁻ turn. Cleanin' out the "shit in the stream" is refreshing.

15. I view people who say they don't want to manipulate as being **insecure** and irresponsible. Change involves risktaking and knowing where you're going.

16. There **can** be a marriage between head and gut to make a more introspective and effective person and that person is me—personally and professionally.

17. This is a tremendous learning experience. Getting to know coworkers better. Clarifying my own techniques; learning there are more sides to all of these issues.

18. Will trust the process of this workshop (seminar); strive to work on cooperation between gut and head; I don't work **for** anyone. I work **with** people.

19. On a roller coaster. Gained a lot of personal benefit to help me do my job, but not sure we can resolve organizational issues; feedback influence: I blush a lot!

20. Not enough trust. Need more in the group between facilitator and participants.

Lessons Learned

What I learned from the "still small voice within" is that I had help **whenever** I needed it if I **asked** for it every step of the way for this seminar. The Universe (God) is always with me but it makes me consciously and willingly cooperate by **asking with emotion** (expressing my desire) for what I need and want. This is true of all of us on earth. Funny thing. The Bible is very clear on this subject:

Ask and you shall receive;
Seek and ye shall find
Knock and it shall be opened unto you. (Matthew 7:7)

At this point in my life, application and testing were my whole approach to the spiritual. I **knew** in my heart I was vibrating to the words I was reading in all the books I could get my hands on. So what was left but to **do** it? I stepped out in faith (the substance of things hoped for, the evidence of things **not** seen) and was determine to **know** whether or not my mind and my thoughts were **truly** in charge of my life. Faith is also a **F**antastic **A**dventure **I**n **T**rusting *Her.*

An important central aspect to the development program at the Human Resources Management Center was counseling and "talking with" the men about issues and problems on all types of subjects. There was pent-up frustration not only with the Navy but with friends, wives, girlfriends and in one case, a boyfriend. I was engaged during breaks, lunch, after hours over drinks at the officers club or with the noncommissioned officers at a restaurant near the base. I was definitely giving out and sharing my knowledge and my under-standing with others. Some days I felt like I was a storyteller, weaving parables, myths and fables to get a point across.

This process was very rewarding *and* draining. I was absolutely a dishrag at the end of the day and had to find ways to replenish my energy for the next morning's effort. It was under these stressful cir-cumstances that I began my learning about The Breath in earnest, as well as yoga.

In Louisiana there is a term called *lagniappe* which means "a lit-tle something extra." Well, these men provided me with a great deal of *lagniappe* for which I now believe I should have paid the Navy. It was such an affirming and broadening experience in my life.

Feedback and Musings

What did I say about manipulation? I defined *manipulation* as "the ability to artfully **influence** the behavior and actions of others. Webster (2nd College Ed. p. 862) identifies the root words as *manus* meaning a hand and *plere* to fill. It says about *manipulate*: to work, operate, or treat with or as with the *hand* or *hands; handle* or *use,* esp. with skill. Two other definitions imply unfair, fraudulant or false ways to handle matters. These are the ways in which the word is perceived by *most* people.

The first meaning, however, is really worth reviewing and using, at least mentally accepting the possibilities inherent in the word use. I told the seminar participants that a good way to get a picture of the right way to use the word was to visualize a man holding his penis in his hand and gently stroking it for pleasure. They all chuckled and said *that* was masturbation. Yes, I said, and it's **also** manipulation because you are "filling your hand" with your penis. The same could apply to a woman "filling" her hand with her vulva. They agreed and began to see what I was referring to when I talked about "artfully" influencing the behavior and actions of others. This means with awareness, understanding, skill and purpose. Let me also point out that the word *manipulation* adds up to a 10 or 1 in numerology. **One** stands for assertiveess, leadership, pioneer effort, individuality, and much more. In other words, it is a *power* word most people use incorrectly, indiscretely or not at all. Manipulation is generally considered to be negative, but it's all in how one "sees" it! Most individuals are afraid of *power* and *power words* but they unconsciously, that's right, for the most part unconsciously, *use* them. In the military *power* is used overtly, though in my experience I learned many men had never given it conscious thought. As one officer said, "It's just 'what I do.'"

In my developmental process, I introduced elements of language—words that were familiar, like *manipulation, power* (and all its variations), *sex, race, stereotype, failure, success*—and established vehicles that opened the men up to *new meanings* relative to what they had considered to be "true" prior to our discussions. It's clear that the word *manipulatio*n rang their bells and became an important anchor in reality checks about *other* aspects of their lives they had thought were fixed, until they *thought* about it. I got ribbed a lot about manipulation and my "creative" discussion of hands and the penis. But they got the point and that's what mattered.

See what I mean about language driving behavior? Now, what are *you* **really** thinking?

This is how my life developed after my "fall" at the university. I was a learner and a teacher and I was serious about it all. Over the years, the more I used my own unique consulting approach, the more effective my consulting became. I used the following framework:

1. Process, Process, Process.
2. Use words people can understand. **Communicate, translate and Integrate** (My CTI Principle) which I discovered and employed in my work in the Human Resource Management Center (HRMC).
3. Find ways to convey spiritual and psychological principles through words that people can **understand** and therefore more readily **accept** without being obviously spiritual and/or psychological.
4. Provide honest feedback. The consultant is **not** always right about content. Invite and receive amiable disagreement.
5. Take full responsibility for the process and outcome of what I do and always do more than requested. (OK, so I was more of a *workaholic* then! The princple still applies. Do 110% always. It just takes a *little* more effort.)
6. **Always go first class. No matter what you do.** First class facilities for sessions and consulting. No dirty rooms or restroom facilities. No mess on the floors.
7. Environments play a very strong role in the outcome of behavioral interactions. Let rooms you use be well lit, pleasant and reflect an appropriate use of color in walls and furniture. **Everything counts.**

That's where the action is. People have been saying the same things for millenia. The questions were raised in my mind: How do I make what **I** do so well **stickable, useable, and something that makes a difference in people's lives?** How do **I** contribute something that will help them **"be"** who they really **want** to be? Answer: I can be a catalyst for inspiring them to do three things: (1) lay a foundation in their lives that answers the question **Who Am I?**, (2) seek information and knowledge and (3) choose processes for growth. Yes. I can **do** *these things. Yesssssssss!*

In Due (DO) Time . . .

Making a difference in people's lives by providing inspiration, processes and information became my purpose. I knew that would be impossible to achieve unless I did it for my Self first and made it a continuous life process. So, I would walk along the coast at La Jolla Shores in the late afternoon, sometimes catching a sunset, and talk to my Self about what I was doing and what *else* I wanted to do. What kept surfacing was the desire to change my own life and to demonstrate how information, process, integration and knowledge of Self can make a difference in, and change other people's lives if they are ready to do so.

> *One must* **be** *something to be able to* **do** *something.*[2]

Seems pretty elementary, one would think, considering I was and am a psychologist. But life is not that easily categorized. We're all unequal in our individuality regardless of our professions. I wanted to do something *different.* Something that would make all the lofty phrases in psychology and spirituality come together and create a new paradigm that women and men could use to make their choices and pay their price tags **consciously.** That was it—I wanted to **wake people up to their own power!**

It was a pretty lofty but exciting goal and one I was finally prepared to engage and **do.** So, "in due (do) time," (which means you have already done the work in your head, now be patient and let the Universe find the right energy grid to put you on and the right people to magnetize to you.) you receive what you think about with focused emotion. My thoughts were out there anyway because I had already **spoken them.** The Universe pointed me to the path *I had chosen* to take. **Remember,** "in due (do) time means **do time—action time**—for the Universe (God). When you do your thinking, expressing desire in your heart with emotion, and move in the direction you need to go **as if** you already have what you desire, you move into "due (do) time" space. Be conscious of it. Believe it. "As a man thinketh in his heart, so is he." "Heart" refers to emotions. Your energy **always, always** follows your thoughts! **Always!**

With a few valleys and turns in the road, *of course!*

I had never lost my dream goal of being rich, being in total control of my life, being whole and happy, and having a home to come "home to" on a more permanent basis while I worked and traveled the world. Included in that travel was learning as well as consulting.

Little did I know what a monster I was unleashing when I made these decisions.

> *Your energy* **always, always** *follows your thoughts!* **Always!**
> —Vikki Ashley

So what did I do? I started my own consulting company to capitalize on my strengths: communications, leadership, organization, process, and management. Though I had never finished the last year of college, I had been on the Dean's List throughout my college career. I continually took courses and seminars, read voraciously (a book was always in my purse and briefcase!), and sought sources of knowledge and learning. I did complete my PhD while working at the university. Not easy but doable! The price tag was high, literally and financially, but I **did** have my professional "ticket" to ride—in organizational psychology and management.

I received my doctorate through the Union Institute in Cincinnati in a program expressly designed for working professionals with life experience as well as intellectual and application knowledge. I strongly recommend that anyone with experience, a passion for knowledge, a willingness to do the work and **apply** the knowledge, look into Union's program, which is still going strong. It provides credit for experience and makes you put your knowledge to use in society *before* you are granted a degree. I am an applied scientist and have a passion for seeking creative ways to make things *work!* So this type of program worked for me. I enjoy that appellation: **applied scientist!**

COMBINING REASON, LOGIC, REVELATION AND FAITH

When my business was launched I was by then pretty well connected. I obtained several contracts to teach unemployed people skills they needed to obtain jobs. I hired and trained people to help me. I did very well in the beginning. But I hired a number of people who wanted to be around *me* but didn't have, finally, what it took to sustain the business. My daughter and youngest son joined me in the business for a while, but in the end I had to let this all go because I found that dependency on Federal contracts was not a healthy way to **build** a business. Such contracts may help one get started and can even provide an "edge" but they can't become the core of your business because you are subject to all sorts of political whims, problems, etc. One *must* diversity. **What** we were doing had value. The **how** and **where** deserved attention and strategic planning. I also had to have a better way to "pick" people with whom to work. I proved to be an overwhelming presence to my staff. In fact, I learned that they "depended" upon me. I had the fantasy that I had hired people who would help me build my business because that was what they had the skills to do according to their vitas, references and their own descriptions. What I did not have the capability to do at that time was to **know** what their behavior patterns and emotional tendencies were in order to judge whether or not they fit what I needed and wanted in *each position*. What I learned later was that my staff's dependency was fostered by *me*. I was the "oldest child in a family of twelve" again. Not consciously of course, but when *that* thought finally seeped into my consciousness, I had one of my "Oh, shit" revelations. "This will *never* do," I said to my Self. "I *know* there's another way to find people who can do their jobs and walk on their own two feet. I've got to find a way."

I sought and found a variety of instruments helpful but not ultimately useful for what I wanted. I continued my search. By the time I discovered what I am going to share with you, I was "out of business" and back to independent consulting.

I had continued to learn during all of this time that the question **Who Am I?** was the most important anyone could ask and seek answers to. **People just didn't know who they were, what their values were or how they consciously impacted other people.** The cost in lives ruined, money lost through conflict in the workplace and in homes, and the increase of stress (which is the root of **all** health problems) is staggering—in the billions and billions of dollars. So I was open and ready for the Universe to bring me information I could use to assist me and it turned out it was perfect for my clients and their staffs and everyone else on the planet—if they but **knew** about it.

Know Thy Self

I was deeply seeking and exploring my inner space to **know** my Self. I was already 37 years old. What **had** I been doing all those years? Gaining experience and insight and being prepared for the Universe's next steps I had chosen. Pay attention here and you can get a head start. Fact is, what I am going to share with you should be standard issue for all junior high school, high school and college students. Talk about credit cards and "don't leave home without it." This is even better, "Don't **live** without it." What is "it?" The **P³ Baseline and Growth Package.** And I kid you not.

In the process of developing my consulting business, I was introduced to some self-assessment instrumentation that made *the* most significant impact on *my* life and has proven useful, accurate and practical in an on-going way. I am going to introduce it to you right now.

Today, I don't even begin a consulting assignment without obtaining agreement up front for the process I am going to share with you, nor do I see a psychological or clinical hypnotherapy client without their prior agreement to "the package" you will be introduced to below. It's absolutely **essential** to:

1. **know thy Self,**
2. **grow thy Self,**
3. **appreciate thy Self and**
4. **represent thy Self to the world.**

The P³ Baseline and Growth Package

Based on my three purposes noted above, what follows is what I call **The P³ Baseline and Growth Package**. (**P³** is my consulting company and I describe its meaning and mission on page 338.) The three instruments provide information and feedback on **your** (**1**) behavior and emotions, (**2**) values, beliefs and attitudes, and (**3**) your perception of you through your "work environment," whatever that "work" is. If I know your behavior, values and perceptions, I know *you* as well as another human being *can* without being *in* your

> *Rule #1 for leadership:* **Know Thy Self!** *Rule #1 for growth:* **Know Thy Self!** *Rule #1 for spiritual development:* **Know Thy Self!**
> —Vikki Ashley

body. The most important thing is, though, if *you* know your behavior, values and perceptions, *you* know *you* in a way you never did before and you now have a strong foundation for growth, power, conscious use of your energy and eventual integration of *SpiritMind EmotionsBody (SMEB)* and wholeness.

Keep in mind the words of Lao-Tse:

> *Those who know much about others may be learned,*
> *but those who understand their Selfs are even wiser.*
> *Those who control many may be powerful,*
> *but those who have mastered their Selfs are even more powerful.*³

Also:

> *Know Thy Self*⁴

Rule #1 for leadership:: *Know Thy Self!* Rule #1 for growth: *Know They Self!* Rule #1 for spiritual development: *Know Thy Self!* Always pay attention to anything that comes in threes! *"Know thy Self,"* there is nothing else to seek.⁵

All right now, have you **got** it? Good. Now here are those foundational as well as growth evaluating, self-assessment instruments (SAIs).

I'll describe the instruments

I. STYLE ANALYSIS PROFILE (SAP)   **7 MIN.**

Describes your behavior as **you** see it, not as someone outside you sees you. A good measure of your own perception of **You.**

2. PERSONAL INTERESTS, ATTITUDES AND VALUES (PIAV)   5 MIN.

You identify **your** values, beliefs, interests and attitudes *as they are* at the time you complete this instrument. These are your "Hidden Motivators" **and** identify **why** you do what you do.

3. THE WORK ENVIRONMENT (TWE)   **5 MIN**

You have an opportunity to describe the **behavior** required to **do** the job **itself.** Not you **in** the job but the behavior you perceive as necessary to effectively do the job. (This will be compared to your own behavioral style.) It often describes people who are square pegs in round holes who are not effectively using their energies to get the maximum out of their lives. This can be used for mothers who stay at home full time or part time as well. It is especially revealing for them. After all, what **are** the behaviors required to "mother?" This instrument will show your perception of what the "job" takes. The "job" speaks for its Self.

After completing the demographic data asked for on each instrument, the actual assessment is timed. The purpose is to avoid rationalization, mulling over, indecision and, more importantly, illusion. This whole process is about you and honesty. Not your **ideal** of who you wannabe. But **who you are** *today.* **This moment. Who do I say I am? What are those behaviors? This is the foundation, the beginning.** This is the *Seven Second Syndrome (S³)* meeting with your Self.

The resultant report **(the P³ B&GR)** contains of the three instruments and will provide information you need for continued growth efforts, including counseling, therapy, work evaluation and feedback, and personal review and evaluation. It is a **workbook. You** write in it, mark your disagreements, ask questions, share the report with others and seek their feedback. "Do I *really* talk to you like that?" *"Oh, no. I can't believe you see me this way? Wow. I've got to take a good look at me."* "No! I don't do *that*, do I?"

Everyone of us has all four of the behaviors described in the **Style Analysis Profile (SAP).** The four are: ***Dominant, Influencing, Steadiness, and Compliance/Conservative.*** Once you know your dominant tendencies, you can then *consciously* apply this knowledge and use any one or more of the four behaviors to accomplish whatever is needed or to help you decide what kind of help you need from others.

Style Analysis Profile

The **Style Analysis Profile** report will tell you (based on **your** information):

1. General Characteristics
2. Checklist for Communicating (how best to communicate with you—the **Do's)** and how **not** to communicate with you (the **Don'ts)**—Two of the most powerful pages in the whole **SAP**!
3. Communication Tips
4. Perceptions
5. Descriptors of your **true** behavior (Graph II of the report)
6. Your natural **and** your adapted style (your true behavior vs your mask and projected style)
7. Adapted style
8. Keys to motivating
9. Keys to managing (as important for you as for anyone you work for.) After all, we manage our Selfs; are led by others, and **we** manage things and process.
10. Areas for improvement
11. Action Plan
12. Style Analysis Graphs
13. Behavioral Factor Indicator (Specific factor analysis of 12 behavioral skills displayed in bar graphs (adapted and natural)—Very powerful.

Personal Interests, Attitudes and Values

The **Personal Interests, Attitudes and Values** report will provide information on the relative prominence of six basic motivating forces (values) in your behavior:

1. Theoretical (How you define Truth and handle information)
2. Utilitarian (How you handle money, resources, talents, practical matters)
3. Aesthetc (How you handle form, beauty, harmony in your life)
4. Social (How you feel about people and handle interpersonal issues. Humanitarian disposition)
5. Individualistic (Primary interest is power and how you use it. Includes responsibility, freedom to control destiny, individuality in relationships, independence)
6. Traditional (Are you traditional in your views, conservative, religious or not?)

> *Trinity of Change!*
> *Chaos, Crisis and Significant Emotional Events (SEEs).*
> —Vikki Ashley

This report provides interesting perceptions that will permit you to review where you are on your beliefs, values and attitudes—most of which have been "given" to you by family, schools, and churches. Change your own views if you **want** to change your behaviors. You've got to *"get ready"* to *"be ready"* for change. Then, it's possible to act, if you choose to act.

My experience as a human being and a psychologist has proven to me that people need three things to give them an opportunity to change. I call it the *Trinity of Change:*

1. Chaos
2. Crisis
3. Signficant Emotional Events (SEEs)

Oh, yes. These three stimuli **make** you "see." Now, what will you do about **what** you now "see?"

The Work Environment

Checks your perception of reality. Remember this: "My perception of reality **is** my reality until new information changes **my** perception." (V. Ashley)

This instrument indicates the behavioral demands of your job, position, project. Keep in mind that your perception of what you **do** may vary widely from your own behavioral style and emotional capability to **do** the job. If so, this report will give you the information you need to either (1) make shifts in your own behavior, (2) maintain *status quo* or (3) or find another job, husband, etc, etc. Your choice!

Impact on My Life

I was stunned the first time I completed the **Style Analysis Profile**. I was shocked at the accuracy and actually got pretty uncomfortable and defensive at what I was reading. This was a good sign that I had been very honest with my Self. What I read made such a difference to me, I decided then and there to make it my business to learn more about what I had just done and became a distributor for the programs: First with Carlson Learning Company and now, for the last nearly 10 years with Target Training International (TTI) in Scottsdale, AZ. The TTI materials are the only self-assessment instruments I have found that work for people from **every background,** under **every condition,** from leader to cook (who can read at the sixth grade level at least). They form the foundation and base for **Know Thy Self** and they provide the information for personal growth, team building, eliminating personal and workplace conflict and lead one ever so subtly toward the basis for spirituality, which is *energy* and how each of us uses it, though this is *not* proclaimed by TTI as a result. This is *my* statement based on years of use and feedback from clients.

Every year I do a **P³ Baseline and Growth Package.** I call it my *"annual psychup."* It has become my behavioral, values and perception annual checkup and is just as important to me as the one given me by my internist. In my view, no counselor, psychologist, psychiatrist, human resource manager, or health professional should begin any process involving the development of people without *grounding* the process in use of this package. No team members should be picked until the people responsible for the choices have identified the type of behavior need for each position on the team and *then* made sure the prospect pool candidates have all taken the **P³B&G Package.**

Listen up! For a 17-minute investment on the front end, the return on *that* investmnt is immense on the back end. Personally *and* professionally you will only benefit from **knowing thy Self** thoroughly. There is no downside. These data led to my asking questions of my Self I would not have gotten to in who-knows-how long? These data provide a way to ensure that employees bring the *energy, behavior, values* and *perception* that fit the environment *and* the job. What happens then is up to each individual in the environment he/she chooses to be in.

If **you** are interested in taking advantage of this unusual opportunity for your Self, turn to page 447 in the **Bitch's Book Bag** to find out how you can complete the self-assessment package and begin to answer the **Who Am I?** question and support your growth as you walk the loose gravel path on this earth. These instruments have been translated into more than eight languages.

The results of the 17 minutes you spend with these three self-assessment instruments are the most valuable you will have ever experienced.

1. The behavioral **SAP** is based on the universal language of behavior called **DISC**. Research supporting this instruments is based on William Moulton Marston"s **The Emotions of Normal People,** Carl C. Jung's work, **Psychological Types**, and over 30 years of experience in use around the globe. (See Bibliography, page 465, Bonstetter.)

2. The research of Bill Bonstetter of TTI has validated the **Personal Interests, Attitudes and Values** and **The Work Environment** as well as provided the software for the computer-based reports for the **P³ Baseline and Growth Package.**

3. Your return-on-investment of 17 minutes will change your view of you and give you the foundation you **need**, *regardless of age*. When is the last time **you** have seen a reflection of your view of **you** on paper? My best guess? Never or rarely.

ACTION WORDS FOR MORE EFFECTIVE COMMUNICATION

> **Power is an inside job.**
> —Vikki Ashley

Next, combine the foundation of **you** with more effective communications. Absolutely essential to being a **bitch** *with style.*

In all my work with organizations and individuals, I emphasize the importance of action words and the active, not passive, voice. I hereby share these words with you because to learn to put **I** before these words, *with no modifiers,* is a declaration of intention to do what these words identify.

Example: **"I communicate what I want to others."** Much stronger than **"Sometimes I let people know what I would like to have."** Or, **"I will balance this approach."** Or, **"I empower my Self. No one has the power to do that but I."** The whole *empowerment movement* is backwards in my view. It simply represents the "flavor-of-the-month" approach in the billion dollar consultant industry. Truth is, no one else can empower me. Power is an *inside* job. And that's up to you and I. So empower **your Self** by using **action words!**

ACTION WORDS FOR PERSONAL EMPOWERMENT			
Accept	Determine	Initiate	Produce
Achieve	Develop	Inspire	Recognize
Act	Discover	Integrate	Regulate
Balance	Empower	Know	Replace
Build	Establish	Lead	Report
Confront	Examine	Learn	Review
Communicate	Find	Link	Reward
Conduct	Finance	Manage	Seek
Consider	Format	Measure	Select
Coordinate	Gain	Modify	Sell
Create	Identify	Monitor	Set
Cultivate	Implement	Organize	Support
Decide	Improve	Plan	Test
Define	Impress	Process	Translate

There are more power words but these should get you started.

Presentation of Thoughts, Beliefs, Ideas, Values

Dr. Albert Mehrabian of University of California, Los Angeles has written on the subject of effective presentation. In a nutshell, his information has been ripped off by all manner of speakers and writers, with atttribution, but he ultimately determined through his research that there are three **V's** of spoken communication:

What counts in speaking with others.

Verbal	7%	**Words**
Vocal	38%	**Tone of Voice**
Visual	55%	**Nonverbal Behavior**

When the vocal and visual components of any message are inconsistent with the verbal content, your message will *not* be believed. It will be considered incongruent with your intention (tone) and behavior (visual) and therefore considered suspicious if not untrue.

Keep in mind that there is no harmony *without* conflict but let not your communication project conflict regarding where **you're** coming from. Be clear, concise, and specific. Your voice must be natural and it must be **yours.**

You can't give what you don't have. Continuous learning and applying the various processes and skills being discussed are essential to communications and growth. I want us all to embrace **CANILEAD**™ philosophies of living (pronounced *Can-é-lead*):

***C**ontinuous and **N**ever-Ending **I**mprovement, **L**earning, **E**nlightenment, **A**ccomplishment and **D**evelopment.*

It also contains a question: Can I Lead? Well, *yes, you **can**, but will you **choose** to?* And, who will you lead? Why, **YOU, of course!** (**Keep in mind: people are led by Self and others and process and things are managed. Animals—nonpeople type—are *trained!*)**

Remember: **Language drives behavior,** verbally, nonverbally and on paper/email/internet. Make **your** language *move* your thoughts, behavior, beliefs and values **forward.**

Never bullshit. If you don't know the answer or don't know what you are doing, say so or say nothing. That's the whole point here: **Know Thy Self!** That means you *must* know **S**trengths, **W**eaknesses, **O**pportunities and **T**hreats **(SWOTs)** *Own* your own stuff! Then it becomes incumbent on you to find out what you **need** to know. Find someone, a book, a class, a video or cassette tapes to assist you in **learning** what you **need** to know. Make the car a classroom.

Or, better yet, find some people out there you want to learn *from*, no matter who, and *go to school in their heads!*. Make contact and ask them to be helpful. Surprise! Most will be flattered and most will be of assistance. It still works 99% of the time: "Ask and you shall receive." It's **how** you ask that does the trick. Process, again!

So, the lesson here for all aspiring **bitches**, *with style* is:

Walk Your Talk, Y'all !!!

—Vikki Ashley

P³

My management consulting and communications company name is **P³** which stands for *Peace, Power and Prosperity.*

My company's mission is to provide **information, knowledge** and **processes** to individuals, organizations and corporations so that they may choose to take quantum leaps on their loose gravel paths to success. We specialize in communications, leadership, transformation and change.

My logo stands for *Thought, Word* and *Action* or *Father, Son* and *Holy Spirit.* Thought *(Father)* is the *Circle,* Word (vibration) *(Son)* is the *Triangle* and Action **(Holy Spirit)** is the *Square*—which stands for earth, the only place humans can demonstrate and manifest . . . "on earth *(square)* as it is in heaven (thought/*circle*)." The Word sets the **intention** in Mind through vibration—"speak the Word" *(triangle)*, thus assuring **attention** will be given to the **thought** and it will manifest through action. This happens when you say **"It is done."**

P is the sixteenth letter of the alphabet. To square anything is to extend it. To cube something is to take a quantum leap. So, $16^2 = 256$; $16^3 = 4096$. See the difference between **256** and **4096**? That *is* a quantum leap! Numerologically, **256** = **13** = **4**. 4 is the number of roots, of psychological and physical foundation building, of posterity. 4 is the number of a solid foundation *(four square)*, of the 4 corners of the earth *(North, South, East and West)*, of building something solid. **16** also equals **7**, the number that sets the pattern, the number of **Jesus**, who *set the pattern* of divinity for men when he became the **Christ**. 4096 = 19 =10 =1. 1 is the number of unity, of divinity, of pioneers who dare to risk, and people with "unity" of mind. 1 is adventure, new paths on the loose gravel of life. 1 is the number of new beginnings. It is the number of **Self**, *I Am.*

PART FOUR

Climbing Venus' Ladder

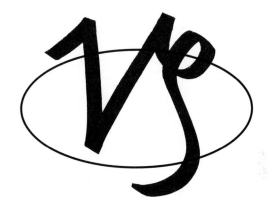

STEP TEN

I Am A Gateway To The World!

Be ye a doer of the word, then,
not a hearer or an instructor only.[1]

Doing our "deanly" duty at an alumni function—Bob and Vikki—1992

BITCHHood 1001
Self-Experience: I *Build*, Therefore I Am.

" **N**ext steps" are ways to test what you know about your spiritual growth. I was tested mightily when closing my company and looking toward my future in the world. I have already mentioned my purpose as **"making a difference in people's lives"** and making the "how" of what I do **stickable and useable.** It seems I always work to integrate the practical with the theoretical or, put another way, demonstrate that the spiritual and material are exactly the same, only on differing planes of reality. I am still doing that and the mix is working **for me,** as it will for you. The process has been long, arduous and challenging. Some times I wonder how much I stood in my own way because of the need to control what was happening **around** me? I am sure I did that a lot. It is also clear that the most wonderful events in my life occurred when I was just "flowing" along, "just passing through."

Meeting My One True Love

Early in my consulting with the midwestern university I mentioned earlier, the president asked me to take on an evening assignment that involved dressing up and going to a dinner at a 5-star restaurant in order to participate in an interview of a gentleman who was a candidate for a top academic administrative post.

Dressed to the nines, I entered the restaurant, walked up a staircase into the room and directly into the line of vision of a very handsome gentleman (and my destiny, though I didn't know it then). We stared at one another intently. I had never seen him before (in this life). He looked at me as if to say, "Where the hell have you *been?*" I was so startled I could only manage a "hello" and held out my hand. We exchanged pleasantries and I moved on to meet others enjoying the cocktail hour. Later, I felt someone behind me. It was he. He wanted to know if I was sitting with someone and, if not, would I sit next to him so we could talk further. "Yes," I said brightly. What a memorable "yes" that was. He had deep brown eyes that penetrated. I was up to the "eye feedback" my Self. My dark brown eyes also penetrated. The heat was building up so strongly, I could feel it in my bones.

We talked with the candidate and others at the table. About 30 minutes into dinner I felt something on my *knee!* It was *his* hand! He was feeling my leg and I couldn't smack him, yell at him or do *anything* without embarrassing my Self and definitely embarrassing him. I put my hand to my side and attempted to move his hand away, but he didn't budge. I had never then, nor have I ever since, had *anyone* play kneesies with me. What a brazen son of a bitch, I thought. Right out in broad dinner light! But it was clear no one was looking at us since attention was focused at the head of the table and our candidate. He *knew* that, of course. We talked about banalities and chit chat when we weren't focused on the candidate and my knee. I asked the usual questions about family, children, etc. He had all of the above—wife and children. Son of a gun! What was going *on?*

If you have never had this occur to *you,* let me assure you, it *can* be a thrill, especially when you've been celibate for a long, long time!. An embarrassing thrill, to be sure, but then rationality took over and I wondered whether or not this man of high station and responsibility was *also* a sex fiend or a slasher or a stalker. How was I to know? I'd *just* met him.

Just as dinner broke up, I stood up and without saying good night to anyone, fled the scene, got a taxi and returned to my hotel. I was leaving for San Diego the next morning after briefing the president, so I busied my Self with packing and wondering: what was this evening all about. Who *was* this man?

BE CAREFUL WHAT YOU ASK FOR

Back in San Diego I worked on my project with the schools. It was politically volatile, educationally dynamic and I was having fun as well as being challenged. This was the work I had been doing just before I was actually hired to work at the midwest university. One week later, my sexy friend called and indicated he would be in San Francisco on business. Might he come to San Diego and take me to dinner? Would I mind if he dropped by to see the project? Yes. No.

One month later, I showed him my creative imagination that had been manifested and was doing well. He met the staff and asked a lot of questions. He was impressed. I had built a building, outfitted it with real paintings and lovely furniture, as well as relaxing, colorful bean bags for seminaring and environmental support. He thought it was very unique and different. After the tour, as we parted, I responded positively to an invitation to meet him at the Shelter Island Inn for dinner.

As I drove up, he was leaning on his rented car in the parking lot. I walked over, put out my hand and he grabbed me, kissed me and whispered in my ear "I want to fuck you." I nearly fell over. I told him to "fuck off" and said I was leaving. "What kind of person are you anyway? Do people know you *act* this way? Why me? Don't answer. I'm outta here."

As I turned to leave, he came after me and told me that he didn't know *what* was happening. All he knew for sure is that he couldn't keep his hands off of me and had wanted to touch me from the first minute he'd seen me. "I'm not like this, I assure you. I just can't tell you what's going on! Please, please have dinner with me and let's talk about this." My curiosity just wouldn't let me leave. I, too, wanted to *know* what was going on.

After an evening with this handsome hunk, I found out he had some depth to him, a sense of humor and was quite open in discussing his life. I won't go into all of that detail, but it turned out to be a very interesting and, for me, an exciting evening. I could feel my Self liking this nutty guy, whom I still thought of as a "strange man," and wondering what kind of woman his wife was. What were his children like? Why was he doing what he was doing *with me*? I asked, "Is this your mid-life-crisis *modus operandi?*" He laughed and said that, actually, he was a real klutz at this type of game and that he really didn't know *how* to behave in these circumstances. He indicated his approach to me as evidence of his klutziness. True. But there was something about his way and his need to touch my hand, even over dinner, that made me wonder if this was a past-life meeting come to life.

Many new spiritual experiences had entered my life during this period and I began to wonder immediately why I was attracted to this guy. What **was** it?

Later, when I was hired at the university, I occasionally saw this man. We'd have lunch and he was very supportive. His eyes always twinkled when he saw me and he provided me a very solid source of feedback and information.

Over the almost three years I was at the university, I *knew* he was going to make a run at me and, even though it would be awkward, in my own heart I *wanted* it to happen. It did. And it was a total disaster. It was my first experience with male stage fright, ending up in inability to execute. He was disappointed and so was I but we sat and talked about what guilt can do to someone's psyche and how, after all that blustery start, I was *certain* he had his sexual act together. Well, he didn't and I was to find out that he really hadn't had any experience *outside* of marriage, except with his wife and it had occurred when they were in their late teens—just before marriage. In his mind, therefore, he had been a technical virgin and so was she. In our initial effort, he was a technical sexual flop. But he was damned romantic and I found that part of him resonated with a strongly romantic part of me.

I was not *that* sexually experienced but I *knew* what it was about and I had a built-in ability to make my way around a man's body sensually. It came in handy on this first encounter when I discovered what oral sex can do for a frightened partner! I also learned the power of giving!

He was not critical of my "splotched" body nor did he comment or even ask questions about why I had a two-color skin. That was curious. But then he was a doctor and I chalked it up to his knowledge, graciousness and not minding, anyway. He seemed to care for me, splotches and all.

We didn't "do sex" any more during our relationship. We became good friends. He was supportive, instructive, playful and respectful. I was the same. We discovered our core val-

ues, thinking on politics (we didn't agree), children and relationships. I had strong views and so did he. I uncovered his
agnosticism and total skepticism about anything religious and
his very doubtful and almost contemptuous thinking about
matters spiritual He always stuck to the scientific line regarding "there is no proof," and I indicated that was fine, "just don't
laugh at me or my thoughts about these things." He didn't. It
turned out to be a good beginning for events down the road
neither of us could foresee.

IN DUE (DO) TIME

When I was terminated from my position, I said goodbye
to my friend and left. I did not see him again for over seven
years (ten years from the time we had met atop the stairs in
the restaurant.)

During that time my life changed drastically. The next turn
in the road after the Kitty Hawk was politics. I ran for office
for a state senate seat and lost. It was great fun and I learned
a great deal. Richard Nixon, Ronald Reagan and Pete Wilson
took pictures with me and I met people I would not have otherwise met, like Bob Dole. I was *not*, however, an ideologue. I
was socially moderate and fiscally conservative (like the core
of Republicans *then*—and I believe still are) but very compassionate and a real trail blazer on education. I knew how much
it meant to be educated, even though I also understood that
wasn't *all* it took. Still, it was a head start from all other bases
I could see.

The loss of the race put me in a state of both apprehen-
sion and chaos. Now I *really* had to decide what to do about
my life. Luckily (I know, there are *no* accidents in the universe!),
a friend called and suggested I take his place at an Aspen
Institute conference on the big island of Hawaii. He said, "It will
give you a chance to chill out and will put you in touch with
dynamic people." I said "yes," and he was right. It was what I
needed.

Walks on the black sand beaches and sitting under the
Hawaiian sky every chance I got really began to blow my tubes

out and I was thinking clearly and spiritually again. One night just before the close of the institute, I took a pad of paper out to a bench by a light, breathed in the wonderful night air, and began to write down all the things I was going to do with my life. At the top of the list were:

1. Do something about your vitiligo².
2. Go somewhere in the country where there are seasons and meet some new people. Leave San Diego!
3. Return to consulting and pursue your purpose. Hire only those people you **need** to get the job done. Otherwise, work alone.
4. Pursue my spiritual development. Too many unanswered questions.

I loved and, still love, politics. I did believe that I could pursue my purpose as a politician for the people. I still believe that's possible if you don't want to be a professional politician and only want to serve for ten years or so as a political stateswoman. However, the rough and tumble of getting elected (and, boy, is it ever *rough*!) isn't pretty. It can be fun now and then, but it isn't pretty or easy. Raising money is the closest thing to being a beggar or prostitute I have ever known. I decided that "ask and you shall receive" works in any arena—and it *does*, but the doublespeak of politics always has its *quid pro quo* and you *know* it and so do the donors. People who already have money sometimes take a different tack. They are like bettors at the race track. They bet on politicians not horses and have a great time gambling. They love winners. They, too expect a payoff down the line but can afford to wait to define their own terms for what they want. Interesting and real.

Abortion was a huge issue when I ran in the late '70s, as it is today. I was prochoice then and still am. That was where the moderates of the Republican party were and still are. Two stories about the race and abortion:

1. A young doctor from the University of California, San Diego School of Medicine was heading a prolife committee and interviewing all candidates. When he visited me, he simply said he wanted my position on abortion.

   I told him that I believe in a woman's ownership of her own body and her inviolate right to choose for her Self. Whatever decision she makes is between her and her God. And that I nor anyone else had a right to intervene in that decision.

   He was aghast, of course, and asked me if he could change my mind. "No," I said. But let me ask *you* a question: "When was the last time *you* were pregnant and bore a child?" "Why, never!" And he looked at me incredulously. "You *know* men can't do *that!*"

   "Well, then," I said, "When you *can*, then you'll have a right to discuss the subject. Until then, don't come back. Good afternoon."

2. I was asked to speak at a gathering in Chula Vista. I expressed my views but deliberately left the abortion question for the Q&A. I had already made my statements about education, equal opportunity for all, etc.

   The first question concerned my position on abortion. I expressed my Self a little differently this time since there were many older couples in the audience. I added: "You all are aware that abortion has been with us from the beginning of time. Women have found ways and always will when being forced to bear children for reasons other than their own desire and creative urge." I indicated that in the days when contraception was not universally available here in our own country, there were other ways—some very dangerous, like back-alley hacks and abortion mills. **"So, let me ask you?** Do you prefer to support choice and clinical abortion in hospitals with good, sanitary medical care for our women (no matter the age) or do you want to support the underworld and illegal operation of abortion? The point being, it will be with us forever as it has been so far. Who are **you** to judge women who make that choice? Who are you to judge one another, period?"

Silence! There was no answer and no further questions on the subject. We moved on to other issues.

As I prepared to leave, men and women came up to me and suggested they had never thought of abortion the way I had discussed it and thanked me for another point of view.

How did they vote? Well, I know most of them voted for my opponent, but I did get some votes in their precincts. I like to think some of them were the ones to whom I suggested "There is another way of looking at this." (**A Course in Miracles,** W,50)

I lost the race and was offered a seat on the City Council. The votes were there but my head wasn't. I wanted to play in a bigger pond. I declined.

There were some scary aspects to politics, I found, like being "followed" all the time. Having my children threatened, since whomever hired the "shadow" knew how important my children were to me. After I lost the race, the "shadow" revealed him Self and told me that they could find "nothing" on me. I didn't even cheat on my income tax or fuck around like lots of the men did. But they knew that if they had to "deal" with me they *could* do so through my children! He was right on. I would *never* jeopardize my children for any reason on this earth. None! (I wouldn't even send my kids to my mom and dad when I wanted to go to law school in 1968 because I knew those three years with my parents in that crazy little town called Xenia! would **ruin** them and jeopardize their futures So I chose not to return to law school.) The "shadow" was very flattering toward me regarding my talent, ability to speak and my integrity. "*They* don't like people like you," he said, "because you're hard to control. But *they* find ways." He reiterated to me how one by one powerful women in Congress were leaving. No matter what these women say their reason for their going is," he said, "they've been given a choice. Leave or be ruined. Either way, you're leaving." Scumbags!

I gathered the children at a local restaurant and told them about the meeting with this asshole—knowledgeable asshole about us as he was. I gave them my plan: I won't be in the city council; I am planning to depigment my vitiligo, and I am going to leave San Diego. My oldest son felt I was crazy not to take the council seat since I wanted to be in politics. Youth is brash and he could not then understand the scope and depth of my feelings for their security and safety. My conversation with my campaign "shadow" had shaken me to my roots. I had mixed feelings about local office anyway and the shadow made me pause and rethink politics, period. I chose not to continue down *that* path.

My oldest son and my daughter were upset with my plan to depigment. My youngest son, Alan, said "Go ahead and do what you want, Mom." None were too surprised that I wanted to leave San Diego. Consulting and doing a business there is like pulling teeth. It's not a headquarters town and I was always on airplanes going somewhere *else* to work.

THE BIG MANIFESTATION AND TRANSFORMATION

The trauma of having white and tan splotches on my body began at age 11. I paid little attention to them until about age 14 when I began to notice that these spots on my feet, hands and waist, no longer just little, were spreading across my toes, and the back of my hands, and down and up my waist where noticeable. My parents weren't interested in doing anything about these spots because Dr. Lee, our "country family practitioner," said he didn't know what caused it, nor did anyone, and there was no cure or suitable treatment he was aware of. It was hard in gym to conceal my "problem." I was discouraged.

I knew a woman in town, Thelma Harper, who was thoroughly "dalmationed," as I called it, but she was dynamic and didn't seem to pay any attention to it. I had an outgoing personality, too, and decided to ignore what I could do nothing about.

In my first marriage, my husband's behavior and his abusive language began to target my vitiligo as a way of humiliating me. "Look at you, you spotted leopard! No one will *ever* want you looking like *that*! You're lucky *I* married you." It was the worst feeling I have ever had and even as I write these words today, tears fill my eyes. I was in terrible psychological pain. I really *did* feel no other man would ever want me looking like I did and so I decided to just settle in and make the best of a bad situation.

During the years, though, my curiosity drove me to begin investigating vitiligo in the literature. It had all sorts of speculative prospects: hypothyroidism, or hyperthyroidism, or Addison's disease, or leprosy. Truth is, *no one* knew the origins of this disorder and no one knew its cure.

After my divorce, I began in earnest to search out experts across the country every opportunity I had in my business travels. As a result, I decided to *repigment* my Self. I used oral and topical treatments and ultraviolet light. What a disaster! I burned my skin; had very bad reactions to the sun and essentially had no results. Doctors were very unfriendly and professionally unprepared to treat someone as determined as I was. The last doctor I went to for guidance on how to handle vitiligo simply asked me how long I had had it. At that point I told him about 35 years. "Then live with it," he said. Turned on his heels and left the room. I was angry and stunned. But I knew then it would be *my journey to make* if I wanted to do anything about **my** condition.

I then happened on an article (no accidents in the universe) in a magazine I was reading in flight and noticed that someone named Dr. James Nordlund at Yale University was doing research in vitiligo and looking at depigmentation. (He is now chairman of dermatology at the University of Cincinnati Scool of Medicine.) I also simultaneously learned of a doctor at Freedman's Hospital in Washington, D.C. who had successfully depigmented several patients who had vitiligo. I also learned that over 40 million people in the world suffer from this skin disorder! After all this research, I made up my mind to be "whole" again. I just wanted to be one color all over and to know what that felt like. I decided to *depigment*.

I could not find a dermatologist willing to cooperate with me in this endeavor and provide the on-going supervision and prescriptions for Benoquine I would need. I thought of a plan. I met with the chairman of the UCSD Department of Dermatology, told him what I planned to do. He suggested I was taking a terrific risk and that he could *not* be responsible for any outcomes related to what I was planning. I then made him an offer: "I will give you a written release and total immunity from *any* responsibility or liability if you will provide me with an open-ended prescription for Benoquine. Further, you will never see me again." He did it and I never saw him again. (He's dead now! I hope he's looking down and taking note of how well things worked out!)

I didn't want to stop my treatment, once begun, so I went to the bank, told my banker what I wanted to do, presented him with the medical information and waited for an answer. He said he'd have to think about it because he had never heard of such a thing but was intrigued with what I proposed. That was Friday. On Monday, he called and told me to pick up my $3000. At that time Benoquine was $7.99 + tax per tube. Today it is around $50 + tax per tube!

I was guided internally to put the Benoquine in a carrier oil I made up and had already been using to moisturize my body. The oil was a formula[3] devised by Edgar Cayce, the famous sleeping prophet, consisted of 6 oz. peanut oil, 2 oz. olive oil, 2 oz. rose water, 1 tbs. dissolved lanolin. Over time, I adjusted this formula to 6 oz. Cold-pressed peanut oil, 2 oz. cold-pressed virgin olive oil and 2 tbs. Vitamin E. I found I did not want the rose water *in* the mix but used it alone to splash on my face as an astringent and tightener. To my adjusted Cayce formula (now found in health stores as Home Health Care Almond Glow) I added one tube of Benoquine. I now call the compound ***Atalaria Lotion***. I mixed it in my electric mixer, poured it into 2 8-oz plastic bottles, went to the bathroom, took a hot shower to open my pores, looked in the mirror and said to the Universal Life Energy within me (God), "It's you and me, baby" and began to apply what I was visualizing as a "magic formula."

Every morning **immediately** after my shower, I put on my formula. I then went about my business in completing my toilette. I continued to use all the "goop and guk" I put on my face to cover my spots, which had ruined more clothes than I can count, but what's a body to do? Cover it up, of course!

I soon learned that my body absorbed the oil pretty fast, that I did not have to use a lot because it spread well, and that my skin continued to be soft, soft, soft. Thirty days later, my face was absolutely clear. Before I found that out, though, I had an embarrassing experience related to my experiment.

I went to a political reception in Del Mar, California. I enjoyed the company of political associates, had some wine and then went to the bathroom. I looked into the mirror to refresh my lipstick and screamed! What looked like skin on both cheeks was separated at the bottom at the chin bone! I was aghast, startled and scared out of my wits. What had I *done* to my Self?

Crying, I left the party, drove back to San Diego, ran to the bathroom, and cried out to my God, **"Now what do I do?"**

Came the answer (as I live and breathe), " Get your bottle of Happy Hands and Feet and a thick wash cloth dipped in warm water. Put the Happy Hands and Feet gently on your face. Slowly massage it off with the warm wash cloth. Now, what do you see?" I took off my dress and followed instructions. After all, I had no medical help or supervision, and *I* certainly wasn't an expert. So, I followed the voice's orders.

I freaked! Staring back at me was this lovely clear face that was totally white, no, porcelain! Not a blemish was in sight. I could *not* believe it. Really? Yes! I cried and cried for joy for about 15 minutes. I was so deeply affected by seeing my face looking like *someone else,* I just didn't know *what* to do. So, I went into my living room and laid down on the floor, began deep breathing and a vision of what I imagine Jesus looked like came to me:

I was a very little girl holding his hand. He walked me across a beautiful park-like carpet of green up a gently sloping hill. As we walked, I grew physically but he remained the same. By the time we reached the top of the hill, I was a young lady. I was standing on a precipice and before me was what I would describe as a very broad, deep chasm spread into eternity with beautiful light structures that looked like buildings, and other things, like the whole world, spread out before me in glorious orange, pink, lavender and gold light.

Jesus said the words I have since carried in my soul:

"Tell me what you want to know. Tell me what you want to see. Tell me where you want to go. Tell me what you want to do."

He held my hand tightly and I *believed* him. I *knew* it was real. And I vowed to **tell him** what I wanted to know, see, do and where I wanted to go **from that moment forward.**

When I "returned" from my inner experience, I remember getting up and looking in the mirror again. That was the "voice" that had guided me in what to do about the hanging skin. Say what you will, I *know* it happened and I have benefitted from that experience ever since. Today, I share what I know with other individuals struggling with vitiligo. (I send out information about my depigmentation. If you're interested, there is a form in the **Bitch's Book Bag.** It's without charge.) There's so much to say about the psychological effects of this disease. People ask you whether or not you were burned in a fire, or "Do you have leprosy?" or "What happened to *you?*" *Ignorance is the original sin,* remember? People who are ignorant are insecure and therefore cruel as a defense against their own ignorance. Yes, these comments often hurt when I was small and even early in my adulthood But I got over it because that was just the way it was. Now, the way it *is* is psychologically and personally enlightening.

NOBODY KNOWS ME ANY MORE, BUT I KNOW ME!

One week after my "miracle," I saw old friends in a shoe store in Mission Valley. I said "hello" to them and they just stared at me, not acknowledging my greeting. I asked how they were and they smiled limply. I was so taken aback I could not *believe what had just happened*. It had. And it continued. My first lesson: the "color" of your skin, otherwise known as your pigment, *matters!* But it is, after all, *only* skin deep. I am living proof of *that*. Now, though, I was to find out that people really don't look at one another or even *know* at whom they are looking.

My two oldest children needed some time to get use to what was happening to me. Alan always knew and was supportive. "Hey, Mom, your hair's too dark for your skin," he said, laughing. "You need to lighten it." He'd tell me how pretty I looked and was a constant source of psychological and loving support.

I was now moving in a world *I* knew but did not *know* me. I had to reintroduce my Self to people I had known for over 20 years! What an experience. It was clearly time for me to move on and leave San Diego. New people would never know what I looked like before.

My vitiligo depigmentation progressed nicely. I would discover parts of my body peeling all of a sudden. I was no longer shocked but expected it. I can't recount how many times I peeled, but the final result is a body of exceptionally lovely skin all over, and I like to say it's as soft as a baby's "behind." And so it is. Still, after I completed the depigmentation (it took about 18 months altogether), I continued with my Cayce lotion *without* the Benoquine. I use the Almond Glow lotion to this day, immediately after my shower. I use no other body moisturizers and my sun block (Neutrogena 30 SPF) and Clinique foundation go over it without any topical or internal chemical reactions.

I have always been sun sensitive, even *before* depigmentation and now I am *really* sun sensitive. The antidote to that is to stay out of the sun completely or wait until evening and late afternoon when the sun goes down to go outside without a hat. It's inconvenient, to be sure. What to do? Wear hats, of course. And, since it was going to be a medical necessity for the rest of my life, why not make it a part of my clothing and my image? Why not, indeed! And so it is. Hats are a complete and total part of who I put into the public view. Since taking them on and off can be a problem for the hair, I just never take them off in public. Period. I have an enormous collection and carefully select my hats to reflect me and coordinate with what I'm wearing. I have become The Hat Lady!

One of my books in the future will be about vitiligo and the devastating psychological and emotional damage it causes. It is **not** "merely" cosmetic as so many physicians have told their clients. *It is a deep down bone issue which I am now convinced relates to past life "stuff."* In my case, I have always seen race as a superficial issue for *individuals*. I know how explosive it is culturally and politically, but after I found out personally how people use the color of your skin to "*not* know who you are," I have redoubled my own efforts to share with people how much more important it is to **know thy Self** and to answer the question **"Who Am I?"** than to care what people think about you or the color of your skin. It's what **you** think about **you** that counts. Period.

Had I *not* been on the path to spiritual development, I am confident I would not have been able to engage my inner physician and heal my Self of this disorder. Had I not had the reversals in my life, I feel certain I would not have been able to "take" the heat of rejection and of being "overlooked" because my exterior shell was very light in complexion. Had I not **known** who I was, I might have taken on a personality or some type of image totally out of kilter with my soul and its purpose. It was a perfect time to go hide and never return to my old life. But it was also the perfect time to stop and take stock of where I'd been and where I was going again, and "go and grow."

This time, though, I was miles down the road and had some principles to live and work by and to share. Those principles follow on page 367.

TIME TO BE ALONE IN THE WORLD

I decided it was time in my life to apply my new perspectives, use my growing sense of the power of my vision with Jesus to "tell me what you want to know, see, do and where you want to go,"

I went to Houston and spent time with an old friend, Cindy Reinhardt. While there I needed to make money, so I decided (with my advanced degree) to return to temporary work as a secretary to reduce pressure and stress on me while I took a spiritual sabbatical. I had no trouble finding work and was put into executive offices in finance and investments. I was so much more knowledgeable than any other support staff in those offices that I was asked each and every place I went to "come to work for us." That was good for my ego, but I knew they wouldn't be able to handle the "real" me who was seeping through my seams in spite of my desire to contain her. I needed the "down" time to read, go to classes, travel to seminars, and just "be" with my Self.

I had told my children when I left San Diego that I was "running away from home" and that I would never be back— not in the way they would remember "home" to be. I knew I was at a fork in the road and that I would not turn around. Well, I *could* have, but I *chose* not to. And I counseled each of them to move on with their lives and find out who *they* were as well.

I "chilled out" for nearly two years. I was seeking new information, reading, applying what I read. I undertook the practice of yoga in earnest, finally going beyond just deep breathing. I studied Hatha Yoga and it not only helped me physically, but renewed my energy for meditation and internal dialogue with my Inner Knower. I began to eat more nutritiously and to exercise. I needed this. My family has a genetic disposition in the females toward small breasts and big butts and thighs. I fortunately had a flat butt but it was wide. And the breasts, well . . . they followed the genes!

I began a continual battle with my own image and dieted up and down and every way possible.

Finally, I decided to just eat well, do yoga and *some* exercise, and let it go at that!

I was (and still am) into holistic living and healing in a big way. All of it was focused on healing *me*. I *knew* it was a journey I had to take and there were more things out there as a psychologist I just *had* to know in order to fulfill my true purpose. I had many past-life regressions. I already use guided visualizations in my work and in my own life. Meditation was very important and still is. Music became even more important to me because of the knowledge I was then gaining about its impact on healing, along with color. I was soaking it all up and putting it to use on me and my friends. Every step, I espoused my **Principles to Live and Work By,** see page 367. I use them to this day and they keep me straight as I walk my talk.

RECONNECTING WITH THE WORLD

Finally, it was time to recycle my Self and reemerge into the world. It was "**due (do) time.**" I reconnected with business contacts in Washington, D.C., obtained several contracts, and moved to Washington.

I kept in physical touch with my children by occasionally visiting San Diego. On one of my return trips to D.C., I stopped off in Columbus, Ohio. After all the years and no communication, I called Bob. Remember Bob at the dinner table and in the parking lot? I asked if he'd help me put a protocol together to assist my parents in helping my youngest sister who had been diagnosed bipolar (manic-depressive). I wanted to "try out" some of my newly found holistic approaches with vitamins and herbs and I needed some medical advice. Would he help? Of course. Just like nearly eight years had *never* happened.

We met at the Columbus airport, I was waiting for him and decided to not greet him to test my new persona. True to my experience, he *walked right past me!* He didn't recognize me, either. In my newly acquired skin, I was truly a stranger! Wow, I thought. What a test! How could he not have *known* who I *was?*

But he didn't. And that's the point!. We do not take time to really *notice* people or to look in their eyes to see who they really are. Not even the people we love. Oh, well . . .

Our reconnect was instant, however. He had been busy since I'd last seen him. He had divorced his first wife and married again. And, he said, was planning to divorce again, but had not yet started the proceedings. So, after our work on my sister's protocol, he asked if, when he was in Washington, could he take me to dinner? "Of course," I responded; "be sure to call first."

Within the next month, he called and said "Set up Dinner at Cantina D'Italia. I'll be in town for two days. May I stay with you?" "Yes." And he did. And it started all over again. This time, though, I was ready.

He came and went for the next year and finally divorced. I worked very hard all over the country on my assignments and he joined me whenever he could. It wasn't long before he asked me to marry him. Of all the things in the world I wanted to do, that was the very last. He told me he wasn't going to give up. I told him I would live with him but not marry him. I was still skittish about men. I wanted my freedom and I could not imagine having the type of freedom I had in mind within a marriage. Clearly, the memory of my first marriage had not yet been expunged. It was lurking in my subconscious, tweaking all of my nerves whenever Bob asked. Actually, I did *not* want to commit my Self to a relationship that would undermine my growth. And, by now, I was beginning to see his authoritative side very clearly. Being an authoritative type my Self, this wasn't going down very well.

I had also changed my name before reconnecting with Bob. I did it as a spiritual development that went along with my transformation. I needed new energy in my *nom de plume* to go along with my new self. I was "given" my current name by my Inner Self. I included it in a list of names I sent to my counselor, Gregge Tiffen, in Dallas. The only name that worked "energywise" was the name I had been "given"—Vikki Ashley. I formally changed my name on February 3, 1983 at 1:50 P.M. in

Cincinnati, Ohio. That's when I got the report from Gregge that this was the *only* name that worked.

One thing was for sure. I loved Bob. I cared for him. We were already friends. He was caring, supportive and, yes, dammit, *directive*. I kept telling him he did not have to treat me like he did his other wives—as appendages. I was not only his peer, I was very aware that I could live without him.

Still, we met all over the country. I began to rationalize that this might work, but not in marriage. Yes, I would move in with him. After all, one of **my** values is that I will not enter a marital relationship without a trial experience. I believe strongly in premarital relationship development and I do **not** support ignorance in the sexual realm. It is not only damaging to the individual psyche, but the notion that a woman should be a virgin at marriage is absolutely designed to keep women subservient to men and is outmoded and outdated. How do women find out there is more to sex and love than they are learning with their one mate? How do you grow in marriage without threatening the marriage, especially sexually? Remember, *Ignorance is the Original Sin!*

The warmth of sex eventually wears off and the cold hard reality of relationship takes its place. This is not only a youthful phenomenon; it occurs whenever you take on a new mate. Fortunately, if you've grown and if you have more knowledge, you have some tools with which to work. Still, adjustment is a **bitch**—and a **Being In Total Control of Her Self** finds out just what she does and doesn't know **about** her Self in such circumstances. For a while, not much. I regressed in my desire. Deep down I wanted to make this relationship work. We both did. But Gregge Tiffen told me that he *never* says this to *anyone*, but **"Do not marry this man.** Play with him, have fun with him, but **do not marry him!"**

Needless to say, my soul decided differently. **In due (do) time**, we came to New Orleans and finally were married at 1:30 P.M. on December 31, 1986. New Year's Eve. A new year. A new beginning.

My approach to our children was simply to leave it up to

them when, or even if, they met Bob and whether or not they would be able to "like" one another as people. I had reared my children to respect their Selfs and to extend that respect to all whom they met. Bob had done the same. I didn't foresee any problems and there were none.

THE VALLEY OF THE SHADOW OF DEATH

My youngest son, Alan, whom you met in the Introduction, was a creative and dynamic individual. Everyone loved him and he was a salesman *par excellence*. He did his best to get through college, but he didn't go past his sophomore year. He was in retail and sold high-end crystal, silver, etc. and wound up in men and women's high-end clothing, including furs and leather. He provided me with some beautiful gifts but the most wonderful gift he gave was him Self. He had a premonition he would die young. He also "knew" he had strong spiritual assistance that kept him out of trouble and turned his steering wheel more than once, he told me, when he was in danger of death.

For three years, Bob was totally supportive of Alan throughout all of his trauma; financially, sometimes emotionally, *and* verbally. Bob saw to it that Alan had an apartment of his own in downtown San Diego across from Horton Plaza—where Alan *wanted* to live. He made sure he was totally financially supported. After he understood I was going to "be there" for Alan whether *he* liked it or not, he really put his energy into supporting both of us. I want to publicly acknowledge his generosity of spirit in fact and in deed. He was *there* and never, ever said "no" to anything that was needed.

I returned home after Alan's death in February, 1991, to grieve. I felt totally withdrawn after the almost simultaneous deaths of my dear friend Avis Johnson, my dad, Alan, my mom. I was done in emotionally. My spiritual energy was low.

My sex drive was absolutely gone. I didn't want anything to do with anything or anyone. Our marriage was taking a body blow and I simply refused to do anything about it. What

I wanted to do was find out what had happened? What was the message in all of this *death?*

I decided to go into therapy and stayed for a year. It was the best thing I could have possibly done for my health. I left therapy the day after I had a dream of a large blue whale breaking out of a huge tank and swimming away into the ocean. The significance of that dream was not lost on *me.* I knew I had broken through and that therapy was over.

I truly found out that what you want in your life you have to be-come your Self. There is no other way to put it. *What I wanted in my life, I had to become.* Then I knew I would mag-netize that very thing or person to me. So, remembering what Jesus had said to me, I decided to *be* exactly what I wanted in my life by becoming the "real" me. And I told him (my Internal Physician) what those things were. I claimed everything I wanted with deep desire and intense emotion.

My personal healing and that of my relationship began to take place when I told my husband who I was and what I want-ed for me. I let him know I wanted to share my future with him as an equal, but that it no longer was a requirement for my hap-piness that he be present in my life. I changed the way *I* viewed everything about our relationship. I described my primary rela-tionship as being the one I had with my Self and the Universe. I was comfortable with that and knew it would work for *me.* I told him that I knew we had both come into each other's lives for a reason. I had learned a lot of lessons in the relationship, the most important being tolerance for differences and accep-tance of him *just as he was.* Now he had to accept me just as I was and we would have to count on direct and unvarnished communications to take us further, if we chose to go further. I was willing to accept that we had individual differences that would never change. That was fine with me. But I also recog-nized all those good things and basic core values we shared. But they had to manifest in reality and go well beyond words and talk. They had to be visible to me, in due (do) time!

I had chosen. Now it was his turn.

August 12, 1988

HAPPY BIRTHDAY, BOB!!!   A NEW YEAR BEGINS...

Dear Darling:

It's very easy to write you a love letter because I love you without conditions. That's it!! Pure and simple.

But that doesn't tell you how much...

1.   I appreciate you.
2.   I respect you.
3.   I enjoy making love to (and with) you.
4.   I treasure your support - in all ways.
5.   I treasure your being a mirror for me and reflecting back to me a lot of
       things we both have in common.
6.   I love your sense of humor--when you let it show!
7.   I enjoy being hugged by you.
8.   I accept you as you are and as you continue to *choose* to be!
9.   I continue to grow and change.
10.   I appreciate your accepting me as *I* am.

Love is the most powerful emotion on this earth. I now understand the importance of loving me. It leaves so much more positive energy for loving you, as my mirror.

Be assured, my darling spouse that there s no thing, at this moment in our relationship, that I regret. It is all good (even the spats) for me; I hope, for you.

Remember, I give you these gifts of love. Accept them with that understanding and enjoy them.

Here's to your continued health and growth in understanding of *you*. Face it, you'll probably *never* understand me totally. But, that's OK. We've got more than enough to keep this partnership going, and going well!

I love you.

Vikki

Your sexy Gemini lover, partner, playmate and
Spouse

PRINCIPLES TO LIVE AND WORK BY

The following principles provide each individual with a foundation that reinforces the importance of individual responsibility and the impact of being **aware** of **who you are, what you want in life, and how you want to go about achieving** your goals and those of your chosen organization or entrepreneurial effort.

1. You create your own reality. Make it what you *truly* want!

2. My perceprion of reality *is* my reality, until new information changes *my* perception!

3. You are responsible for your choices and therefore the **consequences** of those choices.

4. Put names *with* behavior. No rumors allowed. If you **say** it, be prepared to name it, where it comes from, and then own it. If you don't want to do the foregoing, *then don't say it!*

5. Assume nothing. Ask! Otherwise, it makes an ass/u/me.

6. **All** choices have price tags. Be prepared to pay for what you choose to do or say. Remember: there are rewards to *you* in retaining your own integrity. Remember: the choices you make may *not* always fit with the vision, mission, goals and choices of the organization or enviroment you are in. When they do, rejoice. When they *don't*, be prepared to leave.

7. Know your **S**trengths, **W**eaknesses, **O**pportunities, and **T**hreats **(SWOTs)**. Be prepared to **use** your strengths and compensate for your weaknesses—but *not* by hiding them. **Own** them. Then either do something about them (weaknesses) or live with the **consequences of doing nothing.**

8. **You** must know your Self in order to effectively know others. We mirror with one another what it is we need to assess, accept, own and release in our Selfs. Put another way, **You reap what you sow; What goes around, comes around.**

9. *Love your Self. Think for your Self. Act for your Self. Question everything, including your Self. Seek answers **within** your Self.* When you know y-o-u, then you can *effectively* communicate with, and relate to others.

10. It's **ok** to be unique and different. Once you *accept* this, you can face, rather than *avoid*, difficulties and the outside world.

11. Every move's a move and **every** move counts! **Trust the process!**

12. Leadership and communications are the Siamese twins of change, process, and organization.

STEP ELEVEN

I Reach the Stars through Vision and Mastery!

To change your mood or mental state,
change your vibration.
—The Kybalion

*We enjoy our **partnership**—1997*

Bitchhood 1101
Self-Detachment: I *See*, Therefore I Am.

K nowledge, like wealth, is intended for use. Possession of knowledge, unless accompanied by a manifestation and expression in action, is like hoarding precious metals or money—it's foolish. They are intended for circulation. "The Law of Use is Universal, and (he) *she* who violates it suffers by reason of *her* (his) conflict with natural forces.:" (*The Kybalion, p. 214*) (As ammended by the author.)

To be a mental miser is violating the Law of Use and so having information, studying axioms and aphorisms is useless unless you *practice* them also. So, a **Bitch *With Style*** must *walk her talk*. No ifs, ands, or buts.

My Bridge To Self

For me, *walking my talk* meant sharing with my spouse all of the things I was doing to change *my* life. I always assured him that I was not asking *him* to change. I was only changing me. If he didn't like where I was going with those changes or if they stepped on his soul in a way he could not accept, he would have to decide whether or not he could make a life with *me*. As for me, I now recognized that I must, no matter what the price—even if that included divorce—make the changes in my life necessary for me to be happy. I hoped these changes would be *in* our marriage but, if not, *outside* our marriage would have to do.

I consider this period in my life (1990-1994) to be the completion of the bridge to my highest Self that I had been building for over forty years and I was going to complete this crossing no matter what and be totally whole. "High time," I thought. This business of integrating ***SpiritMentalEmotionsBody (SMEB)*** energy is tough sledding until you pass the crisis or go through chaos or a significant emotional event (SEEs). This, of course, happens many times along the way and at each point, you must decide to go forward or remain stuck. Each time, during each event, it's *your* call and **no one** can decide *for* you because you must ultimately pay the price for *your* choice.

Responsibility for every aspect of your life is just *that!* **You create your own reality. Make it what *you truly* want!.** I had been saying that for over thirty years. I had been living what that belief and principle stood for my whole adult life. So it's clear to me there are **no** victims and there are no boogey men. "Only I can deprive my Self of anything. Do not oppose this realization, for it is truly the beginning of the dawn of light" says **A Course in Miracles** (T, 136) Yeah! That means "I'm *it*," I kept telling my Self. "I'm *it* and that's *that*."

STEPPING INTO THE WIND

My vision for my life has always included freedom and equality *in* relationship at *all* levels—mental, sexual, financial, social, and professional. It's clear, from some of the episodes in my life that I have shared with you, that I did not always *act* on that belief based on where I was at that time and based on the choices I made or chose not to make. The choices I made on my path provided the experiences I needed to finally confront what, indeed, this vision is all about. These experiences provide the information, practical knowledge and recognition of consequences that are absolutely essential for a **bitch, *with* style's** growth. I had been "testing" it all along the way, reevaluating my behavior, values and perception of what *my* reality was so that my actions gradually and consciously began to reflect *exactly* who *I am* and who I was consciously be-coming.

> *My definition of courage is:*
> **C**ultivate and
> **O**rganize your
> **U**nlimited
> **R**esources
> through **A**ction
> which
> **G**uarantees
> **E**nlightenment!
> —Vikki Ashley

The crisis of death I had confronted during 90-91 had put before me an undeniable opportunity to deal with my beliefs and values and placed in my hands the gifts of *opportunity, clarity, truth and courage* and asked me to embrace each one without fear by looking into the mirror of my own soul without regard to anyone else in my life. Therapy had provided the *opportunity*. My posttherapeutic evaluation provided the *clarity*. My acceptance of my deep desire for freedom and equality *in* relationship as *my truth* cinched my decision. My communications to my spouse of *my* decision to grow took *courage*.

I wrote that definition of *courage* on January 7, 1992, during an evaluation of my life. By this definition I was able to accept that I had at various stages in my life exhibited courage, even in the face of fear of loss of income, relationships, and support. I am comfortable sharing it with you because I know how hard it is to act in the process of confronting one's true Self, but confront it we all must if we are to enjoy health. St. John's "dark night of the soul" is not a one-time occurrence. All of us who work with individuals, groups and/or businesses know that this time comes not once, not twice, but many times on the loose gravel path to enlightenment and dynamic change.

The **bitch *with style*** understands that she must live with her Self 100% of the time and that enlightenment opens her spirit to information *that she must use* to walk her talk. Her enlightenment (to be in knowledge of) regarding who she is remains the most important part of her growth and power.

The day a **bitch *with style*** *decides* to walk into the service of loving her Self (focusing her thoughts and emotion on her desires) is the day she plugs back into her power and reclaims all the scattered pieces she has strewn around the environment in which she lives and works. She consciously replaces her "shorted out" cord with a new one, capable of handling her "amped up" circuits. Her conscious understanding of the importance of using her energy to execute her dreams, hopes and wishes reminds me of Marshall Field's statement "give the lady what she wants." That is *exactly* what God/the Universe does once you learn how to focus your emotion and desire on your *own* priorities. You then magnetize to you whatever your thoughts continue to focus on. Best you put this energy to work in the service of *your* soul.

Now, does that mean you never provide service to others. *Au contraire*. You are better able to serve others when your cup is full and you have enough to share. Remember, anger and resentment, born of lack, do not hurt those toward which they are directed. They hurt *you*, the sender. They disturb your internal chemistry and disrupt your energy flow even to the point of illness if there is no intervention on *your* part. Your chakras in your etheric body and your aura (soul energy) reflect every single thought you have. Language, internal and external, does indeed drive your behavior and your health. *You create your own reality—always, always, always!*

So, keep in mind, whatever else you consider important, the following five magic, spiritual words:

My thoughts control my life!

ACTIONS SPEAK LOUDER THAN WORDS!

I decided that I would no longer have my spouse asking me detailed questions about money or overseeing what I did financially. We would agree in advance on what had to be done and I would proceed to do it, making whatever adjustments necessary to accomplish the results. We had agreed to his, hers and ours bank accounts in order to ensure he had the very same access to the "ours" but that we each had our own checking/savings accounts for which we accounted to no one. That was a big step. I had looked over my financial prospects and determined that I could, indeed, "make it" in the outside world alone because I knew I would not only be able to take care of me but that my spouse would also provide some type of support. If he had not accepted my proposal, I committed to me that I would terminate the marriage.

I had made a compromise during my husband's tenure in office and had agreed to not work in one of my natural marketplaces (health) to avoid conflict with his job and his decision making regarding his career (we were working in the same pond!), so I was more than ready to take that situation on again. This time without his decision-making authority, since he no longer held the top spot in his organization.

Socially, I was not at all concerned, although I knew that in New Orleans divorced women who were formerly married to "top" men in the city would lose out on most big social opportunities. "So what?" I thought. I'd manage. And, as far as I know, planes fly in and out regularly and I have contacts all

Vikki and Donna, May, 1988

over the country. Not a problem. Besides, the social aspect of being divorced was not at the top of my priority list nor did it occupy a prominent place in my value system.

Spiritually, I was very sure that I was "walking into health" and had committed my Self to the "straight and narrow" with regard to my spiritual goals. I knew in my heart that the Universe would be carrying me and I felt secure inside.

I had not talked to the family about the issues and problems we were having. It was none of their business. Should a divorce be imminent, then I would tell them because there were various legal and personal issues that would ultimately involve them (i.e., wills, trusts, etc.).

When I finally mentioned to my daughter that Bob and I were having some difficulty, she told me, in no uncertain terms, "to stay put and sit tight." "You're always going off on your own to do your own thing," she said. "What's wrong with you? Why can't you just be satisfied where you are?"

I didn't argue because I knew I was not going to pay attention to her insecurities or feedback. A **bitch *with style*** may indeed speak to others, but she decides in spite of what others say. She knows what is right for her Self. She does not act out of fear. Fear, after all, is simply **F**alse **E**xpectations **A**ppearing **R**eal! She walks into the things she seemingly fears and consciously confronts them in order to put them behind her. Always, always, always, she does her homework, consults her Inner knower and then proceeds forward. Easy? No way. It does, however, get easier *with time*. Trust me on this.

So, I took the following steps to change my vibration:

1. I detached my Self from the outcome, knowing I could only take one step at a time, one minute at a time, one day at a time. Trust the process, I decided.

2. I established my own vision of who I was be-coming, since I already knew who I am, and established that as my *intention*. I actually visualized how I would look, etc. I would brook no compromise on quality in my life, of that I was certain. (It only costs 10% more to go first class—well, maybe a bit more—but you get the point.)

3. I fixed my attention on this vision of my desirable state. I reinforced my perception of my reality through my vision. I used my imagination fully, without any constraints, and shaped my mental picture of my future. It has almost all come true. The rest is embedded in the turn in the road I have taken as I walk on this loose gravel path into my next professional arena, that of author, speaker, educator.

4. I focused my vision and emotion on this desired state and, by so doing, changed my vibration and ensured that my vision would come to me. I **willed** my new state of affairs by **concentrating my thoughts on the polarity I desired—freedom and equality** *in* **relationship—to my spouse and to all others with whom I would be associated in my new future.** I killed the undesirable (lack of freedom and insecurity) by changing its polarity. You, too, can do the same. Concentrate on the positive pole of whatever

situation you desire. Focus your thoughts with all the desire and emotion you can muster (that's love, remember?) And then move forward knowing it **has** come to pass.

This whole process is scientific, not magic, though it appears to be so. Just keep in mind that a mental state and its opposite are merely the two poles of one thing and that, by mental transmutation, the polarity can be reversed. We psychologists use this principle all the time to help clients break up undesirable habits by asking them to focus on the opposite qualities. We hypnotherapists also use this principle to support clients in their desire to seek change in their behavior toward positive goals.

> *Don't "kill" fear;*
> *Cultivate Love*
> *and courage!*[1]
> *And the fear will*
> *disappear!*
> *Love, courage*
> *and fear cannot*
> *reside in the*
> *same space.*
> —Vikki Ashley

Thought is the ultimate creator.

Whatever you **think** and then allow yourself to **feel** becomes the **reality** of your life.

Reread Number 4. It is very heart and soul of how to be a **bitch with style**.

My resolve to make radical changes in my life direction had been building up during the marital strain that began when I spent nearly a year in San Diego during Alan's fatal illness and death. I had a lot of time to think about every aspect of my life with my children and with my spouse. In a sense, something in me was dying, too. One cannot watch one's youngest child waste away, helpless to change *his* course or his karma, without feeling emotional pain as well as awareness. My spirit did *not* fail me. My human Self simply wept with despair that there was *nothing* I could do to change the inevitability of his soul's journey. I came to grips with the fact that I *could* not and *would* not change a whit of it. Yet my soul and spirit were buoyed up by *his courage* and *his* acceptance of his transition into another life. When I recall how I sat and planned his funeral *with* him, right down to the music, I have to smile. He told me what to include from Minnie Ripperton and Barbra Streisand, two of his favorite artists. We played the music together.

My son *knew* there was "another side." He *knew* and assured me of three things:

1. "I will live to see my 30th birthday, September 7, 1990." He did.
2. "I will be here for Christmas." He was.
3. "I won't leave, Mom, until *you're* ready to let me go." He didn't.

I released him, with love, on New Year's day, 1991. "Alan, you can go anytime *you're* ready. I can handle it now." He passed over January 22, 1991 at 6:15 am. I wasn't ready, really, to hear him draw his last breath, but my spirit and his spirit were intertwined forever in love and I knew he would remain a part of my life always. In spirit, I *was* ready. In body, I was devastated, but accepting. Alan had prepared me and taught me well.

As I've stated, when I returned to New Orleans, my libido was **gone**. I went into therapy and spent a year there, finishing when the "whale" broke out of the aquarium into the freedom of the ocean.

DECISIONS, DECISIONS

We were moving toward some type of denouement in our relationship when Bob's stroke began late in the afternoon of Thanksgiving 1993 at Herb and Maija Kaufman's home in Slidell. He actually drove us back to New Orleans in this condition. He is *strong willed*. It became full blown the next morning when he couldn't move his left side. I called his neurologist, Austin Sumner, and internist, Cathi Fontenot, and rushed him to the University Hospital. He received the best of diagnostic care but declined hospitalization. He told them I would be his physical therapist. Of course, he had not bothered to ask *me!* So I asked the doctor to step away while I discussed this with him. I told him that I would be his physical therapist on one condition: He must do *everything* I asked him to do. He agreed and we began a very powerful and spiritual walk into health together.

WALKING INTO HEALTH—BOTH OF US

I asked Bob to agree to three things:

1. He would *never ever* again say that he was "useless" and would no longer be any good. No negative language would be accepted or allowed.
2. He would affirm his recovery every day. "It is already done," I said, "but *you* must *say* so." You must *claim* it in advance. I asked him to have faith in the outcome.
3. We would "walk **together** into health."

Through his tears he agreed.

The first thing I taught him to do was use yogic breathing and his right knee as a crutch so that he could turn him Self over and get up if he fell when no one was around to help him. He proved an apt pupil of something he used to laugh about when he saw me practicing my yoga, but he learned how to raise him Self even in his debilitated condition and thus gained a bit of security.

We decided to go to Gulf Shores, AL to do his rehabilitation. Before leaving we obtained some exercises from the rehab specialist. I loaded up the car with the Nikken Magnetic products (the pads that go over the mattress, the magnetic pillows which helped me stop snoring, the magnetic insoles that he would wear 24 hours a day for the next six weeks and beyond, the Kenko creator roller which I used to massage his body, the magboys—magnetic balls) that I used to massage his body and which he used to help his left hand regain some motion and feeling. We were magnetically ready!

We started walking on the beach boulevard and I would whistle and sing Sousa marches while walking on his left side and swinging his arm. Slowly, slowly he began to have some rhythm in his gait. Because of Parkinson's disease, he already had a slightly hesitating walk with his left leg, so it was important to work carefully with it and restore some regularity to his gait. Every day, in every way, he was better and better and better. (Thank you, Emile Coué!)

Every day I would start our day out with yoga breathing and yoga exercises. Slowly we began to see the evidence of his strong speech and his body beginning to respond. In six weeks he was ready to go home to New Orleans and return to work, seeing members of his executive team at home. Cathi Fontenot was amazed. People were incredulous. I was not.

We had been working with Bob's energy and the magnets were part of a perfectly scientific way of tapping into his energy field and supporting his thoughts that established that he was already healthy again. So, he had no negative thoughts interfering with his internal chemistry or obstructing the energy of his chakras and his aura! We were constantly affirming his health and accepted the fact that, if we did our part together, if his thoughts were positively polarized on his health, and if the magnets assisted his blood flow and oxygenation of his blood, and if he continued to walk rhythmically and then, through yoga, strengthen his body—well, then, health was simply a matter of due (do) time. So we walked each day and each step toward his goal. I was a helpmate, truly, and a task master for him. Our love for each other (focused emotion) was the glue that put it all together in a six-week package and held it in place. I, for one, *knew* he was recovered because I *knew* that the **Law of Use** was in motion with the **Law of Polarity**. I explained to him the importance of his masculine and feminine energies working together. When we were out on the road walking to Sousa's marches, it was imperative that he use his masculine energy. When we were in the house doing yoga, it was imperative that he use his feminine energy and go within and not resist or put active barriers in his mind to the movements of his muscles I was prescribing.

We continue our yoga and continue to use our Nikken magnets and pads. We sleep on the pads and pillows to this day and both of us wear the magnetic insoles every day. We are doing *very* well!

ONE MORE STEP TO FREEDOM

Then, though, there was also the matter of his answer to my challenge, seemingly interrupted by his stroke. I wondered, "Did *I* cause this by creating a too-stressful situation for him? Did he cause this by working too many hours/day and creating a too-stressful situation for him Self?" But, actually, it was all of one piece.

I continued my physical therapist role and my support role, excited at the "breakthrough" I was experiencing in his agnostic thinking. Surely, I thought, he will see the benefit of what has occurred and be open to learning more about the mind and the body and how the two *must* work together in a spiritual marriage! It was not long before, with my encouragement, insistence and support he was driving again. He had wanted *me* to drive, getting him to work and picking him up. No. Another way had to be found. He could do it him Self. He had to get over his own fear. I began to ride with him to events instead of driving us, and that built up his security in driving once again. There were several close calls, but I *knew* he could do it and kept telling him so. He did it and still does.

It is not unusual for a powerful, physically active man who is forced to "cut back" on his time and be forced to utilize his energy *for him Self* to, in fact, be resentful of that and other things because of his "misfortune." I hadn't foreseen the *intensity* with which my spouse would begin to resent my own good health and even find ways to be legitimately incapacitated to (a) make me feel guilty, (b) sabotage my plans for more travel and/or even (c) seek greater control over my life because he was aware of my dedication to *his* health and (d) worry about how he would eat if I weren't around for a day or two or three.

I was perfectly in sync with the fact that what I was doing to support Bob was not only for him but also for me. I had knowledge to use in his recovery that he didn't possess. I wanted to share it with him and I kept telling him that we were the guinea pigs for use of new knowledge so we could share it with others later. He with his medical degree and years of credibility in his job and I with my doctorate in psychology and learning and training in the spiritual realm, well, together we might be able to open up some minds and hearts to alternatives and complementary methods to healing. He would smile at me and say nothing. He never said "no" nor did he say "yes." He just smiled and let me go on and on.

Our relationship was better in many ways. I was so happy about his improving health and that he was still with me, but the rumbling that I felt and psychologically knew was there was taking its toll. It didn't take long to refocus our relational energy and for both of us to begin the dance with each other that eventually led to the following letter and another significant emotional event (SEEs).

This is how a **bitch *with style*** deals with an important decision that affects her life if she has the courage. She knows that, in our physical realm, until you put something on paper, it doesn't *really* exist. So . . .

THE LETTER

September 17, 1994
From: Vikki Ashley
Subject: The State of Our Relationship

This letter is intended to put on paper where I view our relationship today. I continue to hope that what I feel inside is absolutely not true, but I know that the inside never lies. So . . . when you asked me last Saturday if I was happy, I answered truthfully, "Yes, I am," I said. "I have never been happier."

Today that statement is still true—for me. I am no fool, however, and I understand that you may feel differently than I do. Clearly this is the case.

This morning you began by telling me that to go to the symphony would require "giving up" some activity or activities in *that* week and how I do not think about priorities and I do the impossible (or try to) without concern for anyone or anything and that I had problems with my children because of my desire to do what *I* do.

Then you said "I am resigning now *because of you*. You're to blame. I don't want to resign now, but you are forcing me to resign by going to Atlanta." Then you said, "I will blame you for the rest of our lives together." Then you reiterated all of this over again, once on your own and then when I repeated these statements to make sure I understood you clearly. I *did* understand you clearly, and so I hope you understand *me* clearly in what I say next.

There is no doubt in my heart that I love you. I want only the best for you—health and a long life. I have always made a real solid contribution to you and our relationship. I am confident that my love, assistance, support and therapy have made it possible for you to be where you are now, in less than nine months. I would do it all over again without hesitation.

However, Bob, there is and always has been this undercurrent in our relationship that rears its ugly head whenever you begin to *feel as though you are being abandoned and are "losing control."* **First things first.**

1. I am not responsible for *your* feelings. You are. How you handle them is a statement about you and your ability to *know your Self.*

2. I am not responsible for your choices. You are. If you resign and blame me, you only demonstrate what I said years ago—you are playing the boyish control "blame game" with your mother and I will have none of it.

3. There are ways to solve problems. There are always ways to solve problems, but you must *want* to. You clearly don't want to solve the problem of how to take care of *you* when I'm not here. There are probably two or three solutions, but you must be open to them.

4. I will not live with a resentful human being for the rest of *my* life. This attempt to control an outcome *you* desire at *my* expense is clearly beneath you. You don't care what *I* want or how *I* feel at this moment. You have just thrown down the gauntlet without any con-

cern for the fact that work and opportunity are coming to me that I have worked for over these past eight
years.   Rather than rejoice *with* me, you want to
undermine me. *I won't stand for it.* Not after all of the
"talk" I have taken from you about how my work has-
n't been financially rewarding or useful, for that matter—from *your* perspective anyway. I have been persistent and have continued to move forward in spite
of it all. Yes. I could sit on my ass and do nothing and
be dead in ten years from depression, anxiety and
anger toward my Self for being so gutless and spineless for *whatever* reason. I am *not* gutless or spineless
and I intend to die when the time comes going somewhere or doing some thing.

5. This high blood pressure problem does not scare me
and it is *not* going to shorten *my* life. I intend to take
care of it and will take time for my Self more than I
do.   Still you have been part of the picture and you
have absolutely no sensitivity to how your behavior
(supportive and otherwise) plays out.   It's there
because I have known for at least two months that
this was going to happen. I knew that when I began to
be more involved, you would lower a boom. You did;
this morning. I could blame you for my blood pressure, but I won't. It's my fault that I have high blood
pressure. I should have brought up what *I* was thinking, but I let it "hang." I wanted to believe I was wrong
about you and us. I wasn't.

   Yes. You have done more for me than any other
human being on the face of this earth—materially. I
deserved every bit of it and I have given to you in a
way you have never experienced before. I do not consider what you have done any less *than you should
have.* People who love one another are good to one
another. Isn't that so?

6. You *know* that I have stayed out of the "when I am
going to resign" game because I *knew* I did not want

to have any part of it. I felt you would blame me *no matter what you decided to do.* You have so much shit around women that there's nothing more I can do to help you see that you are always mentally manipulating every personal situation to *always* get your way when it counts the most. You "give in" to trivial, unimportant issues like what to eat, where to go, what movie to see and things that, in the end, don't matter. On all *important* issues, you always want to have *your* way. You get angry when what you want to happen doesn't—as a result of a decision I make **contrary** to your wishes. I see those times as two adults doing what two mature, caring, loving people do. *Disagree and then move on!* You don't. You immediately jump to blame . . . who? Why, *me,* of course.

Well, Bob, no more. I have enough on my own plate to take care of—plus you. I will no longer subject my Self to a simmering volcano (you) and *pretend* everything is all right. Either it is going to be on-top-of-the-table all right or I refuse to be party to this sick game any more.

MY PROPOSAL

I am willing to discuss ways to handle your needs when I am traveling. At this time, I do not know what kind of travel schedule is involved with Atlanta. Nonetheless, it is only 2 hours by air, so its not far. The problem solving will also take some therapy to get past your current hostile position and your mental predisposition to undermine and manipulate to get your way rather than work out alternatives through honest communication.

There are ways to handle food and whatever else you need. All it takes is an open mind on your part and we will come up with a solution.

If this is unacceptable to you, then on the day you submit your resignation as you are proposing—*because of me*—I intend to file for a divorce.

I am *not* a masochist. Nothing on earth will keep me in this relationship with an angry, resentful, hateful man. Nothing.

Deal with it, Bob. Let me know what *you* intend to do: (1) solve the problem, or (2) get a divorce *and* resign—before you want to—according to you. Or . . .   /s/ Vikki

---

I have always said in my work with executives and managers that "leadership and communications are the Siamese twins of change, process, and organization." Once again, it proved to be true. I organized my own thinking and demonstrated leadership in our relationship by "dealing with" a synthesis of our relationship issues *on paper.* Quite frankly, I was at the stage in my life where I had only one choice to make—walking on my own two feet and stating where *I am!* In so doing, I created a new environment for decision making by asserting my own perception of reality. Bob could agree or disagree but he had to *act* and no longer take anything for granted.

Bob was stunned by the directness of my observations and depth of my feelings about our situation. He was also struck by the fact that he was not going to have a "reason" to resign except his own. That was simply a threat for my benefit, essentially saying my resource pool would be reduced and essentially sucking his thumb and not accepting responsibility for his own feelings. His blame game backfired and all of his thinking had to be reversed if we were to have a way to reverse the negative energy in the *relationship. However,* **I had clearly changed my vibration!** *Significantly!* By changing my polarity I found I could master my moods, change my mental states, remake my disposition, enhance my character*, change* my behavior and reassert my own values.

It worked for us *because* there was a reservoir of professional respect, a deep and strong love that I believe is part of our past lives together, and ultimately, the ability to communicate—when it finally is obvious that we *must.* Talking is *not* communicating, of course. A **bitch *with* style communicates.** She hears and listens and provides feedback based on what is said. Critical!

SO WHAT HAPPENED?

1. We both acknowledged our caring and love for one another.

2. Bob agreed to communicate with me about people and things *at the time these occurred.* He agreed not to harbor resentments (they were undermining *his* health) and to be more open and vulnerable emotionally.

3. I agreed to accept our differences and focus on our agreements. He said he would do the same because that acceptance would permit the his-ours and mine relationship that provides space for each of us to be individuals and to choose how much time we would spend in relationship. That "space" requirement changes with each person depending on what is happening in the cycles of each person's life.

4. We agreed to the his-hers and ours banking process. This relieved a lot of tension and resentment. It also began the process of eliminating Bob's personal fear of poverty and his beginning understanding of where abundance *really* comes from. He began to enjoy our material comforts. I always did.

5. Slowly, through our communications, my sharing of what I knew about positive polarization began to make a difference in his life as well as mine. He smiles at my optimism but accepts its power in our lives.

6. I prepared food in ways that made it possible for Bob to take care of him Self while I was away. I still do. It works and we are both free of the craziness his fear of abandonment once held for him.

7. We agreed that he, as an only child, and I, as the oldest of twelve, had different perspectives of reality. I was strongly into orchestrating teams and groups. He was strongly into one-on-ones. We compromised in our social engagements by doing mostly groups (smile).

8. I looked at Bob through a new framework, one that was guided by the fact that **I** must become **all** that **I** wanted in a husband. I felt I was coming late to the gate on this in our relationship, but it proved to be an accurate way to bring peace and understanding to our relationship. I no longer secretly feared his anger but confronted issues when I saw them coming regardless of what I expected from him. Turns out most of the time his response is very much the way I put the situation on the table.

9. We became teachers for one another. Bob is an extremely capable negotiator. I can be sometimes very quick on the trigger, though not as much lately. I have learned a great deal from him in this regard. What he learned from me is that you sometimes have to assert yourself regardless of the circumstances in order to make a point, albeit intensely. Even-temperedness comes with knowing what's *inside* you. Even then there is a time for anger and intensity if it is *consciously* under your control.

10. We agreed that I would continue my policy of staying totally out of his decisions related to his work and that *he and he alone* would decide when to retire. I told him I do not intend to retire, ever. My professional life will change, but retirement is not in the cards. So, if he thinks there will be a time for him when two old people will be sitting around in rockers deciding what to do with their lives, I suggested he look elsewhere for a companion since I would not be available! **My intent is to live actively to be 130 years or more and drop dead on a tarmac going somewhere!** Is there any wonder health is my highest value?

11. We sat in bed and did a review of our **P³ Baseline and Growth Package** and renewed our understanding of each other's strengths and weaknesses. They exist and we agreed to lead with our strengths and work on our mutual weaknesses. We also laughed

a lot which is really balm for the soul. Neither of us blames the other for what happens to us. We accept responsibility fully for our own behavior. What a difference it makes in the relationship.

12. Mental stimulation and the exchange of ideas and strategies keeps each of us alive! He has his own environment of work and I have mine. We have mutual friends. We don't do as much official entertaining as we used to but we do host more social events because we enjoy people. Naturally, that is my province and he knows I do it well.

   I am convinced people who don't confront that "dark night of the soul" each time it occurs in their lives and who isolate their Selfs and forgo mental and social stimulation—for whatever reason—often retreat into chronic depression, Alzheimers and other diseases of withdrawal from reality. And yes, there is chemical involvement in these and other diseases. Why wouldn't there be? We are, after all, miracles of biochemical and electrical wonders. And since *your thoughts control your life,* they also control your chemistry and electrical circuitry and therefore the health of the body and mind.

13. Our relationship has grown and thrived since our crisis. We are both very happy with our individual lives and our relationship. We know nothing is written in stone and we live each and every day as fully as is possible. We love and enjoy our children, his and mine, who are now "ours." Our grandchildren are enjoyable and part of our lives. We cherish the love they bring as well as the benefits of being part of their growth. We welcomed our ninth grandchild into our fold on January 2, 1999 (Mahea Lani Daniels) and will enjoy the wedding of a daughter Lynn, on February 13, 1999. We wish them all happiness but are clear we provide love and support, not interference in their destinies. Where our experiences are relevant, we share them.

Where not, we keep our mouths shut. We know full well that each of us must make our own choices and mistakes so that our experiences are ours to own and *use* for our soul's growth and development.

14. My life is changing and I will be asking him to go on trips with *me* more often. We both *love* to travel and do so well with each other. We are world travelers and have much more of the world to enjoy.

15. Yes. We disagree but not disagreeably.

16. It is now rare for a cross word to pass between us. If it happens, it is caught and immediately corrected. We consciously work at being who we want each other to be in our lives, so we live the truth that **you must become the person you are looking for.**

The Dark Night of The Soul—Defined and Explained

"Dark night of the soul" means those episodic moments in life when we are mentally, emotionally and physically in chaos, crisis, fear, disorganized, down in the dumps, depressed, confused, blue, don't know where to turn or where to go for solace, direction and, above all, peace of mind. "The dark night of the soul" is also when we are disturbed, unsettled, in disarray, seriously perplexed, "discombobulated;" disoriented, excessively nervous, cluttered, hysterical—a lot or on too many occasions, prone to anxiety attacks, agitated, in a state of breakdown and don't want to call it by its rightful name; embarrassed by little things that *really* don't count, except they do to you; in a tizzy, going round and round and unable to make decisions; in a jam, fix, pretty mess, a pretty pickle, a snafu, or experiencing a *significant emotional event (SEEs)* that you **must** face and *go through* to get to the "other side" where peace and stability beckon from the far shore of enlightenment.

Do any of those descriptors sound like moments in time in *your* life? Of course they do. You are a member of the human race, so these are some of the experiences we must undergo *individually* in order to grow into our **bitch,** *with style* or **bitch** *with style Selfs!*

St. John of the Cross, who originated the phrase "dark night of the soul" clearly had his demons to fight in order to reach his sainthood. And so we each on this earth have *our* demons to fight to reach enlightenment (which means to be "in knowledge of"). That's what it is all about, y'all! The walk through the "valley of the shadow of death," (that's from the 23rd Psalm, the Lord is my Shepherd, remember?) which is also the same as the "dark night of the soul." What is *that?*

When we open our mouths and make that first sound and take that first breath, we put our soul's foot on the earth to make that walk into the valley of the shadow of death—to go darkly and without knowledge—one more time—to experience the dark night of the soul, which is living on *this* earth *until we wake up and become conscious of Who we are!* When we *wake up!* and experience the enlightenment, when we walk into the light of knowledge, we walk out of the valley of the shadow of death and out of the dark night of the soul. We are microcosms of the macrocosm, so our individual "dark nights" reflect the large earthly "dark night of the soul." When we are in knowledge of who we each are—God—spirits having another earthly experience—when *that* happens, nothing we do, say or become, can ever again be done in darkness. We must then be totally aware, responsible for, and conscious of our every thought, word and deed because *we know* each is recorded in the Akashic Records of our very subconscious, which is the recorder of our soul.

Makes sense, doesn't it? Nothing will stop those individual episodic dark nights but the conscious recognition of Who we are. And, each of us must take this journey alone. No one else has your blueprint though we meet others who bring us lessons, light and love—not always in the same individuals. Still, remember that we magnetize the lessons of our blueprint to us *until* we *decide* to take our destiny into our own hands and use our spiritual powers to design our lives the way we want them to be because we know that we *can.*

At this stage of our lives we are rid of the *shoulds, oughts and musts* that have set up the fears in our lives based on someone else's blueprint—not ours! We use words like *I will, I did, I have decided to, I can achieve this, and—the most potent—It is done! I Am walking into* .... *and put in that blank space whatever it is you have decided* YOU *want.*

Other people in your lives, if your energies are harmonious and blend well, will be able to "walk into ...." with you, support you, and take joy and delight in *your* happiness and achievement. Others will envy you, be jealous, and seek on occasion to undermine you. When and if that happens, you will "feel" those vibrations and you must decide to either allow those negative energies to come into your life and undermine you or, in love, depart from those negative energies and the people who hold them. That's right. Sometimes you must walk away from loves, parents, children, employers, so-called friends, whomever you intuit has energies that are *not* supportive of *you*.

If you **must** be a part of a negative environment for your own learning and out of necessity until you can make changes to leave, then you **must** program your subconscious to support you when in the presence of these negative energies until you can take your leave. You do that by:

1. Silently saluting the Christ, Buddha, or Krishna or whomever is your version of Christ, that is internal to every-one—*regardless of their behavior.* You silently say: "The Christ in me salutes the Christ in you." This small thought is a large one in action. It assures that you will not fly off the handle or become defensive in the presence of the per-son with the negative energy. That way, you will not make bad matters worse. In time, you will have a beneficial effect if you choose your words wisely with this individual and use your knowledge of behavior to help you understand where *that* person is coming *from*.

2. Communicate, Translate and Integrate. Here's where the **CTI Principle** comes in handy. Always talk about how what is happening relates to *you*, not the other person. If you are in what *could* be an argument or fight, think ahead and say things like:
   "What you just said makes *me* feel uncomfortable. I do not want to *feel* uncomfortable. What can you tell me that will help me change this feeling. Then I will be better able to hear what you're saying to me."

"I find the language you are using offensive. If you can't find another way to express yourself on this subject, I'll have to talk with you later, after you've had a chance to reconsider what you're saying." Listen to what the other person says next. If there is no improvement or of it's clear the person wants to pick a fight, turn on your heel and walk away. Do it swiftly and without looking back.

"I refuse to remain in places with anyone whose energy is negative toward me. I've got to go." In a case like this, I can see a manager, who is the person with the negative energy, saying something like "Well, then, you should leave." At this point you've got a choice and your decision *will* determine your immediate destiny—position, money, benefits, and on and on it goes.

"I can't help you with your problem because it doesn't relate to me. It sounds to me like *your* perception of *my* reality is incorrect. I am willing to sit down with you and tell you what *my* reality *is*. Perhaps with new information, we can both begin to share a *new* reality."

There is much more to learn about how to use your consciousness and communication skills plus your knowledge of Self, your behavior, values and perception to make your world more enlightened. It's also true that you spread light when you approach sharing information as part of the process of growth. Unless something is a government secret or your most cherished patent from which *you* are earning your living, *nothing is secret* and even those two items are **not** *secret* in this information age if someone wants to find them out. Therefore, self-disclosure is not a negative; it's decidedly a positive when done with sensitivity, timeliness and appropriateness to the topic being communicated.

I do **not** advocate "spilling your guts" to every Tom, Dick, Jane and Mary. What I **do** advocate is using your own experiences *when relevant* to what is being discussed to ensure, by sharing, with another human being that he/she is **not** in this world alone and that there are common issues among us that we need to know about each other. Who knows which one among us is the trigger to that next rung of enlightenment for us—though the occasion for that trigger may appear to be "chance." Well, you know by now there is no such thing as "chance." There are **no** accidents in the Universe!

So you see, that "dark night of the soul" is really our walk through "the valley of the shadow of death." It is, in a word, *life!* When we *Wake Up!* we will "fear no evil" nor will we fear death. We will know that evil is just one end of the polarity of good and that we have to decide which one to focus on. We *know* we have the power to make *that* choice. And with regard to death, we now know there is no death. It's a transition into another dimension where life goes on. The soul's full *intention* for coming here again is to wake up to the light sooner and with more information and tons of experience so that unity with the divine will make the darkness disappear altogether and while we are still on earth, we can radiate that light and share it with others through our *health, wealth, love* and *perfect self-expression.* At that point, y'all, when we transition, we can decide to come back to earth to help or we can decide to stay "home!"

> **There are no accidents in the Universe**
> —Vikki Ashley

Mastery

The Mind is All. "The mastery of polarization is the mastery of the fundamental principles of Mental Transmutation or Mental Alchemy, for unless one acquires the art of changing his own polarity, he will be unable to affect his (her) environment. An understanding of this principle will enable one to change his own polarity, as well as that of others, if he (she) will but devote the *time, care, study* and *practice* necessary to master the art. The principle is true but the results obtained depend upon the *persistent patience and practice* of the individual.

". . . there is a higher plane of consciousness as well as the . . . lower plane and a master (each of us who are students of the 'know thy Self' school", dwells on a higher plane mentally and raise our mental vibrations of the ego above those of the ordinary plane of consciousness. It is like rising above a thing and allowing it to pass beneath you. (In hypnotherapy, we often instruct a client to rise above a situation that could otherwise be traumatic.) The master polarizes her Self at the positive pole of her being, the "I Am" pole rather than the pole of the personality and stands firm in her ability to allow the pendulum of rhythm (time) to swing back on the lower plane without changing her polarity.

"Any individual who has attained any degree of self-mastery whether she understands the law of rhythm or not refuses to allow her Self to be swung back by the pendulum of mood and emotion, and by steadfastly affirming her position, the master remains polarized on the positive pole. Said another way, a master lives completely *in the moment*. The **bitch *with style*** lives from moment to moment, *knowing* that by doing so her future is assured through her focused emotion *in* the moment.

A master uses her will to attain a degree of poise and mental steadfastness almost impossible of belief on the part of those who allow their Selfs to be swung backward and forward by the mental pendulum of moods and feelings. Just bear in mind that you can never destroy rhythm. It is an inexorable law of the universe and is indestructible. One simply overcomes one law by counterbalancing it with another and thus *maintains equilibrium*. The laws of balance and counterbalance are in operation on the mental and physical planes and understanding these laws enables a **bitch *with style*** to seemingly overthrow the law when actually she is simply exerting a counterbalance. (Think of scales! The goal is balance not extremes.)

In time, a **bitch *with style*** becomes *a cause* instead of *being* caused. By mastering her own moods and feelings and by being able to neutralize rhythm (maintain balance), she is able to escape many of the problems of cause and effect. Unconscious people are carried along, obedient to their environment, socialization, religious training and the wills and desires of *others* stronger than their Selfs. Some are impacted by inherited tendencies, suggestions of those in authority and other *outward* causes. They are pawns on the chessboard of life. A **bitch *with style*,** however, seeks a higher plane of mental action. She controls her moods, focusing her emotions, impulses and feelings, and remaining conscious and aware of who she is *in every moment*, creates for her Self new characteristics, qualities and powers by which she overcomes her "ordinary" environment and becomes a player instead of a mere pawn in the chess game of life. She does not resist change. She consciously invites and controls change in her life. She uses the principle of cause and effect instead of being used *by it*.

Your thoughts control your life! You create your own reality; make it what you *truly* want. What you resist, persists!

Everyone in the universe is subject to cause and effect, but a person who understands the laws of mental alchemy is a master on earth instead of a slave. By so doing, the **bitch *with style*** becomes part of the principle instead of opposing it. As a wise woman, the **bitch *with style*** uses her knowledge to change her vibration and thus her life. She is like a swimmer who turns this way and that way, going and coming as she will. Quite unlike a log that is carried here and there. Still, she knows and humbly acknowledges that wise women and fools are *equally* subject to the laws of nature.

> **What you resist persists!**
> —Vikki Ashley

It is the understanding and *use* of knowledge that puts a **bitch *with style*** well on the road to mastery and keeps her there.

So, how does one influence one's own environment? Through the use of *mental power*. The universe is wholly mental and can be ruled only by use of the mind. Mental transmutation *must* change the conditions and phenomena of the Universe. It follows therefore that if the Universe is mental, the Mind must be the highest power affecting its phenomena. This helps to explain "miracles" and "wonder workings". They are mental transmutations as a result of the use of thought. *Thoughts are things—energy. Mind is mental and emotional energy combined.* So, to use vision and mastery to reach for the stars, I and all others who want to know their Selfs and use their Selfs to achieve their individual purposes on this earth must remember these sayings: *My thoughts control my life. I create my own reality. I make it what I truly want.*

> **Consciousness and energy create the nature of reality.**[2]

BEFORE NEW ORLEANS AND THE WEDDING

Bob and Vikki—1986

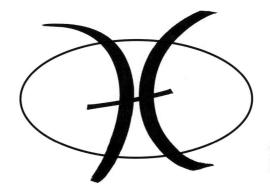

STEP TWELVE

Holding the Hand of God!

Shall We Dance?

It came upon a midnight clear! Love is where it's at! Christmas—1997

Bitchhood 1201
Self-Acceptance: I *know*, Therefore I Am.

Self-acceptance *is* Self-realization. Now that I *know* who I Am, I no longer worry about what being on this earth is all about. I know I am a spirit having an earthly experience! So is each of us, though accepting this fact is different for each of us. My earthly experience is designed for my soul to come to an understanding of its powers for use in moving toward integration and unity with the Universe and for me to come to an understanding that All is mind and All is One. The idea that every single person, animal and thing in our solar system is part of the same energy is a mind blower but it is true. The apparent difference relates to our rate of vibration and density on this earth. Wow!

Energy and consciousness do indeed create the nature of reality. I have said this repeatedly and I want you to understand how important it is that you *believe* it and eventually *know* it. At this stage of my life, I am beyond belief. I am a knower and can say that, in my own experience, I know this to be true . . . I am a spirit having an earthly experience. When my belief turned to knowing **that's when I "got" it and that's also when I understand that, now that I've "got" it, I must share it and use it.**

The "it," by now, you know is my personal power to manifest and to control my own life—my universe, which is a microcosm of the macrocosm. *The secret to all of this is that, in my universe, I am God! I Am that I Am!*

I spent nearly two years in Houston on my spiritual sabbatical. On my 48th birthday, a small voice said: "You've got a lot to do—so get on with it . . . " What a powerful birthday gift! I did "get on with it" and am still "gettin."

My search for truth continues to this day. I have my truth and I want to **C**ommunicate, **T**ranslate and **I**ntegrate *(CTI Principle)* this information in such a way that it can be seen as "truth" by others as well. I recognize that anyone who adopts the name "**bitch *with style***" must be above all else curious and tenacious in the pursuit of information and understanding. That pursuit begins with the individual and answering the question "Who am I?" I continue to reiterate that question because it serves as the foundation for the quantum leap you will all take when you are *ready* to answer it. My experience indicates (and this is not scientific but experiential) that women tend to seriously begin to answer that question around the ages of 42-45. Some men do too. But most men don't even begin to *think* of this question seriously until about ages 55-60, usually stimulated by a crisis, chaos or a significant emotional event (SEEs)! The point is, it will be done in this life or the next or the next or . . .

I will spend the rest of my life researching and interpreting all types of data (I have a very high value regarding information that translates eventually into practical manifestations), but I have answered that very powerful and basic question *for me*. I **know** who I am. Spiritually and, therefore psychologically, I walk today in a **personally** secure place. No one can shake my knowledge base where spirit/energy is concerned. I am very comfortable spiritually and as a psychologist with the awesome potential and creative power of the subconscious mind. I always find my work with clients both rewarding and awe inspiring. As a result, I continue my teaching and learning with a secure inner core, going wherever my "nose for data" takes me. I am enjoying an exciting life which I built in my mind long before it appeared on earth. I am also having fun and each day presents me with many more opportunities than challenges. I ordered it that way and I am enjoying it. You can do the same for yourself. Have faith and believe in yourself, for things which are "seen" and visualized in your mind's eye have substance **before** they appear. Your subconscious mind is your partner. Reprogram it with whatever you want and desire. It is a willing and faithful servant and is totally neutral. It doesn't care what it provides for you and puts no labels on anything since *everything* is contained therein. Keep in mind it's your personal version of the Universal Akashic Records. You have the will to change anything written thereon. *So, **do it!*** Throughout this book I keep reiterating the most important ideas for you to keep and hold:

ASHLEY PRINCIPLES

1. Walk in health *SpiritMindEmotionsBody (SMEB)*.
2. Spirit is energy. Energy is God. You are total energy. You are God.
3. Love yourself first and positive energy will flow *from* you and magnetize your desires *to* you.
4. Your thoughts control your life. Mind is ALL!
5. Your perception of reality *is* your reality, until new information changes *your* reality. It's your world. Get on with it.
6. You create your own reality. Make it what you *truly* want.
7. Walk into your power and utilize it for your growth and development. You are *never* late for your appointment with destiny.
8. When you accept that *I Am That I Am* and *know* these things to be true for you, you will change your life and shift your paradigm of living.
9. You make time for love and what you focus your emotion on comes to pass. Always.
10. Review and remember the Seven Natural Laws of the Universe. *They never change. They are for* knowing *and* use.
11. Review and remember the seven chakras (energy wheels) and consciously keep yours spinning.
12. Review and remember the colors, sounds, body part correlations and each and every day consciously thank the Universe for the miracle that you are (and *I AM)*.

A **bitch** *with style* also has a high experiential quotient. She wants to "do" things, test information and applications and learn by doing. She is also capable of developing theoretical constructs, but gets the greatest bang for the buck from "be-ing" there . . . wherever "there" is. Long ago I read that if you told your *Inner Knower* when you want to wake up each day, you *will* wake up at that exact time or *before*. I decided to practice doing

> **Faith is the substance of things hoped for, the evidence of things not seen.**
>
> (Hebrews 11:1)

that and guess what I found out? It works! As a result I have been waking up without an alarm clock ever since. I simply tell my Self when I want to be awakened and most of the time I wake up *before* the time I require. Try it. It works.

That's a small example, but how many of you would have enough faith to experiment with it and find out if it works for you? Well, a **bitch *with style*** will do just that. Do it at first on week ends. Then do it on vacation. Then do it every day. It will work if you work *it*.

Goethe was absolutely right: "Whatever you can do, or dream you can, begin it. Boldness has genius, power and magic in it." He goes on to say that when you move, Providence moves with you. When you do, it does. Remember *"Ask and you shall receive; seek and ye shall find; knock and it shall be opened unto you."* *(Matthew 7:7)*

Communication, Translation and Integration
The Seven Second Syndrome (S³)

Self-acceptance requires that you use the CTI Principle. To effectively communicate about yourself demands energy—whatever level you possess, and before you speak, your words are "heard," your energy and that of the person you are talking to is *felt*. *Immediately,* you know whether or not the communication is going to "go" or "not go." I call this the *Seven Second Syndrome (S³)* (See Step Six, page 198.) because it's my experience you can "feel" and "know" all you really need to know about anyone in seven seconds and you make necessary adjustments based on your knowledge and understanding of people and yourself. (Remember that **P³ Baseline and Growth Package?** It helps you to "tune in" and use your *Seven Second Syndrome (S³)* to make the changes necessary to handle whatever interpersonal or group situation you're dealing with.) Remember, too, that seven sets the pattern of anything that is going on in one's mind or life. That pattern is then either manifested or redone.

Then, take whatever concepts and mental visuals you desire to convey and *translate* them into words that can be *understood* by the other person. And, *finally,* you *integrate* the verbal, vocal and visual energies of you and the "other." At this point, if you are authentic and not projecting your mask and personality. You connect it all together in a meaningful way. You are an *individual.* If you're not authentic and congruent, the other person will pick this up and whatever you convey will be undermined by your own lack of congruency. Kids call it being phoney. Grownups do too, but they are reluctant to act on their intuitive response to reality because of their socialization and acceptance of some of the *social shields* we're told to use to "protect" people from "being hurt."

That's really a phoney reason. What it really means is that the person who should be telling the other person the truth is a chicken and doesn't want to hurt her Self. So, she projects onto the individual in question her own reluctance.

What I suggest is this: Understand that truth, except for natural law (the sun rises and sets, man cannot control Mother Nature's weather cycles, etc.) is relative as is any individual's perception of reality until new information changes their perception. So, by finding a way to tell the person the truth (give truthful feedback), you are providing "new information" which may or may not change their perception, but your integrity and feeling of wholeness are still in tact. Keep in mind what **A Course in Miracles** says about this: "There is another way of looking at this." (W,50)

There is. Cruelty, pettiness, harshness are not called for in transmitting the truth. Sometimes anger is, and while that is a legitimate emotion in some circumstances, it just does not have to be accompanied by ugliness, name calling and physical altercations, though it often is. This is a signal that the individual who is sharing her anger is not centered or in charge of her own energy. She is pouring it out indiscriminately and it will boomerang on her.

No, anger, as a focused emotion, can be used in the service of truth and in the service of growth. If for no other reason, the release of anger is necessary or it is turned inward and creates an environment where health of the body cannot thrive. Repressed anger and fear, in my mind, are chief causes of the compromising of the immune system and activation of dis-ease, most especially cancer, and most especially, in women.

Each of us must learn to "speak up" and "speak out" for our Self. No one else can do that for us. This must be done individually and in relationship to groups (personal, social, local, national and international.) The process is the same and in the world of spirituality, *process is everything.*

Believe it or not, the foregoing material correlates with what I learned when studying the psychology of groups and leadership, all used in group work and in organizational development assignments (systems change). Another example of integration. The following information for leadership training groups applies to one-on-one communications and team building as well. It encourages descriptions of individual behavior and encourages and permits specific feedback to each individual. You will have no trouble integrating the *CTI* principle nor the 3 *V's*. Take note. More importantly, use these processes in your daily life.[1]

TASK FUNCTIONS

  1. **Define problems**—Overall purpose of group is outlined and problems defined
  2. **Give information**—Offer facts or general information about group problems, methods to be used. Clarify suggestions.
  3. **Seek opinions**—Ask for opinions of others relevant to the discussion.
  4. **Give opinions**—State beliefs and/or opinions relevant to the discussion.
  5. **Test feasibility**—Question reality. Check practicality of suggested solutions

BUILDING AND MAINTENANCE FUNCTIONS

  6. **Coordinating**—Recent statements are clarified and related to another statement in such a way as to bring them together (integrate). Proposed alternatives are reviewed.
  7. **Harmonizing—Mediating**—Intercede in disputes or disagreements. Attempt to reconcile them. Highlight similarities in views.
  8. **Facilitating—Orienting**—Keep group on track. Point out deviations from agreed-upon procedures or from direction of group discussion. Help group process along. Propose other procedures to make group more effective.

9. **Supporting—Encouraging**—Express approval of another's suggestion. Praise others' ideas. Be warm and responsive to the ideas of others. Provide supportive specific feedback.

10. **Following**—Go along with the movement of the group so long as that movement is in agreement with your beliefs, values and personal feelings. Accept ideas of others. Express agreement if you, in fact, agree.

INDIVIDUAL FUNCTIONS

---

11. **Blocking**—Interfere with the process and progress of the group by arguing, resisting and disagreeing beyond reason. Returns to same "dead" issue later. An obstructionist behavior.

12. **Out of field**—Withdraw from discussion. Daydream. Do something else while other person is talking. Whisper to others. Leave the room, etc.

13. **Digressing**—Get off the subject. Lead discussion in a "personally oriented direction" contrary to the agenda. Make a brief statement into a long, nebulous, rambling speech (verbal camouflage).

When I was very young there was a radio show called "The Shadow." The announcer used to say in a very somber voice "The Shadow *knows"* Well, he was right for a different reason. The Shadow in each of us *does* know and each of us uses our individual shadows, our subconscious minds, to help us *know* everything.

Sounds easy, doesn't it. Truth be told, it *is* simple, direct and can be taught, but it is *not* easy. Dr. Albert Mehrabian[2] at University of California, Los Angeles did research on the effectiveness of presenting your messages to people and came up with the following breakdown for impact. Let me reiterate it again:

> **Believe in your Self!**[3]

Verbal (words) 7%   Vocal (tone) 38%   Visual (Nonverbal) 55%

When the *vocal* and *visual* components of your message are inconsistent with the *verbal* content, your message will not be believed. Point: *Walk your talk!*

Words are important because language *drives* behavior, but tone (vocal) and the body language (visual) count much more in the presentation of your *total* self. When your foundation, self-knowledge, self-acceptance and self-projection are in sync, you're "doing it, baby!" And a **bitch** *with style* makes sure she is "doing it" with consciousness and awareness each moment of every day so that her message is knowledgeable, her voice authentic, and her behavior congruent with who she truly *is!*

Sharing these thoughts brings back all those times in my life when I was "tuning in" to the "other side" and when my channels for acceptance of information were wide open. Now they are open all the time!!

The Subconscious Mind: Key to Holding the Hand of God

The Universe is very consistent in its use of mathematical and energetic formulae throughout. Everything and everyone has duality. Feminine and masculine energy is essential for life at *every* level. The Universe is also startling in its establishment of form: Every thing is made up of lines, circles, squares and triangles! Further, sometimes when you are looking at an object you don't immediately "see" the true larger form, but it is there. People, for example, are five-pointed. The body fits into a pentagram. We have a head (top), two arms (sides) and two legs (bottom) and this configuration fits neatly in a circle. Furthermore, you can draw two triangles over the body and have what we all recognize as the Star of David. Where's the square? The whole body fits neatly into either a square or a rectangular. The whole body also fits neatly into an egg shape, the shape of our aura or electromagnetic field surrounding every body of everything on earth. Use your imagination to see how this works.

As you can see, the chakras that provide our etheric body (our double) with energy as well as our physical body are usually "out of sight and out of mind" for the average individual. But they are there, just not as active as if they were consciously being utilized. Conscious

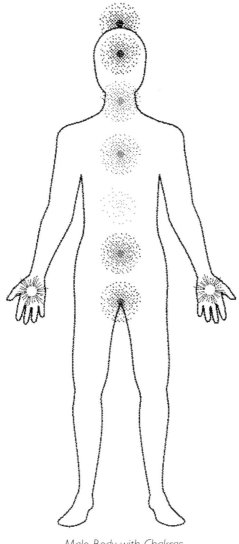

Male Body with Chakras

utilization involves focus, emotion and desire, proper breathing and body exercises (yoga is excellent as noted earlier in this book—for the health of the body).

Now, remember that these seven chakras (energy wheels), and indeed, every aspect of our lives, have color . . . the spectrum of the

CHAKRA ENERGY CORRELATION CHART

Chakra Name	Number	Color	Sound	Endocrine Glands	Body Correlations
Root Security Beginnings	I	Red	Do	Adrenals	Kidneys, spinal column, elimination
Sacral Cooperation Sexuality, family	2	Orange	Re	Gonads	Reproductive systems
Solar Plexus Intuition immortality, authority, name, fame	3	Yellow	Mi	Pancreas	Stomach, Liver, Gall bladder, Intestines, Nervous System
Heart Love, faith, devotion, duty Practical living, building	4	Green	Fa	Thymus	Heart, blood, Vagus nerve, circulatory system, Back, Spine
Throat Knowledge change	5	Blue	Sol	Thyroid	Bronchial, vocal, lungs, alimentary canal
Ajna Third Eye. Realization, clairvoyance induction, austerity Responsibility	6	Indigo (Navy blue)	La	Pituitary	Lower brain, left eye, ears, nose, nervous system
Crown *Knowing* setting the pattern, union	7	Purple/ violet	Ti	Pineal	Upper brain, right eye

rainbow, sound (vibration) and that they relate to each part of our body.

You have the power to integrate every aspect of your life, **SpiritMindEmotionsBody (SMEB),** and physical, by learning how everything around you in nature works and how you correlate with everything else. You have to *want* to do this, of course. Like everything else in life. If you do not *want* to learn, grow and be healthy, then your *shadow*, your **subconscious mind** will take care of everything just dandy, thank you, and you will be so much less than you want to be, ought to be, or could choose to be. But that is *your* choice and only *you* can make it. But here is a recapitulation on some of the essential information required to **support** you in your search for the true you.

The next integration of information for your review and use is the astrological signs with our body parts.[4] (See page 412 and page 413.)

A Few Notes on Body Parts

I am a great fan of Chinese medicine. I believe strongly they've been "onto" something for the past 5000 years that makes a significant difference in our lives today: herbal medicine, qi (pronounced "chee", which means energy/vital force), acupuncture (now "legitimatized" by the National Institutes of Health), nutrition—critical to survival and use of the mind. Well, we all know there's nothing new under the sun, but it is so easy to forget this with all of the technological "miracles" invading our lives and the television advertising bombarding us with all of the latest pharmacological wonders for our use for this, that and the other infirmity.

Note that the Chinese have **five** elements: wood, fire, earth, metals and water. We Westerners have **four** elements: fire, earth, air and water, though I believe *we* have **five** elements as well. We in the west always leave out *ether*, but the scientists account for it and it does **exist even though we can's see it.** It conducts all that electricity and magnetism "out there." It is the *everything* and overall *unified energy field* of physics! In fact, the Chinese account for it directly. They also account for the minerals in the Universe and our bodies by including **metal**, which is absolutely required for life on the earth and *in* universe. Next, the Chinese have **four** natures: cold, cool, warm and hot.

NUMBER	NAME	BODY PARTS
1	Aries	Head, face, brain, eyes (except nose) See Scorpio
2	Taurus	Neck, throat, tonsils, ears, teeth, jaw
3	Gemini	Shoulder, arms, fingers, lungs, thymus gland, upper ribs
4	Cancer	Stomach, diaphragm, chest, lymph system, liver, gall bladder
5	Leo	Heart, aorta, back, spine
6	Virgo	Colon, small intestine, pancreas, nervous system, spleen
7	Libra	Kidneys, bladder, inner ear, and sometimes by association, skin
8	Scorpio	Nose, genitals, rectum, colon, blood, urethra
9	Sagittarius	Hips, thighs, liver, veins
10	Capricorn	Teeth, bones, joints, skin
11	Aquarius	Calves, ankles, varicose veins, circulatory system
12	Pisces	Feet, toes, sometimes by association—lungs, bodily fluids.

Five flavors: sour, bitter, sweet, spicy and salty. **Four** directions which agree with the four seasons: summer is floating; fall is descending; winter is sinking and spring is ascending. Makes sense, no? **Two** systems of organ and meridian classification (this is only several hundred years old!!): Yin organs of transformation and Yang organs of transportation.

As you have probably surmised, I am unalterably fascinated with the *numb*ers and the mathematical precision of the Universe! Aren't you? Mathematics is the perfect language and provides us with the most basic information if we would but **use** this knowledge!

I want to someday do a full *CTI Principle* on the Chinese approach to *everything* but this book simply wants to make you aware of its beauty and contemporary utilization as a way of staying healthy as well as using this knowledge to eliminate disease. I view it as an incredibly accurate diagnostic and prognostic system.[5]

Well, listen to this . . .

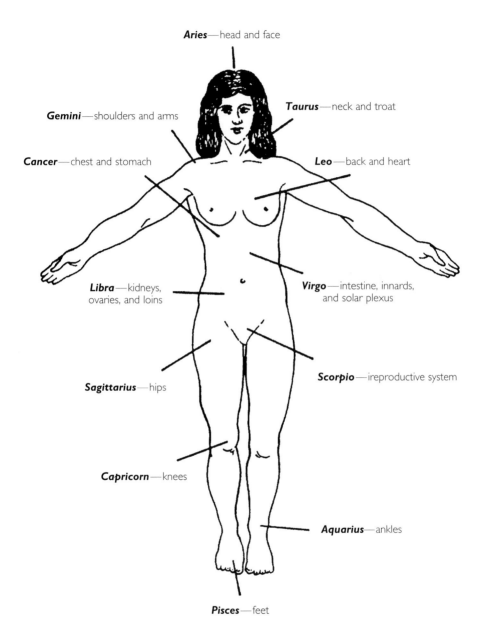

Women's Body With Astrological Correlations to Body Parts

1. "The sages follow the laws of Nature and therefore their bodies are free from strange diseases. They do not lose any of their natural functions and their spirit of life is **never** exhausted. (Emphasis added.) (*Nei Ching.* Referred to as *The Inner Classic*)[6]

2. "Those who act with bravery and courage will overcome diseases, while those who act out of fear will fall ill."[7]

CREATION AND CONTROL CYCLES[8]	
Creation Cycle (Yang)	**Control Cycle (Yin)**
Wood burns to make	**Wood** is cut by **Metal**.
Fire whose ashes decompose into	**Fire** is extinguished by **Water**.
Earth where are born and mined	**Earth** is penetrated by **Wood**.
Metals which enrich	**Metal** is melted by **Fire**.
Water which nourishes trees (**Wood**)	**Water** is channeled and contained by
(That completes the creation cycle.)	**Earth**.

As you review this information, keep in mind the following:

Spirit/Energy/Fire are the same and includes our minds.. **Metal** equates to minerals. **Earth** is physical and includes our bodies (not our mind or emotions) **Wood** equates to purification, burning away the dross. We use **wood** when we desire something so badly that we focus our full attention and emotion and get rid of everything else (purify) standing in the way of that desire. **Water** equates to emotion which, just like water, can drip one's body into total erosion if not controlled by the mind and focused appropriately through love (focused emotion), the most powerful emotion in the world.

Now, pay close attention to the following passages:

Yin Organs of Transformation[9]

The **lungs** rule the **skin** and are involved with the production of mucus. Most colds, flu and skin diseases, for instance, are considered superficial diseases. Sweating or diaphoretic herbs are said to affect the energy of the lungs because they *open the surface of the skin,* helping to clear skin blemishes and . . . the initial stages of simple acute colds and flu. The **lungs** are considered to partake of the energy of metal and are associated with paleness and whiteness. Thus, herbs that are white and mucilaginous are often used to moisten and tonify the lungs.

The **kidney-adrenals** dominate the urinary and hormonal systems of the body. They are characterized by the **water** element and are associated with the color black. Herbs that are diuretic, aphrodisiac, tonic and nourishing and are heavy and black in color are regarded as working on the kidney organ and meridian.

The **liver** is classified as **wood** element and is represented by the color green. Most green, leafy vegetables, herbs that release bile or possess the green-yellow color of bile and calm hypertension are believed to affect the **liver** organ and meridian.

The **heart** partakes of the **fire** element and is represented by the color red. It is said to dominate the blood and circulation. Most herbs that are red and bitter and that clear cholesterol from the veins and arteries are said to affect the **heart** organ and meridian.

The **spleen-pancreas** is of the **earth** element and is represented by the golden-yellow color of the sun. It rules the processes of digestion and assimilation. Herbs that are tonic, nutritive, warming and beneficial to digestion are said to affect the **spleen-pancreas** organs and meridian.

The Yang Organs of Transportation[10]

The colon is the yang of metal and counterbalances the lungs. It is affected by herbs that have a laxative action.

The bladder is the yang of water and counterbalances the kidney. It is affected by herbs that have a lighter, superficial, diuretic action as opposed to the heavier, deeper tonic effects of herbs associated with the kidneys.

The gall bladder is the yang of wood and counterbalances the liver. It is usually affected by lighter herbs which promote the secretion of bile.

The small intestine is yang of fire and counterbalances the heart. It is associated with digestion and its disorders may produce blood in the urine. Herbs that arrest this symptom are said to affect the small intestine organ and meridian.

The stomach is the yang of earth and counterbalances the spleen. It is affected by herbs that are more carminative and digestive rather than sweet-flavored tonics.

Finally, the Chinese assign the organ functions, including the triple warmer and pericardium meridians, to the fire element. The triple warmer is affected by herbs that have a combined action of aiding digestion and regulating the circulation of fluids. The pericardium meridian is the emotional companion of the heart and is affected by herbs that act on the heart.

Ayurveda Medicine

Just for the record, let me state that Chinese medicine equates very closely with Ayurvedic medicine. Keep in mind that none of these systems makes an exact one-to-one correlation except in their fundamentals and they all agree with the need for classifications that acknowledge **energy**. Ayurveda recognizes **five** elements: earth, water, fire, air, and ether. In Ayurveda the humors describe three constitutional types based upon qualities of these elements.

Vata: the **air** humor, relates most directly to the nervous system and combines the **air** and **ether** elements. Described as being dry, cold light, mobile, subtle rough, hard, irregular and clear. It embodies the very essence of the life energy and is considered the most powerful of these three humors. **Vata** can carry and/or combine with either of the other two.

Pitta: the **fire** humor, is light, fluid, subtle, malodorous, soft and clear. It is catabolic or destructive and transforming (living tissue is changed into waste products; destructive metabolism) and governs thermogenesis and all chemical reactions. **Pitta** governs digestion, circulation, heat, visual acuity, hunger, thirst, skin luster, intelligence, courage, determination and pliability and softness of the body. In a deranged condition it will cause a jaundiced appearance or yellowish color of the urine, feces, eyes and skin. This may be accompanied by inflammatory and burning symptoms, insomnia and greater hunger and thirst.

Kapha: The water or mucous humor, is cold, wet, heavy, slow, dull, smooth, and cloudy. It is anabolic or building, (the process by which food is changed into living tissue; constructive metabolism).

Kapha governs bodily stability and strength, body fluids and lubrication of the joints and fosters peacefulness, love and patience. In a deranged state it will cause a diminution of digestive power, excessive phlegm and mucus, exhaustion, heaviness of the body and mind, pallor, coldness difficult breathing and excessive desire for sleep.

Mental and spiritual qualities are attributed to the three biological humors. Temperament types may be classified by observing how the humors combine in an individual and which predominates.

In Ayurveda there are seven *dhatus* or vital tissues: plasma, blood, muscle, fat, bone marrow and reproductive tissues. Herbs and foods of particular properties are used to counterbalance and remedy the diseases that affect them. The fundamental essence and strength of a given organism, however, is considered to derive from its healthy functioning as a whole and the Ayurvedic term for this is **ojas**. This literally means "to invigorate' and includes the functioning of the autoimmune system and the hormonal balance of the body. *Ojas* results from the *refined functioning of all seven vital tissues, particularly the reproductive tissues or semen.*

The difference between traditional Chinese and Ayurvedic systems of diagnosis and treatment is primarily one of emphasis The *traditio* system is the heart of Ayurveda. The prescription of diet and herbal therapy, counseling as to *health-promoting lifestyle* and *exercise, understanding of emotional problems* and *recommendations of spiritual practices*—all are based on diagnosis of the humoral balance. Like Chinese medicine, it, too, is based on a *mind-body unity.*[11]

These foregoing charts and information hardly touch the essence of the wonders of Chinese medicine and Ayurveda, but Deepak Chopra has made the latter very familiar with his books, tapes and seminars and Chinese medicine is "picking up steam" in the western world, especially through use of herbal therapies, acupuncture and acupressure. Check out *reflexology*, a discipline that utilizes and integrates all of the above information. The only difference is that it is utilized on your **feet, which are said to reflect your whole body.** And they do. Ever had an aching foot? What happened to your whole system? That's right! You ache from head to toe! Check it out. Somewhere out there is another God just waiting to hold your hand and lead you into new information **for your use.**

None of the information I am sharing with you is prescriptive. It is all informational and for your review. You must seek more information for yourself and *take responsibility for its use.* Each of us though made on the *same pattern* is distinctly unique in our *purpose* and *reason* for this reincarnation. *So one size in spiritual terms does **not** fit all.* These data simply support and amply display the point I am making for your use and that is: *nature and the universe are more intriguing than you can imagine. We are in deed and in fact the microcosm of the macrocosm.* More to the point, *you* are just as intriguing as any of nature's wonders but go even beyond everything else in nature as a result of your mind! Think a minute: plants and animals do what plants and animals do. People, on the other hand, are the **only** members of the Universe who can **decide**:

1. Who am I?
2. What is my purpose?
3. What do I want to do with my **Self**
4. How do I want to do it?
5. When do I **want** to do it?
6. Where do I **want** to do it?
7. Why do I **want** to do it?

We are the only be-ings who can use both our minds and emotions based on personal **choice!**

And, furthermore, **you can have whatever you truly want in this world—anything at all.** You have the power to actually transform any thought backed by emotion and desire into concrete form. It doesn't matter **what** it is. It can be yours. Think of **that?**

You walk every day of your life **holding the hand of God.** That hand belongs to **you!** It also belongs to each and every one of us. It is up to you, however, to reach out and *ask, seek, knock* and *find.* **How does that occur?** Consciously and with full awareness of who you are! And who is that? **You are a spirit having an earthly experience. You are God!** You are the only person on this earth who can introduce her Self as "I am . . . ." **followed by the name YOU have accepted as your own.** Think about that! It's been you all along who's in total control of her Self! "Hello!"

My Soul and My Aura

I am now convinced *in my soul* that the soul incorporates the mental and emotional parts of me. I *know* this to be true because I have concluded from my research and experience that there is no way to separate the two. (Refer back to Step One, page 72) My mind and emotions are the chief duality of my being: my thoughts and my desire constitute my "mind" in the *SpiritMindEmotionsBody (SMEB)* equation. The energy is my soul Self *reflecting* the heat and fire of the universal mind (i.e., Unified Energy Field). There are ways to prove my energy field exists, as an energy field surrounding everything in the universe, including you and me. But it is my own view that the soul interpenetrates the body and inflows near the solar plexus, the heart and the pineal gland. Some mystics have said that if *the body is weighed before and after death, it will be 10 ounces lighter immediately after death.* It is important to know that the thymus is critical in the development of the immune response in the newborn and begins to shrink at puberty. This is when our awareness needs to be developed in order to maintain its functioning via our consciousness and use of our mental powers. Instead, our immune system is often deteriorated during our 20s and 30s and only when a crisis, chaos or significant emotional event (SEEs) occurs do we take over and rejuvenate our lives through the use of consciousness and energy and thereby create a new reality for our Selfs.

Be that as it may, it makes sense to have the energy field *(soul/aura) connected* to the internal source of life in the body (the heart) and near the *thymus gland.* "This gland is an unpaired (rare in nature for anything to be unpaired, which makes it significant) organ located in the mediastinal *cavity* anterior to and above the heart. It consists of two flattened symmetrical (pyramidal shaped) lobes (ah, there's the pair!), each enclosed in a capsule from which trabeculae extend into the gland and divide each lobe into many lobules. These contain a cortex and medulla. The cortex is composed of dense lymphoid tissue containing many cells (thymocytes) closely packed together. The medulla also contains thymocytes but they are less numerous. It also contains characteristic thymic (Hassall's) corpuscles.

When T Cells enter the circulation they are small and medium-sized lymphocytes and may survive up to 5 years. These cells are important in the body's cellular immune response, since they migrate from the bone marrow to the *thymus gland* where it develops into a mature differentiated lymphocyte that circulates between blood and lymph. Immature T cells are called thymocytes. Mature T cells are "antigen specific" meaning that each one responds to only one antigen. T cells are identified by surface protein markers called clusters of differentiation (CD). All T cells have the CD3 marker; additional markers differentiate different T subsets. CD4+/CDs-Helper T cells serve primarily as regulators, secreting lymphokines that influence the activities of other immune cells during inflammation and T-cell-mediated immunity.

CD4+ cells also secrete *gamma interferon*, one of the strongest stimulators of macrophage activity. Cds+CD4-T cells are effector cells that directly lyse (kill) organisms. Natural killer cells were originally believed to be a subset of T cells but are now recognized as being a third type of lymphocyte.

"T cells cannot recognize foreign antigens without the help of macrophage processing. However, once the macrophage has helped them *identify* an antigen as *"non-self,"* T cells dominate the specific immune response directing macrophages, B Cells and other T cells in the body's defense.

T cells also play a major role in graft rejection, hypersensitivity reactions, and recognition and destruction of tumor cells because of the unique antigens these cells carry. (Emphasis added.)[12]

Cancer is one of this nation's most virulent health challenges. It is clear that a compromised immune system can increase the risk of cancer and other disease in the body. It is therefore important for those of us who believe thoughts are things and *do* matter to provide road signs for the beginning journey many will make to *overcoming* the ravages of disease through the proper use of their *spiritual powers.*

Knowledge and understanding precede change and new behaviors. Pay attention to how you *feel* and what is happening *inside of you.* Reprogram your subconscious to focus on positive outcomes in your life based on your vision of your life *here* and *now.* The shadow *knows* but the shadow is expelled by light—the light of the soul/aura that surrounds your body and tells the tale of your thoughts and emotions more clearly than any other mechanism available to us today.

Aura Proof

I wish to share pictures of my aura and ones recently taken with Bob and one taken when I put my hands on Bob's. They are here just to show that the energy field (soul/aura) *does* exist and that you can find out how yours is doing by finding the closest aura photography center nearest you. Often bookstores that concentrate on spiritual development, personal growth, health, etc. either have, or know who has, an aura camera. See the Resource Directory in the **Bitch's Book Bag** at the end of this book.

Self-Acceptance As a Spiritual Entity Having an Earthly Experience

These pictures are being shared with my readers so that they will see and know that energy is real and all encompassing. These pictures have been taken at different times and will show where I was "at" when they were taken.

Remember that the energy enters our field from the left side and its use is indicated by our right field.

The soul/auric field is *real*. The photo on page 425, lower, taken in 1995, demonstrates how my energy field is full of white light, so much so it obscures my face. It does, however, reflect my state of mind and my development spiritually. I am concentrating my energy around my body and focusing on higher issues. That was, in fact, the case.

Shall we Dance?

I am convinced the "game of life" requires us to dance with the spirit, doing every conceivable type of step along the way: bump, grind, fox trot, tap, waltz, jitter bug, swing, macarena, you name it. Dance requires the use of our energies physically, but the coordination of our steps requires the use of all of our faculties, especially our minds, nerves and emotions (fuel).

A **bitch *with style*** knows that she is going to continue the dance of life because her soul is full of the light of love and acceptance of *who she is*. She is certain that her way is lighted and that any small missteps will be corrected almost immediately by that powerfully developed consciousness that is the fruit of years of hard but joyous work and her walk along that loose gravel path of life.

Her's is a grateful and thankful heart. She understand and *uses* the seven Hermetic natural laws and has a secure place for her Self where it counts—*in her center*. She has a built-in crap detector, uses the *Seven Second Syndrome (S³)* and employs a self-correcting compass, her intuition, that she follows every day, every conscious moment and every second of her life. She affirms her substance and moves out to accomplish her goals *knowing who she is: A* **bitch** *with style* who dares to say to her Self and the world: I am one with Universal Life Energy. It flows through me now. I feel it.[13]

> I am **one** with Universal Life Energy. It **flows** through me now. I feel it.[13]

This wonderful, powerful affirmation will work for you 100% of the time. You will always *know* who you are and where your strength and energy *really* come from.

A BITCH *WITH STYLE'S* MAXIMS FOR LIFE[14]

1. My thoughts control my life.
2. My decisions decide my destiny.
3. My perception of reality *is* my reality until new information changes *my* perception.
4. I create my own reality. I make it what I *truly* want.
5. I am *never* late for my appointment with destiny.

The Auric Energy Field—The Soul

Following are pictures of my energy field at different times since 1992. The colors change and the width may vary on occasion. Keep in mind that the left side is the side of entry for the energy and the right side is the side indicating how the energy is being used in the world. From a brain point of view, energy entering on the left relates to the right side of the brain. Energy used on the right relates to the left side of the brain. My aura indicates that I operate **simultane-ously** out of both sides of my brain. So does Bob, as you will see in his very first—in life!—aura photos.

Remember that the *left hemisphere* of the brain is the analytical, linear, logical, vertical, deductive convergent and rational side. The *right hemisphere* is the visionary, insightful, analogical, lateral, induc-tive, divergent, integrative and intuitive side. I say all of the time that *management, control, order, logic and details are* left hemisphere func-tions, while *leadership, vision, intuition* and *big picture thinking* are right hemisphere functions. And so it is!

The Adjournment

This is where I leave you on the loose gravel path of life. See you later along The Way. I can truly say it is great fun being a **bitch *with style***. I have indeed created my *own* reality and I'm right on time with my date with destiny!!

Christ said "Go forth and multiply."

I say, **"Go forth and bitchiply!"**

1992
Yellow/orange on both sides
tinged with red and purple.
Green in the middle. White
covering all of the front side.

1993
Green on both sides with large
white aura edged with yellow
surrounded by indigo and purple.

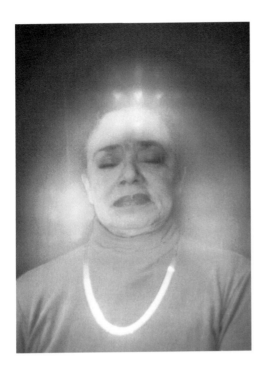

1994
White and purple with three small channels appearing over forehead. Green on right side near neck. White coving all of the front side.

1995
Pure white and very wide. Yellow, red and purple edges. I'm wearing my **bitch with style** *tee shirt!*

January, 1996
Bringing in green, yellow, red, blue. Large green and blue section near right side of head. Red and orange near right shoulder. White covers all of the front side. A very large bright and deep white channel has opened on the left side and is clearly visible.

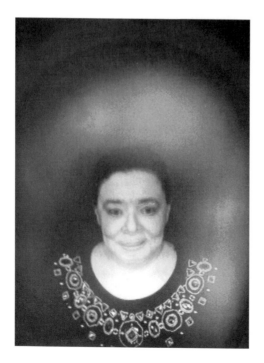

August, 1996
Purple all around integrated with red and gren. A lot of green directly over my head. White covers all of the front side.

August 7,
Left side full
White overhea~
channels open dir~
Right side deep purp~
red (hard to see in a b~
white photo, but there).

June 9, 1998
Total field of purple and red from
left to right—looks like a two-
color ring—covered by white all
over the front side.

le, blue and
ack and

October 28, 1998
My aura looks like a rainbow—
very orange and red on the lower
left side, moving to green and
white and then indigo and purple
on the lower right. White covers
all of the front side.

October 28, 1998
Left field green and white mixed,
with red and then purple all
around the outside. Moves to
more red on the right side, mixed
with orange. White covers all the
front side.

October 28, 1998
Bob first ever aura photo shows
he is in a total ring of red and
purple with white covering the
total front side.

October 28, 1998
I put my left hand on top of
Bob's left hand. The aura is
"amped up" greatly, showing a
large white aura with red, green
and blue evenly dispersed on
both sides of the aura with the
whole aura totally surrounded
by purple. White covers the
front so greatly it almosts wipes
out his face. I know we are
integrated spirits!

October 28, 1998
I put my right hand on top of
Bob's right hand. Again, the aura
is "amped up" greatly, showing a
large white aura, but this time the
colors are very pronounced.
Entering on the left are white,
red, purple with green near Bob's
head. On the left side upper
head is a wide window of purple.
On top, in the center, begins
a wide sweep of a rosy color,
followed on the right by pure
white near his right shoulder.
Purple surrounds the whole field.

NOTES

INTRODUCTION
1. Gibran, Kahlil. *The Prophet*, "On Children." New York: Alfred A. Knopf, 1980, p.17.
2. Ibid.
3. Ibid.
4. Gibran, Kahlil. *The Prophet*, "On Work." p. 26.

STEP TWO
1. **A Course in Miracles.** ©1975, 1985. Foundation for Inner Peace. Tiburon, CA.W,50.
2. Nathaniel Branden. **The Six Pillars of Self-Esteem.** ©1994. New York: Bantam Books. X1, 26-27.
3. William J. McGrane, CPAE. ©1995. **Brighten Your Day With Self-Esteem.** Hummelstown, PA: Success Publishers. 3, 10, 12
4. Foundation for Inner Peace. ©1975 **A Course in Miracles.** Tiburon, CA.**W,50**

STEP THREE
1. Jeff Rovin. **1001 Great One-Liners.** ©1989. New York, NY: Penguin Books.ccc

STEP FOUR
1. Barbara Ann Brennan. **Light Emerging.** ©1993. by Barbara Ann Brennan. Art by Thomas J. Schnirder and Joan Tartaglia. Bantam Books, NY. p. 21
2. Linda Rector Page. **Healthy Healing: A Guide to Self-Healing for Everyone.** ©1996. Tenth Edition. Healthy Healing Publications.
3. Evelyn Lip. **Feng Shui For the Home.** ©1986. Torrance, CA: Heian International Publishers. 1.
4. Derek Walters. **The Feng Shui Handbook.** ©1991. San Francisco, CA: Thorsons. An imprint of *Harper Collins Publishers.*
5. *I Ching.* Based on the translation by James Legge. ©1971. New York: New American Library. 23, 24.

STEP FIVE
1. **Managing For Success©** materials. Dr. Ashley is a Target Training International (TTI) Distributor, Scottsdale, AZ.
2. This material is from the **Managing for Success©** Software Series that is the property of **TTI** (Target Training International), Scottsdale, AZ. Dr. Ashley is a distributor for TTI and its self-assessment instruments and other materials.
3. Random House. Ibid. Geo (earth) + Metry are combination forms of Greek roots that make geometry the science of measuring the earth! In this sense, it is critical knowledge and is explained in the use of numbers. Thank you, Pythagoras!
4. Harish Johari. **Chakras: Energy Centers of Transformation.** ©1987. Rochester, VT: Destiny Books.
5. Ibid. 18

6. Ibid.
7. Mikel A. Rothenberg, MD. **Dictionary of Medical Terms For the Nonmedical Person.** ©1994. New York: Barron's Educational Series. p. 479.
8. David V. Tansley. **Subtle Body.** ©1977. New York: Thames and Hudson. p. 57 (pineal gland).
9. **Llewellyn's Astrology Datebook 1997.** ©1997. St. Paul: Llewellyn Publications.
10. Peter Stratton and Nicky Hayes. **A Student's Dictionary of Psychology.** ©1993. New York: Routledge, Chapman and Hall, distributor. 145.
11. **Dorland's Illustrated Medical Dictionary.** ©1994. Philadelphia: W.B. Saunders Company. p. 1295.
12. **Stedman's Medical Dictionary.** ©1995. Baltimore: Williams & Wilkins. p. 1367.
13. David V. Tansley. Ibid. p. 57.
14. Rom Harre and Roger Lamb,. Eds. **The Dictionary of Physiological and Clinical Psychology.** ©1986. Cambridge, MA: The MIT Press. 214-215
15. Paul Arthur Schilpp. **Albert Einstein: Philosopher-Scientist.** New York: Tudor.
16. Edith Hamilton. **Mythology.** ©1940, 1942, 1969. From the Norse *Elder Edda.* This line shows wisdom.

STEP SIX
1. An original working maxim of Vikki Ashley, PhD
2. Stedman. Ibid. 1752
3. Alice A. Bailey. **Esoteric Healing.** ©1963. Albany, NY: Fort Orange Press. 140.
4. Harold I. Kaplan, MD and Benjamin J. Sadock, MD. **Pocket Handbook of Clinical Psychiatry.** ©1990. Baltimore, MD: Williams & Wilkins. 145.
5. Vikki Ashley.
6. Pat Muller. "Practical Harmlessness and Right Speech." **Journal of Esoteric Psychology.** V. IX, No. 2, Fall 1995. 73f.
7. Dusty Bunker. **Numerology, Astrology and Dreams.** ©1987. Atglen, PA: Whitford Press. 97ff
8. Corinne Heline. Ibid. 40.
9. Ibid.90.
10. Barbara Walker. **Women's Encyclopedia of Myths and Secrets.** ©1983. San Francisco: Harper and Row. 1016.
11. Pauline Wills & Theo. Gimbel. Ibid. 112-3
12. Pauline Willis and Theo. Gimbel. Ibid. 123.
13. Multiple references:
    1. Charles Klotsche. **Color Medicine: The Secrets of Color/Vibrational Healing.** Sedona, AZ: Light Technology Publishing.
    2. Corine Heline. **Color & Music in the NewAge.** ©1964. Marina del Rey, CA: DeVorss and Company.
    3. Alice A. Bailey. Ibid.
14. Reinhold Ebertin. **Astrological Healing: The History and Practice of Astrological Medicine.** ©1972, 1989. York Beach, ME: Samuel Weiser. 143.

15. **Myers Briggs Type Indicator**. Determines psychological preference, is based on Carl Jung's work that represents the four functions of consciousness. **Perception** is how I take in information. **Judgment** is how I make decisions. **Introvert** and **extrovert** refers to my *energy source* — inner or outer world preference.

    Sensing relates to the world of the five senses or our outer world experience and focuses on details, practicality, reality and present enjoyment. The orientation is to live life *as it is*. The orientation is to prefer using learned skills, pays attention to details, is patient with details and makes few factual errors. **Intuition** refers to the sixth sense and possibilities. The focus is patterns, innovation, expectation, and future achievement. The orientation is to change and rearrange life. Looks at the "big picture," and is patient with complexity. **Thinking** relates to use of the intellect and focuses on the logic of a situation, things, truth and principles. The work environment is brief and businesslike, impersonal and the thinker seeks to treat others fairly. Contributes to society through intellectual criticism, exposure of wrongs, solutions to problems. **Feeling** relates to people, human values and needs, tact, harmony. Feelers are naturally friendly, personal, and treat others as they need to be treated. They exhibit enthusiasm and zest for living and demonstrate care and concern for others as well as support for whatever they are involved with. **Judgment** relates to behavior that is decisive, planful, self-regimented, purposeful and exacting. Focus is on *completing* the task; makes decisions quickly and wants only the essentials of the job. **perception** relates to curiosity, spontaneous behavior, flexibility, misses nothing, is adaptable and tolerant. Focuses on *starting* a task as opposed to completing it; often postpones decisions and wants to find out all about the job. **Extroversion:** a person's *energy* is directed outward toward people and things. Focuses on changing the world; is a *civilizing* genius. Has a relaxed and confident attitude; is understandable and accessible. Likes a varied and action-oriented work environment; prefers to be around and with others and has interests are broad. Is an *afterthinker*. **Introversion:** a person's *energy* is directed inward toward concepts and ideas. Focuses on understanding the world. Is a *cultural* genius. Has a reserved and questioning attitude. Is subtle and often impenetrable. Is a *forethinker*. Prefers a quiet and concentrated work environment; prefers to be alone and her interests have depth.

16. Target Training International Self-Assessment Instruments - DISC measures behavior and emotions. Most effective instruments on the market. Packaged with values and work perception provides a thorough **baseline** from which to **know thy Self** and answer the question **Who am I?**

17. William Bridges. **The Character of Organizations.** ©1992. Palo Alto, CA: Consulting Psychologists Press.

STEP SEVEN
1. **Metaphysical Bible Dictionary.** ©1931 Unity School of Christianity, Unity Village, MO. P.557
2. Sybil Leek. **Reincarnation: The Second Chance.** ©1974 by Sybil Leek. Stein and Day, New York. P.159.

3. Paul Pitchford. **Healing With Whole Foods.** ©1993 by Paul Pitchford. North Atlantic Books, Berkeley, CA. P. 9ff
4. **Metaphysical Bible Dictionary.** *Ibid. P. 314.*
5. **Instant Synonyms and Antonyms.** ©1981. Compiled by Donald O. Bolander. Career Publishing, Little Falls, NJ. P.130.
6. **Webster's New World Dictionary.** Second College Edition. ©1982. Simon and Schuster, New York. P. 669-70.
7. Bolander. *Ibid.,* P. 312.
8. *Ibid.,* P. 68.
9. **Life.** Special Issue: Medical Miracles for the Next Millennium . 21 Breakthrough That Could Change Your Life in the 21st Century: Gene Therapy/Edible Vaccines/Memory Drugs/Grow Your Own Organs. Fall, 1998.
10. A quote attributed to Loewi by his nephew and shared after his death in 1961. From Sherwin B. Nuland. **The Wisdom of the Body.** ©1997. Alfred A. Knopf, New York. P. 73.
11. Richard Houck. **The Astrology of Death.** ©1994. Groundswell Press, Gaithersburg, MD. P. 120-121.
12. **Brain Facts: A Primer on the Brain and Nervous System.** ©1993 by the Society for Neuroscience, Washington, D.C. P. 11
13. Nuland, *Ibid. P. 79.*
14. **The Kybalion.** ©1912, 1940. Yogi Publication Society. Chicago, IL.

STEP EIGHT

1. **Dorland's** *Illustrated* **Medical Dictionary.** ©1994. W.B. Saunders Co. A Division of Harcourt Brace & Company. Philadelphia, PA. p. 924.
2. Joseph Murphy, DRS, PhD, DD, LLD. **The Power of Your Subconscious Mind.** ©1963. Prentice Hall, Englewood Cliffs, NY. P.100.

STEP NINE

1. Napoleon Hill. **Think and Grow Rich.** ©1960. Hal Leighton Printing Co., North Hollywood, CA 96605. P. 33.
2. Johann Wolfgang von Goethe. Conversation with Johann Peter Eckermann, October 20, 1818. Bartletts Familiar Quotations, p. 350.
3. Lao Tse (7th Century A.D.)—Chinese Philosopher
4. Inscription at the Delphic Oracle. From Plutarch, *Morals.* One of many sayings throughout antiquity attributed to the Seven Sages. The list is commonly given as Thales, Solon, Periander, Cleobulus, Cjilon, Bias, Pittacus.
5. A Course in Miracles. J, 132.

STEP TEN

1. Cayce, Ibid. The complete sentence continues: "...For that thou has attempted is well, provided it is in accord with the universal consciousness that is in the truth and the way which was manifested in Jesus of Nazareth, Jesus who became the Christ." **Psychic Awareness.** P. 310. The Bible: James 1:23.
2. **Vitiligo:** An acquired cutaneous disorder characterized by white patches, surrounded by areas of normal pigmentation...cause unknown. **Taber's Cyclopedic Medical Dictionary.** ©1997. F.A. Davis Company, Philadelphia, Pa. P. 2095.

3. Edgar Cayce Readings: Individual Reference File. ©1970, 1976. Edgar Cayce Foundation. Virginia Beach, VA. P. 94.

STEP ELEVEN
1. **The Kybalion,** p. 215 (amplified by the author.)
2. Steven Lee Winbert (ed.) **Ramtha.** ©1986. Sovereignty, Inc. Eastsound, WA.

STEP TWELVE
1. Hedley G. Dimock. **Groups: Leadership and Group Development.** ©1966,1970, 1986, 1987 by Hedley G. Dimock. University Associates, San Diego, CA. p. 95.
2. Albert Mehrabian. **Three V's of Spoken Communication.** Based on Dr. Mehrabian's research done at UCLA.
3. Listen to Lena Horne's song **Believe in Yourself!**
4. Ute York. **Living By The Moon.** ©1997 Garret Moore & Bluestar Communications Corporation. Woodside, CA. p. 104
5. Read these books (there are many more) but they will help you get started if Chinese medicine interests you: **Planetary Herbology** by Michael Tierra; **The Tao of Balanced Diet** by Stephen T. Chang; **Asian Health Secrets** by Letha Hadady; **Chinese Tonic Herbs** by Ron Teeguarden; **Chi Gung** by L. V. Carnie; and **Fundamentals of Chinese Acupuncture** by Ellis, Wiseman and Boos. These will get you started!!
6. Nei Ching (The Inner Classic) An ancient Chinese medical classic, more completely translated as *The Yellow Emperor's Classic of Internal Medicine*, has been revered by Chinese healers for ore than 3000 years.
7. Ibid.
8. Paul Pritchford. **Healing with Whole Foods.** ©1993 by Paul Pritchford. North Atlantic Books, Berkeley, CA. P. 267 ff Taken from the Nei Ching, *The Inner Classic*
9. Michael Tierra. **Planetary Herbology.** Edited and Supplemented by Dr. David Frawley. ©1988 by Michael Tierra. Lotus Press. Twin Lakes, WI. p.35 ff.
10. Ibid. p. 36
11. Ibid. P. 38-9
12. Taber's **Cyclopedic Medical Dictionary.**
13. Eugene Ferson. **Science of Being.** ©1970 by The Lightbearers. The Lightbearers, Seattle, WA. p.23.
14. Developed by Vikki Ashley, PhD

OUR FAMILY

THE
ASHLEY-DANIELS
SUCCESS EXPRESS

We're like a good jigsaw puzzle . . .
All the parts are different.
But everything fits together perfectly!

FAMILY PHOTO ALBUM

Vikki and Donna
May, 1988

Alan, Vikki, Donald
May, 1988

Bob and Vikki on their Wedding Day
December 31, 1986
New Orleans, At Home

LSU Committee of 100
June 6, 1996

Bob and Vikki—The Night Bob was honored by his peers with a chair named
The Robert S. Daniels Chair for Leadership and Management
LSU School of Medicine

Our grandchildren in our beautiful New Orleans garden with one of the world's most beautiful live oak trees!
L to R: *Barret, Rebecca, Carlen, Emily, Zachary and Mariah (center), Daniels.*
Missing: Kara Shea and Shawn D'Andrea
June 6, 1996

Bob and Vikki surrounded by family and friends on Bob's big night—June 6, 1998
All children were present and are in this picture: Donald Rickman II, Donna Rickman, Stephen Daniels, MD,PhD, MPH; Allen Daniels, EdD; Judith Daniels, EdD; Lynn Daniels. Alan Rickman looked on "from on High." One more grandchild in this picture: Kara Shea D'Andrea. Her brother, Shawn, was on an educational assignment in Africa.   The other grandchildren are identified in the garden picture.
First row standing: Jennifer Rainford, Mary-Berenice McCall, Mimi Pelton, Bridgett Pincus (Allen's spouse); Judy Daniels; Kara Shea D'Andrea; Emily Daniels; Rebecca Daniels, Dee Daniels, Lynn Daniels, Donna Rickman, Sandra Pailet, Joan Petro and Yvonne Lupella.
Back Row: **L to R;** Donald Rickman II, David Pelton, PhD; Robert Lupella, PhD; John McCall, PhD; Michael D'Andrea, PhD; Stephen Daniels, MD; Allen Daniels, EdD; Steve Freeman, Vivian Leavell, Walter Leavell, MD and Ray Timmerman, MD.
Mahea Lani Daniels was born January 2, 1999 in Honolulu, HI to Judy Daniels and Michael D'Andrea.

The Bitch *With Style's*

DAILY AFFIRMATION

I have been saying this affirmation for 23 years.
I say it every morning in the shower (which serves as a trigger).
If it resonates with your soul, use it. If not, make up your own.

I Am One with God's rich and abundant resources and wealth.

Therefore, I have power, prestige, and money unlimited.

My Mind holds only what I think with God.

God is but love and, therefore, so am I.

I Am not a body. I Am free, for I Am still as God created me.

This holy Instant do I give to Thee, be Thou in charge,

For I will follow Thee, certain that Thy direction gives me Peace.

I Am Health, Wealth, Love and Perfect Self-Expression.

I Am healthy, wealthy, happy, beautiful, thin and young.

I Am That I Am.

I Am God.

And so it is!

—Vikki Ashley, PhD

PART FIVE

The Bitch *With Style*
Book Bag

Instructions for taking the P³ Baseline and Growth Package

This package covers your:

1. Behavior via the **Style Analysis Profile;**

2. Values and attitudes via the **Personal Interests, Attitudes and Values;**

3. Perception (how you take in and use information) via **The Work Environment.**

Follow these instructions **exactly.**

1. Complete the Information page and read the instructions **first** for each instrument. Timing begins *after* you have completed the information side and read the instructions. (See below for timing of each instrument.)

2. These are self-assessment instruments, *not* tests, and thus reflect where you are at *this point in time* in each of the categories being assessed.

3. **You cannot pass or fail.** You will receive information that will identify **SWOTS:** Strengths, Weaknesses, Opportunities, Threats and how others can effectively communicate with *you.* You will obtain information about your basic beliefs, values and attitudes. You will also obtain information about your perception of the behavior required to do your job or carry out your position. Finally, you will receive information on your behavior related to who you *really* are versus who you *think* you are under the "mask" the public sees.

4. Be very honest. This is *you* talking to *you* and you must respond *only* as you perceive yourself, not as you *think* others see you.

5. Timing is exact. However, please remember to do the following:
   a. Fill in *every* block according to instructions.
   b. Look at the example block. Make sure each **completed block looks exactly like the example** for each instrument.

6. Timing:
Style Analysis Response Form	7 minutes
Personal Interests, Attitudes and Values	5 minutes
The Work Environment	5 minutes

   On **The Work Environment,** complete the form *as if* you are hiring someone else to do your job. Ask yourself, "What behaviors are really required in this position to be effective?"

January 1, 1999

Vikki Ashley, PhD • 1712 Delachaise Street • New Orleans, LA 70115
504-895-7968 • fax 504-891-0863 • email Drvikki@Drvikki.com

Style Analysis Response Form

Seven Minutes to Increased Success

In just seven minutes you can complete the Style Analysis Response Form and begin a process of self-understanding that will benefit you both personally and professionally. After completing the instrument, the **Managing For Success®** software will be used to generate a valuable report full of information that may change the rest of your life.

Your report merges sophisticated behavior analysis with computer software operations to provide you with unique personal insights. This comprehensive report will help you discover qualities about yourself that could be the key to opening new doors of opportunity. You will be able to better understand your work and/or management style from the information provided, and develop an action plan that can enhance your personal and professional growth.

NAME _____   DATE _____

BUSINESS/ORGANIZATION NAME _____

BUSINESS STREET ADDRESS _____   BUS. PHONE ( )_____

CITY _____   STATE _____ ZIP _____

YOUR POSITION/TITLE _____   YEARS W/COMPANY _____

HOME STREET ADDRESS _____   HOME PHONE ( )_____

CITY _____   STATE _____ ZIP _____

SINGLE ☐   MARRIED ☐   DIVORCED ☐   DATE OF BIRTH _____

CHILDREN: NUMBER _____   AGES _____

Directions

On the other side of this sheet there are 24 blocks of four words/phrases each.

1. First: look at the words/phrases.

2. Next: put one "x" by the *one* that *most* describes how you *perceive* yourself *at this time.*

3. Next: put one "x" by the *one* that *least* describes how you *perceive* yourself *at this time.*

Do this for each of the 24 blocks. Be sure that your description of you is *your honest perception* of you and not how *others* perceive you. This is a *forced-choice process. You must complete all 24 blocks.*

You have *seven* minutes to complete this process. REMEMBER: This is *you* talking to you *about* you! Your "gut" response is what is required. Do not ponder or intellectualize about your choice.

If you finish in less than seven minutes, *do not go back and reconsider.*

REMEMBER: one "MOST" *and* one "LEAST" *per block.*

Refer to the following example before proceeding:

Example:

M   L

● ◯ Gentle, kindly
◯ ● Persuasive, convincing
◯ ◯ Humble, reserved, modest
◯ ◯ Original, inventive, individualistic

Dr. Vikki Ashley ▪ 1712 Delachaise Street ▪ New Orleans, LA 70115 ▪ 504/895-7968 ▪ Fax 504/891-0863 ▪ Email Drvikki@Drvikki.com

Name _____ Company _____ Female ☐ Male ☐

MOST	LEAST		
⬯	⬯	Gentle, kindly	**1**
⬯	⬯	Persuasive, convincing	
⬯	⬯	Humble, reserved, modest	
⬯	⬯	Original, inventive, individualistic	
⬯	⬯	Attractive, charming, attracts others	**2**
⬯	⬯	Cooperative, agreeable	
⬯	⬯	Stubborn, unyielding	
⬯	⬯	Sweet, pleasing	
⬯	⬯	Easily led, follower	**3**
⬯	⬯	Bold, daring	
⬯	⬯	Loyal, faithful, devoted	
⬯	⬯	Charming, delightful	
⬯	⬯	Open-minded, receptive	**4**
⬯	⬯	Obliging, helpful	
⬯	⬯	Willpower, strong-willed	
⬯	⬯	Cheerful, joyful	
⬯	⬯	Jovial, joking	**5**
⬯	⬯	Precise, exact	
⬯	⬯	Nervy, gutsy, brazen	
⬯	⬯	Even-tempered, calm, not easily excited	
⬯	⬯	Competitive, seeking to win	**6**
⬯	⬯	Considerate, caring, thoughtful	
⬯	⬯	Outgoing, fun-loving, socially striving	
⬯	⬯	Harmonious, agreeable	
⬯	⬯	Fussy, hard to please	**7**
⬯	⬯	Obedient, will do as told, dutiful	
⬯	⬯	Unconquerable, determined	
⬯	⬯	Playful, frisky, full of fun	
⬯	⬯	Brave, unafraid, courageous	**8**
⬯	⬯	Inspiring, stimulating, motivating	
⬯	⬯	Submissive, yielding, gives in	
⬯	⬯	Timid, shy, quiet	
⬯	⬯	Sociable, enjoys the company of others	**9**
⬯	⬯	Patient, steady, tolerant	
⬯	⬯	Self-reliant, independent	
⬯	⬯	Soft-spoken, mild, reserved	
⬯	⬯	Adventurous, willing to take chances	**10**
⬯	⬯	Receptive, open to suggestions	
⬯	⬯	Cordial, warm, friendly	
⬯	⬯	Moderate, avoids extremes	
⬯	⬯	Talkative, chatty	**11**
⬯	⬯	Controlled, restrained	
⬯	⬯	Conventional, doing it the usual way, customary	
⬯	⬯	Decisive, certain, firm in making a decision	
⬯	⬯	Polished, smooth talker	**12**
⬯	⬯	Daring, risk-taker	
⬯	⬯	Diplomatic, tactful to people	
⬯	⬯	Satisfied, content, pleased	

MOST	LEAST		
⬯	⬯	Aggressive, challenger, takes, action	**13**
⬯	⬯	Life of the party, outgoing, entertaining	
⬯	⬯	Easy mark, easily taken advantage of	
⬯	⬯	Fearful, afraid	
⬯	⬯	Cautious, wary, careful	**14**
⬯	⬯	Determined, decided, unwavering, stand firm	
⬯	⬯	Convincing, assuring	
⬯	⬯	Good-natured, pleasant	
⬯	⬯	Willing, go along with	**15**
⬯	⬯	Eager, anxious	
⬯	⬯	Agreeable, consenting	
⬯	⬯	High-spirited, lively, enthusiastic	
⬯	⬯	Confident, believes in self, assured	**16**
⬯	⬯	Sympathetic, compassionate, understanding	
⬯	⬯	Tolerant	
⬯	⬯	Assertive, aggressive	
⬯	⬯	Well-disciplined, self-controlled	**17**
⬯	⬯	Generous, willing to share	
⬯	⬯	Animated, uses gestures for expression	
⬯	⬯	Persistent, unrelenting, refuses to quit	
⬯	⬯	Admirable, deserving of praise	**18**
⬯	⬯	Kind, willing to give or help	
⬯	⬯	Resigned, gives in	
⬯	⬯	Force of character, powerful	
⬯	⬯	Respectful, shows respect	**19**
⬯	⬯	Pioneering, exploring, enterprising	
⬯	⬯	Optimistic, positive view	
⬯	⬯	Accommodating, willing to please, ready to help	
⬯	⬯	Argumentative, confronting	**20**
⬯	⬯	Adaptable, flexible	
⬯	⬯	Nonchalant, casually indifferent	
⬯	⬯	Light-hearted, carefree	
⬯	⬯	Trusting, faith in others	**21**
⬯	⬯	Contented, satisfied	
⬯	⬯	Positive, admitting no doubt	
⬯	⬯	Peaceful, tranquil	
⬯	⬯	Good mixer, likes being with others	**22**
⬯	⬯	Cultured, educated, knowledgeable	
⬯	⬯	Vigorous, energetic	
⬯	⬯	Lenient, not overly strict, tolerant of others' actions	
⬯	⬯	Companionable, easy to be with	**23**
⬯	⬯	Accurate, correct	
⬯	⬯	Outspoken, speaks freely and boldly	
⬯	⬯	Restrained, reserved, controlled	
⬯	⬯	Restless, unable to rest or relax	**24**
⬯	⬯	Neighborly, friendly	
⬯	⬯	Popular, liked by many or most people	
⬯	⬯	Orderly, neat, organized	

Personal Interests, Attitudes and Values

Personal values are those interests, goals and preferences which guide our lives and careers. This instrument is designed to help you determine which particular area of preference is most important to you.

Please read the directions completely and print your data.

Name: _____

Company: _____

Position: _____

For Research Purpose only:

☐ Male   Age: ☐ Under 21   ☐ 40-50
☐ Female   ☐ 21-30   ☐ 50-60
                  ☐ 30-40   ☐ Over 60

There are twelve categories for response, each with six (6) items for you to consider. Please complete this form in **five minutes**.

Directions

Mark your personal preference in each of the twelve areas listed. *Rank each of the six statements* by indicating your choices in numerical order. Your first choice is #1, your second choice is #2, your third choice is #3, etc. *Each number must be used once* in each of the twelve groups, and *each blank must be completed.*

Example

My favorite subjects to study:	**1**
6	Math/Science
4	Political Science
3	Theology
1	Fine Arts
5	Financial Planning
2	Social Studies

P³

Dr. Vikki Ashley ▪ 1712 Delachaise Street ▪ New Orleans, LA 70115 ▪ 504/895-7968 ▪ Fax 504/891-0863 ▪ Email Drvikki@Drvikki.com

My favorite subjects to study:	1	If I were given $500,000 I would:	7
☐ Math/Science		☐ Purchase an art collection	
☐ Political Science		☐ Start my own business	
☐ Theology		☐ Give some to charity	
☐ Fine Arts		☐ Save some/invest some	
☐ Financial Planning		☐ Take courses to gain knowledge	
☐ Social Studies		☐ Donate to church fund	

My personal interests are:	2	I think our tax money should be spent on:	8
☐ Independence		☐ Help for the homeless	
☐ Joining a group with traditions		☐ Military/Defense	
☐ Appreciation of the beauty of nature		☐ Education	
☐ Financial security		☐ Funding of the Arts	
☐ Service to others		☐ Reducing the federal deficit	
☐ Knowledge		☐ Drug control	

Leisure activities that I enjoy:	3	People I admire as role models:	9
☐ Volunteer work		☐ Humanitarians	
☐ Studying new things		☐ Military leaders	
☐ Sports		☐ Entrepreneurs	
☐ Investing or spending money		☐ Artists	
☐ Going to museums		☐ Scientists	
☐ Thinking about life		☐ Ministers	

Personal motivators for me are:	4	The way I would like to contribute to society:	10
☐ Being a leader		☐ Helping the sick and disadvantaged	
☐ Continuing education		☐ Being a business person	
☐ Being a good citizen		☐ Being a team player	
☐ Helping others		☐ Protecting the environment	
☐ Increasing my net worth		☐ Being an inventor	
☐ Arts/crafts		☐ Initiator of community activities	

My career goals:	5	My personal goals:	11
☐ Artist		☐ Reformer	
☐ Researcher		☐ Elected official	
☐ Business owner		☐ Economic freedom	
☐ Manager		☐ Discovering new technology	
☐ Historian		☐ Artistic expression	
☐ Social Reformer		☐ Personal growth	

My desire for improvement may include:	6	My outside interests:	12
☐ Spiritual growth		☐ Teaching	
☐ Helping others		☐ Acting	
☐ Leadership roles		☐ Community projects	
☐ Security for retirement		☐ Part-time business	
☐ Additional education		☐ Politics	
☐ Beautification of personal surroundings		☐ Church activities	

Work Environment

The Work Environment System was developed to assess the behavior that is needed for successful completion of a particular job. This system allows the individual to focus on the behavioral demands of the job itself, *not* the behavior of the person performing the job. Complete the form *as if* you are hiring someone else to do your job. Ask yourself, "What behaviors are really required in this position to be effective?"

Directions for response

From the 14 groups of statements rank, in order of importance or relevance to the *job*, each of the four statements in each group. Please complete this form in **five minutes**.

1 = **high importance, 4 = least importance**

Example

This job calls for:

3	A. Analysis of data and facts before acting. **1**
1	B. Tactful decisions.
4	C. Quick and forceful decisions.
2	D. Logical thinking before making decisions.

Date: _____

Work environment, job or position (define by as many words as necessary, or in a general sense):

_____

_____

Name of organization: _____

As viewed by: _____

Dr. Vikki Ashley ▪ 1712 Delachaise Street ▪ New Orleans, LA 70115 ▪ 504/895-7968 ▪ Fax 504/891-0863 ▪ Email Drvikki@Drvikki.com

This job calls for:

1 A. Analysis of data and facts before acting.	**8** A. Motivating others.
B. Tactful decisions.	B. Concentrating on details.
C. Quick and forceful decisions.	C. Challenging assignments.
D. Logical thinking before making decisions.	D. Exhibiting patience.

2 A. Few changes.	**9** A. Contacting people.
B. Some change.	B. Following directions.
C. Many changes.	C. Getting results.
D. No change.	D. Performing to standards.

3 A. Clean, tidy and organized work station.	**10** A. Following procedures to perfection.
B. Freedom to act independently.	B. Solving people problems.
C. Consistent performance.	C. Bold, aggressive actions.
D. High trust levels.	D. Routine work.

4 A. Work to be completed accurately the first time.	**11** A. High quality controls.
B. Being flexible.	B. Creative and original thinking.
C. Planning ahead on a large scale.	C. Optimistic outlook.
D. Identification with the team.	D. Working within the system.

5 A. A systematic way to do things.	**12** A. Complete authority to carry out responsibilities.
B. Contact with many people.	B. Analysis of facts and data.
C. Making quick decisions.	C. Many people interactions.
D. Being diplomatic and cooperative	D. Patience.

6 A. Avoiding trouble	**13** A. Freedom from excessive detailed work.
B. Solving problems.	B. Task-oriented concentration.
C. Verbalizing thoughts and ideas.	C. Balanced judgment.
D. Working with things.	D. Friendly work environment.

7 A. Staying at one work station.	**14** A. More emphasis on quality than efficiency.
B. Expediting action.	B. Freedom from conflict and confrontation.
C. Adhering to procedures.	C. Highly persuasive communications.
D. Generating enthusiasm.	D. Accepting and initiating change.

P³
P.O. Box 15349
New Orleans, LA 70175

24 hr credit card ordering
TOLL Free
1-800-900-2161

Ordered by:

Name_____

Street Address _____

City _____

State_____ Zip_____

Day Phone (   ) _____

Shipped to: (if different from "Ordered By")

Name_____

Street Address _____

City _____

State_____ Zip_____

Day Phone (   ) _____

Gift Message_____

_____

Payment Method:

_____Visa   _____Mastercard   _____Check   _____Money Order (Send NO cash)

Card Account Number _____ Exp. Date _____

Issuing Bank_____Customer Signature_____

Qty.	Description	Unit Cost	Amount
	P³ Baseline and Growth Package (Behavior, Values, Perception)	150.00	
	Vitiligo Depigmentation Information Pkg. W/Q&A	No Charge*	
	Nikken Magnet Information Package	No Charge*	
	Shipping & Handling	13.95	
	*If ordered without P³ Package, Shipping & Handling	3.00	
	Additional Ship-To Addresses	3.95	
	Add in applicable taxes: 9%, Orleans Parish; 4%, other Louisiana residents		
	TOTAL		

You may send order by mail, as noted above. Or FAX to: 402-345-7700.
Or, order via our web site: www.Dr. Vikki.com.

A *PHOTOCOPY OF THIS FORM IS ACCEPTABLE*.

Speaker Request Form

Dr. Ashley is available for speeches, lectures, conferences, seminars and panels. She will happily do TV and radio. Please complete the following information and mail, fax, phone or put on the web site to:

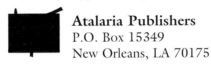 **Atalaria Publishers**
P.O. Box 15349
New Orleans, LA 70175

Phone: 504-895-8312   Fax: 504-891-0863
Email: Atalariapublishers@Atalariapublishers.com
Web Site: www.Atalariapublishers.com

Name of Organization/Group/Institution/Person _____

Street Address _____

City_____State_____ ZIP_____

Phone (   ) _____   Fax (   ) _____

Email_____ Web Site _____

Check as appropriate: ___Profit ___Nonprofit ___Educational ___Religious

___Community-based ___International

Explain briefly what the event is:_____

_____

_____

_____

What dates are planned? _____

Are they scheduled? ___Yes   ___No   Any flexibility? ___Yes   ___No

Expenses Paid: (*Check all that apply to this request*)   ___Travel   ___Hotel

___Honorarium   ___Consulting Fee

___Speaking Fee. You make all arrangements and advise? ___Yes   ___No.

Someone will meet Dr. Ashley ___Yes   ___No

How many people do you expect to be present? (*Size is Not the determining factor regard-*

ing acceptance.) _____

Is the space where the event will take place wired for multimedia? ___Yes   ___No.

If not, what are sound, projection availability? _____

Recording: ___Cassette   ___Video   ___Film   Satellite: ___Yes   ___No

How do you plan to publicize this event? (*Dr. Ashley will provide a press kit.*)

_____

_____

What is your policy on Back-of-the-Room sales of books and products?_____

_____

Who is your contact person? _____

Address _____

City_____State_____ZIP _____

Phone (   ) _____   Fax (   )_____

Email_____ Web Site_____ Beeper (   )_____

Please use the bottom of this document to add any comments to any section of this request.
Thank you.

_____

_____

_____

_____

_____

_____

_____

HOW TO BE A
BITCH^
WITH STYLE

DR. VIKKI ASHLEY
▲ BEING IN TOTAL CONTROL OF HERSELF

Book Order Form
P.O. Box 15349
New Orleans, LA
70175

24 hr credit card ordering
TOLL Free
1-800-942-7552

Ordered by: **Shipped to:** (if different from "Ordered By")

Name_____	Name_____
Street Address _____	Street Address _____
City _____	City _____
State_____ Zip_____	State_____ Zip_____
Day Phone ( )_____	Day Phone ( )_____
	Gift Message_____
	_____

Payment Method:

_____Visa   _____Mastercard   _____Check   _____Money Order (Send NO cash)

Card Account Number _____ Exp. Date _____

Issuing Bank_____Customer Signature_____

Qty.	Description	Unit Cost	Amount
	The Book: **How To Be A Bitch *With Style*:** **Being In Total Control of Herself**	29.95	
	Vitiligo Depigmentation Information Pkg. W/Q&A	No Charge*	
	Nikken Magnet Information Package	No Charge*	
	Shipping & Handling	3.95	
	*If ordered without Book, Shipping & Handling	3.00	
	Additional Ship-To Addresses	3.95	
	Add in applicable taxes: 9%, Orleans Parish; 4%, other Louisiana residents		
	TOTAL		

You may send order by mail, as noted above. Or FAX to: 402-345-7700.
Or, order via our web site: www.Atalatiapublishers.com.

Please allow 3-4 weeks for delivery

A PHOTOCOPY OF THIS FORM IS ACCEPTABLE.

PRODUCTS

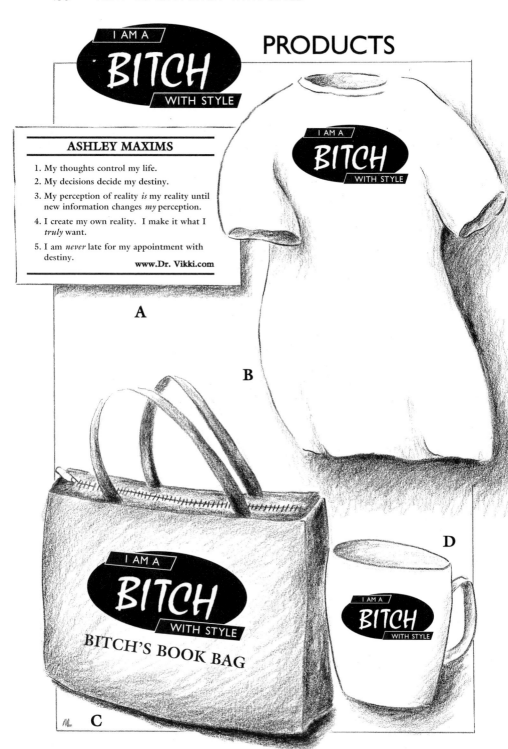

ASHLEY MAXIMS

1. My thoughts control my life.
2. My decisions decide my destiny.
3. My perception of reality *is* my reality until new information changes *my* perception.
4. I create my own reality. I make it what I *truly* want.
5. I am *never* late for my appointment with destiny.

www.Dr. Vikki.com

I AM A BITCH WITH STYLE

A

B

I AM A BITCH WITH STYLE
BITCH'S BOOK BAG

C

I AM A BITCH WITH STYLE

D

PRODUCTS
P.O. Box 15349
New Orleans, LA
70175

Ordered by:

Name_____

Street Address _____

City _____

State_____ Zip_____

Day Phone (   )_____

Shipped to: (if different from "Ordered By")

Name_____

Street Address _____

City _____

State_____ Zip_____

Day Phone (   )_____

Gift Message_____

_____

Payment Method:

_____Visa   _____ Mastercard   _____Check   _____ Money Order (Send NO cash)

Card Account Number _____ Exp. Date _____

Issuing Bank_____Customer Signature_____

Item	Qty.	Description	Unit Cost	Amount
A		Ashley Maxims Magnetic Card	4.95	
B		Bitch *With Style* Tee Shirt ___M ___L ___XL	17.95	
C		Bitch's Book Bag	29.95	
D		Bitch's *With Style* Mug	8.95	
E		From a Bitch *With Style* Post-it Note Pad – 6x4	4.95	
F		Bitch's Tool Kit	19.95	
		S&H: Under $50, add $6.95; $51-100, add $11.95. More than $100, add $13.95		
		Additional Ship-To Addresses	3.95	
		Add in applicable taxes: 9%, Orleans Parish; 4%, other Louisiana residents		
			TOTAL	

You may send order by mail, as noted above. Or FAX to: 402-345-7700.
Or, order via our web site: www.bitchwithstyle.com.
Please allow 3-4 weeks for delivery

A PHOTOCOPY OF THIS FORM IS ACCEPTABLE.

2-27-88 Houston Airport 6:00pm. On Way to NOL (So. Amer.)

I've just been given the Bitch of the Year award. And, I've decided to take it. I'm a Bitch with style!

(I came first!)

Blend
In
The
Caring
Heart

Better to be Bold and
Independent
Than
Conduct,
Helpless.

B
Informal
T
C
H

Bright
Independent
Thinking
Caring
Humble

my Boundless
Intellect
Thinks
Constantly of
Heaven.

B
Information gatherer
T
Cultured
Hale

Bad
Information and
Thoughts
Can
Hurt

Beautiful
Informed
Thoughts
Can
Heal

Be
Impressive
Thoughtful,
Collaborative
Healing

I have
Beauty
Integrity
Talent
Competence
Health (Humor)

I am
Bold
Idiosyncratic
Thoughtful
Centered
Haughty

I am also
Believable
Informed
Trustworthy
Compassionate
Helpful

Blessed
Inner-directed
Transformed
Certain
Happy

Boundless
Intense
Tuned-in
Communicator
Home

Bountiful
Intelligent
Truthful
Contented
Holy (Holistic)

Make a Bitch Board

I am —
Blessed   Blameless
Infinite   Innocent
Thoughtful   Trusting
Cherished   Creative +
Holy   Heavenbound

I have —
Beauty/rain
Influence
Taste (style)
Choice
Health

I am a
Beacon
Initiator
Teacher
Conductor
Harmonizer

I am a
Bridge builder
Illuminator (light of the world)
Translator
Communicator
how-to-do-it person

This is the Best
Informed
Training
Curriculum
Here (on earth)

Builder
Interpreter
Transformer
Communicator
Humanistic

Bright (Bold)
Imaginative
Thankful
Complete
Hopeful + Needful

Title?
I am a
BITCH WITH STYLE!

Will = Wonder
Illumination
Light
Love

With = Will it to happen

Style — Self-esteem
Thinking
Youthful
Love
Energy

Self-esteem that
yearns to lead with ?
energy!

Self-esteem =
thoughts from
you that radiate
love and
Energy! (Enthusiasm)
(Enlightenment)

Being
in total
control of
Herself —

RESOURCE DIRECTORY
OF
THE BITCH'S BOOK BAG
MARCH 3, 1999

Please contact any of these groups that interest you and request their literature and any information you specifically desire.

If you wish to have an aura photo taken, please call:

Aura Imaging
319 Spruce St.
Redwood City, CA 94063
1-800-321-2872.
You will be directed to the nearest center or bookstore that has this special camera equipment. There are about 200 such cameras in the United States and about 600 in the whole world!

In New Orleans, contact:

Life's Journey Bookstore
504-885-2375.

———————————

American Association of Naturopathic Physicians (AANP)
P.O. Box 20386
Seattle, WA 98102
206-323-7610

American Chiropractor Association (ACA)
1701 Clarendon Boulevard
Arlington, VA 22290
703-276-8800

American Counseling Association (ACA)
5999 Stevenson Avenue
Alexandria, VA
703-823-9800

American Dietetic Association (ADA)
216 West Jackson Boulevard,
Suite 800
Chicago, IL 60606

American Holistic Medical Association (AHMA)
4101 Lake Boone Trail, Suite 201
Raleigh, NC 27606
919-787-5181

American Osteopathic Association (AOA)
142 East Ontario Street
Chicago, IL 60611
312-280-5800

American Association of Acupuncture and Oriental Medicine (AAAOM)
4101 Lake Boone Trail, Suite 201
Raleigh, NC 27607
919-787-5181

American Massage Therapy Association (AMTA)
1130 West North Shore Avenue
Chicago, IL 60626-4670
312-761-2682

Associated Professional Massage Therapists and Body Workers (APMT)
1746 Cole Boulevard, Suite 225
Golden, CO 80401
303-674-8478

American Psychiatric Association
(APA)
1400 K Street, NW
Washington, DC 20005
202-336-5662
www.psych.org

American Psychological
Association (APA)
750 First Street, NE
Washington, DC 20002-4242
202-336-5500
www.apa.org

American Society of Clinical
Hypnosis (ASCH)
2200 E. Devon Avenue, Suite 291
Des Plaines, IL 60018
847-297-3317

Association for Humanistic
Psychology (AHP)
1772 Vallejo, Suite 3
San Francisco, CA94123
415-346-7929

C. G. Jung Foundation for
Analytical Psychology
28 East 39th Street
New York, NY 10016
212-697-6430

Institute of Core Energetics
116 East 23rd Street
New York, NY 10010
212-505-6767

International Society for the
Study of Subtle Energies and
Energy Medicine (ISSSEEM)
356 Goldco Circle
Golden, CO 80403-1347
303-425-4625
www.nekesc.org/issseem

Mind/Body Medical Institute
(Herbert Benson, MD)
Beth Israel Deaconess
Medical Center
330 Brookline Avenue,
East Campus
Boston, MA
617-632-9530

National Board for
Hypnotherapy and Hypnotic
Anaesthesiology
(NBHHA)
7841 W. Ludlow Drive, Suite A
Peoria, AZ 85381
602-843-2215

National Vitiligo Foundation, Inc.
P. O. Box 6337
Tyler, TX 75711
Ph: 903-531-0074
Fax: 903-531-9767

The Academy of Chinese Healing
Arts
505 S. Orange Avenue
Sarasota, FL 34236
941-365-5768
www.acha.net

Integrative Medicine Program
(Andrew Weil, MD)
College of Medicine
Arizona Health Sciences Center
University of Arizona
Tucson, AZ
520-621-2211

The Chopra Center For Well
Being
7630 Fay Avenue
La Jolla, CA 92037
619-551-7788
www.chopra.com

BIBLIOGRAPHY

A Course in Miracles. ©1975, 1985. Foundation for Inner Peace, Tiburon, CA.

Addington, Jack Ensign. *The Hidden Mystery of the Bible.* ©1969. DeVorss & Company, Publisher, Marina del Rey, CA.

Airola, ND, PhD, Paavo. *Every Woman's Book.* ©1979. Health Plus Publishers, Phoenix, AZ.

Alcamo, PhD, I. Edward. *Anatomy Coloring Workbook: An Easier and Better Way To Learn Anatomy.* ©1997. Random House, Inc., New York, NY.

Alessandra, PhD, Tony and Michael J. O'Connor, PhD with Janice Alessandra. *People Smart: Powerful Techniques for Turning Every Encounter into a Mutual Win.* ©1990. Keynote Publishing Company, La Jolla, CA.

Alessandra, PhD, Tony, Gary Couture, Gregg Baron. *The Idea-A-Day Guide to super Selling and Customer Service: 250 Ways to Increase Your Top and Bottom Lines.* ©1992. Dartnell, Chicago, IL.

Alvarado, Luis. *Psychology, Astrology & Western Magic: Image and Myth in Self-Discovery.* ©1991. Llewellyn Publications, St. Paul, MN.

Anonymous. *Christ in You.* 1910, 1997. DeVorss Publications, Marina del Rey, CA.

Aquarian Gospel of Jesus the Christ. ©1907, 1935, 1964. DeVorss & Co., Marina del Rey, CA.

Arroyo, Stephen. *Astrology, Karma & Transformation: The Inner Dimensions of the Birth Chart.* ©1978. CRCS Publications, Vancouver, WA.

Arroyo, Stephen. *Stephen Arroyo's Chart Interpretation Handbook.* ©1989. CRCS Publications, Sebastopol, CA.

Arroyo, Stephen. *The Practice and Profession of Astrology: Rebuilding Our Lost Connections With the Cosmos.* ©1984. CRCS Publications, Reno, NV.

Ashley, Adrienne. *The Zodiac: A Pattern for Meditation.* ©1979. New Age Bible and Philosophy Center, Santa Monica, CA.

Astrology: A Guide to the Stars. ©1992. Ariel Books/Andrews and McMeel, Kansas City, MO.

Avery, DMs, Kevin Quinn. *The Numbers of Life: The Hidden Power In Numerology.* ©1977. Dolphin Books/Doubleday & Company, Inc., Garden City, NY.

Bailey, Alice A. *A Treatise on Cosmic Fire.* ©1951, 1979. Lucis Publishing Company, New York, NY and Lucis Press Ltd., London, England.

Bailey, Alice A. *A Treatise on White Magic.* ©1951. Lucis Publishing Company, New York, NY and Lucis Press Ltd., London, England.

Bailey, Alice A. *Discipleship In the New Age, Volume II.* ©1955. Lucis Publishing Company, New York, NY and Lucis Press Ltd., London, England.

Bailey, Alice A. *Education in the New Age.* ©1954. Lucis Publishing Company, New York, NY and Lucis Press Ltd., London, England.

Bailey, Alice A. *Esoteric Astrology: Volume III, A Treatise on the Seven Rays.* ©1951. Lucis Publishing Company, New York, NY and Lucis Press Ltd., London, England.

Bailey, Alice A. *Esoteric Healing: Volume IV, A Treatise on the Seven Rays.* ©1953. Lucis Publishing Company, New York, NY and Lucis Press Ltd., London, England.

Bailey, Alice A. *Esoteric Psychology: Volume I, A Treatise on the Seven Rays.* ©1962. Lucis Publishing Company, New York, NY and Lucis Press Ltd., London, England.

Bailey, Alice A. *Esoteric Psychology: Volume II, A Treatise on the Seven Rays.* ©1970. Lucis Publishing Company, New York, NY and Lucis Press Ltd., London, England.

Bailey, Alice A. *From Bethlehem To Calvary: The Initiations of Jesus.* ©1937, 1965. Lucis Publishing Company, New York, NY and Lucis Press Ltd., London, England.

Bailey, Alice A. *From Intellect to Intuition.* ©1960. Lucis Publishing Company, New York, NY and Lucis Press Ltd., London, England.

Bailey, Alice A. *Glamour: A World Problem.* ©1950, 1978. Lucis Publishing Company, New York, NY and Lucis Press Ltd., London, England.

Bailey, Alice A. *Initiation, Human and Solar.* ©1951. Lucis Publishing Company, New York, NY and Lucis Press Ltd., London, England.

Bailey, Alice A. *Letters on Occult Meditation.* ©1950, 1978. Lucis Publishing Company, New York, NY and Lucis Press Ltd., London, England.

Bailey, Alice A. *Problems of Humanity.* ©1964. Lucis Publishing Company, New York, NY and Lucis Press Ltd., London, England.

Bailey, Alice A. *Telepathy and The Etheric Vehicle.* ©1950, 1978. Lucis Publishing Company, New York, NY and Lucis Press Ltd., London, England.

Bailey, Alice A. *The Consciousness of the Atom.* ©1961. Lucis Publishing Company, New York, NY and Lucis Press Ltd., London, England.

Bailey, Alice A. *The Destiny of the Nations.* ©1949. Lucis Publishing Company, New York, NY and Lucis Press Ltd., London, England.

Bailey, Alice A. *The Externalization of the Hierarchy.* ©1957, 1985. Lucis Publishing Company, New York, NY and Lucis Press Ltd., London, England.

Bailey, Alice A. *The Labours of Hercules: An Astrological Interpretation.* ©1974. Lucis Publishing Company, New York, NY and Lucis Press Ltd., London, England.

Bailey, Alice A. *The Light of the Soul: The Yoga Sutras of Patanjali.* ©1955. Lucis Publishing Company, New York, NY and Lucis Press Ltd., London, England.

Bailey, Alice A. *The Rays and The Initiations: Volume V, A Treatise on the Seven Rays.* ©1960. Lucis Publishing Company, New York, NY and Lucis Press Ltd., London, England.

Bailey, Alice A. *The Reappearance of the Christ.* ©1948, 1976. Lucis Publishing Company, New York, NY and Lucis Press Ltd., London, England.

Bailey, Alice A. *The Soul and Its Mechanism.* ©1930, 1958. Lucis Publishing Company, New York, NY.

Bailey, Alice A. *The Unfinished Autobiography.* ©1951, 1979. Lucis Publishing Company, New York, NY and Lucis Press Ltd., London, England.

Bailey, Foster. *Changing Esoteric Values.* ©1954. Lucis Publishing Company, New York, NY and Lucis Press Ltd., London, England.

Bailey, Foster. *Running God's Plan.* ©1972. Lucis Publishing Company, New York, NY and Lucis Press Ltd., London, England.

Ball, Carolyn M. *Claiming Your Self-Esteem.* ©1990. Árati Books, Houston, TX.

Becker, MD, Robert O. and Gary Selden. *The Body Electric: Electromagnetism and the Foundation of Life.* ©1985. William Morrow, New York, NY.

Benjamine, Elbert. *Astrodyne Manual.* ©1950. The Church of Light, Los Angeles, CA.

Benson, MD, Herbert with Marg Stark. *Timeless Healing: The Power and Biology of Belief.* ©1996. Fireside/Simon & Schuster, New York, NY.

Berger, Ruth. *Medical Intuition: How to Combine Inner Resources With Modern Medicine.* ©1995. Samuel Weiser, Inc., York Beach, ME.

Berger, Ruth. *The Secret Is In The Rainbow: Aura Relationships.* ©1979. Samuel Weiser, Inc., York Beach, ME.

Besant, Annie and C.W. Leadbeater. *Talks on the Path of Occultism: Light on the Path, Volume III.* ©1926. The Theosophical Publishing House; Madras, India; London, England; Wheaton, IL.

Besant, Annie. *Man and His Bodies.* ©1912. The Theosophical Publishing House, Madras, India.

Bettelheim, Bruno. *Freud & Man's Soul.* ©1982. Alfred A. Knopf, New York, NY.

Bills, Rex E. *The Rulership Book, A Directory of Astrological Correspondences.* ©1971. Macoy Publishing & Masonic Supply Co., Inc., Richmond, VA.

Bishop, Clifford. *Sex & Spirit: Love Mystics & Creation Myths, The Union of Souls, Ritual & Taboo.* ©1996. Time-Life Books, Alexandria, VA.

Bletzer, PhD, June G. *The Donning International Encyclopedic Psychic Dictionary.* ©1986. Whitford Press, division of Schiffer Publishing, Ltd., West Chester, PA.

Bliznakov, MD, Emile G. and Gerald L. Hunt. *The Miracle Nutrient: Coenzyme Q^{10}.* ©1986. Bantam Books, New York, NY.

Bonnstetter, Bill J., Judy I. Suiter and Randy J. Widrick. *DISC, The Universal Language: A Reference Manual.* ©1993. Target Training International, Ltd., Scottsdale, AZ.

Boston Women's Health Collective. *The New Our Bodies, Ourselves: A Book By and For Women.* ©1984, 1992. Touchstone/Simon & Schuster, New York, NY.

Bott, MD, Victor. *Spiritual Science and the Art of Healing: Rudolf Steiner's Anthroposophical Medicine.* ©1984. Healing Arts Press, Rochester, VT.

Brain Facts: A Primer on the Brain and Nervous System. ©1993. Society for Neuroscience, Washington, DC.

Breiling, Psy.D, Brian and Bethany ArgIsle, editors. *Light Years Ahead: The Illustrated Guide to Full Spectrum and Colored Light in Mindbody Healing.* ©1996. Celestial Arts, Berkeley, CA.

Brennan, Barbara Ann. *Hands of Light: A Guide to Healing Through the Human Energy Field.* ©1987. Bantam Books, New York, NY.

Brennan, Barbara Ann. *Light Emerging: The Journey of Personal Healing.* ©1993. Bantam Books, New York, NY.

Bridges, William. *The Character of Organizations: Using Jungian Type in Organizational Development.* ©1992. Consulting Psychologists Press, Palo Alto, CA.

Brinker, MD, Francis. *Formulas for Healthy Living.* ©1995. Eclectic Medical Publications, Sandy, OR.

Brinkley, Dannion with Paul Perry. *Saved By The Light.* ©1994. Villard Books, New York, NY.

Brown, Sylvia and Antoinette May. *Adventures of a Psychic: The Fascinating and Inspiring True-Life Story of One of America's Most Successful Clairvoyants.* ©1990. Hay House, Inc., Carlsbad, CA.

Browne, Sylvia. *Adventures of a Psychic: The Fascinating and Inspiring True-Life Story of One of America's Most Successful Clairvoyants.* ©1990. Hay House, Inc., Carlsbad, CA.

Bruyere, Rosalyn L. *Wheels of Light: Chakras, Auras, and the Healing Energy of the Body.* ©1989, 1991, 1994. Fireside/Simon & Schuster, New York, NY.

Buess, Lynn M. *Synergy Session: Holistic Counseling Toward The New Age.* ©1980. DeVorss & Company, Marina Del Rey, CA.

Buess, Lynn M. *The Tarot and Transformation.* ©1973. DeVorss & Company, Publishers, San Diego, CA.

Bunker, Dusty. *Numerology and Your Future.* ©1980. Whitford Press, a division of Schiffer Publishing, Ltd., West Chester, PA.

Bunker, Dusty. *Numerology, Astrology and Dreams.* ©1987. Whitford Press, a division of Schiffer Publishing, Ltd., West Chester, PA.

Bunker, Dusty. *Quintiles and Tredeciles: The Geometry of the Goddess.* ©1989. Whitford Press, a division of Schiffer Publishing, Ltd., West Chester, PA.

Burt, Kathleen. *Archetypes of the Zodiac.* ©1988. Llewellyn Publications, St. Paul, MN.

Burton Goldberg Group, compiler. *Alternative Medicine: The Definitive Guide.* ©1993, 1994, 1995. Future Medicine Publishing, Inc., Fife, WA.

Capra, Fritjof. *The Tao of Physics.* ©1975, 1983. Bantam Books, New York, NY.

Capra, Fritjof. *The Turning Point: Science, Society and the Rising Culture.* ©1982. Bantam Books, New York, NY.

Carey, George Washington and Inez Eudora Perry. *The Zodiac and the Salts of Salvation: Homeopathic Remedies for the Sign Types.* 1932, 1989. Samuel Weiser, Inc., York Beach, ME.

Carlson, PhD, Richard and Benjamin Schield, editors. *Healers on Healing.* ©1989. Jeremy P. Tarcher/G.P. Putnam's Sons, New York, NY.

Carnie, L.V. *Chi Gung: Chinese Healing, Energy, and Natural Magick.* ©1997. Llewellyn Publications, St. Paul, MN.

Carper, Jean. *Stop Aging Now!: The Ultimate Plan for Staying Young & Reversing the Aging Process.* ©1995. HarperCollins Publishers, Inc., New York, NY.

Carroll, Lee. *Alchemy of The Human Spirit (a guide to human transition into the New Age): Kryon Book III.* ©1995. The Kryon Writings, Del Mar, CA.

Carter, Mildred and Tammy Weber. *Body Reflexology: Healing At Your Fingertips.* ©1994. Parker Publishing Company, West Nyack, NY.

Carter, Mildred. *Helping Yourself With Foot Reflexology.* ©1969. Parker Publishing Company, Inc., West Nyack, NY.

Cathie, Bruce L. *The Energy Grid: Harmonic 695, The Pulse of the Universe.* ©1990, 1997. Adventures Unlimited Press, Kempton, IL.

Cayce, Edgar. *Edgar Cayce Readings. Individual Reference File and V. 1-11.* Compiled by Gladys Davis Turner and Mae Gimbert St. Clair. ©1970, 1976. By Edgar Cayce Foundation. Association for Research and Enlightenment. Virginia Beach, VA.

Chang, Dr. Stephen T. *The Complete Systems of Self-Healing Internal Exercises.* ©1986. Tao Publishing, San Francisco, CA.

Chang, Dr. Stephen T. *The Tao of Balanced Diet: Secrets of a Thin & Healthy Body.* ©1987. Tao Publishing, San Francisco, CA.

Chang, Dr. Stephen T. *The Tao of Sexology: The Book of Infinite Wisdom.* ©1986. Tao Publishing, San Francisco, CA.

Chia, Mantak. *Awaken Healing Energy Through the Tao.* ©1983. Aurora Press, Santa Fe, NM.

Chopra, MD, Deepak. *Ageless Body, Timeless Mind: The Quantum Alternative to Growing Old.* ©1993. Harmony Books, New York, NY.

Cicero, Chic and Sandra Tabatha Cicero, editors. *The Golden Dawn Journal, Book II, Qabalah: Theory and Magic.* ©1994. Llewellyn Publications, St. Paul, MN.

Cicero, Chic and Sandra Tabatha Cicero. *Experiencing the Kabbalah.* ©1997. Llewellyn Publications, St. Paul, MN.

Cicero, Chic and Sandra Tabatha Cicero. *Secrets of a Golden Dawn Temple: The Alchemy and Crafting of Magickal Instruments.* ©1992. Llewellyn Publications, St. Paul, MN.

Cicero, Chic and Sandra Tabatha Cicero. *Self-Initiation into the Golden Dawn Tradition: A Complete Curriculum of Study for Both the Solitary Magician and the Working Magical Group.* ©1995. Llewellyn Publications, St. Paul, MN.

Cichoke, DC, Anthony J. *Enzymes & Enzyme Therapy: How to Jump Start Your Way to Lifelong Good Health.* ©1994. Keats Publishing, Inc., New Canaan, CT.

Clark, John. *Matter and Energy: Physics in Action.* ©1994. Oxford University Press, New York, NY.

Cleary, Thomas, translator. *The Taoist I Ching.* ©1986. Shambhala Publications, Inc., Boston, MA.

Cole-Whittaker, Terry. *Love and Power in a World Without Limits.* ©1989. Harper Paperbacks/Harper & Row, Publishers, New York, NY.

Cole-Whittaker, Terry. *The Inner Path From Where You Are To Where You Want To Be.* ©1986. Fawcett Crest, New York, NY.

Cole-Whittaker, Terry. *What You Think Of Me Is None Of My Business.* ©1979. Jove Books, New York, NY.

Collier, Robert. *Riches Within Your Reach: The Law of the Higher Potential.* ©1947. Robert Collier Book Corporation, Ramsey, NJ.

Collier, Robert. *The Secret of the Ages, Volume Seven.* ©1926. Robert Collier, New York, NY.

Connolly, Eileen. *Tarot: A New Handbook for the Apprentice.* ©1979, 1990. Newcastle Publishing Company, Inc., North Hollywood, CA.

Connolly, Eileen. *The Connolly Book of Numbers, A new path to ancient wisdom: Volume I, The Fundamentals.* ©1988. Newcastle Publishing Company, Inc., North Hollywood, CA.

Cooper, David A. *God Is A Verb: Kabbalah and the Practice of Mystical Judaism.* ©1997. The Berkley Publishing Group, New York, NY.

Cooper, J.C. *An Illustrated Encyclopaedia of Traditional Symbols.* ©1978. Thames and Hudson, New York, NY.

Cousens, MD, Gabriel. *Spiritual Nutrition and The Rainbow Diet.* ©1986. Cassandra Press, San Rafael, CA.

Cousins, Norman. *Head First: The Biology of Hope and the Healing Power of the Human Spirit.* ©1989. Penguin Books, New York, NY.

Covey, Stephen R. *The 7 Habits of Highly Effective Families.* ©1997. Golden Books, New York, NY.

Crowley, Aleister (The Master Therion). *The Book of Thoth (Egyptian Tarot).* 1985. Samuel Weiser, Inc., York Beach, ME.

Crowley, Brian and Esther. *Words of Power: Sacred Sounds of East & West.* ©1991. Llewellyn Publications, St. Paul, MN.

Daily Planetary Guide 1998. ©1997. Llewellyn Publications, St. Paul, MN.

Daily Planetary Guide 1999. ©1998. Llewellyn Publications, St. Paul, MN.

Dale, Cyndi. *New Chakra Healing: The Revolutionary 32-Center Energy System.* ©1996. Llewellyn Publications, St. Paul, MN.

Dale, PhD, ND, Theresa. *Transform Your Emotional DNA: Understanding the Blueprint of Your Life.* ©1995, 1996, 1997. The Wellness Center for Research and Education, Inc., Los Angeles, CA.

Daly, Mary with Jane Caputi. *Webster's First New Intergalactic Wickedary of the English Language.* ©1987. Beacon Press, Boston, MA.

Davison, R.C. *The Technique of Prediction.* ©1955, 1971, 1977, 1979, 1983. L.N. Fowler & Co. Ltd., Romford, Essex, England.

Decker, James A. *Magnificent Decision.* ©1963. Unity Books, Lee's Summit, MO.

Dee, Miss. *Health, Astrology & Spirituality.* ©1984. American Federation of Astrologers, Tempe, AZ.

Dee, Miss. *The Yod: Your Special Life Purpose.* ©1983. American Federation of Astrologers, Tempe, AZ.

Dernay, Eugene. *Longitudes and Latitudes in the U.S.* ©1945. American Federation of Astrologers, Tempe, AZ.

Devlin, Mary. *Astrology and Past Lives.* ©1987. Para Research, Inc., distributed by Schiffer Publishing Ltd., West Chester, PA.

Diamond, Harvey and Marilyn. *Fit For Life II: Living Health—The Complete Health Program.* ©1987. Warner Books, New York, NY.

Diamond, M.C., A.B. Scheibel, L.M. Elson. *The Human Brain Coloring Book* ©1985. Harper Perennial, a division of HarperCollins Publishers, New York, NY.

Dimock, Hedley G. *Groups: Leadership and Group Development.* ©1966, 1970, 1986, 1987. University Associates, Inc., San Diego, CA.

Doane, Doris Chase. *Astrology: 30 Years Research.* ©1956. American Federation of Astrologers, Inc., Tempe, AZ.

Doane, Doris Chase. *How to Prepare and Pass an Astrologer's Certificate Exam.* ©1973. American Federation of Astrologers, Inc. Tempe, AZ.

Doane, Doris Chase. *How to Read Cosmodynes: An Astrological Guide to the Use of Personal Power.* ©1974. American Federation of Astrologers, Inc., Tempe, AZ.

Doane, Doris Chase. *Progressions in Action.* ©1977. American Federation of Astrologers, Inc., Tempe, AZ.

Doane, Doris Chase. *Time Changes in the USA.* ©1966. American Federation of Astrologers, Inc. Tempe, AZ.

Dorland's Illustrated Medical Dictionary. ©1994. W.B. Saunders Company, a division of Harcourt Brace & Company, Philadelphia, PA.

Dostoyevsky, Fyodor. *The Brothers Karamazov.* Penguin Books, New York, NY.

Douglass, MD, William Campbell. *Color Me Healthy.* ©1995, 1996. Second Opinion Publishing, Inc., Atlanta, GA.

Douglass, MD, William Campbell. *Hydrogen Peroxide Medical Miracle.* ©1992. Second Opinion Publishing, Atlanta, GA.

Douglass, MD, William Campbell. *Into the Light: The exciting story of the life-saving breakthrough therapy of the age.* ©1993. Second Opinion Publishing Inc., Dunwoody, GA.

Dumont, Theron Q. *The Master Mind.* Yoga Publication Society, Jacksonville, FL.

Dunn, Joseph. *Tranformed Lives.* ©1998. A.R.E. Press, Virginia Beach, VA.

Dychtwald, PhD, Ken and Joe Flower. *Age Wave: How the Most Important Trend of Our Time Will Change Your Future.* ©1990. Bantam Books, New York, NY.

Eadie, Betty J. *The Awakening Heart: My continuing journey to love.* ©1996. Pocket Books, New York, NY.

Eadie, Betty J. with Curtis Taylor. *Embraced By The Light.* ©1992. Gold Leaf Press, Placerville, CA.

Eastern Systems for Western Astrologers: An Anthology. ©1997. Samuel Weiser, York Beach, ME.

Ebertin, Reinhold. *Astrological Healing: The History and Practice of Astromedicine.* ©1982, English translation ©1989. Samuel Weiser, Inc., York Beach, ME.

Edinger, Edward F. *Goethe's Faust: Notes for a Jungian Commentary*. ©1990. Inner City Books, Toronto, Canada.

Ellis, Andrew, Nigel Wiseman and Ken Boss. *Fundamentals of Chinese Acupuncture*. ©1991. Paradigm Publications, Brookline, MA.

Erbe, Peter O. *God I Am: From Tragic To Magic*. ©1991, 1997. By Triad Publishers, Cairns, Qld, Australia. P. 205-206.

Farber, Barry J. *Diamond in the Rough: The Secret to Finding Your Own Value—and Making Your Own Success*. ©1995. Berkley Books, New York, NY.

Farber, Monte (devised by). *Karma Cards: A New Age Guide to Your Future Through Astrology*. ©1988. Penguin Books, New York, NY.

Farrell, Patricia. *Numerology*. ©1997. Element Books Limited, Rockport, MA.

Ferguson, Marilyn. Updated by Wim Coleman and Pat Perrin. *Marilyn Ferguson's Book of PragMagic: Pragmatic Magic for Everyday Living—Ten Years of Scientific Breakthroughs, Exciting Ideas, and Personal Experiments That Can Profoundly Change Your Life*. ©1990. Pocket Books/Simon & Schuster, New York, NY.

Fersen, Eugene. *The Fundamental Principles of Science of Being*. ©1976. The Lightbearers, Seattle, WA.

Fillmore, Charles. *The Twelve Powers of Man*. Unity School of Christianity, Unity Village, MO.

Flack, Rudy and Diane. *American Presidents and Their Wives (includes horoscopes)*. ©1996. A is A Publishing, Ltd., Belleville, IL.

Flowers, PhD, Stephen Edred, editor. *Hermetic Magic: The Postmodern Magical Papyrus of Abaris*. ©1995. Samuel Weiser, Inc., York Beach, ME.

Foley, Dennis, Eileen Nechas and the Editors of *Prevention* Magazine. *Women's Encyclopedia of Health & Emotional Healing: Top Women Doctors Share Their Unique Self-Help Advice on Your Body, Your Feelings and Your Life*. ©1993. Rodale Press, Emmaus, PA.

Fraser, Antonia. *The Warrior Queens*. ©1988. Alfred A. Knopf, New York, NY.

Fromm, Erich. *Man For Himself: An Inquiry into the Psychology of Ethics*. ©1947. Rinehart and Company, Inc., New York, NY and Toronto, Canada.

Garfield, Charles. *Second To None: The Productive Power of Putting People First*. ©1992. Avon Books, New York, NY.

Geddes, Sheila. *Astrology & Health*. ©1992. Foulsham, London, England and New York, NY.

Gerber, MD, Richard. *Vibrational Medicine: New Choices for Healing Ourselves*. ©1988, 1996. Bear & Company, Santa Fe, NM.

Gerson, MD, Max. *A Cancer Therapy: Results of Fifty Cases and The Cure of Advanced Cancer by Diet Therapy: A Summary of 30 Years of Clinical Experimentation*. ©1958, 1975, 1977, 1986, 1990. The Gerson Institute, Bonita, CA in association with Station Hill Press, Barrytown, NY.

Gettings, Fred. *Dictionary of Astrology*. ©1985. Routledge & Kegan Paul, London, England and Boston, MA.

Glynn, Patrick. *God, The Evidence: The Reconciliation of Faith and Reason in a Postsecular World*. ©1997. Forum/Prima Publishing, Rocklin, CA.

Godwin, David. *Godwin's Cabalistic Encyclopedia: Complete Guidance to Both Practical and Esoteric Applications*. ©1979, 1989, 1994. Llewellyn Publications, St. Paul, MN.

Goldsmith, Joel S. *A Parenthesis in Eternity: Living the Mystical Life*. ©1963. Harper San Francisco/Harper Collins Publishers, New York, NY.

Goodwin, Matthew Oliver. *Numerology, The Complete Guide, Volume One: The Personality Reading*. ©1981. Newcastle Publishing Company, North Hollywood, CA.

Goodwin, Matthew Oliver. *Numerology, The Complete Guide: Volume Two: Advanced Personality Analysis and Reading the Past, Present and Future*. ©1981. Newcastle Publishing Company, Inc., North Hollywood, CA.

Gordon, Rochelle. *Body Talk: Whey You Really Get Sick And Why It Need Never Happen Again!* ©1997. International Rights, Ltd., New York, NY.

Grayson, Dr. Stuart. *Spiritual Healing: A Simple Guide for the Healing of Body, Mind and Spirit*. ©1997. Simon & Schuster, New York, NY.

Green, Jeff. *Uranus: Freedom From the Known*. ©1988. Llewellyn Publications, St. Paul, MN.

Greene, Liz and Howard Sasportas. *The Inner Planets: Building Blocks of Personal Reality; Seminars in Psychological Astrology, Volume 4.* ©1993, Samuel Weiser, Inc., York Beach, ME.

Grove, Daisy E. *The Mystery Teaching of the Bible.* 1925, 1962. The Theosophical Publishing House Ltd., London, England.

Guiley,l Rosemary Ellen. *Harper's Encyclopedia of Mystical & Paranormal Experience.* ©1991. Harper Collins Publishers, New York, NY.

Guttman, Ariel and Kenneth Johnson. *Mythic Astrology: Archetypal Powers in the Horoscope.* ©1993. Llewellyn Publications, St. Paul, MN.

Hadady, Dac, Letha. *Asian Health Secrets: The Complete Guide to Asian Herbal Medicine.* ©1996. Three Rivers Press, New York, NY.

Hall, Calvin S. *A Primer of Freudian Psychology.* ©1954. Mentor Books/New American Library, New York, NY.

Hall, Judy. *The Hades Moon: Pluto in Aspect to the Moon.* ©1998. Samuel Weiser, Inc., York Beach, ME.

Hall, Manly P. *Pluto in Libra: An Interpretation.* ©1971. Philosophical Research Society, Los Angeles, CA.

Hall, Manly P. *Questions and Answers: Fundamentals of the Esoteric Sciences.* ©1965. The Philosophical Research Society, Inc., Los Angeles, CA.

Hamaker-Zondag, Karen. *Foundations of Personality: Combining Elements, Crosses, and Houses with Jungian Psychological Concepts in Horoscope Interpretation.* ©1984, 1988. Samuel Weiser, Inc., York Beach, ME.

Hamaker-Zondag, Karen. *Planetary Symbolism in the Horoscope.* ©1985. Samuel Weiser, Inc., York Beach, ME.

Hand, Robert. *Essays on Astrology.* ©1982. Whitford Press, a division of Schiffer Publishing Ltd., Atglen, PA.

Hand, Robert. *Horoscope Symbols.* ©1981. Para Research, Inc., Gloucester, MA.

Harré, Rom and Roger Lamb, editors. *The Dictionary of Physiological and Clinical Psychology.* ©1983, 1986. The MIT Press, Cambridge, MA.

Harrison, Nick. *365 Daily Answers to What Would Jesus Do?* ©1998. HarperSanFrancisco, a division of HarperCollins Publishers, New York, NY.

Harvey, Charles and Suzi. *Sun Sign, Moon Sign: Discover the Key to Your Unique Personality Through the 144 Sun-Moon Combinations.* ©1994. Aquarian/Harper Collins Publishers, San Francisco, CA.

Hay, Louise L. *Heal Your Body: The Mental Causes For Physical Illness and the Metaphysical Way to Overcome Them.* ©1982, 1984. Hay House, Inc., Santa Monica, CA.

Hay, Louise L. *Your Personal Colors and Numbers.* ©1987. Hay House, Santa Monica, CA.

Heindel, Max. *Mysteries of the Great Operas.* ©1921. The Rosicrucian Fellowship Press, Oceanside, CA.

Heline, Corinne. *Beethoven's Nine Symphonies Correlated With the Nine Spiritual Mysteries.* ©1971. New Age Press, Inc., Los Angeles, CA.

Heline, Corinne. *Color & Music in the New Age.* ©1964. DeVorss and Company, Publishers, Marina del Rey, CA.

Heline, Corinne. *Esoteric Music of Richard Wagner.* 1986. New Age Bible and Philosophy Center, Santa Monica, CA.

Heline, Corinne. *Healing and Regeneration Through Color.* ©1987. DeVorss & Company, Marina del Rey, CA.

Herter, George Leonard. *How To Live With A Bitch.* ©1969, 1971. Herter's Inc., Waseca, MN.

Hickey, Isabel M. *Astrology: A Cosmic Science.* ©1992. CRCS Publications, Sebastopol, CA.

Hickey, Isabel M. *It Is All Right.* ©1976. New Pathways, Waltham, MA.

Higgins, Frank C. *Hermetic Masonry: The Beginning of Masonry and AUM "The Lost Word."* Kessenger Publishing Company, Montana.

Hill, Napoleon and W. Clement Stone. *Success Through A Positive Mental Attitude.* ©1960. Prentice-Hall, Inc., Englewood Cliffs, NJ.

Hill, Napoleon. *Law of Success.* ©1979. Success Unlimited, Inc., Chicago, IL.

Hill, Napoleon. *The Think and Grow Rich Action Pack!: Think and Grow Rich* and *Think and Grow Rich Action Manual.* ©1972. Hawthorne Books/W. Clement Stone, Publisher, New York, NY.

Hills, SRN, Margaret. *Curing Illness The Drug-Free Way.* ©1988. Sheldon Press, London, England.

Hodson, Geoffrey. *The Hidden Wisdom In The Holy Bible, Volume I.* ©1963. The Theosophical Publishing House; Madras, India; London, England and Wheaton, IL.

Hodson, Geoffrey. *The Hidden Wisdom In The Holy Bible, Volume II.* ©1967. The Theosophical Publishing House; Madras, India; London, England and Wheaton, IL.

Hodson, Geoffrey. *The Hidden Wisdom In The Holy Bible, Volume III.* ©1971. The Theosophical Publishing House; Madras, India; London, England and Wheaton, IL.

Hodson, Geoffrey. *The Hidden Wisdom In The Holy Bible, Volume IV.* ©1980. The Theosophical Publishing House; Madras, India; London, England and Wheaton, IL.

Holy Bible, New International Version. ©1978. Zondervan Bible Publishers, Grand Rapids, MI.

Houck, Richard. *The Astrology of Death.* ©1994. Groundswell Press, Gaithersburg, MD.

Hulse, David Allen. *The Key of It All: An Encyclopedic Guide to the Sacred Languages & Magickal Systems of the World, Book One: The Eastern Mysteries.* ©1993. Llewellyn Publications, St. Paul, MN.

Hulse, David Allen. *The Key of It All: An Encyclopedic Guide to the Sacred Languages & Magickal Systems of the World, Book Two: The Western Mysteries.* ©1994. Llewellyn Publications, St. Paul, MN.

Husain, Shahrukh. *The Goddess: Creation, Fertility, Female Essence; The Sovereignty of Women; Worship, Love, Abundance.* ©1997. Time-Life Books, Alexandria, VA.

Hutchinson, William. *The Spirit of Masonry.* ©1982. Bell Publishing Co., New York, NY.

Hyatt, PhD, Christopher S. and Lon Milo DuQuette. *Sex Magic, Tantra & Tarot: The Way of the Secret Lover.* ©1991. New Falcon Publications, Tempe, AZ.

Igram, Dr. Cass with Judy K. Gray, MS. *Eat Right or Die Young.* ©1989. Instant Improvement, Inc., New York, NY.

Institute of Noetic Sciences with William Poole. *The Heart of Healing.* ©1993. Turner Publishing, Inc., Atlanta, GA.

Iyengar, B.K.S. *Light on Yoga.* ©1966, 1968, 1976. Schocken Books, New York, NY.

Jansky, Robert Carl. *Astrology, Nutrition and Health.* ©1977. Para Research, Rockport, MA.

Javane, Faith and Dusty Bunker. *Numerology and The Divine Triangle.* ©1979. Whitford Press, a division of Schiffer Publishing, Ltd., West Chester, PA.

Jocelyn, John. *Meditations On The Signs Of The Zodiac.* ©1970. Harper & Row Publishers, San Francisco, CA.

Johari, Harish. *Chakras: Energy Centers of Transformation.* ©1987. Destiny Books, Rochester, VT.

Johnson, Kenneth. *Jaguar Wisdom: Mayan Calendar Magic.* ©1997. Llewellyn Publications, St. Paul, MN.

Johnson, Tom. *You Are Always Your Own Experience.* ©1982. Los Arboles Publications, Redondo Beach, CA.

Jones, Marc Edmund. *The Guide to Horoscope Interpretation.* ©1941, 1969. The Theosophical Publishing House, Wheaton, IL; Madras, India; and London, England.

Jones, Marc Edmund. *The Sabian Symbols in Astrology.* ©1953, 1966, 1969. Sabian Publishing Society, Stanwood, WA in association with Shambhala Publications, Inc., Berkeley, CA.

Joy, MD, W. Brugh. *Joy's Way, A Map for the Transformational Journey: An Introduction to the Potentials for Healing with Body Energies.* ©1979. J.P. Tarcher, Los Angeles, CA.

Judith, Anodea. *Wheels of Life: A User's Guide to the Chakra System.* ©1987. Llewellyn Publications, St. Paul, MN.

Jung, C.G. *Aion: Researches Into the Phenomenology of the Self.* ©1959, 1969. Princeton University Press, Princeton, NJ.

Jung, C.G. *The Undiscovered Self.* ©1957, 1958. Atlantic-Little Brown, Boston, MA.

Kaptchuk, OMD, Ted J. *The Web That Has No Weaver: Understanding Chinese Medicine.* ©1983. Congdon & Weed, Inc., Chicago, IL.

Kast, Verena. *Imagination As Space of Freedom: Dialogue Between the Ego and the Unconscious.* ©1988, translation ©1993. Fromm International Publishing Corporation, New York, NY.

Keirsey, David and Marilyn Bates. *Please Understand Me: Character and Temperament Types.* ©1978, 1984. Prometheus Nemesis Book Company, Del Mar, CA.

Khalsa, MD, Dharma Singh with Cameron Stauth. *Brain Longevity: Regenerate Your Concentration, Energy, and Learning Ability for a Lifetime of Peak Mental Performance.* ©1997. Warner Books, New York, NY.

Klotsche, Charles. *Color Medicine: The secrets of color/vibrational healing.* Light Technology Publishing, Sedona, AZ.

Knight, Gareth. *Experience of the Inner Worlds.* ©1975. Samuel Weiser, Inc., York Beach, ME.

Knox, Bernard, editor. *The Norton Book of Classical Literature.* ©1993. W.W. Norton & Company, New York, NY and London, England.

Korf, Bruce R. *Human Genetics: A Problem-Based Approach.* ©1996. Blackwell Science, Cambridge, MA.

Kozminsky, Isidore. *Numbers, Their Meaning and Magic.* 1980. Samuel Weiser, Inc., New York, NY.

Kroeger, Rev. Hanna. *The Seven Spiritual Causes of Ill Health.* ©1988.

Kul, Kuthumi and Djwal. *The Human Aura: How to activate and Energize Your Aura and Chakras.* ©1971, 1974, 1982, 1996. Summit University Press, Livingston, MT.

Kulvinskas, Viktoras, edited by Richard Tasca, Jr. *Life in the 21st Century.* ©1981. Omangod Press, Woodstock Valley, CT.

Lansdowne, PhD, Zachary F. *The Chakras & Esoteric Healing.* ©1986. Samuel Weiser, Inc., York Beach, ME.

Lansdowne, Zachary F. *Rules for Spiritual Initiation.* ©1990. Samuel Weiser, Inc., York Beach, ME.

Lawlis, PhD, G. Frank. *Transpersonal Medicine: A New Approach to Healing Mind-Body-Spirit.* ©1996. Shambhala, Boston, MA and London, England.

Leadbeater, C.W. *The Life After Death.* ©1912. The Theosophical Publishing House; Madras, India; London, England and Wheaton, IL.

Leary, PhD, Timothy. *The Game of Life.* ©1979. New Falcon Publications, Phoenix, AZ.

Leek, Sybil. *Reincarnation: The Second Chance.* ©1974. Stein and Day Publishers, New York, NY.

Leichtman, MD, Robert R. *From Heaven to Earth: The Hidden Side of Science.* ©1979, 1980, 1992. Ariel Press, Atlanta, GA.

Leo, Alan. *The Complete Dictionary of Astrology.* ©1983. Destiny Books, Rochester, VT.

Lewi, Grant. *Astrology for the Millions.* ©1940, 1942, 1950, 1969, 1978. Llewellyn Publications, St. Paul, MN.

Lewi, Grant. *Heaven Knows What.* ©1998, 1994, 1990, 1984, 1978, 1977, 1971. Llewellyn Publications, St. Paul, MN.

Lewis, Jim with Kenneth Irving. *The Psychology of Astro*Carto*Graphy.* ©1997. Penguin Books, New York, NY.

Lewis, PhD, FRC, H. Spencer, prepared under the supervision of. *Rosicrucian Manual.* ©1918, 1941, 1966, 1978. Supreme Grand Lodge of AMORC, San Jose, CA.

Lewis, PhD, FRC, H. Spencer. *Self Mastery and Fate with the Cycles of Life.* ©1929, 1954. Supreme Grand Lodge of AMORC, Inc., San Jose, CA.

Lindbergh, Anne Morrow. *Gift from the Sea.* ©1955, 1975. Vintage Books/Random House, New York, NY.

Lip, Evelyn. *Feng Shui For Business.* ©1989. Heian International, Inc., Union City, CA.

Lip, Evelyn. *Feng Shui For The Home.* ©1986. Heian International, Inc., Torrance, CA.

Lofthus, Myrna. *A Spiritual Approach to Astrology.* ©1983. CRCS Publications, Reno, NV.

Lucas, Richard. *Secrets of the Chinese Herbalists.* ©1987, 1977. Prentice Hall, Paramus, NJ.

Lundsted, Betty. *Planetary Cycles: Astrological Indicators of Crises & Change.* ©1984. Samuel Weiser, Inc., York Beach, ME.

Lynch, Dudley. *The Brain Map Workbook: A Leader's and User's Guide to The Brain Map™.* ©1985, 1987. Brain Technologies Corporation, Fort Collins, CO.

Magi Society. *Astrology Really Works!* ©1995. Astro Room, a division of Hay House, Inc., Carson, CA.

Mann, A.T. *The Divine Plot: Astrology and Reincarnation.* ©1986. Element, Inc., Rockport, MA.

Mann, A.T. *The Round Art: The Astrology of Time and Space.* ©1979. Mayflower Books, New York, NY.

March, Marion D. and Joan McEvers. *Astrology: Old Theme, New Thoughts.* ©1984. ACS Publications, San Diego, CA.

March, Marion D. and Joan McEvers. *The Only Way to Learn...Astrology, Volume II.* ©1977, 1981. Astro Computing Services, San Diego, CA.

March, Marion D. and Joan McEvers. *The Only Way To...Learn About Horary and Electional Astrology, Volume VI.* ©1994. ACS Publications, San Diego, CA.

March, Marion D. and Joan McEvers. *The Only Way To...Learn About Relationships, Volume V: Synastry Techniques.* ©1992. ACS Publications, San Diego, CA.

March, Marion D. and Joan McEvers. *The Only Way to...Learn About Tomorrow: Current Patterns: Progressions, Directions, Solar and Lunar Returns, Transits.* ©1988. ACS Publications, Inc., San Diego, CA.

March, Marion D. and Joan McEvers. *The Only Way To...Learn Astrology, Volume I: Basic Principles.* ©1976, 1981. Astro Computing Services, Inc., San Diego, CA.

March, Marion D. and Joan McEvers. *The Only Way To...Learn Astrology, Volume III: Horoscope Analysis.* ©1982. ACS Publications, San Diego, CA.

Marks, Tracy. *Your Secret Self: Illuminating the Mysteries of the Twelfth House, A Guide to Using astrology & Your Dreams for Personal Growth.* ©1989. CRCS Publications, Sebastopol, CA.

Martin, Stephen Hawley. *Beyond Skepticism: All the Way to Enlightenment.* ©1995. Oaklea Press, Richmond, VA.

McBarron, Dr. Jan. *Lose Weight and Keep It Off!* ©1998. Globe Communications Corp., Boca Raton, FL.

McEvers, Joan, editor. *Spiritual, Metaphysical & New Trends in Modern Astrology.* ©1988. Llewellyn Publications, St. Paul, MN.

McEvers, Joan, editor. *The Astrology of the Macrocosm: New Directions in Mundane Astrology.* ©1990. Llewellyn Publications, St. Paul, MN.

McEvers, Joan, editor. *Web of Relationships: Spiritual, Karmic & Psychological Bonds.* ©1992. Llewellyn Publications, St. Paul, MN.

McEvers, Joan. *12 Times 12: 144 Sun/Ascendant Combinations.* ©1980, 1983. ACS Publications, San Diego, CA.

McGrane, CPAE, William J. *Brighten Your Day With Self-Esteem: How to Empower, Energize & Motivate Yourself to a Richer, Fuller, More Rewarding Life.* ©1995. Success Publishers/Markowski International Publishers, Hummelstown, PA.

McKellar, Peter. *Abnormal Psychology: Its Experience and Behaviour.* ©1989. Routledge, London, England and New York, NY.

Merivale, Philippa. *Healing With Color: An Experience of Aura-Soma.* ©1998. Element Books Limited, Boston, MA.

Metaphysical Bible Dictionary. Unity School of Christianity, Unity Village, MO.

Michaud, Ellen, Alice Feinstein and the Editors of *Prevention* Magazine. *Fighting Disease: The Complete Guide to Natural Immune Power.* ©1989. Rodale Press, Emmaus, PA.

Michelsen, Neil F. *The American Ephemeris for the 20th Century, 1900 to 2000 at Midnight.* ©1980, 1983, 1988, 1990, 1991, 1994, 1995. ACS Publications, San Diego, CA.

Mikaels, Leslee and Jecobie Roberts. *Unveiling the Secrets of the Soul.* Dream Dancer Publications, Springfield, MO.

Millard, MD, Margaret. *Casenotes of a Medical Astrologer.* ©1980. Samuel Weiser, Inc., York Beach, ME.

Millenium: Fears, Fantasies & Facts. ©1996. ACS Publications, San Diego, CA.

Miller, PhD, Daniel Weiss. *The Unseen Universe: Of Mind and Matter.* ©1993. Beyond The Realm Publishing, Brooklyn, NY.

Miller, Ruth. *The Mystical Origin of the United States.* ©1976. New Age Bible and Philosophy Center, Santa Monica, CA.

Moacanin, Radmila. *Jung's Psychology and Tibetan Buddhism: Western and Eastern Paths to the Heart.* ©1986. Wisdom Publications, Boston, MA.

Moody, Jr., MD, Raymond A. *The Light Beyond.* ©1988. Bantam Books, New York, NY.

Moore, Marcia and Mark Douglas. *Astrology: The Divine Science.* ©1978. Arcane Publications, York Harbor, ME.

Morse, MD, Melvin. *Closer To The Light: Learning From the Near-Death Experiences of Children.* ©1990. Villard Books, New York, NY.

Most Valuable Book Ever Published. ©1997. American Publishing Corporation.

Muktananda, Swami. *Play of Consciousness.* ©1978. Harper & Row, San Francisco, CA.

Murphy, DD, PhD, LLD, DRS, Joseph. *How to Use the Laws of Mind.* ©1980. DeVorss and Company, Marina del Rey, CA.

Murphy, DD, PhD, LLD, DRS, Dr. Joseph. *The Power of Your Subconscious Mind.* ©1963. Prentice Hall, Englewood Cliffs, NJ.

Murphy, Michael. *The Future of the Body: Explorations Into the Further Evolution of Human Nature.* ©1992. Jeremy P. Tarcher/Perigee Books. The Putnam Publishing Group, New York, NY.

Murray, ND, Michael and Joseph Pizzorno, ND. *Encyclopedia of Natural Medicine.* ©1991. Prima Publishing, Rocklin, CA.

Myss, PhD, Caroline. *Anatomy of the Spirit: The Seven Stages of Power and Healing.* ©1996. Three Rivers Press, New York, NY.

Mysteries of the Qabalah, Volume II. ©1922. The Yogi Publication Society, Chicago, IL.

New York Public Library Desk Reference. ©1989, 1993. Stonesong Press/Prentice Hall General Reference, New York, NY.

Nielsen, Greg and Joseph Polansky. *Pendulum Power: A mystery you can see, a power you can feel.* ©1977, 1987. Destiny Books, Rochester, VT.

North, John. *The Norton History of Astronomy and Cosmology.* ©1995. W.W. Norton & Company, New York, NY.

Nuland, Sherwin B. *The Wisdom of the Body.* ©1997. Alfred A. Knopf, New York, NY.

Oken, Alan. *Alan Oken's Complete Astrology.* ©1980. Bantam Books, New York, NY.

Oken, Alan. *Alan Oken's Complete Astrology: As Above, So Below; The Horoscope, The Road and Its Travelers; Astrology: Evolution and Revolution.* ©1980. Bantam Books, New York, NY.

Oken, Alan. *Soul-Centered Astrology: A Key to Your Expanding Self.* ©1990. Bantam Books, New York, NY.

Oman, Maggie, editor. *Prayers for Healing: 365 Blessings, Poems & Meditations.* ©1997. Conari Press, Berkeley, CA.

Orsborn, Carol. *Inner Excellence: Spiritual Principles of Life-Driven Business.* ©1992. New World Library, San Rafael, CA.

Ouseley, S.G.J. *The Power of the Rays: The Science of Colour Healing.* ©1951. L.N. Fowler & Co. Ltd., Essex, England.

Page, ND, PhD, Linda Rector. *Healthy Healing: A Guide to Self-Healing for Everyone.* ©1996. Healthy Healing Publications, Sonora, CA.

Pagels, Heinz R. *The Cosmic Code: Quantum Physics as the Language of Nature.* ©1982. Bantam Books, New York, NY.

Palmer, Lynne. *Lynne Palmer's Astrological Almanac for 1999.* ©1998. Star Bright Publishers, Las Vegas, NV.

Parrish-Harra, PhD, Carol E. *The New Dictionary of Spiritual Thought: The definitive guide to understanding over 1,100 of today's most important Western and Eastern esoteric and spiritual concepts.* ©1994. Sparrow Hawk Press, Tahlequah, OK.

Parry, Robert. *In Defense of Astrology: Astrology's Answers to Its Critics.* ©1991. Llewellyn Publications, St. Paul, MN.

Paul, Helen and Bridget Mary O'Toole. *Interpreting the Houses.* ©1976. Astro-Analytics Publications, Van Nuys, CA.

Payne, PhD, Buryl. *The Body Magnetic.* ©1988. Santa Cruz, CA.

Payne, Stanley L. *The Art of Asking Questions.* ©1951, 1979. Princeton University Press, Princeton, NJ.

Phelps, MSW, Stanlee and Nancy Austin, MBA. *The Assertive Woman: A New Look.* ©1975, 1987. Impact Publishers, San Luis Obispo, CA.

Picknett, Lynn and Clive Prince. *The Templar Revolution: Secret Guardians of the True Identity of Christ.* ©1997. Touchstone, New York, NY.

Pierrakos, Eva. *The Pathwork of Self-Transformation.* ©1990. Bantam Books, New York, NY.

Pike, Albert. *Morals and Dogma of the Ancient and Accepted Scottish Rite of Freemasonry.* ©1871. Supreme Council of the Thirty-third Degree for the Southern Jurisdiction of the United States.

Pitchford, Paul. *Healing With Whole Foods: Oriental Traditions and Modern Nutrition.* ©1993. North Atlantic Books, Berkeley, CA.

Podesta, Connie. *Self-Esteem and the Six-Second Secret.* ©1990. Corwin Press, Newbury Park, CA.

Ponder, Catherine. *The Millionaire Moses: His Prosperity Secrets For You!* ©1977. DeVorss & Company, Marina del Rey, CA.

Pottenger, Maritha. *Astro Essentials: Planets in Signs, Houses & Aspects.* ©1991. ACS Publications Inc., San Diego, CA.

Pottenger, Maritha. *Astrology: The Next Step, Complete Horoscope Interpretation.* ©1998. ACS Publications, San Diego, CA.

Pottenger, Maritha. *Healing With The Horoscope: A Guide to Counseling.* ©1982. ACS Publications, San Diego, CA.

Powell, Robert. *Christian Hermetic Astrology: The Star of the Magi and the Life of Christ.* ©1991. Golden Stone Press, Great Barrington, MA.

Puryear, Herbert B. *The Edgar Cayce Primer: Discovering the Path to Self-Transformation.* ©1982. Bantam Books, New York, NY.

Quinn, Daniel. *Providence.* ©1994. Bantam Books, New York, NY.

Redd, Ry. *Toward a New Astrology, The Approach of Edgar Cayce: An Entirely New Look At Whey the Stars & Plants Affect You So Much!* ©1985. Inner Vision Publishing Company, Virginia Beach, VA.

Reed, Henry; Charles Thomas Cayce, editor. *America's Greatest Psychic Edgar Cayce on Channeling Your Higher Self.* ©1989. Warner Books, Inc., New York, NY.

Regarde, Israel. *The Golden Dawn.* ©1971, 1986, 1989. Llewellyn Publications, St. Paul, MN.

Reid, Daniel P. *The Tao of Health, Sex, & Longevity: A Modern Practical Guide to the Ancient Way.* ©1989. A Fireside Book/Simon & Schuster, New York, NY.

Robbins, John. *Diet For A New America.* ©1987. Stillpoint Publishing, Walpole, NH.

Roberts, Peter. *The Message of Astrology: The New Vitalism and What It Means for Our Future.* ©1990. The Aquarian Press/Thorsons Publishing Group, Wellingborough, Northamptonshire, England.

Robertson, Jon and the Editors of the A.R.E. *The Golden Thread of Oneness.* ©1997. A.R.E. Press, Virginia Beach, VA.

Robertson, Marc. *The Engine of Destiny: Cosmopsychology, Planets and Personality.* ©1976. American Federation of Astrologers, Inc, Tempe, AZ.

Rogers-Gallagher, Kim. *Astrology for the Light Side of the Brain.* ©1995. ACS Publications, San Diego, CA.

Roob, Alexander. *The Hermetic Museum: Alchemy & Mysticism.* ©1997. Taschen, Köln, Lisboa, London, New York, Paris, Tokyo.

Rudhyar, Dane. *Astrological Insights into the Spiritual Life.* ©1979. ASI Publishers Inc., New York, NY.

Russell, Robert A. *God Works Through You.* ©1957. Shrine of the Healing Presence, Denver, CO.

Sakoian, Frances and Betty Caulfield. *Astrological Patterns: The Key to Self-Discovery.* ©1980, Harper & Row Publishers, New York, NY.

Sakoian, Frances and Louis S. Acker. *That Inconjunct—Quincunx—The Not So Minor Aspect.* ©1972. Copple House Books, Inc., Lakemont, GA.

Sanford, Linda Tschirhart and Mary Ellen Donovan. *Women & Self-Esteem: Understanding and Improving the Way We Think and Feel About Ourselves.* ©1984. Penguin Books, New York, NY.

Saraydarian, Torkom. *The Symphony of the Zodiac.* ©1980. Aquarian Educational Group, Sedona, AZ.

Schermer, Barbara. *Astrology Alive! Experiential Astrology, Astrodrama, and the Healing Arts.* ©1989. The Aquarian Press/Thorsons Publishing Group, Wellingborough, Northamptonshire, England.

Schick Anatomy Atlas. American Map Corporation, Maspeth, NY.

Schiegl, Heinz. *Healing Magnetism: The Transference of Vital Force.* ©1987. Samuel Weiser, Inc., York Beach, ME.

Schönberger, Dr. Martin. *The I Ching & The Genetic Code: The Hidden Key to Life.* ©1992. Aurora Press, Santa Fe, NM.

Schulman, Martin. *Karmic Astrology: The Karma of the Now.* ©1979. Samuel Weiser, Inc., New York, NY.

Schulman, Martin. *Karmic Astrology: The Moon's Nodes and Reincarnation.* ©1975. Samuel Weiser, Inc., New York, NY.

Schulman, Martin. *Karmic Relationships.* ©1984. Samuel Weiser, Inc., York Beach, ME.

Schwartz, PhD, David J. *The Magic of Thinking Big.* ©1959. Wilshire Book Company, North Hollywood, CA.

Segerberg, Osborn Jr. *The Immortality Factor.* 1974. E.P. Dutton & Co., Inc., New York, NY.

Seymour-Smith, Martin. *The New Astrologer.* ©1981. Macmillan Publishing Co., Inc., New York, NY.

Shealy, MD, PhD, C. Norman and Caroline M. Myss, MA. *The Creation of Health: The Emotional, Psychological, and Spiritual Responses that Promote Health and Healing.* ©1988, 1993. Stillpoint Publishing, Walpole, NH.

Shealy, MD, PhD, C. Norman. *Miracles Do Happen: A Physician's Experience With Alternative Medicine.* ©1995. Element Books, Inc., Rockport, MA.

Sheehy, Gail. *New Passages: Mapping Your Life Across Time.* ©1995. Random House, New York, NY.

Sherman, Sylvia and Jori Frank. *Uranian Astrology Guide plus Ephemeris.* American School of Astrology, West Orange, NJ.

Silva, José and Philip Miele. *The Silva Mind Control Method.* ©1977. Pocket Books, New York, NY.

Sjöö, Monica and Barbara Mor. *The Great Cosmic Mother: Rediscovering the Religion of the Earth.* ©1987. Harper and Row, Publishers, San Francisco, CA.

Skalka, Julia Lupton. *The Instant Horoscope Reader: Planets by Sign, House, and Aspect.* ©1994. Llewellyn Publications, St. Paul, MN.

Smith, Tony. *Parzival's Briefcase: Six Practices and a New Philosophy for Health Organizational Change.* ©1993. Chronicle Books, San Francisco, CA.

Spence, Lewis. *An Encyclopedia of Occultism: A Compendium of Information on the Occult Sciences, Occult Personalities, Psychic Science, Magic, Demonology, Spiritism, Mysticism and Metaphysics.* ©1960. University Books, New Hyde Park, NY.

Starck, Marcia. *Astrology: Key to Holistic Health.* ©1982. Seek-It Publications, Birmingham, MI.

Starck, Marcia. *Healing With Astrology.* ©1997. The Crossing Press, Freedom, CA.

Starr, Aloa. *Prisoners of Earth: Psychic Possession and Its Release.* ©1987. Light Technology Publishing, Sedona, AZ.

Stearn, Jess. *Intimates Through Time: Edgar Cayce's Mysteries of Reincarnation.* ©1989. Signet/The Penguin Group, New York, NY.

Stedman's Medical Dictionary. ©1995. Williams & Wilkins, Baltimore, MD.

Stehling, Wendy. *Thin Thighs in 30 Days.* ©1982. Bantam Books, New York, NY.

Stephenson, James. *Prophecy on Trial: The Dated Djwhal Khul to Alice Bailey Prophecies Analyzed.* ©1983. Trans-Himalaya, Incorporated, Greenwich, CT.

Storr, Anthony. *Music and the Mind.* ©1992. Ballantine Books, New York, NY.

Subtle Energies & Energy Medicine. Volume Seven, Number Three. ©1966. The International Society for the Study of Subtle Energies and Energy Medicine, Golden, CO.

Sun-tzu. *The Art of War.* ©1994. Barnes & Noble Books, New York, NY.

Tansley, DC, David V. *Chakras–Rays and Radioneics.* ©1984. C.W. Daniel Company Limited, Saffron Walden, Essex, England

Tansley, DC, David V. *Radionics & the Subtle Anatomy of Man.* ©1972. C.W. Daniel Co. Ltd, Saffron Walden, Essex, England.

Tansley, DC, David V. *Subtle Body: Essence and Shadow.* ©1977. Thames and Hudson, New York, NY.

Taylor, Ariel Yvon. *Numerology Made Plain.* ©1930. Laidlaw Brothers, Chicago, IL and New York, NY.

Teeguarden, Ron. *Chinese Tonic Herbs.* ©1984. Japan Publications, Inc. Distributed in the United States through Oxford University Press, New York, NY.

31 Days of Wisdom & Praise. ©1990. Zondervan Publishing House, Grand Rapids, MI.

Thomas, MD, MPH, Clayton L., editor. *Taber's Cyclopedic Medical Dictionary.* ©1997. F.A. Davis Company, Philadelphia, PA.

Thompson, John W. *The Human Factor: An Inquiry Into Communication and Consciousness.* ©1983. Coleman Publishing, Farmingdale, NY.

Three Initiates. *The Kybalion: Hermetic Philosophy.* ©1912, 1940. The Yogi Publication Society, Chicago, IL.

Thurston, PhD, Mark and Christopher Fazel. *The Edgar Cayce Handbook for Creating Your Future.* ©1992. Ballantine Books, New York, NY.

Tierney, Bil. *Dynamics of Aspect Analysis: New Perceptions in Astrology.* ©1983. CRCS Publications, Sebastopol, CA.

Tierra, CA, ND, Michael. *Planetary Herbology.* ©1988. Lotus Press. Twin Lakes, WI.

Troward, Thomas. *The Edinburgh Lectures on Mental Science.* ©1909. G. Putnam's Sons, New York, NY.

Turner, Gladys Davis and Mae Gimbert St. Clair, compilers. *Individual Reference File of Extracts from the Edgar Cayce Readings.* ©1970, 1976. Edgar Cayce Foundation/Association for Research and Enlightenment, Inc., Virginia Beach, VA.

Two Disciples. *The Rainbow Bridge: First Phase, Link with the Soul.* ©1975, 1988. Rainbow Bridge Productions, Danville, CA.

Tyl, Noel Jan. *Holistic Astrology: The Analysis of Inner and Outer Environments.* ©1980. TAI Books, McLean, VA.

Tyl, Noel. *Astrological Timing of Critical Illness: Early Warning Patterns in the Horoscope.* ©1998. Llewellyn Publications, St. Paul, MN.

Van Praagh, James. *Talking to Heaven: A Medium's Message of Life After Death.* ©1997. Dutton/Penguin Books, New York, NY.

Vanzant, Iyanla. *One Day My Soul Just Opened Up.* ©1998. A Fireside Book/Simon & Schuster, New York, NY.

Vogel, Dr. H.C.A., *The Nature Doctor: A Manual of Traditional and Complementary Medicine.* ©1952, 1991. Instant Improvement, Inc., New York, NY.

Wade, Carlson. *Inner Cleansing: How to Free Yourself From Joing-Muscle-Artery-Circulation Sludge.* ©1992. Prentice-Hall, Paramus, NJ.

Walker, Barbara G. *The Woman's Encyclopedia of Myths and Secrets.* ©1983. HarperSanFrancisco/HarperCollins Publishers, New York, NY.

Walsch, Neale Donald. *Conversations With God: An Uncommon Dialogue, Book 1.* ©1995. Hampton Roads Publishing Company, Inc., Charlottesville, VA.

Walsch, Neale Donald. *Conversations With God: An Uncommon Dialogue, Book 2.* ©1997. Hampton Roads Publishing Company, Inc., Charlottesville, VA.

Walsch, Neale Donald. *Conversations With God: An Uncommon Dialogue, Book 3.* ©1998. Hampton Roads Publishing Company, Inc., Charlottesville, VA.

Walsch, Neale Donald. *Conversations With God: An Uncommon Dialogue, Book 1 Guidebook.* ©1997. Hampton Roads Publishing Company, Inc., Charlottesville, VA.

Walsch, Neale Donald. *Meditations from Conversations With God: An Uncommon Dialogue, Book 1.* ©1997. Berkeley Books, New York, NY.

Walters, Derek. *The Feng Shui Handbook: A Practical Guide to Chinese Geomancy and Environmental Harmony.* ©1991. Thornsons/HarperCollins Publishers, London England and San Francisco, CA.

Washnis, George J. and Richard Z. Hricak. *Discovery of Magnetic Health: A Health Care Alternative.* ©1993. NOVA Publishing Company, Rockville, MD.

Weil, MD, Andrew. *8 Weeks to Optimum Health: A Proven Program for Taking Full Advantage of Your Body's Natural Healing Power.* ©1997. Alfred A. Knopf, New York, NY.

Weinberg, PhD, Steven Lee, editor with Randall Weischedel, Sue Ann Fazio and Carol Wright. *Ramtha.* ©1986. Sovereignty, Inc., Eastsound, WA.

Weschcke, Carl Llewellyn and Stan Barker. *The Truth About 20th Century Astrology.* ©1989. Llewellyn Publications, St. Paul, MN.

Whitcomb, Bill. *The Magician's Companion: A Practical & Encyclopedic Guide to Magical & Religious Symbolism.* ©1993. Llewellyn Publications, St. Paul, MN.

Wilkinson, Robert. *A New Look At Mercury Retrograde.* ©1997. Samuel Weiser, Inc., York Beach, ME.

Wills, Pauline and Theo. Gimbel. *16 Steps to Health and Energy: A Program of Color & Visual Meditation, Movement & Chakra Balance.* ©1992. Llewellyn Publications, St. Paul, MN.

Wilson, James. *Dictionary of Astrology.* 1978, 1974, 1971, 1969, 1880. Samuel Weiser, Inc. New York, NY.

Windsor, Joan Ruth. *Dreams & Healing: A Step-By-Step Guide to Health Through Dream Awareness.* ©1987. Berkley Books/The Berkley Publishing Group, New York, NY.

Winters, Samuel J. *Wave Therapy: Your Power to Heal.* ©1998. Winters Publishing, Wichita, KS.

Witkov, Harold S. *Keys to Spiritual Awakening: A Journey into Mysticism and Kabbalah.* ©1995. DeVorss & Company, Marina del Rey, CA.

Wright, Cedric. *Words of the Earth.* ©1960. Sierra Club, San Francisco, CA.

Wright, Paul. *Astrology in Action: How Astrology Works In Practice, Demonstrated by Transits, Progressions & Major Chart Themes in Famous People's Lives.* ©1989. CRCS Publications, Sebastopol, CA.

Wright, Paul. *The Literary Zodiac.* ©1987. CRCS Publications, Sebastopol, CA.

Yancey, Philip. *The Jesus I Never Knew.* ©1995. Zondervan Publishing House, Grand Rapids, MI.

Yott, Donald H. *Intercepted Signs and Reincarnation: Astrology and Reincarnation, Volume 2.* ©1977. Samuel Weiser, Inc, New York, NY.

Yott, Donald H. *Retrograde Planets and Reincarnation: Astrology and Reincarnation, Volume 1.* ©1977. Samuel Weiser, Inc., New York, NY.

Zain, C.C. *Astrological Signatures: Evolution of the Soul and the Nature of Astrological Energies.* ©1994. The Church of Light, Los Angeles, CA.

Zain, C.C. *Esoteric Psychology: Success Through Directed Thinking and Induced Emotion.* ©1996. The Church of Light, Los Angeles, CA.

Zain, C.C. *Natal Astrology: Progressing the Horoscope.* ©1934, 1962. The Church of Light, Los Angeles, CA.

Zoller, Robert. *The Lost Key to Prediction: The Arabic Parts in Astrology.* ©1980. Inner Traditions, New York, NY.

Zukav, Gary. *The Seat of the Soul.* ©1989. Simon & Schuster, New York, NY.

LEADERSHIP, TRANSFORMATION & CHANGE

Bauermeister, Erica, Jesse Larsen and Holly Smith. *500 Great Books by Women: A Readers Guide.* ©1994. The Penguin Group, New York, NY.

Bennis, Warren and Burt Nanus. *Leaders.* ©1985. Harper & Row Publishers, New York, NY.

Bennis, Warren and Joan Goldsmith. *Learning to Lead: A Workbook on Becoming A Leader.* ©1994. Addison-Wesley Publishing Company, Reading, MA.

Bennis, Warren and Michel Mische. *The 21st Century Organization: Reinventing Through Reengineering.* ©1995. Pfeiffer & Company, San Diego, CA.

Bennis, Warren. *An Invented Life: Reflections on Leadership and Change.* ©1993. Addison-Wesley Publishing Company, Reading, MA.

Bennis, Warren. *Leaders on Leadership: Interviews with Top Executives.* ©1992. Harvard Business Review, Boston, MA.

Bennis, Warren. *On Becoming A Leader.* ©1989. Addison-Wesley Publishing Company, Reading, MA.

Bennis, Warren. *Why Leaders Can't Lead.* ©1989. Jossey-Bass Publishers, San Francisco, CA.

Blanchard, Kenneth and Norman Vincent Peale. *The Power of Ethical Management.* ©1988. William Morrow and Company, Inc., New York, NY.

Blanchard, Kenneth, Patricia Zigarmi and Drea Zigarmi. *Leadership and the One-Minute Manager.* ©1985. William Morrow and Company, New York, NY.

Block, Peter. *Stewardship.*

Block, Peter. *The Empowered Manager.* ©1987. Jossey-Bass Publishers, San Francisco, CA.

Bridges, William. *Managing Transitions.* ©1993. Addison-Wesley Publishing Company, Reading, Massachusetts.

Bridges, William. *Transitions: Making Sense of Life's Changes.* ©1980. Addison-Wesley Publishing Company, Reading, MA.

Cousins, Norman. *The Pathology of Power.* ©1987. W.W. Norton & Company, New York, NY.

Covey, Stephen R. *Principle-Centered Leadership.* ©1990. Simon & Schuster, New York, NY.

Covey, Stephen R. *The 7 Habits of Highly Effective People.* ©1989. Simon & Schuster, New York, NY.

Cribbin, James J., *Leadership.* ©1981. American Management Association, New York, NY.

Dalziel, Murray M. and Stephen C. Schoonover. *Changing Ways: A Practical Tool for Implementing Change Within Organizations.* ©1988. American Management Association, New York, NY.

Drucker, Peter F. *Innovation and Entrepreneurship: Practice and Principles.* ©1985. Harper & Row Publishers, New York, NY.

Drucker, Peter F. *Management: Tasks, Responsibilities, Practices.* ©1973, 74. Harper & Row Publishers, New York, NY.

Drucker, Peter F. *The Frontiers of Management.* ©1986. Harper & Row Publishers, New York, NY.

Drucker, Peter F. The New Realities: In Government and Politics/Economics and Business/Society and World View. ©1989. Harper & Row Publishers, New York, NY.

Farlas, Charles M. and Philippe De Backer. *Maximum Leadership: The World's Leading CEOs Share Their Five Strategies for Success.* ©1996. Henry Holt and Company, New York, NY.

Farson, Richard. *Management of the Absurd: Paradoxes in Leadership.* ©1996. Simon & Schuster, New York, NY.

Fisher, Roger. *Beyond Machiavelli: Tools for Coping With Conflict.* ©1994. Harvard University Press, Cambridge, MA.

Gardner, Howard. *Leading Minds: An Anatomy of Leadership.* ©1995. Basic Books, Harper Collins Publishers, New York, NY.

Hamiltom, Edith. *Mythology.* ©1940, 1942, 1969. From the Norse *Elder Edda.* This line shows wisdom.

Hyland, Brice and Merle Yost. *Reflections for Managers.* ©1994. McGraw-Hill, Inc., New York, NY.

Jay, Anthony. Management and Machiavelli: An Inquiry Into the Politics of Corporate Life. ©1967. 7th Printing 1978. Bantam Books, New York, NY.

Jones, Riki Robbins. *The Empowered Woman.* ©1992. S.P.I. Books, New York, NY.

Kanter, Rosabeth Moss, Barry A. Stein and Todd D. Jick. *The Challenge of Organizational Change: How Companies Experience it and Leaders Guide it.* ©1992. The Free Press, Maxwell Macmillan International, New York, NY.

Kilmann, Ralph H. *Managing Beyond the Quick Fix.* ©1989. Jossey-Bass Publishers, San Francisco, CA.

Kotter, John P. *The Leadership Factor.* ©1988. The Free Press. McMillan, Inc., New York, NY.

Kotter, John P. The New Rules: How to Succeed in Today's Post-Corporate World. ©1995. The Free Press, New York, NY.

Kouzes, James M. and Barry Z. Posner. *The Leadership Challenge: How to Get Extraordinary Things Done in Organizations.* ©1987. Jossey-Bass Inc. Publishers, San Francisco, CA.

Kuczmarski, Susan Smith and Thomas D. Kuczmarski. *Values-Based Leadership.* ©1995. Prentice Hall, Englewood Cliffs, NJ.

Lao-Tzu. *Te-Tao Ching (The Book of the Way and Its Power).* ©1989. Translation and new text by Robert G. Henricks. Ballantine Books, New York, NY.

Maccoby, Michael. *The Leader.* ©1981. Simon & Schuster, New York, NY.

Machiavelli, Niccoló. *The Prince.* ©1952. Translation by Luigi Ricci, revised by E.R.P. Vincent. The New American Library of World Literature, New York, NY.

Mandino, Og. *The Greatest Salesman in the World.* ©1968, 1996. Bantam Books, New York, NY.

Mandino, Og. *The Greatest Success in the World.* ©1981. Bantam Books, New York, NY.

Manske, Jr., F.A. *Secrets of Effective Leadership.* ©1987. Leadership Education and Development, Inc., Memphis, TN.

McFarland, Lynne Joy, Larry E. Senn and John R. Childress. *21st Century Leadership: Dialogues with 100 Top Leaders.* ©1994. The Leadership Press, Los Angeles, CA/New York, NY.

Minninger, Joan and Eleanor Dugan. *Make Your Mind Work For You.* ©1988. Rodale Press, Emmaus, PA.

Morgan, Gareth. *Creative Organization Theory: A Resourcebook.* ©1989. Sage Publications, Newbury Park, CA.

Morgan, Gareth. *Images of Organization.* Second Edition ©1997. Sage Publications, Thousand Oaks, CA.

Morgan, Gareth. *Imagin-I-Zation: New Mindsets for Seeing, Organizing, and Managing.* ©1993, 1997. Berrett-Koehler Publishers, Inc., San Francisco, CA.

Morrison, Ann M., Randall P. White, et al. *Breaking the Glass Ceiling.* ©1982. Addison-Wesley Publishing Company, Inc., Reading, MA.

Oakley, Ed and Doug Krug. *Enlightened Leadership.* ©1991. Simon & Schuster, New York, NY.

Parkinson, C. Northcote. *Parkinson: The Law, Complete. The whole truth about the madness of modern management.* ©1957. First American Edition 1980. Ballantine Books, a division of Random House, New York, NY.

Peter, Dr. Laurence J. *The Peter Prescription.* ©1972. William Morrow & Company, Inc., New York, NY.

Peters, Thomas J. and Robert H. Waterman. *In Search of Excellence: Lessons From America's Best-Run Companies.* ©1982. Harper & Row Publishers, New York, NY.

Pitcher, Patricia. *The Drama of Leadership.* ©1997. John Wiley & Sons, Inc., New York, NY.

Roberts, Wess. *Leadership Secrets of Attila the Hun.* ©1985. Warner Books, Inc., New York, NY.

Rost, Joseph C. *Leadership for the Twenty-First Century.* ©1991. Praeger, New York, NY.

Rothenberg, Mikel A. *Dictionary of Medical Terms For the Nonmedical Person.* ©1994. Barron's Educational Series, New York, NY.

Scholtes, Peter R. et al. *The Team Handbook: How to Use Teams to Improve Quality.* ©1988. Joiner Associates, Madison, WI.

Senge, Peter M. and Art Kleiner, Charlotte Roberts, Richard B. Ross, Bryan J. Smith. *The Fifth Discipline Fieldbook.* ©1994. Doubleday, a division of Bantam Doubleday Dell Publishing Group, Inc., New York, NY.

Senge, Peter M. The Fifth Discipline: The Art & Practice of the Learning Organization. ©1990. Doubleday/Currency, New York, NY.

Tregoe, Benjamin et al. *Vision in Action.* ©1989. Simon & Schuster, New York, NY.

Wheatley, Margaret J. *Leadership and the New Science.* ©1992. Berrett-Koehler Publishers, San Francisco, CA.

Winston, Stephanie. *The Organized Executive.* ©1983. Warner Books, Inc., New York, NY.

Zohar, Danah. *ReWiring the Corporate Brain: Using the New Science to Rethink How We Structure and Lead Organizations.* ©1997. Berrett-Koehler Publishers, Inc., San Francisco, CA.

Zukav, Gary. *The Dancing Wu Li Masters.* ©1979. William Morrow & Company, New York, NY.

Zukav, Gary. *The Seat of the Soul.* ©1989. Simon & Schuster, New York, NY.